SO DAMN MUCH MONEY

SO DAMN MUCH MONEY

The Triumph of Lobbying and
the Corrosion of American Government

ROBERT G. KAISER

ALFRED A. KNOPF   NEW YORK   2009

THIS IS A BORZOI BOOK
PUBLISHED BY ALFRED A. KNOPF

Copyright © 2009 by Robert G. Kaiser

Library of Congress Cataloging-in-Publication Data
Kaiser, Robert G., 1943–
So damn much money : the triumph of lobbying and the corrosion of American
government / by Robert G. Kaiser.—1st ed.
p. cm.
Includes bibliographical references and index.
978-0-307-26654-5
1. Lobbying—Corrupt practices—United States.   2. United States.
Congress—Ethics.   3. Political corruption—United States.   4. Cassidy,
Gerald S. J.   5. United States—Politics and government.   I. Title.
JK1118.K35 3009
328.73'078—dc22   2008033862

Manufactured in the United States of America
First Edition

For Paul Corso and Andy Sumner,
who kept me in the game

I seen my opportunities and I took 'em.

— GEORGE WASHINGTON PLUNKITT
OF TAMMANY HALL, EARLY 1900S

Contents

SO DAMN MUCH MONEY

A SCANDAL FOR OUR TIME

In the early hours of February 22, 2004—a cool, clear, late-winter day—copies of the fat Sunday edition of *The Washington Post* landed on doorsteps and driveways throughout the nation's capital and its booming suburbs in Maryland and Virginia. Near the top of the front page, an arresting headline announced a scoop:

A JACKPOT FROM INDIAN GAMING TRIBES
LOBBYING, PR FIRMS PAID $45 MILLION OVER 3 YEARS

This was a seductive come-on in a city where making money was in vogue, and the story lived up to the enticement. The *Post* reported startling details about the exploits of a lobbyist named Jack Abramoff, then forty-six, and a public relations man who collaborated with him, Michael Scanlon, thirty-three. They had persuaded four Indian tribes flush with gambling money to pay huge fees to exploit Abramoff's connections with conservative Republicans in the White House and Congress to protect the tribes' interests. At Abramoff's urging, the tribes also hired Scanlon to do unspecified public relations work.

"The fees are all the more remarkable because there are no major new issues for gaming tribes on the horizon, according to lobbyists and congressional staff," reported the *Post*'s Susan Schmidt. Abramoff persuaded the tribes that they needed his help "to block powerful forces both at home and in Washington who have designs on their money," Schmidt wrote, quoting members of the tribes to this effect. She disclosed that the four tribes had donated millions of dollars to politicians and causes suggested by Abramoff, and had changed their traditional patterns of political contributions by giving less to Democrats and more to Republicans—at his urging. "Some members of the tribes" Abramoff represented "have begun to complain that they are getting little for their money," wrote Schmidt.

Neither Abramoff nor Scanlon was a household name in Washington. But Tom DeLay was, and DeLay's name appeared five times in that *Post* story. DeLay, a successful small businessman who ran an exterminating firm in the suburbs of Houston before he became a politician, was then the most powerful man in Congress. Everyone knew that DeLay had chosen Dennis Hastert of Illinois to become Speaker of the House of Representatives when that job suddenly came open in 1999. DeLay's title was majority leader, technically second-ranking to the speaker, but their colleagues understood that DeLay was smarter and tougher than Hastert, and more influential among House Republicans.

In the mid-1990s DeLay and his colleagues in the Republican leadership had struck a bargain with Washington's lobbyists that was both brazen and remarkably successful: if the lobbyists would help raise hundreds of millions of dollars to support Republicans and help preserve their majority in Congress, DeLay would invite them into the legislative process, and allow them to propose entire bills and suggest changes to legislation proposed by others.

Both sides fulfilled this understanding with gusto. The Republican National Committee and the party's House and Senate campaign committees, which collected $358 million in contributions in the two years prior to the 1994 elections when Republicans won control of Congress for the first time since 1952, reported contributions of $782 million a decade later, in 2003–04—a 220 percent increase. Lobbyists and their clients helped make that possible. And lobbyists for corporate interests won countless legislative provisions from the Republican House and Senate favoring their clients. Under the accepted interpretation of the law on bribery, all of this was entirely legal. The law prohibits a member of Congress from "corruptly" seeking or accepting money in return for "being influenced in his performance of any official act." That adverb "corruptly" speaks to intent, but it speaks vaguely. "Corruptly" has no clear legal definition. Absent evidence that the political contributions directly purchased the legislative results, quid for quo, both the contributions and the favorable legislative provisions were legal.

The *Post* story about Abramoff, Scanlon, and their Indian clients mentioned DeLay in three contexts: as a friend of Abramoff's with whom the lobbyist enjoyed "a close bond"; as Scanlon's former employer (Scanlon had been Representative DeLay's press spokesman in the late 1990s); and as one of the congressional leaders Abramoff had persuaded to defeat a proposal to tax Indian gambling earnings in 1995, when he had just begun representing Indian tribes. Abramoff used the argument then that the tribes were "engaged in the same ideological and philosophical efforts that conservatives are—basically saying, 'Look, we want to be left alone.' "

With DeLay so prominently involved in this story, it quickly qualified as a scandal. Because Washingtonians tend to evaluate a scandal by the rank and power of those involved, this one looked juicy. A good scandal makes life richer and more interesting for nearly everyone in town—apart from the involved parties. The Abramoff scandal arrived with impeccable timing, after eight years of Republican control of the House of Representatives that had brought lobbying and money to the forefront of public consciousness and changed the accepted standards of behavior in Washington.

The *Post* is the house organ of Washington's political class; virtually all its members read the paper every day. Its stories are grist for one of the world's most prolific gossip mills. On Monday morning, February 23, the Abramoff story was Topic A on Capitol Hill and across the city. On Tuesday the 24th, a Republican congressman from the Washington suburbs of Virginia, Frank Wolf, released a letter to the attorney general and the director of the FBI asking them to investigate relations between the Indian tribes and Abramoff and Scanlon. On Thursday the 26th, Senator John McCain announced an investigation by the Committee on Indian Affairs, which he chaired. The reported fees paid by Indian tribes to Abramoff and Scanlon were "disgraceful," McCain said. Now the story had legs.

In a press release on March 3, Abramoff's law firm, Miami-based Greenberg Traurig, announced that he was leaving the firm. Abramoff had brought riches to his partners in the three years he had worked there, but now a member of its executive committee said Abramoff had "disclosed to the firm for the first time personal transactions and related conduct which are unacceptable."

What did "unacceptable" mean? Abramoff operated in a world of huge numbers and vague standards. Lobbying in Washington is traditionally done on a retainer basis—clients pay lobbyists fixed monthly fees, regardless of the hours actually worked or the results achieved. Lobbyists are thrilled to get a $40,000-a-month client; $60,000 a month is considered a bonanza. Abramoff was charging each of his four tribes $180,000 a month. McCain and other members of the Indian Affairs Committee thought the lobbyist was committing grand larceny. "He was ripping off Indians," was the way Senator Daniel Inouye of Hawaii put it. But Greenberg Traurig hadn't complained about the size of the fees or looked very closely at Abramoff's operations until the *Post* story appeared.

Abramoff had acquired a big reputation among his competitors for his success expanding Greenberg Traurig's lobbying practice. In 2000, the year before Abramoff brought his large "book of business" from his previous law firm, Greenberg Traurig's lobbying revenue had been about $3 million. In 2001, it shot up to $16 million, then to more than $25 million in 2003. Suddenly, Greenberg Traurig ranked fourth among the lobbying powers in town. Everyone in the business knew this was Abramoff's doing.

In the lobbying fraternity, reactions to the Abramoff revelations were strong. Nearly everyone was surprised by the amounts, huge by any standard. Abramoff's competitors wondered what he had done for the Indians to justify those fees. Many sensed the odor of malefaction, hardly an unknown aroma in Washington. One man, however, saw an opportunity.

Gerald S. J. Cassidy, then sixty-three years old, had been a Washington lobbyist for three decades when he read that *Post* story. He had never met Abramoff, who was much younger than he and a product of the conservative Republican movement. Cassidy was a liberal Democrat whose circle of acquaintances did not include many brash young conservatives. But he knew about Abramoff, and envied his success.

Abramoff's achievements at Greenberg Traurig came at a difficult time for Cassidy and the firm he ran, Cassidy & Associates. The same year-end statistics that recorded Greenberg Traurig's leap into fourth place in the standings of lobbying firms' revenues showed that Cassidy & Associates had fallen out of first place in 2003. News of that disquieting change appeared in *Roll Call*, a Capitol Hill newspaper, on February 25— three days after the first Abramoff story appeared in the *Post*: "Lobbying shop Patton Boggs replaced Cassidy & Associates as king of K Street last year. . . ." A quarter-century earlier, K Street was the location of many Washington lobbyists' offices; the name had become the city's favorite euphemism for the world of lobbyists. Gerald Cassidy had been in first place for many years, and he did not like being second.

Not that he was in any apparent difficulty. The numbers that described Cassidy's business were all large. At the end of 1999 he had sold his firm to an international advertising and public relations conglomerate, the Interpublic Group, for a little more than $60 million. He continued to operate as an independent unit of IPG, and his fifty lobbyists continued to earn handsome fees. The "revenue number" for 2003, to use the argot of the profession, was $28 million. That was the total of fees paid to the Cassidy firm that were reportable under a law called the Lobbying Disclosure Act. When the numbers came out, Cassidy's spokesperson told *Roll Call* that the firm had received an additional $5 million in fees that weren't covered by the law, so the firm's income totaled more than $33 million that year. But there was no avoiding the fact that in the official standings, Cassidy had fallen out of first place.

First place had suited Cassidy, whose life reminded some of his friends of F. Scott Fitzgerald's Jay Gatsby. Cassidy was a self-invented man, driven to get rich by haunting memories of a violent, impoverished childhood in Brooklyn and Queens. "I remember evictions, repossessions, things you never forget," Cassidy once said. "I'm a big fan of financial security."*

Soon after Abramoff was fired by his firm, he met Cassidy. "Mutual friends" encouraged them to explore the possibility of working together, Cassidy recounted. He declined to name anyone, but others said one who helped bring the men together was Arthur Mason, a vice president of Cassidy & Associates who was also a personal friend of Abramoff's. Mason acknowledged his role, but said he didn't think he was the only one who encouraged Cassidy and Abramoff to get together.

In the lobbying world, nothing is more important than relationships. From a lobbyist's perspective the best business relationships are those that allow you to ask a favor. Scores of Washington lobbyists have such connections to members of the House and Senate who were once their colleagues, or whom they served as staff assistants. Others sustain such relationships with political help, particularly money contributed to the members' campaigns. But business relationships are not the only ones that matter. Washington is also lubricated by the grease of friendly acquaintanceship. Mason's relationships with Cassidy and Abramoff are both good examples.

Mason, who was born in 1941, fought in the Vietnam War, winning a Silver Star and other decorations. In 1976 he ran for Congress in his native Massachusetts as the Republican challenger to Father Robert Drinan, a liberal Democrat. Drinan won, but by a smaller margin than usual. Mason then moved to Washington to practice law, where he got into trouble representing a New York ex-con and shady real estate operator named

* Cassidy generously gave many hours of interviews for this book.

John P. Galanis. In 1987 Mason was indicted in New York State for real estate investment fraud related to Galanis's activities. Mason pleaded guilty to one charge and spent four and a half months in a New York prison. Later he was disbarred by the D.C. Superior Court, which found "a wealth of evidence of wrongdoing" in a case that cost defrauded investors millions of dollars.

Affable, handsome, funny, and a good golfer, Mason had many friends. One was Sheila Tate, press secretary to Nancy Reagan, and to Vice President George H. W. Bush during the 1988 presidential campaign. Tate worked for Cassidy in a public relations firm he launched as an adjunct to his lobbying operation. She brought Mason into the PR operation in the early 1990s. His charm and ability to make friends quickly impressed Cassidy, a rather shy man. Cassidy decided Mason should become a lobbyist.

Soon Mason was successfully plying that trade as a Republican in a firm dominated by Democrats. As an ex-con and disbarred lawyer whom Cassidy had restored to dignity and prosperity, Mason was grateful and loyal to his boss, and sang his praises. "I have to be very careful about what I ask Gerry for," he said once, "because he's such a good human being he'll do it."

Mason's relationship with Abramoff was social, not professional. It reflected the fact that almost no one who works in Washington has roots in Washington. Throughout its history the city has been a magnet for lone adventurers who dreamed of making a mark. Abramoff, who grew up in California, and Mason, a native of the Boston area, were typical of the breed. Like thousands of others, they came to Washington without a long list of friends in the city to provide support, and made their way by building alliances.

Such alliances can have many origins: people who worked for the same politician or in the same administration often remain friends and allies for life; southerners have always tended to band together; old school ties create bonds that endure; so do shared ethnicities. Abramoff and Mason were both Jewish. Abramoff was an observant Orthodox Jew; Mason was more relaxed about his religion. But when his daughter married an Orthodox Jew, according to several friends, Mason turned to Abramoff for advice on how to deal with his new son-in-law.

This led to their relationship, a Washington kind of friendship.

"Arthur was snowed by Jack," according to one former colleague— the more so after Abramoff treated him to a half-day golf lesson from

Mitchell Spearman, known as America's most expensive golf instructor (fee: $600 an hour). Another colleague recalled Mason arriving at work at Cassidy & Associates one Monday morning in autumn, "bragging that he had been in Jack Abramoff's box at FedEx Field" for a Washington Redskins football game the day before. The colleague remembered Mason's enthusiasm: "There were senators there!" Mason liked Signatures, the restaurant on Pennsylvania Avenue that Abramoff owned and used to court the powerful and reward his friends.

In March 2004, when Abramoff unexpectedly found himself a free agent, he told friends he didn't want to work again for a big law firm; he would prefer a straight lobbying operation like Cassidy & Associates, which might be "the only firm big enough" to take him and his group of lobbyists on, he told one person. Abramoff spoke with Mason at this time to ask if there was any interest at Cassidy in him and his team. A meeting between Abramoff and Cassidy was soon arranged. Employees at Cassidy & Associates noticed the short, dapper Abramoff's arrival one day that month. Mason ushered him down the gold-hued carpet of Cassidy's pretentious, Federal-style offices on 13th Street in downtown Washington, to the proprietor's corner office.

Abramoff had nothing on Cassidy in the dapper department that day. The older man, whose barrel chest and broad shoulders were reminders of his high school football career, wore one of his flashy suits custom-made by Alan Flusser, one of New York's most estimable tailors. Flusser's suits cost $3,800 and up. Cassidy favored double-breasted pinstripes and bright silk ties that gave him the appearance of a snazzy defense lawyer for celebrity clients, or the owner of a Las Vegas resort. He carried himself with a self-conscious body language that suggested caution. His favorite pose was prayerful, all ten fingers touching, hands pointed upward. Cassidy's office was decorated with fine antique reproductions; guests were seated on an Empire-style sofa with a high back, beneath a handsome copy of a Gilbert Stuart portrait of George Washington. As Cassidy once explained, all this had a purpose. When potential clients met him, he wanted them to have the impression that they "ought to be paying me a lot of money."

Cassidy proposed an arrangement that would bring three of Abramoff's associates and many of his clients from Greenberg Traurig to Cassidy & Associates. Abramoff would be a "consultant" to the Cassidy firm. His compensation would consist of a nice percentage of whatever fees his clients who moved their business to Cassidy paid to their new lobbyist. Abramoff would have an office in the building that housed Cassidy and his affiliates.

The paths the two men had followed to that meeting in March 2004 had little in common. Abramoff was the child of privilege; his father was an executive of Diners Club. His family wasn't particularly religious, but Abramoff embraced Orthodox Judaism as a teenager. He too played high school football—he was the center on the Beverly Hills High School varsity. He then attended Brandeis, the Jewish university outside Boston. There, during Ronald Reagan's first run for the White House, Abramoff became an active conservative Republican. After graduating from college he won election to the chairmanship of the College Young Republicans, and helped radicalize the organization, making it an arm of the "movement" then pushing the Republican Party to the right. He befriended movement conservatives, as they called themselves, like Ralph Reed, later a leader of the Christian Coalition, and Grover Norquist, a resourceful political entrepreneur who created and ran an ardent anti-tax organization called Americans for Tax Reform. In the 1980s the three supported the Nicaraguan contras and the white apartheid regime in South Africa. When the Republicans won control of Congress in 1994, Abramoff became a lobbyist. He ardently cultivated DeLay, an ambitious and rising member of the new House leadership.

To advertise his influence to his first lobbying employer, the Washington office of the Seattle law firm Preston Gates & Ellis, Abramoff had persuaded DeLay to make an appearance at the firm just weeks after Abramoff joined it in the winter of 1995. This was shortly after DeLay had become the new House majority whip, third-ranking in the new Republican leadership. Abramoff and DeLay never really became friends, but this was the beginning of an intense professional relationship that brought great benefits to both men—for a time. In 2000, Greenberg Traurig lured Abramoff and his team of lobbyists away from Preston Gates with promises of a big share of their billings. This deal proved extremely rewarding both for the Miami firm and for the members of the Abramoff team who joined its Washington office.

Cassidy and Abramoff shared one important experience: both got rich. Cassidy's path to riches began at Villanova University—he was the first member of his poor Irish-American family to go to college, and then the first to get a professional degree, in law from Cornell. After law school he had worked as a legal aide lawyer representing black and brown migrant workers in the poorest part of Florida. There he met Senator George McGovern of South Dakota and other members of the Senate's Select Committee on Nutrition and Human Needs, an important incubator of liberal programs including food stamps and subsidized school lunch and breakfast. The committee went to South Florida to hold hearings on poverty and hunger. Cassidy subsequently talked his way into a job on the committee staff, which took him to Washington in 1969. He played a bit part in McGovern's 1972 presidential campaign.

In 1975 he and a colleague on the committee staff, Kenneth Schlossberg, decided to go into business together as "consultants" who could help people solve problems in Washington. Soon they were seeking favors from Congress for their clients, who were companies, universities, and medical centers. They helped invent tricks no predecessor had thought of to assist their clients extract money from the federal government. They came up with what became known as "earmarks," provisions added to appropriations bills passed by Congress for specific projects for named beneficiaries, such as a new chemistry lab for Columbia University. Their operation became one of Washington's first lobbying firms—not a law firm whose attorneys sometimes sought to influence government decisions, but a lobbying firm devoted entirely to influencing the government on behalf of their clients. They worked on retainer—fixed fees, not dollars-per-hour—and they prospered.

But the partnership soured. Cassidy's intensity, his determination to get rich, and a temper he had trouble controlling all aggravated Schlossberg—whose laid-back approach to work in turn aggravated Cassidy. So did Schlossberg's new Russian-born wife. Once close friends, the partners turned on each other. After ten years together, Cassidy forced out Schlossberg, the original founder and president of the firm. To acquire his interest, Cassidy paid Schlossberg $812,600—a lot of money in 1985, but a pittance compared to the money Cassidy was soon earning as sole proprietor of the firm. Within a year or two he was paying himself as much as $5 million a year.

In the small universe of Washington lobbyists, Gerry Cassidy became a big man. He acquired a certain charisma, as successful self-inventors often do. He developed a taste for, then a vast collection of, fine wine. He bought a suburban estate in nearby Virginia and built a replica of a nineteenth-century farmhouse on 165 acres on Maryland's Eastern Shore, on the banks of the Chesapeake Bay, creating a country estate worth $8 million. He bought fine shotguns and fishing equipment, and became a gentleman sportsman. He collected old English hunting prints. In the world of his own company he was a domineering paterfamilias, sometimes terrorizing his employees, sometimes making them blush with his kindness and generosity. He made it a habit to attend a Catholic mass every day. His old friend Bill Cloherty, another Irishman but much easier-going, called the daily visit to church "an insightful self-corrective."

By the time Cassidy met Abramoff he must have been the wealthiest lobbyist in Washington, considerably wealthier than Abramoff. Cassidy's personal fortune exceeded $100 million, a staggering sum for a Washington entrepreneur to accumulate—evidence of the fact that early-twenty-first-century Washington has become a place to pursue great wealth as well as political power.

Despite his success, Cassidy's shyness could make him seem awkward, especially with prominent people. He was drawn to those who had an easy way with others—Arthur Mason was one, and on that day in March 2004, Jack Abramoff became another. "He was very charming when he was in here," Cassidy said later, referring to their first meeting. "Very charming."

Abramoff liked Cassidy too. "People envy Gerry Cassidy," he later told an acquaintance. "He plays on several battlefields at once—a lot of these guys can't conceive of doing that."

Cassidy's deal with Abramoff got almost no publicity. *The Washington Post* reported it deep inside its weekly gossip column on the lobbying business. One of Cassidy's senior associates was quoted by the *Post* as acknowledging the controversy then swirling around Abramoff, but also dismissing it: "Washington is a town full of controversies," said Gregg Hartley, a former aide to the House Republican leadership who had been with Cassidy for a year, and was running the firm's day-to-day operations. "If you over-worry about controversies, you'd end up doing nothing."

In the process of not over-worrying after they struck their deal with Abramoff, Cassidy, Hartley, and their colleagues drove right through a series of flashing yellow lights. Just five days after that item in the *Post* announced their new arrangement, the newspaper published another scoop on the first substantial finding of the Indian Affairs Committee's investigation of Abramoff. Scanlon, the public relations man Abramoff had recommended to his Indian clients, had kicked back at least $10 million to Abramoff, the committee's investigators had learned. "The financial arrangements between the two men were not previously known to the tribes or to Abramoff's firm," the *Post* reported. A month earlier, Abramoff had told the *Post* flatly that he had no financial stake in Scanlon's business.

Another story on May 18 reported that the FBI was "conducting a public corruption investigation of Scanlon's and Abramoff's work for the tribes," looking for evidence of bribes or kickbacks—another ominous sign ignored at Cassidy & Associates.

By his own account Cassidy did not try to contact anyone at Greenberg Traurig to try to learn more about Abramoff. Nor did he contact Preston Gates. Had he done so, he would have heard strong words of caution, according to a senior member of that firm. What Cassidy did do was convene a meeting of his lawyers and Abramoff's attorney to discuss what had happened at Greenberg Traurig. "His explanation at that time seemed credible," Cassidy said later, without specifying what the explanation was.

Why hadn't he checked Abramoff out more thoroughly? "Let me tell you what people thought was going on," Cassidy replied—a classic Washington formulation. He meant, *Let me tell you the inside story.*

A lot of "very good people" who were Abramoff's friends said he had been railroaded by Greenberg Traurig, said Cassidy. He blamed this on a campaign against Abramoff conducted by a rival lobbyist, Scott Reed, who wanted to steal away Abramoff's Indian clients. Reed, a Republican operator who had managed Bob Dole's 1996 presidential campaign, was close to McCain, Cassidy said, suggesting a reason why the Indian Affairs Committee had launched an investigation into Abramoff's business. "There's no truth to it," Reed said later.

Cassidy said "people thought" that Greenberg Traurig "had made a very bad decision about not defending Abramoff," whose actions in fact were "defendable and defensible." Abramoff had "a story to tell that would come out."

Cassidy's longtime lawyer and partner, Lester G. "Ruff" Fant, said later: "Whoever told him 'this guy is getting screwed' knew Gerry very well." Cassidy loved underdogs, Fant explained, and would find it hard to resist such "bait."

Cassidy would eventually acknowledge that this was not his finest hour—that he had failed to do the necessary "due diligence" by checking on Abramoff more carefully. "I thought he was a great marketer. I thought he would find us business," Cassidy said years later. "That was the number one motivation . . . to get somebody who could bring in business."

This is the voice of Cassidy the entrepreneur, the businessman who found ways to exploit the political process in Washington to make a fortune. When he first arrived in Washington a generation earlier, such a person did not exist. There were lobbyists, to be sure, but they were small-time players compared to Cassidy—or Abramoff. Those two were fantastically successful figures in a town that until quite recently hadn't known their like.

Cassidy sensed that despite their different histories and conflicting personal politics, he and Abramoff could be compatible. They both saw the big possibilities in their business; they both wanted the largest rewards attainable; they both put business well ahead of politics. Cassidy's enthusiasm for Abramoff's abilities to attract new business must have helped him avoid the obvious ethical questions about his new consultant.

And the size of the fees Abramoff had collected was stunning. Greg Schneiders, whose public opinion research firm was part of Cassidy's organization from 1996 to 2002, remembered his reaction when he saw the story in the *Post* reporting fees of $45 million: "Cassidy must be apoplectic that someone out there is making so much money from the Indian tribes!"

"Green is a blinding color," observed a former Cassidy colleague.

If indeed the green had blinded him, Cassidy soon regained his eyesight with the help of a telephone call from Senator Inouye of Hawaii, whom Cassidy called "a good friend." Inouye described Cassidy as an old acquaintance, someone he did a lot of business with. The story of their relationship is instructive.

Inouye is another self-invented man. Born in Hawaii in 1924 to Japanese immigrant parents, he volunteered to fight in World War II in the spring of 1943, as soon as the Army dropped a ban on Japanese-American recruits. But he had to accept assignment to a segregated unit consisting entirely of Japanese-Americans. He fought for a country that was holding thousands of Japanese-Americans in internment camps while he was killing Nazis in Italy. In the last days of the war, Second Lieutenant Inouye led his platoon into a fierce fight near San Terenzo, losing his right arm to an enemy grenade but continuing to guide his men. His heroism won him the Congressional Medal of Honor.

After the war Inouye became a lawyer, won a seat in Hawaii's territorial legislature, then in 1959 became its first elected member of the House of Representatives when Hawaii became a state. Three years later he was elected to the Senate, where he has served for nearly half a century.

Inouye is a product of a Senate now all but forgotten, a collegial body of men and the occasional woman that took seriously its oft-claimed status as the "world's greatest deliberative body." Early in his career Inouye learned to legislate, to make deals, and to swap favors. He learned the value of loyalty. He built long-term alliances without regard to partisan considerations. So, for example, one of the most enduring partnerships on Capitol Hill was the team of Inouye and Senator Ted Stevens, Republican of Alaska. For many years, one or the other of them chaired the Senate Appropriations Subcommittee on Defense, which oversaw the Pentagon's enormous budget. (Stevens became chairman for the first time in 1981; Inouye in 1989.) Both believed it was a senator's job to bring home the bacon—to Hawaii and Alaska first of all, then to the states of favored colleagues.

Inouye and Cassidy first met in the early 1970s. Their relations took a dramatic turn for the better in 1990, when Cassidy hired a native Hawaiian named Henry Giugni as a new vice president of Cassidy & Associates. Giugni had gone to work for Inouye in 1957, and remained at his side for decades, a close personal friend and devoted assistant. In 1987, sponsored by Inouye, Giugni became sergeant at arms of the Senate, a largely ceremonial job but with influence over the Capitol police force and a number of patronage jobs. If he had the talent and inclination to do so, the sergeant at arms could easily befriend every member of the Senate, and Giugni had both. He was fun, funny, and warm. People loved him.

Giugni was no intellectual; he did not master complicated legislative issues. But he knew about friendships and favors. His job for Cassidy was to help bring in new business. The lure he offered was his intimacy with Inouye. It often worked. Year after year, Cassidy clients, including many colleges and universities, won earmarks from Congress in the annual defense appropriations bills. Giugni made a lot of money and liked it.

In 1993, Larry Grossman, a young lobbyist who had recently joined the Cassidy firm, sought Giugni's assistance. Grossman hoped to persuade the McDonnell Douglas Corp. to hire the firm to help protect its C-17 military transport plane from critics in the Department of Defense and Congress who were threatening to end production. He needed a contact at the company. Giugni said he could introduce Grossman to Denny Sharon, a former aide to Senator Barry Goldwater who had run McDonnell Douglas's Washington office for many years and still had influence in the company. Giugni arranged a lunch at the 116 Club, a scruffy Capitol Hill restaurant with no charm whatsoever that is frequented by lobbyists, members of Congress, and their aides. "Henry showed up dressed all in green. Shoes, suit, shirt, tie, socks—all green," Grossman recalled. Sharon looked at him and asked: "What are you, the Hawaiian leprechaun?"

"Giugni replied: 'Green is the color of money and that's what I want from you,' " Grossman recalled. McDonnell Douglas hired Cassidy &

Associates for $60,000 a month and also retained the services of its affiliated public relations firm.

Cassidy and his employees supported Inouye in the way they knew best—with campaign contributions. Cassidy and people who worked for him gave Inouye more than $65,000 between 1985 and 2006. They raised a good deal more for him from others, but did not have to report such activity. This is an ordinary way of doing business in Washington.

Did Inouye consider Cassidy a friend? The question was put to him in the summer of 2006. He did not answer directly, instead offering a classic senatorial circumlocution. Inouye obviously enjoys the role of senator, and has cultivated a rotund, oratorical voice that suits the role. "I've known him over all these years—I'd say oh, thirty-five years. In Washington that's a lifetime. So I've seen him rise from an unknown to someone who is, I suppose, in the big leagues now." Inouye also acknowledged teasing Cassidy about the latter's need to make enough money to keep his closet full of custom-made suits. But did that make him a friend? Inouye would not give a direct answer.

But in Washington the distinction between a friend and someone with whom one regularly and rewardingly conducts business is usually insignificant. Inouye made that clear in the spring of 2004, when he placed a phone call to Cassidy and immediately began upbraiding him. Cassidy asked why, and Inouye answered bluntly: hiring Abramoff had been a dumb mistake.

As a member of the Indian Affairs Committee, Inouye was learning the extent of Abramoff's brazen dealings with his tribal clients. "I took it personally," he said. "He was ripping off Indians." Inouye considered native Hawaiians part of the Native American population, and always took a protective approach to Indian issues.

The committee's early discoveries about Abramoff's rip-offs came soon after the news items in the *Post* and *Roll Call* reporting Cassidy's deal with Abramoff. This is what prompted Inouye to pick up the telephone. Inouye said he told Cassidy that if Abramoff remained associated with his firm, "your people won't come into my office"—they would no longer be welcome. The senator told Cassidy he had to fire Abramoff immediately. Cassidy did as he was told.

So nearly four months after the original bargain was struck, Abramoff and Cassidy met again and agreed to part company. Abramoff told friends he realized by then that he was "dead as a lobbyist" because the scandal bearing his name had grown out of control. He remained grateful to Cassidy for resisting "the frenzy going on around me." The members of

Abramoff's lobbying team that Cassidy had hired remained at his firm. Abramoff and Cassidy both released brief statements, which got very little attention in the press. Again, the *Post* used its lobbying column to record that the deal had ended. Cassidy's statement described the Abramoff colleagues he had hired as "tremendous assets" to Cassidy & Associates.

So with that help from his friend—or acquaintance—Inouye, Cassidy had long since separated himself from Abramoff by the time it became clear just how awful an apple he was. Abramoff and Michael Scanlon, his partner in crime, had bilked his tribal clients of more than $80 million. Abramoff had corrupted several members of Congress and congressional spouses. He had established charities that weren't charitable (except to himself and his friends), plied members with contributions and persuaded clients to do the same, and moved money around like an offshore banker. He went into the gambling business by buying (under false pretenses—a crime to which he pleaded guilty) a casino ship in Florida. He exploited (and sometimes exaggerated) his connections with influential people, starting with Tom DeLay and including numerous other members of the House and Senate and old friends from the college Republican movement, including Karl Rove, then in the White House. (Abramoff's personal secretary went to work for Rove in the White House in 2001.) Abramoff sent indiscreet e-mails ridiculing the same Indians who were putting millions into his pocket, making clear how cynical and vile he was despite his protestations of Orthodox Jewish piety. In Cassidy's words, spoken two years after he ended their relationship, Abramoff's transgressions were "beyond anything anyone could have imagined . . . the scale of it, and the boldness of it."

But not the nature of it, which is an important distinction. Abramoff had no self-control, no sense of limits or, certainly, of propriety, but apart from the gambling enterprise in Florida, his transgressions were all familiar to the Washingtonians who played the game that Abramoff and Cassidy and thousands of others played. Once revealed, Abramoff became a kind of caricature of the Washington lobbyist; but he was an extreme example of the breed, not another breed altogether.

His tricks were nearly all familiar: He bought a fancy restaurant (as did many other Washington lobbyists) to entertain the powerful, sometimes in violation of the rules about gifts to members of Congress and their staff or executive branch officials. He bought skyboxes at FedEx Field; at Camden Yards, the Baltimore Orioles' ballpark; and at the MCI Center, where Washington's professional basketball and hockey teams played. He could take important people to the games, and friendly congressmen could use the boxes for fund-raising events. He arranged luxurious free travel for elected and appointed government officials, a common-place favor taken to over-the-top extremes by Abramoff when, for example, he flew DeLay and others to Scotland to play golf on three famous courses that had all hosted past British Opens, with a stop at the Four Seasons hotel in London on the way home.

After he got caught but before he was sentenced to prison, Abramoff used to tell people (according to one who heard him): "I was participating in a system of legalized bribery. All of it is bribery, every bit of it." And every congressman and lobbyist in Washington was involved: "They all participate, all of them." That included two dozen members of the House and Senate who received campaign contributions from Abramoff personally or from his lobbying clients including the tribes. Abramoff had raised more than $100,000 for President George W. Bush. As the scandal thickened in 2006, members returned contributions they had received, or made donations to charity of the amounts they had received from Abramoff and his clients. The rush to return this money was unseemly, but persuasive: Washington had come to a collective judgment that Abramoff had gone over the line.

But where was the line? This was a difficult question to answer. To claim the high ethical ground was easy. On its Web site, for example, Cassidy & Associates boasted of its "tradition of ethics and integrity," citing the firm's "mandatory ethics training and compliance program that is the gold standard of the industry"—meaning the lobbying "industry." This training and compliance program did not protect Gerald Cassidy from his Abramoff temptation, however.

Drawing the line got harder as the money got bigger. Green really could be a blinding color. The ethics of Washington changed; old taboos fell away; things that once just weren't done, at least not openly, became commonplace.

Abramoff's use of the word bribery was hardly new. In a debate on campaign finance reform in 1971, one of the lions of the Senate, Russell B. Long, observed that "the distinction between a campaign contribution and a bribe is almost a hairline's difference. You can hardly tell one from the other." Long spoke at a time when candidates for the House and Senate raised tens or hundreds of thousands to run campaigns every two or six years. A generation later, when Abramoff got into trouble, members of the House and Senate raised millions, or tens of millions, to wage their re-election campaigns. They routinely spent a fourth or a third of their working hours soliciting those campaign contributions that Long and Abramoff both thought looked a great deal like bribes.

Players of the game liked to tell one another—and any outsider who asked—that this soliciting and giving was all just fine. "You have to have money to run," explains a congressman. "I can't buy a member or a vote for a $2,000 contribution," says a lobbyist. These are commonplace reassurances, heard in Washington every day. But they are not universally held. A few outspoken participants in the game will say it is wrong and dangerous.

One is Chuck Hagel, the Nebraska Republican senator from 1997 until 2009. "There's no shame anymore," Hagel observed not long after his party lost control of the Congress in 2006. "We've blown past the ethical standards, we now play on the edge of the legal standards." Money and its pursuit has paralyzed Washington, Hagel thought. Nothing truly important for the country was getting done.

"Legalized bribery" was a good description of the game, according to Leon Panetta, an influential and effective Democratic congressman from California for eighteen years who gave up his seat in 1994 to run President Bill Clinton's Office of Management and Budget, and then served as Clinton's chief of staff. When he left that job in January 1997, Panetta did something that is now rare for Washington players who relinquish their official office: he went home. He turned down several big-money offers to become a Washington lobbyist and instead established, with his wife, the Panetta Institute for Public Policy at California State University. He became a professor. He quit the game.

"Legalized bribery has become part of the culture of how this place operates," Panetta said on a visit to Washington. Today's members of the House and Senate "rarely legislate; they basically follow the money. . . . They're spending more and more time dialing for dollars. . . . The only place they have to turn is to the lobbyists. Members have a whole list of names in their pockets at all times, and they just keep dialing. It has become an addiction that they can't break."

Almost two decades before the Abramoff scandal erupted, in May 1986, a Washington lobbyist had written a stern warning about the ways that lobbyists' political contributions were corrupting the American political process. This was early in the days of the modern Washington money game, when $500 was still a big contribution and a House member with $200,000 in his campaign bank account was pretty nearly invulnerable. But the role of money in political campaigns was growing quickly at the time. Pollsters and the political consultants who used pollsters' findings to concoct candidates' television commercials were pushing up the cost of campaigns, and lobbyists had already become an important source of the money needed to pay for them. The warning, published as an op-ed piece in *The New York Times*, took the lobbying community and the Congress to task.

Some rationalizations used to defend the practice of lobbyists' hustling money for members of Congress "don't ring true," wrote this practitioner, "not least the argument that campaign contributions from special interests, which are often funneled through lobbyists, really don't make a difference because everybody does it. Money does make a difference—and it has changed the character of this town [Washington]. . . . The truth is that money has replaced brains and hard work as the way for a lobbyist to get something done for his client. Washington's atmosphere is reminiscent of what city halls must have been like in the days of Boss Tweed [the corrupt nineteenth-century boss of New York's Democratic machine]— only now the bagmen have fancy college degrees, $500 suits, big cars, the best tables. . . . Within acceptable limits the relationship can be ethical and legitimate. . . . Unfortunately, in today's Washington, those limits are long gone. Nobody can say when all the small cracks created by legal corruption in our legislative and administrative processes will create a disaster," but it was surely coming.

That article came to be prophetic. Its author was Kenneth Schlossberg, who had been the dominant figure in the onetime lobbying firm of Schlossberg-Cassidy & Associates. By his account, differences with Cassidy about the use of political contributions to try to influence members of Congress was one source of the collapse of their partnership in 1984.

The Abramoff scandal looked eerily like the disaster Schlossberg had predicted in 1986. It suggested the total corruption of several members of Congress, and it compromised a potentate of the House, DeLay. Abramoff made Schlossberg's colorful rhetoric about bagmen and Boss Tweed suddenly look utterly apt.

Jack Abramoff was an ideal villain for the early twenty-first century, a man whose crude appetites and brash overconfidence suited the tabloid culture of the time. Even his friends were appalled by the e-mails he had written that belittled his Indian clients as "monkeys" and "idiots." The e-mails, disclosed by congressional investigators, revealed a vain, lying, conniving, and apparently shameless operator hungry for money. One message instructed a colleague on how to inflate a bill to one of the Indian tribes artificially so it would reach $150,000. After it became clear that DeLay had received extensive and valuable gratuities from Abramoff, the most powerful member of the House of Representatives quite suddenly resigned from Congress. Soon after that, the Democrats regained control of the House and Senate.

The Abramoff affair exposed to a national audience trends and influences that had taken deep root in Washington over the previous thirty years. The scandal symbolized and advertised a kind of ethical rot in the nation's capital. The message was unmistakable because the Abramoff affair was so hyperbolic; it provided a vivid definition of "over-the-top." But the truths it revealed were well established, mundane by the time the scandal broke in that Sunday *Washington Post:* the capital city had changed. American politics had changed. Money had changed them both. Even Congress was embarrassed, and began to make some modest reforms.

But there was no obvious way to reform the new, underlying reality: in earlier generations enterprising young men came to Washington looking for power and political adventure, often with ambitions to save or reform the country or the world. In the last fourth of the twentieth century such aspirations were supplanted by another familiar American yearning: to get rich. Abramoff and Cassidy shared that craving.

They were just two of the tens of thousands of lobbyists, trade association executives, and related hangers-on who constituted a new class in Washington. Their posh way of life was often envied by the people they tried to influence—members of Congress, their aides, and officials of the executive branch. But in due course, often just a few years, those people could move beyond envy to share the city's new wealth themselves. They just had to pass through the revolving door from public service to "the private sector," the Washington euphemism for the influence-peddling industry. Once they crossed that threshold, such people could accumulate their own fortunes by influencing the choices and decisions of successor generations of public servants. In their new roles they could become donors of the campaign money that fueled the system, demonstrating their fealty with dollars.

Jack Abramoff became the celebrity and the symbol of Washington corruption. But the man who offered him a job, Gerald S. J. Cassidy, was a much more typical denizen of the new Washington that has evolved over the last three decades—precisely the period that Cassidy has been a lobbyist. Abramoff was an aberration, a kind of political sociopath who used familiar techniques to play the Washington game but overplayed his hand absurdly. Cassidy is a much more representative figure.

Clever men making serious money by influencing (or claiming to influence) official proceedings in Washington are nothing new, of course. At the time Cassidy went into the lobbying business in 1975 the two best-known Washington lobbyists were prominent former officials closely identified with the presidents they had served, Thomas G. "Tommy the Cork" Corcoran and Clark M. Clifford. Corcoran was the author of much of Franklin D. Roosevelt's New Deal legislation of the 1930s; Clifford was Harry S. Truman's right-hand man. Both traded on relationships and reputations acquired as truly important figures.

Cassidy never held an important government job. He had a narrow circle of influential friends and acquaintances. He was justifiably proud of his brainpower and of his ability to devise strategies for making things happen in Washington, but he had no particular stature in the community, no great reputation to trade on. What he did have was a keen business sense, determination, and self-discipline. Clifford worked hard to preserve his standing as a wise elder statesman, one presidents turned to in moments of crisis. Cassidy had no such pretensions. He used his ingenuity and his uncanny ability to exploit the ingenuity of others to get rich. Most of the people who became his competitors—most of the men and a few women who populated the lobbying firms that proliferated in the 1980s, 1990s, and 2000s—were similarly oriented toward business. This was a new class in Washington, hustlers who exploited the public policymaking process for profit. In financial terms, Gerald S. J. Cassidy was probably the most successful of the lot of them.

The story of Cassidy's rise to influence and riches is told in the pages that follow to try to illuminate how Washington has changed over the last three decades. But no individual's story can convey the entire tale, which involves more than the rise of lobbying and the growing role of money. Some of the most important changes have occurred in the ways our politicians run for office and, if they win, do their jobs in Washington. These are the subjects of digressions from the narrative of Cassidy's rise that are intended to provide a fuller sense of Washington's transformation in the modern era.

It is not a pretty tale. Chuck Hagel is certainly correct that the new realities have largely paralyzed political Washington. The arrangements that prevail in the nation's capital today have been entirely satisfactory to those who benefit from them, including lobbyists like Cassidy; the interest groups, corporations, and institutions that they represent; and, often, the members of the House and Senate. At least until 2006, in this era of big money incumbent members of Congress won re-election at unprecedented rates and with relative ease. Resurgent Democrats ended a prolonged period in which incumbents easily won re-election, but they did so in large measure by raising more money than ever. They changed the outcome but not the fundamentals of the game.

It has been a game that ill served the United States. Most obviously, the players have ignored or avoided a great many grave national problems. Hagel put it this way: "Health care, immigration reform, environment—you name the big issues today, we have not been able to move on any of them, because of the power of the process, the power of the special interests. . . ."

In today's Washington, money builds bulwarks that defend the status quo, even when political power changes hands because of election results. The classic example of this is the looming demographic crisis that will threaten the two most important social programs in America, Social Security and Medicare, which have provided protection for older Americans for decades. That these programs are going broke is hardly a secret; demographers and statisticians have been warning of the risks to both for more than twenty years. There is no avoiding the crunch that is coming soon, and which will shake American society to its foundations. Yet neither political party, nor any presidential administration since Ronald Reagan's, has confronted the problem.

Not addressing problems has become easy in a political environment distorted by money. Money allows politicians to run for office without even mentioning important matters that affect ordinary Americans' lives. A pollster and a political consultant making slick thirty-second commercials can fully compensate for a candidate who has no real philosophy of governance nor a coherent view of the world. The result is unreal politics—candidates winning or losing office on the basis of their positions on social issues essentially unrelated to governance, for example. In these three decades when money became so important in Washington, Congress lost much of its effectiveness as a governing institution. Running for re-election became more important than running the country, or keeping an eye on the exercise of executive power—the roles the founders envisioned for the House and Senate. The quality of governance in the United States had declined palpably in these years.

The money needed to sustain this situation can be easily raised from the interests and individuals for whom the politician can do favors of many kinds. The amount of money politicians raise for their campaigns goes up inexorably every two years; the earnings of Washington lobbyists climb in tandem.

The Abramoff scandal advertised the fact that for many of the players in Washington, money had come to matter more than anything else. This is an unpleasant fact, one that contradicts the mythologies of American democracy, and that many in Washington choose not to confront. This is hardly surprising. Political Washington is a village that can be both incurious and ignorant about itself. And Washington is the capital of a romantic, self-deluding country that often prefers its myths to its realities.

Gerry Cassidy accumulated a vast fortune by exploiting the opportunities that fate put in his path. Those were Washington opportunities, for the most part—opportunities of a new kind, opportunities that illuminate a new America.

CHAPTER 2

LOOKING DOWN ON THE CAPITOL

Gerald Cassidy's flirtation with Jack Abramoff astounded many of his old associates. "It was every bit as audacious in this town as doing a daytime bank robbery," one of them observed. "But he got away with it!" That *The Washington Post* was the only major news organization that even mentioned—barely mentioned—the Cassidy-Abramoff deal stunned many of Cassidy's competitors. "It wasn't surprising that he did it," one said. "It *was* surprising that it didn't blow up on him." Who could be so lucky as to make a deal with the man whose criminal behavior set off the biggest political scandal of the era, and never be called to account for it? Gerald Cassidy could.

On May 17, 2005, just ten months after he followed Senator Inouye's instructions and canceled his agreement with Abramoff, a jaunty Cassidy was receiving important Washingtonians at one of the grandest parties of that spring—the thirtieth birthday celebration of his firm. Such longevity for what Washingtonians call a "lobby shop" was rare, and Cassidy had decided to make the most of it. He and his colleagues invited more than a thousand guests. Typically for Washington, most neither accepted nor declined the invitation, so eight hundred nametags were made up for the occasion. They were set out on tables in the wood-paneled, two-story lobby of one of Washington's most splendid office buildings, a new twelve-story behemoth at 101 Constitution Avenue N.W., at the foot of Capitol Hill. Cassidy's offices were a dozen blocks away but he had an indirect interest in this building because he was a principal backer of Charlie Palmer Steak, a grand new restaurant that occupied much of the ground floor. Cassidy & Associates rented the rooftop terrace of 101 Constitution for the birthday party, and Charlie Palmer Steak catered the event.

Nametags for members of Congress were segregated on their own table, scores of them. Hundreds more nametags were lined up in rows on tables farther from the front door. The first guests began to arrive at 5 p.m. They were greeted by a team of smiling young women who doled out the tags, and pointed their owners to the elevators that would take them up to the roof.

It was a perfect spring evening. The temperature was in the low seventies; all over Washington the daffodils were blooming, and the greens of spring painted the tree-lined city. The sun was bright in the western sky; as the party continued for the next several hours, it turned a flaming orange and moved across Washington's vast Mall, passing over the Washington Monument, then the Lincoln Memorial and Arlington National Cemetery in the distance. As it descended the sun cast an angular light across the party on the roof.

For the guests the most striking view was toward the southeast, where the United States Capitol sat on its own hill—Jenkins Hill as it was known in 1791, when Pierre L'Enfant, the brilliant Frenchman who created a timeless and magnificent design for America's new capital city, chose the hill as the location for what he called the "Congress House." A good golf drive hit from the roof of 101 Constitution could have reached the Capitol. Cassidy's guests that spring evening looked out at the sandstone western facade of the familiar, neoclassical structure, lit up by the setting sun. From this unique vantage point the huge structure seemed to shrink into a single field of vision; it almost looked like a toy model.

Ordinarily Cassidy is not a party animal. He has none of the social bravado that pushes many a Washington operator into the center of a crowd. "He hates socializing," as one longtime colleague put it. Cassidy and his attractive wife, Loretta, rarely gave parties or attended the glitziest Washington events. But this was *their* glitzy event, and both Cassidys were enjoying a steady stream of congratulatory greetings from the guests on the roof. Loretta Cassidy's smile lit up the occasion. Cassidy seemed to preen.

He is about five feet, ten inches tall. The lower half of his handsome, square face is now covered with neatly trimmed white whiskers a quarter-inch long. His receding and thinning hair is white too, but his thick eyebrows remain black. He has large ears with huge lobes. Crow's-feet fan out amiably from the outer corners of his eyes.

On this occasion he was turned out in a favorite Alan Flusser double-breasted suit. This one was made for him from dark gray worsted wool with subtle, light gray pinstripes half an inch apart. The suit coat had no vents—the Italian look—and it fit perfectly. Three points of a crisp white handkerchief rose out of the jacket's breast pocket, matching Cassidy's plush white shirt with French cuffs. He wore a black silk tie decorated with white oval dots so it almost looked checked.

One of the first VIPs to appear that evening was a surprise to those who knew Cassidy's history: Robert C. Byrd of West Virginia, the senior-most member of the Senate. Sixteen years earlier, in an angry speech, Byrd had described Cassidy & Associates (not by name, but unmistakably) as "influence peddlers [who] sell themselves as hired guns to the highest bidder." Byrd, at the time chairman of the Senate Appropriations Committee, had been embarrassed by the revelation that his own West Virginia University had employed Cassidy to win favors from Congress. Partly as a result, Byrd sponsored and Congress passed legislation requiring new disclosures by lobbyists and some limitations on how they were paid. The lobbying community considered this "Byrd Amendment" to be an expression of the senator's hostility to Cassidy, which is why Byrd's presence at the party was surprising.

At eighty-seven Byrd was frail; he had to hold his glass of red wine in two hands, and they shook. He was asked why, given his history with Cassidy, he had come to this party.

"I'm here because I'm here," he replied, obviously flustered. "I was invited, and I decided to come." He would not elaborate.

Later another Washington lobbyist offered an explanation: "That's simple. It's his cycle. He's up." Translation: it was Byrd's turn to run for re-election (for the *ninth* time) in 2006. Republicans hoped the old man might be vulnerable, and had put him on their list of prime Democratic targets. Byrd was busily raising money. (By election day 2006, he had accumulated $5,205,708, more than four times the amount he had raised for his previous campaign six years earlier.) Attending Cassidy's party was part of that effort.

Six weeks before the party, Byrd's campaign filings to the Federal Election Commission later showed, Cassidy had made a $2,000 contribution to Byrd's re-election campaign. Six months after the thirtieth birthday party, Cassidy & Associates' political action committee made a $938 "in-kind" contribution to organize and pay the tab for a Byrd fund-raiser at an Italian restaurant in downtown Washington. The reception raised

$16,645 for Byrd, mostly from Cassidy's employees. In the disclosure forms filed later, one of the listed donors was Loretta Cassidy, who wrote a check for $2,000.

When asked later if he had been surprised by Byrd's decision to attend the party, Cassidy said no; he had advance word that the senator was coming.

Byrd was the first of at least two dozen members of Congress to make an appearance at the birthday party. Another was Congressman Edward Markey, a Democrat from Massachusetts, who was—when Democrats controlled the House—chairman of the subcommittee on telecommunications policy, a powerful position that made him an influential figure on big-dollar items like telephone regulation. That evening Markey came striding across the rooftop toward Cassidy with a big grin on his face, shouting "My Cassidy! I'm a fan of yours!"

Markey was part of the first world of pals that Cassidy had made as a lobbyist, the Massachusetts politicians who were part of Tip O'Neill's circle. Thomas P. O'Neill of Cambridge became the Democratic leader of the House in 1973, and the speaker in 1977. Markey became a congressman that year. He was a graduate of Boston College, as was O'Neill and his friend Silvio Conte, a liberal Republican congressman from western Massachusetts. Cassidy was Boston College's lobbyist (two of the college's administrators were also at the party). BC's campus includes the Tip O'Neill Library and the Silvio Conte Forum, the latter an arena for basketball and hockey games. Both were built with federal grants that Cassidy had helped steer through Congress.

Campaign contributions were part of the relationship too. Cassidy and his wife gave Markey's campaigns $23,000 between 1984 and 2006; Cassidy's employees gave an additional $43,300. In Markey's view contributions flowed from friendship: "Gerry is my friend. I've known him back thirty years. He has been my supporter from the beginning. And I think it all does go back to that early era. . . . It goes back so long, over so many years, back to him working for Boston College, that we had all gone to."

George McGovern came to the party—at eighty-two still vibrant and immediately recognizable. His and Cassidy's lives had been intertwined since their first meeting in 1969 in Immokalee, Florida. Cassidy still considered himself a McGovern man, and it was his service on McGovern's nutrition committee staff that launched Cassidy's lobbying career; as noted earlier, Cassidy had worked briefly on McGovern's 1972 presidential campaign. Over the years Cassidy had helped McGovern out of a couple of financial scrapes. At the time of the party Cassidy had been helping raise money for the George and Eleanor McGovern Library at Dakota Wesleyan University, the McGoverns' alma mater. Cassidy personally gave $100,000 to the library. McGovern expressed amazement at the success his old aide had enjoyed. He was happy to accept the invitation to the party.

The only presidential candidate besides McGovern whom Cassidy had personally tried to help was Senator Tom Harkin of Iowa. Cassidy served as one of Harkin's principal fund-raisers in his short-lived campaign for the Democratic nomination in 1992. Cassidy had few real friends in the Congress, but Harkin was one. He had come to Cassidy's defense during a 1986 Senate debate where the lobbyist was criticized by name. And he came to Cassidy's party on the roof.

The most influential guests to appear that evening were not Cassidy's friends, but Gregg Hartley's. Hartley was then a new addition to Cassidy & Associates, hired in 2003 for just less than a million dollars a year, plus a hefty share of the fees paid by any clients he attracted. Hartley ran the firm as chief operating officer.

His politics had nothing in common with Cassidy's. Hartley was a conservative Republican, a friendly, outgoing Missourian who came to Washington with Roy Blunt, who was first elected to Congress in 1996, two years after the Republicans won control of the House of Representatives. Blunt rose quickly into the House leadership, and in 2002 was elected majority whip. Blunt was a staunch conservative who cast himself as part of the religious right. Hartley was his most important aide for eighteen years, and a personal friend too.

In 2003, Hartley decided that the time had come to "go downtown"— to become a lobbyist, as so many senior aides from Capitol Hill had done over the years, especially in recent times. He and Blunt agreed on the timing; Blunt knew Hartley would remain a useful ally after moving downtown, one upon whom he could continue to call for political advice. And Hartley knew he was about to get rich. Cassidy won a bidding war for Hartley's services and quickly made him an important member of his team. It was a characteristic move by Cassidy, who for a quarter-century had found just the right associates and given them just the right degree of autonomy to do their best work and help make him rich.

Cassidy made no effort to deny what had happened—he had given a Republican day-to-day control of his firm, with an understanding that Hartley would hire more Republicans. At a time when Republicans controlled the White House and Congress, this was the only way he could preserve his firm's status as one of the top earners on K Street.

Cassidy had always employed Republicans, but hiring Hartley heralded a fundamental transformation of the firm. As if to advertise the change, Hartley's old boss Blunt appeared at the party wearing his familiar big grin, and then Blunt's boss appeared—Tom DeLay. DeLay was still at the height of his power at the time of the party, and his arrival, surrounded by a bustling entourage, created a stir. By coming to the party DeLay was doing a Washington favor for Hartley, who had served as a member of the leadership's brain trust for years. In the tribal protocol of Washington, to find two of the top three House Republicans at a lobbyist's party was a powerful signal.

Other prominent guests were acquaintances of Cassidy's but friends of another senior employee of the firm, Marty Russo. Russo was a Chicago pol of the old school, a big man, a golfer and locker room habitué, brash and loud. He won a seat in Congress from a suburban Chicago district in 1974; he was one of seventy-four new Democrats elected that year, the famous Watergate class that increased the Democratic majority in the House by forty-nine, to a total of 147. He became a protégé of Congressman Dan Rostenkowski's, whose first name—in newspaper stories, at least—was for many years "powerful chairman of the House Ways and Means Committee." Russo and another Democratic member had been redistricted into the same constituency after the 1990 census, and the other member beat him in a primary in 1992.

The next year Russo went to work for Cassidy & Associates. A former member of Congress becoming a lobbyist wasn't yet a common occurrence. Russo held on to as much of his old status as he could, playing basketball regularly in the House gym (former members were welcome) and hanging out with old pals on the Democratic side of the aisle. For the first four years that he worked at Cassidy & Associates, Russo continued to live in suburban Chicago and commute to Washington—just as he had as a member of Congress. He had calling cards printed that featured a large, golden seal of the United States and identified him first as "Marty Russo, Member of Congress, Retired."

Russo evokes strong emotions. He has a large collection of loyal friends, but a great many people can't stand him. Initially he was popular with his new colleagues at Cassidy & Associates. Then in 1997 Cassidy made him the president of the firm, and his popularity evaporated. He wasn't an effective leader, and his office political style was crude. Ultimately he drove a number of senior people away. More than one told Gerry Cassidy, "It's either Marty or me." Cassidy repeatedly picked Russo, who became his close friend.

Many prominent Democrats in the House were among the Russo loyalists, and a number of them turned out for the birthday party. Nancy Pelosi of California, the Democrats' leader and the future speaker (after the 2006 elections), was there. So was her best pal, Representative Anna Eshoo of California. Senator Richard Durbin of Illinois, a Russo colleague in the House and in 2005 the Democrats' deputy leader in the Senate, was another. Senator Charles Schumer of New York, who had shared a Capitol Hill townhouse with Russo, Durbin, and Congressman George Miller of California, also came to the party. So did Miller, Pelosi's closest ally. Senator Frank Lautenberg of New Jersey came. Congressman Charles Rangel of New York was there, the ranking Democrat then on the Ways and Means Committee, later its chairman when the Democrats reclaimed control in 2007.

Russo was shouting greetings, slapping backs, and hugging people with a hand around the backs of their necks all evening long. For part of the evening he carried a blown-up black-and-white photograph of himself as a young congressman with thick sideburns, showing it off to everyone he encountered. May 17 happened to be George Miller's sixtieth birthday, a coincidence Russo was delighted to exploit. He persuaded Bob Michel, the retired Republican leader in the House (Newt Gingrich pushed him into retirement in 1995, and took his place), to sing "Happy Birthday" to Miller. When he completed that assignment, Michel then sang an off-key happy anniversary song to Cassidy as well.

A guest list like this made the party a big success by Washington's standards, though only a fraction of those invited actually showed up. Most of the "Members of Congress" nametags remained unclaimed at the end of the party. There weren't many senators present, and no recognizable administration officials.

If Tom DeLay had been the host, the crowd would have been a lot more impressive; in Washington the strongest magnets are those with real power. A fixer like Cassidy can be influential, to be sure, but he doesn't scare anyone. For him and his associates, cultivating relationships is the heart of their professional lives. The guests at this party were mostly business acquaintances, the most common Washington version of friends. They came to the party to thank Cassidy or Hartley or Russo, knowing they would accumulate some credit in the favor bank by doing so.

The waiters from Charlie Palmer Steak circulated beneath the big tent that had been pitched on the roof with platters of miniature hamburgers, slices of roast beef, tempura shrimp, and miniature tarts filled with goat cheese and mushrooms. Big platters of cheese and raw vegetables with several dips covered tables in the middle of the party. Several bars served the good stuff. In the course of the three-hour party hundreds of guests passed through. Many were Cassidy clients; many were employees; a few were competitors. Aides from Capitol Hill—harder to recognize than their bosses—were also numerous. Often such giant receptions are cold and mechanical, but this one was boisterous and fun. The weather and the location certainly helped; so did the many high-volume schmoozers among the guests.

Cassidy himself was a disciplined host. He maintained a cheerful, rather formal dignity, and sustained a pleasant game face. Like Fitzgerald's Gatsby, he seemed to enjoy the idea of his party at least as much as the party itself. He sipped a little red wine early on, but took his first drink at 7:30, as the party was winding down. It looked like vodka on the rocks.

He had been disciplined in drawing up the list of invitees as well. Cassidy lived by an Irish code of loyalty. "Loyalty comes before other considerations," he said in one of our long conversations. "You're loyal to your friends if they're loyal to you, until they break that bond in some way." If someone does break the bond, Cassidy remembers it. So he carefully excluded from the list of invitees several dozen former associates who had left his firm, mostly since he had sold it. One such was James Fabiani, Cassidy's employee from 1984 until 2000 and his most important associate in that era. On the evening of May 17, 2005, Fabiani could be found half a dozen blocks down Pennsylvania Avenue, in the offices of Fabiani & Co., the lobbying firm he had opened in 2002.

Toward the end of the party Russo took a microphone and made a very brief speech about the firm's birthday. Then he handed the microphone to Cassidy. As the sun settled low in the western sky above the Lincoln Memorial, the proprietor spoke briefly too.

"All I want to say is it's been a great time, I've enjoyed it. I've had a great time over the years because of all of you. I've loved being in Washington working on important issues. My boss is here, Senator McGovern. He brought me to Washington thirty-five years ago and opened the door to a great life. Thank you."

Cassidy's words meant more to him than the people in this crowd could have known. He had no reason, as a boy, to expect a great life. Many knew he had survived a rough childhood in New York City, but few understood how horrific it had been. This party really was a triumphant moment for a man whose early life featured more hardship than triumph.

CHAPTER 3

THE ART OF SELF-INVENTION

Washington has always been a magnet for ambitious people. From the time the young American republic created a new capital on the banks of the Potomac in the first years of the nineteenth century, the federal city has provided a meritocratic arena where anyone with talent can pursue his ambitions, regardless of personal history. The city's indifference to pedigree has made Washington a mecca for self-invented men and women who have thrived there, unhindered by an absence of social credentials that might have restricted their prospects closer to home.

One such was Gerald S. J. Cassidy. He started out in Brooklyn and Queens as a tough street kid, the product of a poor, violent family poisoned by alcohol. He began inventing himself long before he arrived in Washington, long before he even knew what went on in Washington. His self-creation was a victory of determination over grim circumstance; circumstance might well have prevailed.

Perhaps the best thing to be said about Cassidy's miserable childhood was that it instilled in him a fierce ambition. He was determined to escape from the hell he grew up in and make something of himself. As he grew up he developed parallel ambitions: to do well—to make serious money—and also to do some good.

The miseries he endured as a child were largely the work of Jack Cassidy, a pugnacious drunk who could make life awful for everyone around him. After serving in the Navy in World War II he never had much success in life. His marriage to Cassidy's mother was rocky. As Cassidy described it, "they were an off-and-on relationship, that's just the way it was." When the relationship was on the family lived mostly in Brooklyn.

Jack Cassidy had exploited his status as a veteran to get an apartment in a public housing project in Red Hook, the neighborhood around the Brooklyn docks. When the relationship was off, Cassidy's mother often lived with one of her daughters, in Queens.

Cassidy's mother—"a tower of strength"—earned certification as a practical nurse, and was always the family's principal breadwinner. But there was never much bread. Evictions from cheap apartments and repossessions of items bought on credit—"things you never forget"—were regular occurrences, Cassidy recounted. Some of these he doesn't remember himself but heard about from his sisters. When he was an infant, "we were living in a one-room apartment—a one-room room—my mother, my three sisters, and me." Baby Gerry's crib was repossessed, so he slept in a bureau drawer.

As a child Cassidy had no real home, no safe haven. "I got shuttled around a lot . . . from house to house. It was sort of just a lot of living with who could afford me. I lived with my sister Mickey, I lived with my sister Delores, I lived with my grandparents, I lived with my Aunt Jane." He spent two stints of two years each near Dallas with his beloved oldest sister, Delores, and her Jewish husband, Ted Milkey, a six-foot, six-inch pilot and a particular favorite of Gerry's: "He was a wonderful person."

A photograph of his second-grade class in Dallas shows Cassidy to be the tallest boy in the class by several inches. The corners of his mouth are turned down in a sullen scowl. "I had a lot of problems with grade school. A lot of things got screwed up. . . . When I finished the second grade I was nine years old. . . . I had trouble with learning until I got a fifth grade teacher . . . at P.S. 27 [in Brooklyn] who took a big interest in me and helped me. After the fifth grade, in each class I did better."

When he came home from Texas the second time, Cassidy recounted, "I had a Texas accent. The kids made fun of me. . . . Some of the older kids were picking on me one day and started to punch me around, so I ran for our apartment. It was after school so my father [Jack Cassidy] was home by then and was looking out the window, watching me run. I ran up to the second floor and the door's open, so I think I'm going to run in and be saved. He closed the door and locked it. And I got beat up outside the door. Eventually he opened the door, the kids ran away, he pulled me inside and he told me, 'I don't want to ever, ever see you run away from anybody.' And that was it."

On another occasion Cassidy asked Jack Cassidy's advice about the hoods hanging out on neighborhood street corners in "black leather jackets [and] the Tony Curtis hairdo . . . looking tough. I went home one day and said, There are these guys out there, tough guys when you go by, they're older and they're saying stuff to you. And my father said to me, 'Look, they can dress up and try to look tough, it don't'—and he would talk like this—'it don't make them tough. It's just like if they wear dresses, it wouldn't make 'em women.' That's just how he felt about things. His advice was, hit first, ask questions later. And if you're going to hit, hit in the face because people didn't like that. That's just how he was.

"Dad joined the Navy at sixteen—lied about his age and went in. . . . He boxed in the Navy, he was a pretty good boxer. . . . I never remember him telling a joke, ever, and he was not a frivolous man. He didn't laugh a lot or anything. . . . He was a very traditional Catholic, in that he believed that life was a valley of tears that you went through to your reward in the next life. He really didn't expect much good to turn out about life."

Cassidy's childhood was violent and deprived, but he got glimpses of better alternatives, and they left an enduring impression. One came from his great-aunt Nellie. "My Aunt Nellie was the information lady at Gimbel's [one of the biggest department stores in New York City from the 1920s through the 1970s]. We were all impressed. She was the establishment figure in our little world. She had this job—you walked into Gimbel's main entrance and there was a desk. And there would be my Aunt Nellie, who was my [maternal] grandmother's sister. Her name was Helen but everybody called her Nellie. She was the information lady. And she had adopted this very proper attitude, because she was the information lady. She wanted me to have manners, so she paid for me to go to this school the nuns ran for little kids in the summer, where they would teach you what fork to use. Its name was Foxwood. . . . She was a sweetheart."

Cassidy's mother worked nights and slept during the day, often leaving envelopes containing cash on the kitchen table to pay the bills—utilities, rent, and so on. "We didn't have a checkbook. . . . When I was old enough to find my way around I would go and make these payments," Cassidy said.

Poverty seemed to come naturally in his family. On his mother's side the Millotts were poor rural folk from the west of Ireland who spoke Gaelic. Some of them stuck to their native tongue long after they arrived in America. "These were very troubled people," he said. "The trouble when you have the kind of poverty they experienced, it lasts. People take it with them. They have very low expectations. There's just a lot of heartache."

For Cassidy the family's troubles were compounded by Jack Cassidy's drunken violence: "Jack Cassidy and I didn't get along. There was not a prejudice he did not subscribe to. He was a drinker, a chaser, and a fighter. And a rough guy. He brought me up essentially with an idea that you just didn't take anything from anybody. He was rough all the way around." This included roughing up Cassidy's mother on occasion. "I physically stopped him at some point, that's what stopped his behavior."

Behavior toward his mother?

"Yeah, and toward me. I was sixteen when that happened."

These experiences took a toll. "A lot of who I was and how I was as a kid was very private to me. I didn't let people inside my life. I kept people out. I think in a way it's something I learned to do, and never stopped doing. You know, if you can't trust the people you live with, it's hard to trust other people. So I've always had a wall around me, and I've always felt that I had to be careful with people, and I always felt a level of embarrassment about our situation. . . . Our house was very often a loud place, with my father's behavior. If you walked out and downstairs from an apartment, you felt that everybody—that wasn't happening in their house. So I didn't want friends coming over, I didn't have friends coming over, and I lived my life outside of the house. And pretty much from the time I was thirteen, I sort of ran my own life. I went out, and I came home. So there was a good deal of distance, and not a lot of people were inside my world."

Cassidy's situation improved considerably when he entered Holy Cross, a new Catholic high school in Flushing, Queens. This was the first of a series of academic institutions that helped Cassidy escape from the deprivations of his childhood. His mother had tried to get him into Catholic schools earlier, but without success. "I just had bad grades," Cassidy explained. Holy Cross was a new school that the Brothers of Holy Cross were opening, and Cassidy's mother got him a place in its first class. "She talked my way in." To qualify for admission, Cassidy had to pretend to be a permanent resident of his sister's Queens apartment.

Phil Costanzo, the son of a bricklayer, met Cassidy when both were freshmen in that first class at Holy Cross. "We were each walking home from school. I impulsively picked up a rock and threw it at his book bag, being a wise-ass street kid. We became the best of pals."

Costanzo is another self-invented man. He eventually earned a Ph.D. and became a professor of psychology at Duke University. He drew a complex portrait of the adolescent Cassidy, his closest friend for many years. Costanzo described a real character, a natural leader: "He had a sense of humor and a turn of mind that would ignite those around him," Costanzo said. "His antics . . . were not buffoonery at all. They were the antics of a person who had a real delight in what his connections were." Even before he had a driver's license Cassidy had the use of an uncle's red and white Oldsmobile 88, Costanzo recalled. "He drove it with wild abandon. If you complained he would threaten to get out of the car, and open the door as if to do so."

Members of their gang rewarded Cassidy with stable friendships that helped compensate for his unstable family relationships, Costanzo said. "I think that Gerry used his peer group, always, as partly his family. . . . There was a sense of sanity [in those friendships] that he wasn't getting at home."

At Holy Cross, Costanzo noted, their class of '59 was "king of the manor" for four years. The new school grew by one class each year, so they were the oldest (and only) class as freshmen, and retained senior status throughout. Costanzo thinks the success of many members of that class—which includes professors, college presidents, businessmen, and one professional football player—in part reflected the confidence-building status they enjoyed for four years in high school.

The Holy Cross brothers who ran the school and taught there indulged their charges' high jinks. "They were not as stern with us as the Jesuits might have been. They tolerated our boyishness without letting it get out of hand," Costanzo said. He remembered stealing ice cream out of the cafeteria freezer after football practice. He remembered Brother Martian, the dean of students, poking a stiff finger into the chests of wayward students, impressing on them the need to behave better.

"Very good values were conveyed there: You can be self-seeking as long as you take care of others. . . . The rules of the game are, you can pursue for yourself as long as you look out for those around you."

Holy Cross put the idea of going to college into their heads. Cassidy's mother approved; "my mother always said I was going to college, always." But Jack Cassidy did not see the point. "He told me he had friends who could get me into either the boilermakers union or the operating engineers union, and I could make a good living," Cassidy remembered. "He was not a big believer in education."

Costanzo and Cassidy were both good football players. "We played varsity football in the Catholic leagues even as juniors," Costanzo remembered. But senior year brought an unexpected setback for Cassidy: because of his slow start in elementary school, his nineteenth birthday would come in April of senior year, which made him too old to play that season for Holy Cross.

"So I played on a sandlot team," Cassidy recalled. His teammates and opponents were mostly older men, but "I still did pretty well. . . . I played fullback and linebacker." Villanova University, a Catholic school with Augustinian roots, was then a serious football power. The team's head coach recruited Cassidy. "I understood the coach to say . . . that if I showed up I'd have a scholarship." He did show up and tried out, but the competition was fierce and he failed to make the team. "It was probably the singular disappointment in my life," he said in a conversation nearly half a century later. He spoke these words with a poignancy that was totally convincing.

So Cassidy was a Villanova student, but the football scholarship he had anticipated to pay for school had suddenly evaporated. "The good friars helped me out," Cassidy explained. They gave him an academic scholarship that covered part of his costs, "and I had jobs. I worked. . . . I have always worked—always, always worked." In Cassidy's climb out of the hell of his youth, work was his constant companion.

Phil Costanzo ended up at Villanova with Cassidy on similar terms. He too failed to make the football team. He and Cassidy joined forces in Philadelphia to good effect. In their sophomore year they lived in an apartment in Ardmore, commuting to class and arguing sports with the locals in a bar across the street. The next year they moved back to a dormitory on campus. They had numerous jobs during their undergraduate years. Costanzo remembered cutting lawns for suburbanites living on the Main Line. Cassidy worked for a Philadelphia trucking company— "worked nights on the platform there . . . I worked . . . at the infirmary. I worked at a place in Bryn Mawr called the Showbar . . . a college bar." He was able to send money home to his mother during his four years at Villanova. Cassidy and Costanzo played hard too, though without much money this could require improvisation. "Gerry and I used to get dressed to the teeth," Costanzo recounted. "We got imitation nice suits. Gerry always liked to dress well. We'd go out to the best restaurants in Philadelphia with an umbrella on our arms. We'd eat an elegant dinner at Bookbinder's, leave a nice tip, and beat the check. We did that all over Philadelphia."

Cassidy majored in social sciences. He liked college and did well. He and Costanzo used to share their dreams for the future that, they both hoped, would take them far from working-class Queens.

Costanzo remembers Cassidy's talent for making lemonade from the lemons of his life: "He could always construct in his mind positive futures. He would do this perhaps to run away from the darker side, the more depressed components that were there. I remember lying with him in a bunk bed in Villanova. We both had the dream that we would be with unbelievably beautiful women and we would go to a place like Dartmouth College and teach and it would be beautiful and nice. By the time you finished talking with Gerry you believed in those fantasies and in your ability to make them live."

All of Cassidy's dreams nearly crumbled on Christmas Day in 1961, during his junior year at Villanova. He was home for the holidays at his mother's apartment when his sister Joan and her two children stumbled in. "They were just in bad shape, and hysterical," Cassidy remembered. They had come from their apartment, where Joan's husband, in a drunken rage, had been beating all three of them. Gerry and his mother tried to comfort them. Then Gerry decided to respond.

"I left and I found him at their home. They lived in a second-floor apartment. So I had it out with him. I wanted him to leave the apartment so I threw him out and actually did throw him down the stairs. Neighbors called the police."

The cops came and were about to arrest Cassidy on charges of assault when "a distant cousin of mine, a priest, Father Coffey," arrived serendipitously on the scene and tried to mediate. "He got the police not to take me in." Father Coffey told the cops that this was a fine young man who was trying to protect his sister. He would lose his scholarship to Villanova if they arrested him.

Cassidy did not let the matter drop. "I got my sister to file charges, I got him arrested. Then I got a neighborhood lawyer who I knew through a guy I knew from high school, and he got a restraining order to keep him out of the house and then my sister got a divorce, kept him away. He was a terrible person. But there were a lot of terrible guys like that around. It was not an unusual story for that world. . . . Anytime there's an Irish family and they're called the Ellis Boys or the O'Brien Boys, it's a bad sign. These were the Ellis boys. They were just a bad bunch." Back at Villanova Cassidy and Costanzo debated the relative merits of graduate and professional schools. The idea of becoming a lawyer had been in Cassidy's head since "early in high school," he remembered, though he wasn't sure why. As a boy he never knew a lawyer, nor understood what they did, but he liked the sound of it. As his Villanova career neared an end he decided to apply to law school.

Cornell was not an obvious choice. It was an Ivy League school, located in a small town in upstate New York where the winters were cold and long. Cassidy did not know a lot about law schools or about Ithaca, but he did know from his experience at Villanova that he could compete in the classroom with the brightest students. And those dreams Costanzo remembered had enticed him to reach upward by applying to a really good law school. Best of all, Cornell would have him, and would provide a combination of scholarship and campus job that would make law school financially possible. "I even got a stipend of $50 a month," Cassidy recalled.

And he would not have to go alone. Since his sophomore year at Villanova he had courted Loretta Palladino, a lively young woman from South Philadelphia who people said looked like a smaller, slimmer version of Sophia Loren. They had met by chance on the Villanova campus, which she was visiting with several girlfriends. She was working as a secretary at the time. Cassidy was immediately smitten. Could they go out on a date? She said he would have to telephone her at home, which he did. Then he had to meet her parents, who were suspicious of this Irishman from New York. Her father worked in the post office. "Her aunts would talk to each other in Italian when I was at the house," Cassidy remembered. But the romance was permitted—under strict conditions. "Dating her you had to have her home at ten. Her mother would sit at the front door, waiting for you to come in," he said. Loretta had everything Cassidy did not: a warm home, doting parents, a supportive extended family. He was often invited to the modest row house in an Italian neighborhood, and he liked it. Friends thought the beefy Irishman with the fullback's physique and the diminutive, vivacious Italian made a handsome couple.

Loretta agreed to follow Cassidy from Philadelphia to Ithaca, New York, the hilly college town "far above Cayuga's waters," in the words of Cornell's alma mater. For both of them Ithaca was a long way from home in fact and in spirit. But it was the first stop on their journey out of South Philadelphia and New York City, a journey they hoped would take them to a better life than either Cassidys or Palladinos had known.

As they settled in that fall they decided it was time to get married. Both families had seen this coming, and the young people presumed it would happen easily. All they needed was a marriage license. Cassidy discovered that this would require a copy of his birth certificate. He asked his mother for it.

At the time Beatrice Cassidy lived in a modest apartment with her daughter Joan in a sprawling red-brick housing project for moderate-income tenants in Fresh Meadows, a working-class neighborhood in Queens. She had her son's birth certificate, and his baptismal certificate too, but sharing them with her only son was difficult. Both documents contained a long-hidden family secret that she had kept from him for twenty-three years. She told her son he had better come home.

When he did she gave him the birth certificate. It recorded the arrival on this earth on April 14, 1940, of Gerald Sylvester Joseph McIntyre, the son of Clarence McIntyre, someone Gerry Cassidy had never heard of. His mother now revealed that Jack Cassidy, the man Gerry had called Dad all his life, with whom he had fought physically and psychologically, who had tried to discourage Gerry's ambition to go to college, was actually not related to him. Jack Cassidy had married Gerry's mother shortly after Clarence McIntyre had abandoned his family, when Gerry was an infant.

Gerry was the fourth child in the family, born in 1940. His three sisters were much older—Joan by thirteen years, Mickey by sixteen, Delores by eighteen. They were all McIntyres. They were teenagers when their father abandoned the family. Mickey and Delores were adults by the time their mother married Jack Cassidy. But all three helped their mother keep the secret from their beloved kid brother, whom the women in the family liked to spoil.

The discovery that his father wasn't his father shook Cassidy. He dropped out of Cornell. Through a friend in Queens Cassidy found a job as an insurance adjuster for Liberty Mutual. He and Loretta moved into their own apartment. They were married on March 7, 1964. Phil Costanzo was his best man.

Costanzo considers this year in Queens the crucial moment in Cassidy's early life. His initial experience at Cornell Law School had not been good. "It felt like he didn't belong there," Costanzo remembered—surrounded by privileged kids who acted as if they were entitled to be at Cornell, studying subjects Cassidy considered boring.

When he first came home from Cornell, Costanzo remembered, Cassidy was depressed. He had to struggle with the fact that his real father had abandoned him. Cassidy learned that McIntyre had lived nearby all of Cassidy's life, but had never made an effort to see the son he abandoned, never saw him play football or anything. It took a long time to process these revelations.

Costanzo recalled that Cassidy watched a lot of television. He went to work but had no heart for the job handling insurance claims. "I decided in favor of every claimant that came along. I hated it, hated it," Cassidy recalled.

But he got ahold of himself. Costanzo remembered with admiration the way his friend regrouped as the year progressed. He used the time to generate determination to go back to Cornell, and prevail at law school, his chosen route to a better life. Costanzo thought this persistence reflected an ethos they both learned on the streets of New York: "You beat the things that beat you. . . . It's the characteristic of indomitability that you get from hanging around with working-class kids that wanted something better." Somehow Cassidy always understood that wanting something better was not enough—he had to seize the opportunities that came his way, reach for the brass rings that fate put in his path.

Cassidy still remembers the name of the man who helped him salvage his Cornell Law School career: his original faculty advisor, John McDonald. After the unexpected discovery of his father's true identity, Cassidy discussed with McDonald his desire to drop out for a year. "He was a wonderful man, he understood the situation and said everything would be in place, financial assistance, the scholarships, everything." With his new wife beside him, Cassidy tried Cornell Law again in September 1964.

"Loretta was an important ballast point for Gerry," Costanzo said. "He was less mercurial around Loretta than usual. She loved him; he really loved her." She had encouraged him to resume his legal studies, which he did doggedly, though without much enthusiasm.

"I found law school to be one of the most tedious things—in fact, the most tedious thing I ever did," Cassidy said. But he put up with the tedium. The law degree was going to be his ticket to a better world.

He and Loretta lived quietly in married student housing. She worked as a professor's secretary for $45 a week. He continued to hold multiple jobs, including working an evening shift in the university library. He had few friends. One pal was Robert Cartwright from Chicago, another married student, and his seatmate in many classes because in alphabetical order, Cartwright came just before Cassidy.

Years later Cartwright recalled that he and Cassidy "shared a similar reaction to the law school, which was not entirely complimentary." Surrounded by more privileged students, they shared a similar working-class outlook. Cartwright also had to work to pay his way through law school. They thought the Socratic teaching method was stilted and unnatural, and found many of the professors to be cold fish. Their common attitudes and shared status as married students and neighbors in many classes contributed to a real friendship, Cartwright said. "We even had the same automobile, we both had Volkswagen Bugs."

"Gerry and I were fairly to the left, particularly about the Vietnam War," Cartwright remembered. In 1968 they both supported Senator Eugene McCarthy's antiwar candidacy for the Democratic presidential nomination.

"I'm not sure I would have made it through the place if it hadn't been for his friendship," Cartwright said. "We didn't have a lot of bosom buddies among the classmates. He'd be the only friend I would mention today." They had to push each other to find the discipline to complete the three-year course, but they both made it.

Gerry and Loretta didn't like Ithaca much, but they stayed in town through both summers of his law school career because Cassidy needed the money he could earn on a beer truck. He graduated in 1967 without distinction or humiliation. "I wasn't at the top of the class, and I wasn't at the bottom."

He enjoyed what was going on around him on Cornell's campus more than torts and criminal procedure. "It was a stimulating time, with a lot of issues percolating," Cassidy recalled of the mid-1960s, when the anti–Vietnam War movement swept campuses such as Cornell's and President Lyndon B. Johnson waged a war on poverty. "There wasn't a lot to do there, so we went to a lot of lectures," he remembered—Vietnam teach-ins, lectures on civil rights, on poverty, and on legal assistance to the weak and poor. One of the speakers who made a strong impression on Cassidy was Edgar Cahn, whom he remembers speaking at Cornell each of the three years he was there. Cahn and his wife, Jean Camper Cahn, were the founders of the neighborhood legal services program in LBJ's Office of Economic Opportunity, the headquarters of the war on poverty. The Cahns proselytized in law schools across the country, advancing the idea that the law could be used to promote social justice.

"Poverty really caught me," Cassidy said. "I was really taken by *Harvest of Shame* [the famous Fred Friendly–Edward R. Murrow television documentary on migrant workers in Florida]. . . . I had seen it when it was originally on television [in 1960]. Somebody came to Cornell, I can't remember the name, and showed it and gave a lecture about how things were now."

In his final year at law school Cassidy learned about South Florida Migrant Legal Services, a legal aid program for itinerant farmworkers that was about to start operating in the area where Murrow and Friendly made *Harvest of Shame*. He had talked with some big law firms but had no job offers when he decided to apply for a job with the Florida program, one of the first in the country to try to implement the Cahns' ideas. After three grim years cooped up in Ithaca, Cassidy was ready for an adventure.

This cannot have been an easy choice, because Cassidy was already committed to the goal of making serious money. "He wanted to be rich," Costanzo remembered. Cassidy never hid his desire for the financial secu-

rity which "I didn't have a lot of" as a child. At the same time the spirit of
the 1960s had obviously infected him. His Catholic education had taught
him about his obligations to the less fortunate. And poverty was something Cassidy knew a lot about.

He also had firsthand experience with racial issues. He remembered
his brother-in-law driving him through a black neighborhood in Dallas
"that was just so bad I couldn't understand it. . . . I was five, and I remember just being curious about why black people were in this obviously different situation." Young Gerry put the question to Ted Milkey, his sister's
husband, who was driving. "He explained to me that this was just something that was wrong in our world, and that there was no reason for it, and
it was something I should never engage in in any way."

Cassidy was seven when Jackie Robinson broke the major leagues'
color line by joining the Brooklyn Dodgers, and sixteen when Robinson
retired. "He was my biggest hero. I was so impressed with him, I was crazy
about him. He just personified manliness. I can still see him stealing home
against the Yankees in the '55 World Series. He was one of the old men of
baseball at the time, and he stole home. He was everything."

But the situation was more complicated than simple hero worship. "I
was surrounded by racism growing up. It was just a reality. That's how it
was. Working-class areas, you could root for the Brooklyn Dodgers one
day, and [Roy] Campanella and [Don] Newcombe and [Junior] Gilliam
and Robinson [four black stars for the Dodgers], and at the same time not
want any of them to move into your neighborhood, not want anybody
[black] to work where you are working, use racial epithets about them—
but not about those guys [the ballplayers]. That was a reality." The South
Florida Migrant Legal Services program, created by prominent Florida
lawyers with a board chaired by Chesterfield Smith, president of the
Florida Bar (and later of the American Bar Association), looked like a serious enterprise. The legal aid project offered him a job for just less than
$9,000 a year.

He spent the summer of 1967 studying on his own for the Florida bar
exam. "I expected it to be much harder than it was," Cassidy said. He
passed. After brief training in Washington and Miami, Cassidy and three
other young attorneys were sent to Fort Myers on the west coast, not far
from Naples, which was then a sleepy little town. They would open a new
office there and look for clients among the black and brown fruit and vegetable pickers who flocked to the area for seasonal work every year. Gerry
and Loretta rented a small bungalow on a riverbank in Fort Myers.

Cassidy's colleagues were an interesting group: Mickey Kantor (secretary of commerce three decades later, under President Bill Clinton), William "Willie" Dow (now a white-collar defense attorney in Connecticut), and Michael Foster (who practices law in Tampa). None had any relevant legal experience, but all had enthusiasm. The other three have warm memories of Gerry and Loretta. Local white people were often hostile to the lawyers, whom they considered troublemakers and outsiders. The local bar association shunned them. So the young lawyers and their spouses relied on each other for companionship. Diana Dow, Willie's wife, remembered outings to Busch Gardens, Tampa, and Miami, and good Italian dinners at the Cassidys'.

The Dows and Cassidys became friends. Diana Dow and Loretta Cassidy cooked one Christmas dinner together, and when Dow got pregnant, Loretta helped her sew baby clothes. "They were a fun-loving couple," Diana Dow remembered. "I thought they were very commonsense. And they always were funny. . . . Her dream really was just to be the best wife she could be."

Willie Dow remembered Cassidy as unsure of himself in this new setting. "Gerry was a big, insecure teddy bear," who was overweight at the time and wore sideburns and a mustache. Dow thought Mickey Kantor and his wife, Georgetown University graduates who had already been exposed to Washington political life, were the most mature in their group. "Kantor was politically astute and smooth; Gerry was not. Gerry had some envy of Mickey."

Kantor remembered Cassidy fondly. "He was very, very smart," Kantor said, and was committed to helping the migrant workers they represented. "He really cared." He also recalled Cassidy as "tightly wound" and fiercely competitive: "When he has a cause, whatever it is, you don't want to get in his way."

The senior member of the group was Foster, who had worked as an attorney in the Department of Justice in Washington before coming to Florida. But he had no more experience trying the kinds of cases the four dealt with than any of the others. He too remembered Cassidy's combative nature, which occasionally showed up in court. "Gerry was known for standing his ground. He wouldn't stand down for anybody. A couple of times I had to suggest that maybe we ought to convene in the corner for a minute before things got out of hand."

Cassidy's colleagues had all reached this point in their young careers by paths easier than the one Cassidy took. They were all from middle-class families, and all had less difficult lives. Cassidy did not share with them details of his own past.

The lawyers worked in a storefront. "We had a small office, on . . . the black side of town, with a little grocery store next door to us, and we represented migrant workers in civil matters," Cassidy recalled. Their toughest cases were likely to come from the town of Immokalee, about twenty miles southeast of Fort Myers, the locale where Murrow's *Harvest of Shame* was filmed.

"It was really a dangerous place, in terms of violence and in terms of disease," Cassidy said. "It was just terribly poor, the worst abuses that one heard of in the *Harvest of Shame* were present there, but beyond what I had heard about. . . . They were crews, they were ethnically divided; one camp would be black, another would be Mexican. It was a lot like the coal mining situation: they owed their life to the company store. They were always in debt to the crew boss, or to the farm account. They weren't welcome many places. Living conditions were terrible. They wanted them out as fast as they could get them out of town, once there wasn't work [after the harvest was in]. The schools were a problem because they really weren't welcome in the local schools, though they should have been. They couldn't get benefits that they were entitled to. It was before food stamps—there was a federal feeding program; one of our lawsuits was to get them into that. Labor standards were not enforced and we sued them about labor standards."

The crew bosses contracted with the farmers and then abused the workers, Cassidy said. The bosses dealt harshly with any worker protests. "There was one instance, a woman who was talking to us about a suit, she was living in one of these trailers they had, and she was horribly burned, somebody set it on fire, after she talked to us. She was in the hospital, just burned to pieces. She passed away. And I always thought that we had in some way put her in jeopardy that we didn't quite understand. They were in more danger I think than we initially realized."

Kantor estimated that the young attorneys had a couple of hundred live cases in folders in their desk drawers at any time: landlord-tenant disputes, consumer fraud complaints, a case to desegregate a nursing home, even a slavery case involving trade in young black workers from Mississippi at $20 a head. "The local sheriff would track down any escapees and bring them back, charged with failure to pay debts."

The exploitation of hapless and largely helpless migrants had deep roots in Immokalee, and Cassidy realized that the four of them could not change the system fundamentally: "Around the edges we were helpful to them, but I don't think we changed their situation. We brought attention to it. In some areas I think we got some local enforcement of the labor laws that wasn't happening."

The only palpable accomplishments involved improving the circumstances of individuals. Cassidy won a lawsuit for a Mexican-American crew boss named Pedro Gomez, who brought workers from his hometown of McAllen, Texas, to pick vegetables in Immokalee. Gomez had formally complained about the ramshackle houses that one farmer provided for his crew, which consisted of Gomez's relatives. The houses "were deplorable," Cassidy remembered. But "he could not find anywhere else to live. And then, because he complained, they tried to evict him from there. And during that process there were injuries to the people and the property and so we filed a suit about that. That was my case." Before it went to trial the farmer settled for $45,000. Gomez took this money back to McAllen and opened a grocery store, Cassidy remembered forty years later.

He also recalled Charles Luckey, whom he met as a teenager when Luckey and his mother were trying to help a black woman in Fort Myers become the town's first African-American city councilor. He and his mother both picked vegetables. Luckey "did very, very well in school," Cassidy remembered. He took a liking to the young man.

Luckey remembers Cassidy phoning him at home to ask what his plans were for college. "He was more helpful than my counselors," Luckey said. "He got me books on colleges. Helped me with the applications. He was very instrumental in that."

Luckey did not know about the biggest favor Cassidy had done for him. Cassidy knew a man with ties to Macalester College, a fine liberal arts school in St. Paul, Minnesota. "I helped to get him into Macalester. I helped him apply there, I called there and spoke to the school, he got a scholarship. I don't think he could have gone otherwise."

When asked about these events four decades later, Luckey said he never realized Cassidy had intervened on his behalf. He remembered Cassidy as "tremendously compassionate, very interested, very supportive in every way." Luckey finished Macalester in three years.

The two lost touch. Cassidy thought Luckey had become an FBI agent, but he was wrong. Luckey had considered the FBI and had begun the process of applying to the bureau when he realized he didn't want a job that involved carrying a gun. He became a schoolteacher instead, and then the principal of Harns Marsh Elementary School in Fort Myers, with nearly one thousand students.

The four lawyers spent most of two years in Fort Myers. The biggest event by far of their time in Florida was the visit of the U.S. Senate's Select Committee on Nutrition and Human Needs in March 1969.

The committee was created in 1968 in response to two privately funded studies of hunger in the United States, released in April and May 1968, and a CBS television documentary called *Hunger in America* that was broadcast on May 22. It was a "select" committee, not a "standing" committee, which meant it had no legislative jurisdiction—no direct role in writing new laws. Its purpose was to investigate and educate. The chairman of the committee was George McGovern, who was just beginning his second term in the Senate.

It is difficult now to imagine the atmosphere of that time, when politicians of both parties agreed that the government had to take action to alleviate hunger and poverty. The politicians were influenced by those revelations of poverty in America, but they were propelled into action by the alarming riots in American cities that caused dozens of deaths and massive destruction in Los Angeles in 1965, then in Cleveland in 1966, Newark and Detroit in 1967, and in many cities, dramatically including Washington, after the assassination of Martin Luther King Jr. in April 1968.

The president joined the chorus in that spring of 1969. He sent a message to Congress on hunger: "In the past few years we have awakened to the distressing fact that despite our material abundance and agricultural wealth, many Americans suffer from . . . hunger and malnutrition. . . . Millions may be affected. . . . The moment is at hand to put an end to hunger in America itself for all time. I ask this of a Congress that has already splendidly demonstrated its own disposition to act. It is a moment to act with vigor; it is a moment to be recalled with pride." The president sending this message was no liberal Democrat; Richard M. Nixon had been in the White House since January 20, 1969.

Facing up to the realities of poverty and hunger was in fashion. *The New York Times* assigned one of its best reporters, Homer Bigart, to write a series of front-page articles on hunger, and he consulted with the Senate Committee on Nutrition and Human Needs. When he learned that the committee planned a field hearing in Immokalee, he decided to devote one of his articles to conditions for migrants there. In February 1969, he published a stomach-turning description of Smith's Camp, which, Bigart wrote, "houses some of the migrants who flock here [to the Immokalee area] in winter to pick the vegetable crops.

"The camp consists of a dozen windowless plywood shacks," Bigart wrote, "all without toilets or running water, all painted a dull green and all facing a dark slough choked with bottles and trash. Some distance away there are three smaller shacks, two of them privies, the third a cold-water shower. None shows signs of recent use. Few migrants are hardy enough to take cold showers out of doors in the dead of winter, even in Florida, and the latrines are unspeakably filthy, seats and floors smeared with dried defecation. So the people use the woods."

Properly conceived and executed, the congressional hearing is an art form that skilled legislators can use to attract attention to favorite causes and promote specific legislation. In the 1950s and 1960s the country was entertained and educated by a series of dramatic congressional hearings; many of them had important legislative consequences. McGovern's staff on the nutrition committee hoped to make a splash in 1969 with a series of hearings on hunger.

Two members of the staff went to Florida several weeks before the scheduled Immokalee hearing to explore the situation on the ground and look for potential witnesses. One was Bill Smith, staff director of the committee, a Harvard graduate and a lawyer. The other was Kenneth Schlossberg.

Schlossberg was twenty-nine. He had graduated from the University of Rochester, then earned master's degrees in journalism from Columbia and in international relations from Johns Hopkins. He began work on a Ph.D. at Hopkins, but gave that up to become a newspaper reporter on the tabloid *Washington Daily News*. The spirit of the 1960s infected him. He wanted to help change the world. He took a job as a field investigator for the Office of Economic Opportunity under R. Sargent Shriver, John F. Kennedy's brother-in-law, who was waging the war on poverty. After two years at OEO, Schlossberg joined the 1968 vice presidential campaign of Senator Edmund S. Muskie of Maine, Hubert H. Humphrey's running mate. When Nixon beat Humphrey, Schlossberg joined the nutrition committee staff. By then he had spent seven years in Washington and had a wide circle of friends. He saw the committee job as another opportunity to address issues of social justice. Just a week after he started at the committee, Smith took him to Florida to "advance" the hearings.

"A Senate hearing is like a stage show," Schlossberg said years later. "You have to know what kind of show you want to put on, who the best actors—witnesses—are going to be, and what you want the reviews—the news stories—to lead with." Good advance work contributes to all those objectives.

Smith and Schlossberg could do good advance work because of the help they received from the four young attorneys in the Fort Myers office of South Florida Migrant Legal Services. "The lawyers were able to explain who was who, what was what, take us around, so that we could pick and choose what we thought would make the best show," Schlossberg recalled.

By any measure the two-day hearings were a huge success. The three television networks all covered the senators in Florida, as did *The New York Times* and *The Washington Post*. Local officials were embarrassed on camera by the disbelieving senators when they ducked responsibility for the migrants' living conditions. Foster, leader of the lawyers, testified about the results of medical studies they had done in Miami on the children of migrant workers, which found serious malnutrition. The governor of Florida, Claude Kirk, fumed about outside agitators. It all made for good television.

Schlossberg wrote a statement for McGovern that was picked up widely: "We have seen diet and living conditions these past two days that one might expect to find in Asia, not in America. Most of the cattle and hogs in America are better fed and sheltered than the families we have visited. . . . A country that is powerful enough to rocket men to the moon should be able to feed its own hungry people."

For the four young lawyers, the committee's visit brought a flash of glamour into their utterly unglamorous lives. Each of them tried to look after two of the eight senators who participated. Kantor was assigned to Walter F. Mondale of Minnesota, the beginning of a relationship that has endured for decades. Cassidy drew McGovern and Jacob K. Javits, the formidable liberal Republican from New York.

This was Cassidy's first real exposure to powerful people and to the excitement they and the reporters following them could create. Having labored invisibly for nearly two years, with little tangible impact on conditions in Immokalee, Cassidy suddenly found himself part of a media event that his friends and relations back home could see on television or read about in the newspapers. Was this what it meant to be somebody? He liked it.

Cassidy hit it off with McGovern, and he liked the people he'd met who worked for him. Talking to McGovern prompted the idea that perhaps his next job ought to be in Washington. He saw another opportunity to seize.

Weeks later Cassidy contacted McGovern, who put him in touch with Bill Smith to discuss a job on the nutrition committee. Schlossberg remembered that he was enthusiastic about hiring Cassidy—"biggest mistake of my life," he said years later. At the time he thought Cassidy was like him, "an ethnic kid from the Northeast," who could help with a heavy workload. "Something about it struck me right."

Cassidy said he thought he was taking a brief detour. "Like so many people I thought I would come for a short while—this was exciting, the whole food stamp thing, the whole poverty issue was exciting—I thought I'd do that for a couple of years, then come back to Florida and get a real job," practicing law. Loretta liked Florida, and it was starting to boom. But a sojourn in Washington wouldn't hurt. He could try to do good in Washington for a couple of years, then try to do well as a lawyer in Florida afterward.

So in April, barely six weeks after the hearings in Immokalee, Cassidy and Loretta moved from their riverbank bungalow in Fort Myers to a small apartment in Arlington, Virginia. The construction project called Gerald S. J. Cassidy (born McIntyre) was well under way.

CHAPTER 4

A WASHINGTON THAT WORKED

When Gerald S. J. Cassidy went to work for the nutrition committee in its first-floor office in the Old Senate Office Building, he was joining the staff of a Senate that was much more a club than a venue for aggressive partisan politics. Its members knew one another personally, often intimately. They worked collaboratively across party lines without thinking they were doing anything unusual. In other words, they worked in an environment that is unrecognizable in the twenty-first century.

With very few exceptions, senators then maintained their principal residences in Washington and visited their home states occasionally, not nearly every weekend as most do today. Old institutions now long gone, including the Washington hostess and her offspring, the Washington dinner party, and the traveling delegation of senators making relatively relaxed visits to far-flung places around the world, often called a "junket," still thrived. They provided natural lubricants for the legislative machinery. Senators got to know one another, entertained each other in their Washington homes, talked business when they were socializing and socialized when they were working. Many had the time and inclination to master details of the subjects before them, sometimes by visiting places like Immokalee, Florida, as McGovern and four other members of the nutrition committee did for those hearings on hunger and migrant workers. The professional life of members of the House of Representatives was comparable.

Like the executive branch, Congress had been changing in the 1960s, when the federal government was growing at a fast clip. Quite suddenly Washington got involved in many aspects of American life that had previously been beyond its reach—hunger, for example. The Select Committee on Nutrition and Human Needs was one such instance of how the Senate itself was growing as an institution. The Congressional Staff Directory listed ten members of its staff after Cassidy signed on—ten positions that hadn't existed before the committee was established in 1967.

Its creation contributed to the growth of the total Senate staff from about 2,700 in 1959 to nearly 3,900 a decade later, when Cassidy started his new job. Many in the Senate, particularly older members, thought this was getting out of hand, but growth in the 1960s was modest compared to what was about to happen. In the 1970s total Senate staff would grow to about 7,000 people, where it still stands today. The staff of the House of Representatives also burgeoned: from 3,000 in 1960 to 5,700 in 1970 and 9,300 in 1980 (counting members' and committees' staffs).

But the biggest difference between that Senate and more recent versions was its members' appetite for taking on serious national problems, including many related to poverty and inequality. When John F. Kennedy promised in the 1960 presidential campaign to "get this country moving again," he initiated an era of government activism that fundamentally changed the nation and the federal government.

The nutrition committee was an example. McGovern offered a resolution to create a select committee on nutrition the day the Citizens' Board of Inquiry released its report, "Hunger, USA." McGovern had forty co-sponsors for the resolution, including Republicans, conservative Democrats, and liberals. The first hearing on McGovern's resolution was held on May 23, the day after CBS broadcast its powerful documentary *Hunger in America.* The Senate approved McGovern's resolution unanimously on July 30. It called on the new select committee to recommend ways "to establish a coordinated program . . . [to] assure every United States resident adequate food, medical assistance and other related basic necessities of life and health." The committee's thirteen positions were quickly oversubscribed by eager members of the Senate, both Democrats and Republicans, McGovern recalled.

The spirit of the age had affected both parties, as Nixon's statement on hunger made clear. So in 1965 large, bipartisan majorities in both the House and the Senate enacted the Medicare program, providing government-financed health care for senior citizens, a revolutionary change in American life. Medicare and increased Social Security benefits with an annual cost-of-living adjustment, approved later in the 1960s, transformed the status of older Americans; poverty in their ranks declined radically. Civil rights legislation, court decisions, and executive branch policies completed the metamorphosis of the legal status of black Americans that the Supreme Court had begun in 1954 with *Brown v. Board of Education*. New housing programs helped millions find habitable homes. Head Start offered educational opportunities to preschoolers. Federal urban renewal programs gave cities new resources to cope with urban blight.

All this happened in a political context that looks now like something from another planet in a parallel universe. Lyndon Johnson had obliterated Senator Barry Goldwater in the 1964 election, a landslide that seemed to end the Republican Party's flirtation with conservatism. Nixon won in 1968 on a progressive, centrist platform, and was nearly as much of an activist in domestic affairs as Johnson. He too promoted civil rights, established the first federal affirmative action programs, and vastly extended the reach of federal regulation of business. Nixon created both the Environmental Protection Agency and the Occupational Safety and Health Administration. He presided over a huge expansion of the food stamp program, which served three million people when Nixon became president in January 1969 and nearly fifteen million when he resigned in disgrace in August 1974.

Marlow Cook of Kentucky, a Republican who was active on the nutrition committee, said years later he could recall no partisan divisions in the committee's work. "How could you not work together on something like nutrition?" he said. "How do you choose sides between Democrats and Republicans over whether people are eating the right things, or just eating?"

McGovern agreed: "I think it's fair to say we never had a partisan quarrel on that committee."

The committee's staff felt the magic. Schlossberg called this period "the golden moment of progressive liberalism in the Senate. The country has been living off the moment ever since. It was, in retrospect, almost like a dream to have been in the middle of it."

Cassidy, the newcomer, suddenly found himself playing the Washington game, negotiating with the conference of bishops of his own Catholic church about how to make Catholic schools eligible for the school lunch program, or sitting for weeks with Schlossberg in the conference of House and Senate members trying to resolve disagreements about food stamps. Cassidy realized that one of the more interesting and eccentric senators, Allen J. Ellender of Louisiana, a populist who was once an ally of Huey Long's, had taken a shine to him. "I actually built a very nice relationship with Ellender out of that [Immokalee] hearing," he recalled.

Finding himself in this situation was exhilarating. "It all happened so fast," Cassidy said. "I had never thought about coming to Washington [before the hearing in Immokalee], and I wasn't particularly politically minded, and all of a sudden—" Gerry Cassidy was somebody.

"The Senate was a very different place then: small staffs, members did so much of the work themselves, they were on the floor a lot. You could walk in the cloakroom and find twenty-five, thirty senators at any time. So you did more of the work talking directly to members, which was terrific. If McGovern said 'Go see what Ellender thinks,' he really meant to go see what *Ellender* thinks, you know? So many people today say 'Well, I spoke to him.' What they really mean is they spoke to the staff. But back then you really talked to members a lot. And members knew what they were talking about. They had a lot of time. . . . [They] were very familiar with issues. . . . So it was very interesting, very exciting, and you really thought you were doing something that was important and a good thing to do."

One reason for the exhilaration Schlossberg and Cassidy both felt was the quality of the senators they worked with. The select committee on nutrition was dominated by what Lyndon Johnson called, when he was the Senate majority leader, "whales"—big men with brains and a desire to use their power creatively. The committee was short on "minnows," LBJ's derisive term for senators of little consequence, who were much rarer in LBJ's time than they are today.

McGovern was an ascending whale, just beginning his second term but already influential and effective. The ranking Republican was Marlow Cook of Kentucky, a new member and a smart one. He had succeeded Jacob Javits of New York, one of the brightest men in the Senate, who retained a place on the committee but relinquished the position of senior Republican. Walter Mondale of Minnesota was an important Democratic member; so was Philip Hart of Michigan, one of the giants of the Senate for eighteen years. Besides Ellender there were two southern whales who had long been effective senators: Herman Talmadge of Georgia, a southerner who often hid his progressive instincts from Georgia's voters, and Ralph Yarborough of Texas, a liberal. Bob Dole of Kansas and Chuck Percy of Illinois were smart, influential Republicans on the committee as well. Dole was particularly important on agricultural issues; his decision to embrace a universal, nationwide food stamp program guaranteed its support in the Senate.

Because this was a select committee, which had no jurisdiction over legislation, the nutrition panel had to persuade others to take the hunger issues seriously. "Its power came from the prestige and the status of the senators on the committee," said Marshall Matz, another member of the staff at the time. Its game was to attract attention to its issues.

This was Schlossberg's turf, and he loved to play on it. He was a good writer himself, and loved coming up with new gimmicks. Matz remembered Schlossberg as "the creative member of the team, the guy who had the vision."

Jack Rosenthal was then a reporter in the Washington bureau of *The New York Times* who made the subject of hunger one of his specialties. Schlossberg became a key source. "He was completely enthusiastic, bright-eyed, cheerful, had this impish grin, always had an idea, often a reach. But he was eager to try out ideas all the time. And he was an exceptional salesman, in the sense that a news source can sell stories. And he would do it not simply because he wanted ink, but because he was quite persuasively outraged."

As Cassidy and Schlossberg worked together on food stamps, school lunch, and other issues, they became a team. They got along well together. At first they both worked under Bill Smith, but Smith and McGovern had a falling-out over McGovern's presidential ambitions, and Smith left the committee. McGovern then appointed Schlossberg staff director, and Cassidy general counsel. Now they worked even more closely together.

"They'd always appear together," recalled John Holum, an aide in McGovern's office. "It was Ken-and-Gerry, as if it was one word. Ken would do the talking at a staff meeting or whatever, and Gerry was pretty quiet. He'd nod and maybe chip in a word or two."

"I remember Cassidy as someone who walked behind Schlossberg, was his lapdog," said Eli Segal, who worked briefly with both men on the nutrition committee after the 1972 election. "Cassidy was clearly the junior partner, but it was no partnership at all. He was very much subservient to Schlossberg."

The hunger issues had helped make McGovern a national figure. So did the Vietnam War, which he opposed vigorously. A man of restless ambition, he first offered himself as a presidential candidate in 1968, when Humphrey won the Democratic nomination. He was then the first Democrat to announce his candidacy for the 1972 nomination—which he did in January 1971, much earlier than politicians then considered sensible. But McGovern had a two-year plan to win the White House.

Schlossberg and Cassidy were ambivalent about McGovern's candidacy. They considered it a distraction from the hunger issues, a judgment

McGovern eventually confirmed by suggesting to Schlossberg in 1971 that it was time to begin wrapping up the committee's activities. Rather than succumb quietly to this idea, Schlossberg leaked McGovern's plan to several union officials and other liberal activists who, he knew, would try to persuade McGovern not to let the nutrition committee die.

The gambit worked. McGovern now told Schlossberg that he wanted to preserve the committee and use it to further his presidential ambitions. Schlossberg recalled hearings they organized in the South Bronx to expose McGovern to big-city poverty, something he had never really seen. Schlossberg thought his boss was a good man but unsophisticated. He recalled McGovern asking him, a year or more after they had been working together, "Are you Jewish?" He certainly was—his family ran a Jewish funeral business in Brookline, Massachusetts. "In South Dakota," Schlossberg remembered McGovern saying, "we don't know what anybody is."

Eventually the presidential campaign brought with it an entirely new entourage, led by a young Colorado attorney named Gary Hart, McGovern's campaign manager. Years later Schlossberg admitted that when McGovern told him he planned to make Hart campaign manager, he was wounded, though he had no experience running any kind of political campaign: "I had done so much politically for him, and done it so well, why wasn't he thinking of me as a campaign manager? It bothered the hell out of me."

Presidential fever is a powerful virus; eventually it infected Schlossberg and Cassidy too. They left the committee staff temporarily to work on the campaign, but they were not admitted to the inner circle. They played modest roles on the edges, but they had one moment in the sun.

In March 1972, McGovern's influential press secretary, Frank Mankiewicz, invited the two to draft a speech for McGovern after Alabama governor George C. Wallace had won the Florida Democratic primary. Wallace's success winning blue-collar votes from traditional Democrats alarmed the latter, including the McGovern camp. Mankiewicz wanted McGovern to speak directly to the voters he expected Wallace to court in the next primary, in Wisconsin—white, ethnic, working-class Democrats, largely Catholics—and to acknowledge their anxieties.

"I wrote most of the speech," Schlossberg said, "but the spirit of the thing, in terms of connecting with blue-collar Catholics—this was really Gerry's." In the speech, McGovern described the votes cast by working-class voters who chose Wallace in Florida as "an angry cry from the guts of ordinary Americans against a system which doesn't give a damn about what's really bothering people in this country today." Mankiewicz had added a nice literary flourish, quoting Willy Loman from Arthur Miller's *Death of a Salesman:* "Attention must be paid." The speech was widely covered, and *The Washington Post* praised it in an editorial.

"I had been pushing the campaign to concentrate more on the working class, to look for things where George could reach out to them," Cassidy recounted. "Now here's a guy who got elected in South Dakota, and there isn't a more working-class place that I've been to than South Dakota. He could connect with those people." But too often, the elitists running the campaign—Ivy Leaguers and antiwar activists—had other ideas, Cassidy thought.

"I didn't like the people, to be frank with you," Cassidy said years later, speaking of the campaign team Hart assembled. "A lot of them were why George lost. There was this arrogance about them, this resentment of people who didn't agree with them. . . . They were just a group of people who knew everything. . . . [They imagined] an enlightened class of college graduates who were going to lead the world to their point of view. . . . They were talking about themselves. And that's what I didn't like about them."

Cassidy and Schlossberg anticipated McGovern's crushing defeat long before it happened. Cassidy had returned to the nutrition committee payroll before election day; Schlossberg did so right afterward. Cassidy soon had a job offer from Barbara Mikulski, then a city council member from Baltimore (and now a U.S. senator from Maryland), whom he had met while courting ethnic voters for McGovern. She had become chairman of a panel at the Democratic National Committee established after the McGovern debacle to once again examine the party's delegate selection process. She hired Cassidy as her chief staff man. In January 1973, he left the nutrition committee for the DNC. But he ran into trouble almost immediately.

Mikulski was an accidental chairman of the DNC committee on delegate selection, elevated to that role because the man chosen for the job fell ill. She had no personal influence with the new chairman of the national committee, Robert S. Strauss of Texas, whom the Democrats had chosen to try to repair the wreckage left by McGovern's loss of forty-nine states (he won only Massachusetts and the District of Columbia). Strauss, a Dallas lawyer, was a relatively new Washington player, but an accomplished one. In 1971 he had opened a Washington office of the law firm he had created in Texas; he would quickly become one of Washington's most successful lobbyists. He served briefly as treasurer of the Democratic Party before becoming its chairman in 1973.

Mikulski offered Cassidy the job of staff director and general counsel to her committee apparently without realizing that Strauss was determined to eliminate McGovern people from the DNC. Strauss had important allies in this mission at the AFL-CIO, the headquarters of the American labor movement, then still influential in the Democratic Party. "They viewed me with a lot of suspicion," Cassidy said years later, referring to both Strauss and the labor crowd. "Then I hired this woman Doris Hardesty whose husband was . . . a press guy for George Meany [president of the AFL-CIO], then I fired her . . . for not showing up [for work]. . . . You can't get dumber than that. So they went crazy."

Nine months after he started this job Cassidy was gravely injured in a car accident caused by an uninsured immigrant who drove his car across the median of a divided highway and ran into Cassidy's car. He spent six weeks in the hospital with serious injuries. A colleague at the DNC, Carol Casey, visited him regularly. Before one visit some weeks after the accident, she went to the payroll clerk at the DNC to ask for Cassidy's check so she could take it to him in the hospital. There was no check, she was told—Cassidy no longer worked for the DNC. He had been fired by Mikulski, at Strauss's instruction. Years later both said they had no memory of firing him, but Cassidy remembered it vividly.

Another visitor to the Virginia hospital where Cassidy was laid up was Ken Schlossberg, still the staff director of the nutrition committee. The spectacle of his old sidekick flat on his back with serious injuries and suddenly without a job moved him. "I asked Gerry what he'd think about coming back to work at the committee?" said Schlossberg. "He hated the idea of taking my charity. He didn't accept right away, he called back in a day or so."

At that point—in the fall of 1973—they had known each other for four and a half years. They had socialized together with their wives, shared their life stories, become friends. But they had differences, which later would undermine and ultimately overpower the friendship. At this stage the differences remained minor, if sometimes aggravating. Schlossberg remembered being put out with Cassidy for behaving imperiously toward Nancy Amidei, the woman they left in charge of the nutrition committee staff when they took leave to work for McGovern's campaign. In the brief period when Cassidy was back at the committee but Schlossberg was still campaigning, Cassidy so angered Amidei that she resigned.

These are two complicated men whose lives were closely intertwined for sixteen years and then went their separate ways. Each looms large in the other's personal movie—that moving picture of our lives that we all carry in our heads. Both remember early episodes of their collaboration in remarkable detail, but the details often differ—as they did about this moment in 1973.

Cassidy remembered that the offer to come back to the committee came from McGovern personally, not Schlossberg. "The kindhearted George McGovern took me back," he said. Whereas Schlossberg, the staff director, remembered that "McGovern had mixed feelings about it, but he agreed" with Schlossberg's suggestion to rehire Cassidy. McGovern himself said, when asked, that he couldn't remember just what happened.

Cassidy accepted the job. At first he had to work from home while his recuperation continued. Soon he and Schlossberg were collaborating again. After a while colleagues got the impression they were planning something together. Alan Stone, a new member of the staff, remembered that the door to the office Schlossberg and Cassidy shared was often closed. "They were already scheming how they were going to get out."

Indeed they were. After McGovern won re-election to the Senate in November 1974, he still suffered from presidential fever. "It was pretty clear that McGovern's interest was moving on to national politics, and he was in a lot of pain," Cassidy recalled years later. "He really wanted to be redeemed."

Neither Cassidy nor Schlossberg had the slightest interest in that idea. Cassidy remembered going to lunch with McGovern, probably in the summer of 1974, at the Monocle Restaurant, a favored Senate watering hole close to the Senate office buildings. McGovern wanted to talk about running for president again, and asked Cassidy's advice. "I knew the answer he wanted to hear was yes. . . . I told him that I didn't think he should do it, that maybe someday in the future but certainly not in '76," Cassidy said.

His argument was not persuasive. McGovern was soon talking about bringing people onto the staff of the nutrition committee who could help him run for president again. One he wanted was Bob Shrum, a political operative who had worked on the 1972 campaign, which turned out to be the first of eight losing Democratic campaigns for president that Shrum ran or advised.

Recounting these events decades later, Cassidy said McGovern's obvious eagerness to run again, including his desire to put Shrum and one or two political types on the nutrition committee staff, were all he needed to conclude that "it was time to leave." He talked to a few law firms about a job, he said, "and I disliked the prospect of practicing law enormously." Instead, "starting a lobbying operation was what made sense." So that was what he did. He remembered leaving the committee staff on May 1, 1975.

Schlossberg provided a different account. With tension rising over the idea of hiring Shrum, he remembered, a letter was brought to him in March or April of 1975 that had been dictated by McGovern to his secretary in Washington "from Cairo" (McGovern was making a Mideast tour). The letter instructed him to fire Cassidy to make room for Shrum as the new general counsel of the committee, Schlossberg said.

Did Cassidy remember that? No. "I think that's all baloney," he said when asked about Schlossberg's recollection. "I had told George I was leaving, it was all amicable. I can't imagine we would have maintained the relationship we did [over the years since] if it hadn't been amicable."

"If I fired anyone I don't remember it," McGovern said in 2006.

McGovern's papers are deposited at the Princeton University Library. They include a letter to Schlossberg dictated by McGovern on March 31, 1975—though not from Cairo. The letter was dictated from Damascus.

"Dear Ken," it said, "As you know, I have been thinking for a couple of months about making a change on the Committee. I would like to have you tell Gerry Cassidy that Bob Shrum is coming on board as general counsel. . . . Therefore, Gerry should begin looking for other employment."

Shrum joined the committee staff that spring. He remembered an altercation with Cassidy at the time, which he attributed to Cassidy's anxiety about his future. "He pushed me up against a wall. I said, 'Gerry, this is a lousy way to deal with it.' "

This was the backdrop to Cassidy's and Schlossberg's decision to go into business together. For years, Schlossberg said, he had noticed that "people were making a living in Washington as consultants doing pretty interesting stuff." Why couldn't he do the same? "I figured I could turn my food experience into a successful business, perhaps consulting to the Department of Agriculture, the Agency for International Development, and others." He also thought he could find clients among companies and institutions that had problems in Washington they couldn't solve.

"I wanted to start a lobbying operation," Cassidy remembered. "Ken wanted to have a consulting business, and he pictured this would be largely on social policy issues, public policy issues. I did not believe there was a market for that. So I viewed it that we were going to start a lobbying business. Ken thought of himself at that time as someone who could run for Congress back in Massachusetts and didn't want to be a lobbyist. And that's when we should have parted company right then."

Alan Stone thought so too. "They were so tight, and they were such bosom buddies," Stone said of Cassidy and Schlossberg. "But I knew they would have a falling-out in the end. It just seemed doomed; they were too close."

Friends who knew both men at the time agree that the firm was Schlossberg's idea, and that he was the moving force in its creation. The firm's original name suggests as much: Schlossberg-Cassidy & Associates. Schlossberg was the president, Cassidy the secretary-treasurer. The only "associate" was Loretta Cassidy, who did some secretarial work.

Distracted by a difficult divorce, Schlossberg suggested Cassidy take care of the paperwork to set up the firm, which Cassidy did. They agreed on fifty-fifty ownership ("my mother was very upset with me for doing that," Schlossberg remembered) and Schlossberg accepted a three-member board of directors consisting of him and both Cassidys, "since I was then single. I never gave it a thought in terms of possibly causing me grief down the road."

The official address of Schlossberg-Cassidy & Associates was 623 South Carolina Avenue, Schlossberg's Capitol Hill townhouse. The office was in the basement. The firm's original articles of incorporation, filed in May 1975, described its "purposes" in terms that reflected Schlossberg's original idea: "To provide a broad range of services to industry and government including but not limited to research, counseling, evaluation, planning, policy making and analysis of agricultural, food, nutrition and health programs, policies and products." No lobbying there.

Nor, it soon became clear, was there much business. The two sent hundreds letters to everyone they could think of, announcing the creation of their new firm and offering to help solve problems in Washington. No one responded.

Schlossberg's friend Jack Rosenthal had become the editor of *The New York Times Magazine*, and Rosenthal commissioned an article from Schlossberg on how the food stamp program was changing America. Schlossberg spent weeks on the article, which was published in September 1975. McGovern inserted it into the *Congressional Record*. The *Times Magazine* identified Schlossberg as "president of a private consulting firm on food issues in Washington." That summer the Rockefeller Foundation invited him to give a paper at its conference center in Bellagio, Italy, on nutrition policy—a nice honor, Schlossberg thought, but not one that brought in any money for the new firm.

Schlossberg remembered having a little money in the bank—between $10,000 and $20,000. He remembered lending $5,000 to Cassidy; Cassidy instead remembered a loan from his in-laws to tide him over. For that first summer they were in business, the new firm's earnings were zero. These were not Gerry Cassidy's first hard times, of course. But they would be his last.

CHAPTER 5

A NEW KIND OF BUSINESS

Schlossberg-Cassidy's first real client finally materialized soon after the Rockefeller Foundation conference in Italy. Larry's Foods, a California company run by Larry Goodman, had provided ingredients worth $200,000 to schools participating in a federal lunch program for summer school students, but had not been paid by the Department of Agriculture. Larry's contacted Schlossberg-Cassidy to see if the fledgling consulting firm could help the company get its money.

Cassidy remembered that first client vividly. "I was the one who took the call," he recalled three decades later. "I knew who to call . . . at the Department of Agriculture, and I knew this could be more than just one shot, that we could turn this into a retainer, which we did . . . for a number of years."

Schlossberg had a vivid memory of this episode too—a different one: "It was Larry's son, Chip Goodman, who had attended a hearing on the summer lunch program that I set up [for the Senate nutrition committee]. He came looking for me. Gerry and I met him in a downtown restaurant. We negotiated a $10,000 retainer." Schlossberg remembered Goodman as someone he had known for years from various food conferences and meetings. "He didn't know Gerry from a hole in the wall."

What did Chip Goodman remember? Thirty years later, he said he sought out Schlossberg. "I knew Ken from the industry side of child nutrition programs going back to the late 1960s," he said. Yes, Schlossberg-Cassidy managed to extract a check from the Department of Agriculture, and a continuing relationship was established.

But Cassidy seems to have had the better memory of how they got the check for Larry's Foods. Said Schlossberg: "Who figured out who to call at USDA to solve Chip's problem? Could have been Gerry."

Another early client was the Kellogg Company, the cereal manufacturer based in Battle Creek, Michigan. Cassidy recalled: "I had a very, very good relationship with Phil Hart," the Michigan senator. Hart, who died in 1976, enjoyed a reputation among his colleagues as perhaps the finest senator of his generation. "He got us a meeting with Bill LaMothe, the CEO of Kellogg, and they had a problem with cereals, with getting their products into the school lunch program . . . so we got him as a client."

No, Schlossberg said, this relationship began with a request from his pal LaMothe for help persuading Senator Hubert Humphrey to attend a Kellogg event in Washington promoting the importance to schoolchildren of eating a good breakfast. Schlossberg had attended the Rockefeller Foundation conference in Bellagio with Humphrey, and recalled his "easy access" to the senator. Schlossberg said he had no trouble persuading Humphrey's staff to put the event on the senator's schedule, and asked LaMothe for a $5,000 fee. Later Kellogg signed up as a regular client paying a monthly retainer. "Senator Hart had absolutely nothing, zip, nada, to do with my relationship with Bill LaMothe," Schlossberg said.

Thirty years later LaMothe confirmed Schlossberg's version. And he still remembered that "Humphrey was great with the kids, urged them to come to school with full stomachs." LaMothe pointed out that he did not become Kellogg's CEO until 1979, four years after these events.

Both Schlossberg and Cassidy cast themselves in the leading role in the creation of the firm.

Cassidy's version: "The first year Ken was not around a lot. That summer he was going through a really wrenching and painful divorce, he had two kids and his wife was very difficult. The kids—he just couldn't get to see them, it was just terrible for him. But he went to Bellagio that summer, he was invited by the Rockefeller Foundation, and he was gone. Then he was gone up to his parents' place [a beach house in Massachusetts], he was gone most of the summer. So the business getting started was largely me getting started."

Schlossberg agreed that he was investing "considerable time in my divorce and child custody cases," but added, "because I was single, I had endless time for receptions and trips to drum up business." He had time to write the article for *The New York Times Magazine* on the food stamp program—"what better publicity could we get?" But he also remembered that business picked up in the fall of 1975.

"The next client was the National Livestock and Meat Board in

Chicago. Called for me. We went out to Chicago. The executive director wanted a report for his members on where Congress was going with nutrition policy and how that might affect the cattle industry—$25,000. Who wrote the report? I did. Next client: Joe Danzansky [CEO of a big Washington-area supermarket chain and a family acquaintance of the Schlossbergs']. Called for me. Told me to get together with the executive director of the National Frozen Food Association, work something out. We met. I came up with the idea of doing a survey of Congress on attitudes toward supermarkets and present it [to the association's convention] in Los Angeles—$40,000. American School Food Service Association—I chased them for nine months, a year, going to all their meetings, including their big board meeting in Vail where they canned their founding executive director and hired us to represent them in Washington—$25,000. . . . Next came an executive from Mead Johnson Labs, which was selling baby formula to the government's Women and Infant Children [WIC] feeding program, and wanted their help to keep track of developments affecting that program. . . . He found us in the basement of the townhouse. Was Gerry sitting there? Could have been, I don't remember. But the WIC program was my baby in the Senate [Schlossberg worked on the legislation that set up WIC during 1972] and they were looking for me—$10,000."

"When I started out in the 1970s it was really about knowing the decision-makers," Cassidy said. "And I knew a lot of the decision-makers, both from working in the Senate, the McGovern campaign, the DNC—I just knew a lot of them."

Schlossberg remembered, on the contrary, that "Gerry didn't have a lot of friends or a wide circle of contacts. . . . He didn't know many people, and those he knew didn't like him." Schlossberg saw himself as "the widely known and highly respected staff director of the nutrition committee," with many important friends in the press corps, in the world of food and nutrition, and on Capitol Hill.

Schlossberg was more gregarious, did have many more friends and contacts, could write wonderfully, and had a salesman's gift for gab. Cassidy was harder-working, more attuned to detail, more patient with the nuts and bolts of running a business. Schlossberg's ambitions were diffuse; he wanted to be a player in Washington on nutrition issues, he wanted the respect of journalists and members of Congress, he dreamed of running for Congress himself one day.

Cassidy wanted to be a big-time lobbyist like Claude Desautels, who once worked on John F. Kennedy's White House staff as a liaison to

Congress, then lobbied Congress for Kennedy's longtime political advisor Lawrence O'Brien Jr. when O'Brien became postmaster general, then became an almost invisible but effective and successful Washington lobbyist.

Desautels was one of the people Cassidy consulted when he was just starting out, and his advice made a deep impression: always work on a retainer basis—a fixed monthly fee—and always insist on payment in advance. "He had a lot of very large clients," Cassidy remembered—just what Cassidy wanted himself.

Asked to summarize his ambition for the new firm, Cassidy replied: "I wanted to be successful and financially secure." This would be the theme of his life and career.

Alan Stone, of the nutrition committee, probably had it right when he said their relationship was doomed.

After six months in operation, Schlossberg-Cassidy was a going concern. Pillsbury, Nabisco, and General Mills had joined its roster of clients. Schlossberg and Cassidy had real income, several thousand dollars a month each. "In about December," Cassidy said, "I thought we had enough money to get an office."

This was the sort of matter that he handled. He and Loretta found an office in L'Enfant Plaza, a hulking office complex designed by I. M. Pei then several years old. Part of an urban renewal project, it was wedged between Independence Avenue and the Southeast Freeway, about half a mile from the Capitol. "It was a single office. You could have a little reception area if you put in bookcases to block it off. That was our first office. We moved in there like March or so. We rented furniture," Cassidy remembered.

On its first birthday, Schlossberg-Cassidy & Associates was pretty much what Schlossberg had envisioned: a modest consulting firm specializing in food and nutrition issues. Lobbying Congress was not yet an important part of its repertoire. Its one-room office accurately signified its insignificance on the Washington scene. "We couldn't afford parking," Cassidy remembered, "so we would find parking spaces down on Maine Avenue," near the Anacostia River. Then in the summer and fall of 1976, their world changed.

The agent of this change was a charismatic Frenchman named Jean Mayer, a biologist and physician who earned doctorates from the Sorbonne and Yale, and became famous as a nutritionist on the faculty of the Harvard School of Public Health. His fame grew in the late 1960s when Americans began looking seriously at hunger and malnutrition in their own country. When the Nixon White House called a White House Conference on Food, Nutrition and Health, Mayer was invited to be its chairman, giving him a highly visible national platform.

As an immigrant Mayer was an outsider in American academic life, but this did not diminish his ambition. When a search began for a new president of Harvard in 1971, Mayer threw his hat into the ring. Harvard's trustees picked Derek Bok, a law professor, instead, but the experience whetted Mayer's appetite. Five years later he accepted an offer from Tufts University to become its president.

Tufts, a venerable institution founded in 1852, was located in Medford, Massachusetts, just a few miles from Harvard. But in the academic world the distance between the two was far greater. Tufts had a middling reputation and modest ambitions when Mayer took over in 1976. But he was determined to change its status. "He had a vision of rebuilding Tufts, turning it from a commuter school into an elite school," Cassidy recalled, "and he thought the key to it was federal funding." Even before he was inaugurated as Tufts' tenth president in September 1976, Mayer approached the young partners of Schlossberg-Cassidy to seek their help.

How he approached them is, typically, disputed by Cassidy and Schlossberg. Mayer died in 1993, so cannot resolve the dispute. Cassidy's version: "In June [of 1976] I got a call from Jean Mayer and [he asked] where the hell were we located? He came by, it was the first real business meeting I had in that office. It was me, Jean. . . . He wanted to get [federal] funds appropriated. . . . He wanted to build a national nutrition center."

Schlossberg's version: Yes, Mayer called the office in Washington and reached Gerry, but he asked for Schlossberg, who was then at his family's beach house in Massachusetts. He and Mayer had been working together for years. They became friends at the 1969 White House conference on nutrition that Mayer chaired. Mayer had invited Schlossberg to speak to his class at Harvard, then helped him organize a National Nutrition Policy Conference in the Senate. Schlossberg remembered that "Gerry called me and told me that Jean was looking for me to call him from my beach house at his office at Tufts." So, Schlossberg said, he placed the call.

"Jean said he was going to become the president of Tufts, and invited me to come see him for a chat. . . . I went from my beach house to Jean's office. . . . He said Tufts is a sort of second or third sister to Harvard, it doesn't have wealthy alumni, but I want to do some serious things here. I want to establish a human nutrition research center, and a school of veterinary medicine. Could you help me with this? How?

"I don't know what I can do," Schlossberg remembered saying, "but for $10,000 I'll take a hard look." Mayer agreed to his terms.

The fulfillment of Mayer's dream ultimately changed the way Congress spends much of the money that America's taxpayers provide to their government.

Cassidy and Schlossberg agree about what happened next: Cassidy, the lawyer and detail man, began looking for legislation on the books that they might exploit to help Mayer fulfill his ambitions.

The rules and procedures of the House and Senate can be maddeningly opaque and confusing. One of the most basic is also one of the least understood: the relationship between authorizing and appropriating. Traditionally, to spend the taxpayers' money, both houses must pass two pieces of legislation: the first to authorize the project on which money is to be spent, the second to allocate dollars from the Treasury to that project. This is why, for example, the Senate and House both have armed services committees and appropriations subcommittees on defense. The armed services committees are supposed to write legislation authorizing military programs; the defense appropriations subcommittees work on bills to fund what has been authorized. Eventually, the full House and Senate must approve versions of both kinds of legislation, and the president must sign the bills in order for the money to be spent.

Cassidy found a law on the books "that you could say authorized a national nutrition center," as he put it. It had been sponsored by Senator Quentin Burdick of North Dakota, and money had been appropriated for a project in North Dakota under the authorization. As Cassidy realized, its wording seemed to allow room to fund the facility Mayer hoped to create at Tufts.

Still, there were few precedents for what Mayer was seeking: a specific appropriation of federal funds to a single university for a particular facility, the nutrition research center. In years to come this kind of legislative provision would become so common that it acquired a widely used nickname—an earmark, short for an earmarked, or specifically directed, appropriation. But in 1976 this was an unusual idea.

Mayer was inaugurated president of Tufts on July 1, 1976. A reception was held for the new president, and the local congressman attended. Fortuitously, this was Tip O'Neill, who grew up a stone's throw from Tufts and was then the majority leader of the House of Representatives. Months later he would be its speaker.

Mayer shared some exciting news with Schlossberg and Cassidy after that reception. O'Neill, he reported, had told him he had a soft spot for Tufts. As boys, he and his brother used to sneak onto a football field there to play ball. If there is anything I can do for you while you are president of Tufts, he told Mayer, just let me know.

"Well, you can imagine having something like that fall into your lap," Schlossberg said years later. "It's like being at the casino and pulling the arm on the one-dollar machine with a million-dollar payoff and seeing the thing go *Gzing! Gzing! Gzing!* It didn't take me more than two seconds to start to have my own wheel in my own mind go *Gzing! Gzing! Gzing!* I'm sure it did the same thing with Gerry."

Soon afterward Cassidy and Schlossberg went to O'Neill's office in the Capitol to talk about the possibility of appropriating money for a human nutrition research center at Tufts. Schlossberg recounted a meeting with O'Neill, who "brought in his staff guy and said, 'These two guys work for President Mayer at Tufts. We're going to try to help them out. I want you to work with these guys.' Manna from heaven. We now have what would turn out to be—you know, like a prospector finding the first nugget with gold in it. This was what Tufts University was going to turn into."

Cassidy and Schlossberg threw themselves into the project. They had a contact at the Department of Agriculture whom they persuaded to consider sponsoring it. The department sent a team to Tufts to evaluate Mayer's idea. The team liked it. The first money appropriated was $2 million for a feasibility study of the center. It was part of an agriculture appropriations bill, Cassidy remembered, although the center would be built in Boston's Chinatown, far from rural America.

"We managed the whole thing, from start to finish, over two years," Schlossberg recalled. With O'Neill's active support, Schlossberg-Cassidy enlisted Representative Silvio Conte to help. Conte was a Republican of a kind that no longer exists in Congress, a progressive who thought the government should spend money to help deserving projects and institutions. He was a senior member of the House Appropriations Committee, which is responsible for writing the spending bills every year. O'Neill and Conte, as noted earlier, were personal friends and, on numerous issues involving Massachusetts, political allies. Conte's district in the western part of the state included small cities and towns far removed from O'Neill's urban backyard in Cambridge and Somerville, but Conte understood the importance of alliances, and the Massachusetts delegation in the House often stuck together across party lines. Another early ally of the Tufts project was Senator Edward M. Kennedy, who has had a soft spot for his state's educational institutions since he came to the Senate in 1963.

But "the biggest thing," Schlossberg said, "was O'Neill's relationship with Jamie Whitten," a Mississippian who was then the second-ranking Democrat on the Appropriations Committee and also a power on the House Agriculture Committee. Whitten was a complicated figure, as Cassidy explained many years later: "If you were up in his office he was always very proud to point out this picture he had of himself at the 1932 Democratic convention as a Roosevelt delegate. He was a real progressive, [but] he had to be real careful about what he did," especially on issues that involved race. Helping poor people was fine; demonstrably helping black people was not. Mississippi Democrats were not progressives on anything that touched on race.

The new class of House Democrats elected in the post-Watergate landslide in 1974—seventy-four new Democratic members—was suspicious of Whitten, Schlossberg recalled. Some of the newcomers thought Speaker O'Neill should force him out as chairman of Appropriations. One proposal was to replace him with Edward Boland of Massachusetts, a reliable liberal and O'Neill's best personal friend in the House. But O'Neill was a conservative when it came to House traditions; Whitten had the seniority, and should stay as chairman, the speaker decided. "And by the way," Schlossberg quoted O'Neill as telling Whitten—he couldn't remember how he'd heard this—"there's this project for Tufts University . . ." In the end, "everything worked out," in Schlossberg's words.

In the agriculture appropriations bill for fiscal 1978 (the government's fiscal year, which began on October 1, 1977), Congress appropriated $20 million to build the nutrition center, and an additional $7 million to fund its initial operations. Though attached to Tufts, it would be formally part of the U.S. Department of Agriculture, which would pay its operating expenses for years to come.

The importance of these appropriations was not immediately clear. This wasn't the first time a private university had won money from Congress for its own special project. A precedent of sorts had been established by Georgetown University in Washington, a Jesuit school with only a modest endowment but a great many good friends in Congress. Two charming and resourceful Jesuit priests, Fathers William George and T. Byron Collins, had quietly persuaded important members of the House and Senate to sponsor appropriations for projects at Georgetown worth millions, their real purpose often obfuscated in arcane legislative language.

The two priests and their charismatic boss, Rev. Timothy Healy, president of the university from 1976 to 1989, had their own bag of tricks for
cultivating friends. Members of Congress whose wives were pregnant
were offered free deliveries and care at the Georgetown University Hospital. A regular patient in that institution was Dan Flood of Pennsylvania,
an idiosyncratic and influential member of the House Appropriations
Committee who wore an opera cape and a waxed mustache twisted into
dramatic spikes. Flood was treated gratis for stomach cancer at Georgetown when he was chairman of the Appropriations Subcommittee on
Labor, Health, Education and Welfare. When reporters for *Congressional
Quarterly* and *The Washington Post* caught on to Georgetown's game—
favors for members who reciprocated with favors for the university—the
school's administrators sheepishly ducked questions about its lobbying.
Many years later, Father George refused to give an interview on the subject, saying he had never spoken publicly about the university's lobbying
and wasn't prepared to begin doing so. Fathers Collins and Healy are
dead.

And there was nothing new about members of Congress bringing
home the bacon. Extracting money and other benefits from the federal
government for one's state or district has been part of the job for as long as
there has been a Congress. When O'Neill, Conte, and Kennedy shared
credit for the creation of what became the Jean Mayer USDA Human
Nutrition Research Center on Aging, they performed an ancient ritual by
which members have long advertised their effectiveness to voters. The
fact that Americans understand the phrase "bringing home the bacon" as a
description of one aspect of politics is telling. The *Oxford English Dictionary* says that the origin of this usage involved farmers, not politicians.
Not in America.

But Schlossberg-Cassidy & Associates had brought something new to
an old game by stationing themselves at a key intersection between a supplicant for government assistance, Tufts, and the people who could
respond—members of Congress and the executive branch. Their success
for Tufts would create a new kind of Washington business and a new political art form, the earmark.

Schlossberg's evocation of a slot machine's *Gzing!* says it all. He, Cassidy,
and Mayer all realized that they had stumbled on to something with big
potential. Tufts was paying Schlossberg-Cassidy $10,000 a month. The
federal government was providing the money Mayer needed. The Massa-

chusetts politicians were delighted. This was a winning formula. The participants all wanted to continue applying it.

Mayer's second ambition for Tufts was to create a school of veterinary medicine. He asked Schlossberg-Cassidy if they could find more federal money to pay for it. Cassidy was busy pursuing the nutrition center project, so, he remembered, Schlossberg began looking for a way to get more federal money for the veterinary school. He learned that Washington State University was also trying to create a veterinary school, a fortuitous discovery, because the chairman of the Senate Appropriations Subcommittee on Education and Labor was Senator Warren G. Magnuson of Washington.

Schlossberg proposed a package deal to Magnuson's staff: he would try to win support from the Massachusetts delegation if Magnuson would propose an appropriation to create two new veterinary schools in underserved regions of the country. This worked. But then the University of Pennsylvania, site of the only existing veterinary school on the East Coast, got wind of the scheme and protested through the same Congressman Flood of Pennsylvania who had been so helpful to Georgetown University. Penn feared competition from Tufts. "Someone in Magnuson's office has the idea of putting another $10 million in the bill for Penn," Schlossberg recalled, a maneuver that successfully overcame Penn's concerns. Tufts got $10 million for its new school of veterinary medicine.

While both these projects were in the pipeline, a third opportunity to win federal money for Tufts unexpectedly materialized. It resulted from an improvised alliance between the pioneering lobbying priests at Georgetown University, Fathers Collins and George; the dean of Georgetown's School of Foreign Service, Peter F. Krogh; and former ambassador Edmund Gullion, dean of the Fletcher School of Law and Diplomacy at Tufts. Once again, Schlossberg-Cassidy had a leading role.

Later, when earmarked appropriations for universities, hospitals, and other institutions became commonplace, they sailed through the Congress without much ado, usually without leaving much of a legislative history. But when Dean Krogh decided in 1977 to make a serious attempt to build a new home for his School of Foreign Service with federal money, the idea was new and controversial. Thanks to hearings held by Senator Edward Brooke of Massachusetts, another progressive Republican and a member of the Appropriations Committee, there is an extensive record of this telling moment in the history of the earmark.

The Georgetown School of Foreign Service was founded in 1919, five

years before the Foreign Service itself. Its graduates often became diplomats for the State Department or joined other government agencies that
worked overseas. Krogh, who became the school's dean in 1970, was
proud of the school and embarrassed by its physical surroundings. When
he took over, he recalled, "the school consisted of two offices on the second floor of the Nevils Building, the old hospital. There the dean sat
opposite the men's room, whose door was constantly ajar, never closed.
There's where I was supposed to run the oldest and most prestigious
school of foreign affairs in the U.S."

Fathers Collins and George had won several federal appropriations
for Georgetown to conduct "demonstration projects" that, theoretically at
least, could test innovations—in technology for a university power plant,
for example—that others might adopt. Krogh came up with the idea for a
demonstration project to combine language training, area studies, diplomatic history, and related subjects in one "intercultural center." Collins
asked him to write up the proposal. Krogh remembered Father Collins
vividly—"a chain-smoking, rail-thin, toupee-wearing Jesuit who was very
confident of his capabilities on the Hill [Capitol Hill]. . . . And the next
thing I knew it was in an appropriations bill! One of the fathers slapped a
copy of the *Congressional Record* on my desk; there was my proposal."

Exploiting their connection with Congressman Flood, Collins and
George had managed to get a line item into a supplemental House appropriations bill for the 1977 fiscal year that would have funded the Georgetown Intercultural Center. A supplemental bill provides spending not
covered by the traditional, individual appropriations bills that fund federal
agencies and programs, and has long been a device members have
exploited for pet projects. Often supplementals fund unanticipated or
emergency government spending that enjoys broad support, so sneaking a
provision for something else into one can be a sly way to get approval for
something that might not survive the ordinary procedures.

The Senate Appropriations Committee had blocked this maneuver.
Schlossberg said the committee's staff director, Terry Lehrman, opposed
spending federal funds on a church school like Georgetown. Lehrman
also discovered that Georgetown had slipped a new gymnasium into the
project, an embarrassing bit of overreaching that made it easier to block
the line item.

Months later Georgetown was back with a new wrinkle: it proposed
two demonstration projects, its own and another at Tufts. The Fletcher
School of Law and Diplomacy was the country's second important training school for the Foreign Service and other international work, and it too

needed new facilities. Krogh had long known Gullion, the distinguished retired diplomat who was dean of Fletcher. "I worked for Ed," recalled Krogh. "I can call him and find out if he wants an intercultural center. So I called him, and of course he said, 'You bet.' "

Once this deal was struck, Tufts brought in Schlossberg-Cassidy, now the university's regular lobbyist. Schlossberg quickly discovered that Magnuson's staff including Lehrman still opposed giving federal money to Georgetown. Magnuson was ill so he asked Brooke to hold a hearing on the proposal. This was still the old Senate, where a Democratic subcommittee chairman (Magnuson) could ask his ranking Republican colleague (Brooke) to hold a hearing, as though the two senators were interchangeable. Schlossberg worried that Magnuson's staff had given Brooke the assignment so he could find reasons to block the appropriation for the two intercultural centers.

Brooke called the hearing to order on September 21, 1977. He had done his homework, and was clearly skeptical. He noted that the Department of Health, Education and Welfare, the agency then responsible for federal aid to education, had never recommended that the government support intercultural centers. He expressed dismay that there had been no open competition to allow other schools interested in this idea to make proposals for their own intercultural centers. He noted that the proposal conflicted with the one piece of authorizing legislation on the books, an amendment passed the previous year that permitted expenditures for intercultural centers, but stipulated that no one state should get more than one-eighth of the money spent, which should be allocated by the federal commissioner of education only after consulting "an outside panel of specialists." No such panel had been created, Brooke noted, and the pending proposal would have been divided fifty-fifty between Massachusetts and the District of Columbia.

The first witness was a senior official from HEW who quoted a letter written earlier by the secretary of the department, Joseph Califano, which said the government put a low priority on providing funds for new facilities for higher education programs. "I feel even more strongly," Califano wrote, "that if the Congress wishes to appropriate funds for construction, the grants should be subject to competition on the basis of national needs and objective criteria. The earmarking of these funds for specially selected schools is entirely inappropriate."

Georgetown and Tufts had submitted more than thirty pages of documents supporting their request. In one, Schlossberg, writing as Tufts' representative, reported that the lobbyists had consulted with HEW officials about the plan, implying that they had approved it. Brooke called Schloss-berg to testify—"the first and only time I testified [to Congress] myself"—and asked about this point. The officials he talked to had not encouraged the idea of funding intercultural centers, had they? "At no time did any-body suggest that we not pursue it," Schlossberg replied lamely. Brooke noted that this was hardly an endorsement.

In his testimony, Dean Krogh of Georgetown offered this rationaliza-tion for the project: "The way I would come at it is to say that the idea for the intercultural centers, I believe, originated with our institutions. We believe that we may then be entitled to be earmarked as first, because we initially conceived of the idea." This novel theory—the author of a new idea is entitled to a federal grant to support it—did not appear to sway Brooke.

Krogh and Gullion both testified repeatedly that their two schools were the leading institutions training American diplomats and others who work in international fields. This was their response to Brooke's interest in a competition among schools to see which had the best ideas for intercul-tural centers. Of course, the two deans implied, we have the best ideas because ours are the best schools.

But wait, Brooke interjected, mischievously. He understood from his absent colleague, Senator Magnuson, that Georgetown's first attempt to attract a second school to be a partner in this request had been directed to the University of Washington. How, he asked Dean Krogh, did that jibe with the idea that Georgetown and Tufts had invented the idea of inter-cultural centers, and were the only obvious schools to create them?

Father George quickly realized that his dean was in a jam. Before Krogh could answer George jumped in himself: "Georgetown asked the University [of Washington] if they were interested, if they would consider having an intercultural center. . . . They decided they were not inter-ested." George was confessing, indirectly but unmistakably, that his first gambit had been to try to attract as a partner the university that was widely known to be the favorite institution of the chairman of the education and labor subcommittee, Magnuson.

At this point Krogh realized he had slipped into a trap, and he moved quickly to try to escape from it: "I believe I may have misrepresented this, Senator, and I did so because I am not intimately familiar with the sequence of events here. But I believed the intercultural concept was a Georgetown concept. [Indeed, it was his own idea.] I got involved in the jointness of it at the point [when] we invited the Fletcher School of Tufts University to join us, to pair with us in the model demonstration."

Did Krogh know that Georgetown (no doubt in the person of Father Collins or Father George) had initially approached the University of Washington?

"No," he replied. "With all respect to Senator Magnuson, I don't know anyone at the University of Washington, and it doesn't have much in common with the School of Foreign Service at Georgetown University."

Senator Brooke: "But it has other things to recommend it."

Mr. Krogh: "Oh, a great many, Senator. A good public administration school."

Senator Brooke: "Well, I wasn't specifically speaking of that—" The stenographer transcribing the hearing then noted: "laughter." Brooke was teasing Georgetown about trying to make Magnuson an ally of its scheme to fund a new building for the School of Foreign Service, and about the fact that he had caught them in the act.

Brooke, a graduate of Boston University and, at the time, a member of its board of trustees, had invited that school's colorful and outspoken president, John Silber, to testify at the hearing as well. Evidently, Brooke expected Silber to endorse his view that the $19 million in grants and loans that Georgetown and Tufts were seeking ought not be approved by the federal government without a merit-based competition that would allow other schools to compete for the money.

But Silber, who would soon be seeking his own earmarked federal appropriations to help him realize his large ambitions for Boston University, seemed to disappoint Senator Brooke when he took the witness chair. Though Brooke's comments clearly indicated that he was looking for negative assessments, Silber had only good things to say about the Georgetown-Tufts proposal.

Diplomacy, Silber said, is critical to "national survival," and "These are the two most important, most effective institutions in the training of Foreign Service officers for the United States, and also for a large number of foreign countries." Moreover, "these two institutions have subsidized the Federal Government in the education of Foreign Service [officers] since their founding, and that goes back now for about forty years or more. And that means that they have invested somewhere between $40 million and $60 million in the education [of American diplomats] . . . that the Federal Government and the Federal taxpayer would otherwise have had to support." Silber did not explain why the government would have had to fund activities that two private universities had voluntarily undertaken already.

What about running an open competition for the $19 million in the proposal, or sharing the money more widely? Brooke asked.

"You can take $19 million and divide it eighty-five different ways or 1500 different ways to accommodate all the other places that have [international] education in the United States," Silber replied, "and I don't think you are going to make any of them much better. You know, it is sort of like mixing ice cream and spinach; it doesn't help the spinach, but it ruins the ice cream."

Tufts and Georgetown were the ice cream—"two of the greatest institutions in this area in the United States, and the two that have clearly made the greatest contribution." An open competition would produce no better candidates, but it would "open the doors to the hustle, to 100 very hungry institutions who are perfectly prepared to compete for the Federal dollar."

Silber urged Brooke not to shy away from making a judgment that these two schools deserved something from the government that others did not. "I don't think you are going to find any evidence that is going to prove that some other institution can do it better," he said. "I am not in favor of this because Tufts wants it, or because Georgetown wants it. I am in favor of this proposal because I believe the country needs it."

Silber's ringing rhetoric did not move Brooke, who ended the hearing on the same skeptical note he had introduced at the outset. Noting that the House had already approved the grants, he said the Senate faced "a difficult question of priorities and one which we will have to weigh very carefully."

Brooke had run a smart, effective hearing—something that used to be common on Capitol Hill. Though surprised by Silber's testimony, he had put the case against the earmark clearly on the record with the testimony of executive branch officials and his own skeptical comments. He had raised questions about the appropriateness of designating recipients for $19.3 million without any public competition or real debate. When his gavel fell ending the hearing, Schlossberg knew he had work to do.

To his frustration, *The Washington Post* editorial page picked this moment to offer a sternly negative opinion on the earmark for Tufts and Georgetown. The House vote in favor of the proposal was "one of those weak moments that bring out the worst in Congress," the *Post* editorialized on October 27, 1977. Georgetown and Tufts were worthy institutions, but their "intercultural centers" were not high national priorities and "they shouldn't be getting large amounts of taxpayers' funds from the pork barrel." The Senate should kill this earmark, said the *Post*.

Such editorials can have an impact in arguments like this one. The *Post* tried to cast itself as an honest broker upholding good government. Senators and congressmen could, and often did, shrug off its editorial positions, but members who agreed with the *Post* could use such an editorial to embarrass opponents and win allies.

Schlossberg remembered calling Mayer and Dean Gullion at Tufts when the *Post* editorial appeared. He asked Mayer if he wanted to abandon the effort. "The old resistance fighter said 'No way,' " Schlossberg remembered. He and Gullion hurriedly met with the editorial board of *The Boston Globe*, hoping it would editorialize in favor of the earmark for Georgetown and Tufts. The *Globe* came through on October 30: "Congress has an opportunity to give tangible aid to an already flourishing international program through grants for construction of model intercultural centers at two leading schools of diplomacy, one of them the Fletcher School at Tufts." Schlossberg-Cassidy circulated the *Globe* editorial to members of the House-Senate conference committee that would consider the earmark. Gullion suggested asking his friend Henry Kissinger, then recently retired secretary of state and newly appointed Georgetown professor, to write to the conference committee members. Kissinger, Schlossberg remembered, wrote a strong letter describing the importance of the Fletcher School and Georgetown's School of Foreign Service to the U.S. Foreign Service.

But they could not win the argument on the merits. Magnuson was unmoved. Schlossberg said he realized that only raw politics could save the day.

The conference was to consider hundreds of line item appropriations that had been included in supplemental appropriations bills by both House and Senate. Many of them, like the money for Tufts and Georgetown, had been approved by only one of the houses of Congress. "I read every line of the Senate and House supplemental bills," Schlossberg said. "I discovered that Washington State had something like $500 million in earmarks," including a $75 million bridge over Tacoma Harbor and numerous other infrastructure projects of a kind Magnuson had long been directing to his home state.

Schlossberg then wrote a memo to the Massachusetts members who would participate in the conference committee, pointing out this largesse for Washington State. "Eddie Boland [the senior Massachusetts member on the House Appropriations Committee] asked me if everything in the memo was correct," Schlossberg remembered. "I said it was." In the end a deal was struck—in private, the way conference committees most often strike such deals. Washington State got all its money; Tufts and George-town got their earmarks as well. There is no official record of how the final arrangement was made, no recorded vote or transcript of the confer-ence committee meeting. But fine buildings on the Georgetown campus and at Tufts testify that the deal went through.

The early earmarks for Tufts (another soon followed to help build a med-ical library) marked an unspoken victory for Gerry Cassidy over his part-ner. With them, the debate over Schlossberg-Cassidy's corporate identity ended. This was now a lobbying firm—*Gzing!* could have been the com-pany motto. Schlossberg, making more money than he had ever seen in his life, did not complain, though he had misgivings.

The firm soon acquired a string of university clients, all looking for their own earmarks, each paying a handsome retainer. Cassidy had also brought in a substantial corporate client, a source of tension in the part-nership but also of money in the bank. This was the Ocean Spray cran-berry cooperative, a marketing organization owned by cranberry farmers that promoted and developed cranberry-based products. Ocean Spray was referred to Cassidy by the same Department of Agriculture official who had helped resolve the payment to Larry's Foods. Ocean Spray was having trouble getting cranberry juice approved by the Department of Agricul-ture for the federal school lunch program because its sugar content was high. ("Did you ever try to drink raw cranberry juice?" Cassidy likes to ask, even today. The sugar compensated for the cranberry's natural bitter-ness.) At Cassidy's suggestion, Ocean Spray set up one of the early politi-cal action committees, to funnel campaign contributions from cranberry farmers to politicians who could affect their business. Cassidy would run the PAC and help decide who got its money.

Schlossberg recalled this with discomfort. He remembered Cassidy "explaining to me what was going on in town with the DNC [Democratic National Committee] and corporate PACs [whose money both parties wanted], and what the law was, how this could make us a bigger player and help get things done."

Cassidy asked him to come to an Ocean Spray convention in San Diego, where Schlossberg played golf with members of the board. One of them, he recalled, "delivered a diatribe against FDR and his works—you'd have thought it was 1932." He found the Ocean Spray people distasteful, Schlossberg said. He was taken aback by Cassidy's enthusiasm for the Ocean Spray relationship, which had fulfilled his desire for a corporate client who would agree to set up a PAC. "He never got excited about any-thing the way he did about that," Schlossberg said.

Soon the two of them were making contributions to members them-selves. In the beginning the amounts were small, but the role of money in politics was changing palpably.

So was the role of money in the Schlossberg-Cassidy partnership. They were paying themselves handsome salaries. They moved offices at L'Enfant Plaza, trading in their one room for a more spacious suite. Both bought bigger houses and fancier cars.

Schlossberg had grown up in an upper-middle-class household; living this well wasn't new for him. For Gerry and Loretta the change was more dramatic, and more exciting. They spent many weekends shopping, and began collecting antiques.

Both men had new Washington identities. They had met and made friends as warriors for the hungry and poor—underpaid aides to a Senate committee. Quite suddenly, they looked a lot like fat-cat Washington lobbyists.

CHAPTER 6

CORRUPT OR CORRECT?

When Schlossberg-Cassidy & Associates moved unabashedly into the ranks of Washington's lobbyists, they joined an ancient profession. Lobbyists were present at the first session of the first Congress when it convened in New York City in March 1789, in the persons of wealthy New York merchants eager to delay congressional action on a tariff bill they thought would cost them money. They exploited what quickly became the most typical transaction between moneyed favor-seeker and elected legislator—a good dinner, well lubricated with wine and spirits, allowing the supplicant to make his case to the legislator in congenial circumstances. These merchants offered "treats, dinners, attentions," Senator William Maclay of Pennsylvania wrote in his diary. There would be many more such treats and attentions in the decades and centuries that followed.

Members have always been willing and often eager to be wooed—including some who were otherwise considered distinguished statesmen. One was Daniel Webster, senator from Massachusetts, whose fame as an orator has survived to the present day. In 1833 Webster wrote to Nicholas Biddle, president of the Second Bank of the United States, a controversial financial institution chartered by Congress that existed from 1816 to 1836. Webster reminded Biddle that he was under political pressure to oppose renewing the bank's charter, "which I have declined of course, although I believe my retainer has not been renewed, or refreshed, as usual. If it be wished that my relation to the bank should be continued, it may be well to send me the usual retainer." Indeed.

The Civil War created a boom time for Washington lobbyists. Henry Adams described Mrs. Samuel Baker, her husband's partner in a highly successful lobbying enterprise during that war, though she did not use the term. She characterized herself and her spouse as "agents" when she described their business:

"We had more congressional business than all the other agents put together. Everyone came to us then, to get his bill through, or his appropriation watched. We were hard at work all the time. You see, one can't keep the run of three hundred men [members of Congress] without some trouble. My husband used to make lists of them in books with a history of each man and all he could learn about him, but I carried it all in my head."

Did that mean, Mrs. Baker was asked, "that you could get them all to vote as you pleased?"

"Well! We got our bills through," replied Mrs. Baker.

"But how did you do it?" she was asked. "Did they take bribes?"

"Some of them did. Some of them liked suppers and cards and theaters and all sorts of things. Some of them could be led, and some had to be driven like Paddy's pig who thought he was going the other way. Some of them had wives who could talk to them, and some—hadn't," said Mrs. Baker, with a queer intonation in her abrupt ending.

Mrs. Baker's account of past triumphs is actually a work of fiction, which may explain its candor. It appears in the only great novel ever written about Washington, Adams's *Democracy*. Adams's family tree included two presidents, John Adams, his great-grandfather, and John Quincy Adams, his grandfather. His father, Charles Francis Adams, served as President Abraham Lincoln's minister to London during the Civil War; Henry worked as his father's private secretary there. He then returned to Washington where he became a crusading reporter. *Democracy* was a fine piece of writing, and a devastating portrait of Washington's political community in the second half of the nineteenth century. Adams published the novel anonymously—his authorship became known only when he died in 1918. When it appeared in 1880, the book was a sensation, prompting speculation about who wrote it and who the characters were meant to resemble. Everyone in political Washington seemed to assume that *Democracy* was a roman à clef, because it described a world that all Washingtonians of the day recognized.

Though Mrs. Baker did not use the word, the verb "to lobby" was already in use in the early nineteenth century. It first appears in the *Oxford English Dictionary* in 1808 as an American usage. In the twentieth century a myth arose that the term was born in the lobby of Willard's Hotel, the most popular hangout for politicians in nineteenth-century Washington. The myth had it that representatives of various interests would take advantage of President Ulysses S. Grant's proclivity to visit Willard's lobby in the evening for a glass of brandy and a cigar to approach and try to influence him—hence "lobbying." But in fact, the practice and the term were already well established when Grant became president in 1869.

Lobbyists have always been associated in the public imagination with corruption, and for good reason. Examples of bribes and payoffs by pleaders for special (usually wealthy) interests recur throughout American history. Perhaps the definitive case was the Crédit Mobilier scandal in the late 1860s, an era when the young railroad industry learned to work its will in Congress through complex financial transactions that produced simple outcomes: members were bought and paid for.

Crédit Mobilier was a holding company used as a front for massive corruption involving multimillion-dollar contracts for the construction of the first transcontinental railroad. Shares in the firm were sold at nominal prices to at least fourteen members of Congress who reciprocated by voting for lucrative benefits to the Union Pacific Railroad Company. Thanks to crusading journalism by the *New York Sun*, Crédit Mobilier became a household name in post–Civil War America, but it represented only a fraction of the corruption surrounding the building of the country's great railroads in the late nineteenth century. That era has been called "The Great Barbecue," as in "come and get it!" From 1862 to 1877, Congress passed a series of railroad bills rewarding the companies that were spanning the country with iron rails, a great boon to the lobbying profession, and to members of Congress.

One who benefited was Richard Franchot, who served a single term as a member of the House from upstate New York from 1861 to 1863. He gave up his seat on the House of Representatives railroad committee to become the Central Pacific's Washington lobbyist for $25,000 a year, or five times the salary of a member of Congress. A lobbyist making five times a congressman's salary today would earn $850,000 a year—a handsome stipend, though not an unusual salary in today's Washington.

Franchot's immediate boss was Collis P. Huntington, one of the original partners in the Central Pacific, who became chief lobbyist for the project in Washington. The Central Pacific proposed to build the rail line from California eastward, to meet the line being built westward from

Omaha by the Union Pacific. (The two met near Ogden, Utah, in 1869.) Huntington's exploits in the early years of the Great Barbecue suggest that there were few if any legislative objectives that could not be achieved with the proper combination of carrots.

In the heat of one legislative battle Huntington wrote to a partner in California: "There is a very strong combination against us, but I expect to beat them—but it will cost us something." As it turned out it cost a lot of money and promises of more, cleverly dispensed. To win the loyalty of Senator Henry Winslow Corbett of Oregon, for example, Huntington secretly promised that the Central Pacific would join a partnership with the senator and his friends to build a spur of the transcontinental railroad into Oregon. To assure the allegiance of Representative Ignatius Donnelly, "a first class man on the Land and Railroad Committee," the issue was simpler. Donnelly was "a little short of cash, and I loaned him $1000." Huntington promised Senator James Warren Nye of Nevada an ownership stake in the new town by a big Nevada lake that was expected to develop quickly once the new railroad was operating—Lake's Crossing, it was called then: today, Reno. Nevada's other senator just wanted campaign cash—up to $50,000. Representative Samuel B. Axtell wanted a job, so Huntington put him on the Central Pacific payroll: "I have employed him as our attorney (confidential)," Huntington wrote to his partner.

These details only emerged long after Huntington's machinations. The doings of Sam Ward, on the other hand, were notorious while they were going on, also during the era of the Great Barbecue. Ward was a swashbuckling figure who had married into the Astor family, then the richest in New York, only to have his wife die in childbirth. The Astors turned against him, forcing him to rely on his own considerable wits to make his way in the world, which he did with repeated successes and failures in New York, in California during the gold rush, and then in post–Civil War Washington, where he became known as "King of the Lobby," the most notorious lobbyist in town. "No country except the United States could have produced such a man, and under no [other] circumstances could he have found such diversified opportunities of development," wrote London's *Daily Telegraph* when Ward died. Ward's very public antics contributed to the image of Washington lobbyists as scoundrels, albeit sometimes charming scoundrels. He became the subject of national attention early in 1875 when he was subpoenaed to testify before the House Ways and Means Committee, which was investigating charges that bribes of at least $120,000 had been paid by the Pacific Mail Steamship Company to win government subsidies to carry mail to China and the Far East. The committee had heard from a series of uncooperative and obfuscating witnesses when Ward came to the witness table and gave the impression, at least, of total candor.

Yes, he readily acknowledged, he had been approached by one of the alleged recipients of a payoff—James G. Barrett, a former mayor of Washington—who asked if he could help win support for the subsidy in Congress. "I asked him how much," Ward testified. "He said $500 and $5000 contingent on success. I said, 'All right.' "

Ward's girth was as impressive as his fame, and the two were connected. His specialty was the grand dinner party. He could often be found at Welcher's restaurant on Fifteenth Street, across from the Treasury Department. Ward famously instructed Welcher's cooks on how to prepare elaborate and expensive dinners. They were shared, typically, with members of Congress and other important people whom Ward cultivated. "There is nothing in the world so excellent as entertainments of a refined order," Ward testified to the Ways and Means Committee, an allusion quickly grasped by his audience. "Talleyrand says that diplomacy is assisted by good dinners, but at good dinners people do not 'talk shop.' But they give people who have a taste in that way the right, perhaps, to ask a gentleman a civil question, and to get a civil answer; to get information which his clients want, and that can be properly given." Ward was describing his lobbying technique.

The committee chairman asked Ward for details about what he had done to win support for the Pacific Mail subsidy—"state the nature of the services rendered by you."

"Simply stating on all occasions when it was proper to do so that I was in favor of the measure, that I thought it a good measure," Ward replied. This was easy, he added, because he strongly believed in the subsidy as a way to promote American shipbuilding and the merchant marine. "I thought that a subsidy to the Pacific Mail Steamship Co. was a proper thing, particularly as the Cunard Steamship Co. had a subsidy from the English government and had attained a colossal success. I wanted to see the American flag flying again on the seas, and I would have helped the Pacific Mail Steamship Co. subsidy without one cent of compensation."

So he used his influence to win passage of the measure?

"Certainly," Ward replied.

The newspapers had printed reports that cash payments had been made to members. Did Ward know of "any sum of money being paid, directly or indirectly in connection with the subsidy?"

"Not a penny," Ward replied.

Ward spent "a fortnight" lobbying for the subsidy. Though promised $5,000 if the measure passed—half the money former mayor Barrett had been promised, he had told Ward—Barrett altered the arrangement when the bill did pass. He said that whoever was paying him had reneged on his original offer and reduced his fee from $10,000 to $7,000; there would only be $3,500 for Ward. "Let's take what we can get," Ward quoted himself as replying. "It is all right." Barrett gave him the $3,500 in cash. "I went to New York that night," Ward testified. "I must say that it was very liberal compensation for the moderate amount of work which that subsidy seemed to require."

The chairman asked: "Were you aware that Mr. Barrett, in point of fact, had received $10,000 instead of $7,000"—that he had cheated Ward?

"No, I did not know anything about it until I saw it mentioned in the papers," Ward replied. "It's quite all right; he probably did more work than I did. I was quite satisfied with what I got"—which amounted to 70 percent of a congressman's annual salary for two weeks' work.

The official transcript of Ward's appearance contains numerous references to the laughter in the hearing room that his testimony provoked. He was a genuine Washington character who exploited the character of the times, which was corrupt.

Just a few years later, in a long-forgotten decision that is quite startling to a twenty-first-century eye, the Supreme Court expressed a contrary view of the world Sam Ward lived in, the world of Washington "agents" or lobbyists. A unanimous Supreme Court decided the case, *Trist v. Child*, in 1875. Its decision reflected a puritan, perhaps romantic, view of propriety in Washington that has appeared sporadically throughout the history of the republic. The contrast between Ward's jaunty testimony and its appreciative reception and the Court's scolding opinion in this case captures both sides of a deep American ambivalence about influence peddling, as evident today as it was during the Great Barbecue.

N. P. Trist had made a claim against the federal government, seeking to be paid for services rendered "touching on the Treaty of Guadalupe-Hidalgo," which ended the Mexican-American War. The court record offers no details about those services. The government rejected Trist's request for payment, so he hired Linus Child, a Boston lawyer, to "take charge of the claim and prosecute it before Congress as his agent and attorney." As Sam Ward did in the Pacific Mail matter, Child took the case on a contingency basis. If he persuaded Congress to recognize and pay Trist's claim, Trist would pay him one-fourth of whatever he received. If Child failed, he would receive nothing.

The issue dragged on for several years. Child died. His son and law partner, L. M. Child, took up the matter and pursued it to a successful conclusion. In April 1871, Congress appropriated $14,559 to pay Trist's claim. The younger Child applied for his fee, but Trist refused to pay it. Child then sued Trist and prevailed in the courts of Washington, D.C. Trist appealed to the Supreme Court of the United States, which emphatically reversed the D.C. court and said Child was not entitled to any payment under the contract with Trist.

Specifically, the Court found that the arrangement between the Childs and Trist "was for the sale of the influence and exertions of the lobby agent to bring about the passage of a law for the payment of a private claim, without reference to its merits, by means which, if not corrupt, were illegitimate, and . . . contrary to the plainest principles of public policy." A contract that runs "against the maxims of sound policy" is void, and cannot be enforced in the courts, wrote Justice Noah H. Swayne for a unanimous Court.

The key evidence, according to Swayne's decision, was this letter that the younger Child had sent to Trist early in 1871:

Mr. Trist:

Everything looks very favorable. I found that my father has spoken to C———— and B————, and other members of the House. Mr. B———— says he will try hard to get it before the House. He has two more chances, or rather "morning hours," before Congress adjourns. A———— will go in for it. D———— promises to go for it. I have sent your letter and report to Mr. W————, of Pennsylvania. It may not be reached till next week. Please write to your friends to write immediately to any member of Congress. Every vote tells; and a simple request to a member may secure his vote, he not caring anything about it. Set every man you know at work even if he knows a page, for a page often gets a vote. The most I fear is indifference.

Yours &c, L. M. Child

Justice Swayne absolved the Childs of corrupt behavior: "There is no reason to believe that [their actions] involved anything corrupt or different from what is usually practiced by all paid lobbyists in the prosecution of their business," Swayne wrote. But that was just the point—the machinations of lobbyists to influence members of Congress to vote for measures the lobbyists supported without regard for the public interest undermined values crucially important to the health of the republic, the Court said.

"The theory of our government is, that all public stations are trusts, and that those clothed with them are to be animated in the discharge of their duties solely by considerations of right, justice, and the public good," Justice Swayne wrote. "They are never to descend to a lower plane. But there is a correlative duty resting upon the citizen. In his intercourse with those in authority, whether executive or legislative, touching the performance of their functions, he is bound to exhibit truth, frankness, and integrity. Any departure from the line of rectitude in such cases, is not only bad in morals, but involves a public wrong."

In other words, by asking Trist to encourage his friends to write letters to congressmen seeking support for Trist's bill, the Childs had committed "a public wrong."

The justice wanted no confusion: the contract would have been valid and enforceable if the Childs had stuck to a narrower definition of their role. The Court explicitly endorsed "drafting the petition to set forth the claim, attending to the taking of testimony, collecting facts, preparing arguments, and submitting them orally or in writing, to a committee or other proper authority, and other services of like character." All those were fine, because they "are intended to reach only the reason of those sought to be influenced. They rest on the same principle of ethics as professional services rendered in a court of justice, and are no more exceptionable." On the other hand, "such services are separated by a broad line of demarcation from personal solicitation, and the other means and appliances which the correspondence [young Childs's letter to Trist] shows were resorted to in this case.

> The agreement in the present case was for the sale of the influence and exertions of the lobby agent to bring about the passage of a law for the payment of a private claim, without reference to its merits, by means which, if not corrupt, were illegitimate and considered in connection with the pecuniary interest of the agent at stake, contrary to the plainest principles of public policy. No one has a right, in such circumstances, to put himself in a position of temptation to do what is regarded as so pernicious in its character.

Mr. Justice Swayne here establishes the Supreme Court as an exemplar of high-mindedness. And his very next paragraph makes clear that he understood the implications of the Court's position. The justices were condemning practices that they surely realized were already widespread in Washington:

> If any of the great corporations of the country were to hire adventurers who make market of themselves in this way, to procure the passage of a general law with a view to the promotion of their private interests, the moral sense of every right-minded man would instinctively denounce the employer and employed as steeped in corruption, and the employment as infamous. If the instances were numerous, open, and tolerated, they would be regarded as measuring the decay of the public morals and the degeneracy of the times.

Justice Swayne seemed to be pointing right at Sam Ward and his many colleagues then making market of themselves in Washington.

Henry Adams shared Justice Swayne's disdain. The leading political figure in *Democracy* is Senator Silas Ratliffe, who falls for the book's heroine and central figure, Mrs. Lightfoot Lee, an attractive young widow from New York. Mrs. Lee is about to accept Ratliffe's offer of marriage when she discovers that Mrs. Baker's husband, the lobbyist, had bought a crucial vote from Ratliffe for a bribe of $100,000. Though he had not confessed this to Mrs. Lee, he had given her a more generic confession: "To act with entire honesty and self-respect, one should always live in a pure atmosphere, and the atmosphere of politics is impure." His sentiment was as American as cherry pie.

As the progressive movement gathered strength early in the twentieth century, the corruption of politics became a reformers' target. The ability of the railroads and the gigantic trusts that controlled entire sectors of the economy—including wool, sugar, tobacco, steel, and oil—to work their will in Washington was the topic of a famous piece of muckraking by a novelist named David Graham Phillips, who wrote a series of articles for *Cosmopolitan* magazine under the title, "The Treason of the Senate." Phillips's reporting was eye-opening, and his denunciatory writing style compelling. The combination influenced public opinion.

In Phillips's account, the most effective lobbyists for what he called "the interests," using quotation marks every time he used the phrase, were corrupted members of the Senate. In 1906 (and until 1914) many senators were chosen, under Article I of the Constitution, by their state legislatures, though a steadily growing number of states provided for direct election.

Phillips's thesis was simple: giant corporations—"the great drainage companies fastened upon America's prosperity"—had enriched themselves at the expense of the people whose wealth they "expropriated." They did this by controlling legislatures, both in the states and in Washington, which granted them all sorts of advantages that nearly always defied the public interest. The Senate was "a traitorous band of servants of 'the interests' " who happily took bribes in many forms and provided in return whatever legislative services "the interests" requested. He named the most corrupt, led by Senator Nelson W. Aldrich of Rhode Island, explained how they got paid, held them up to merciless ridicule, and captured the country's imagination.

Phillips's exposé fed and encouraged the reformers pressing for direct election of senators as an antidote to their control by "the interests." His articles resonated with a country already familiar with the corruption of the Senate. Nine senators were formally accused of taking bribes between 1866 and 1905. In 1913 the Seventeenth Amendment was ratified, providing for direct election.

But the Seventeenth Amendment did not end controversy about wealthy interests' influence in Congress and the lobbyists they employed. The last of the progressive presidents, Woodrow Wilson, discovered early in his first term how well-heeled interests could frustrate his plans to reduce U.S. tariffs, and he decided to take them on. In May 1913, barely two months after he became president, Wilson issued a "message for publication," what we would call today a press release, obviously intended to embarrass "the interests" by denouncing their lobbyists.

"I think the public ought to know the extraordinary exertions being made by the lobby in Washington to gain recognition for certain alterations of the Tariff bill," Wilson's statement said. "Washington has seldom seen so numerous, so industrious or so insidious a lobby. The newspapers are being filled with paid advertisements calculated to mislead the judgments of public men . . . [and] the public opinion of the country itself. There is every evidence that money without limit is being spent to sustain this lobby and to create an appearance of a pressure of opinion antagonistic to some of the chief items of the Tariff bill."

Wilson also noted a truism about Washington lobbying then and now when he instructed the citizenry: "It is of serious interest to the country that the people at large should have no lobby and be voiceless in these matters, while great bodies of astute men seek to create an artificial opinion, and to overcome the interests of the public for their private profit. It is thoroughly worth the while of the people of this country to take knowledge of this matter. Only public opinion can check and destroy it."

Of course Wilson was trying to establish himself as lobbyist for the people at large. In this case he succeeded; Congress approved the Under-wood tariff bill, reducing most import duties from 40 to 25 percent, despite the opposition of the trusts, especially sugar and wool.

The 1920s were a relatively quiet time. Corruption thrived in the executive branch under Warren G. Harding and his Ohio gang, but there were no scandals in Congress, and lobbyists for corporate interests had less to do in a Republican era when business and government were rarely at odds.

That all changed as Franklin Roosevelt came to power in March 1933 and instituted the New Deal. Even before FDR was inaugurated an exten-sive and expensive lobbying campaign had prepared the ground for the repeal of Prohibition, which Congress approved in February 1933. Jouett Shouse, a former Kansas congressman, led something called the Associa-tion Against the Prohibition Amendment, which enjoyed generous sup-port from the du Ponts and other wealthy industrialists. This was perhaps the first successful "grassroots" lobbying effort, which provided political cover for members of Congress who were ready to abandon the great experiment in temperance that had been a failure almost from the moment it began in 1920, when the Eighteenth Amendment to the Con-stitution came into force. Popular opinion strongly favored repeal by 1933; it took only months for the requisite three-fourths of the states to ratify the Twenty-first Amendment, which repealed the Eighteenth.

Shouse's campaign was atypical. More routine were the efforts by the titans of finance and industry to block or temper FDR's reforms. Kenneth G. Crawford explained what happened in his stylish and entertaining book on lobbying in the 1930s, *The Pressure Boys:* "The New Deal with its social reform program, its brood of alphabetical agencies and its tendency to ignore advice from Wall Street, frightened enough big businessmen to fatten the entire corps of Washington lobbyists."

Besides goring some very large oxen, the new Roosevelt administra-tion was extending the reach of the federal government into spheres of American life previously ignored by Washington. This produced a great many newly interested parties who wanted to be heard in the councils of government. Politics in Washington have always mimicked Newton's third law of motion: every action produces "an equal and opposite reac-tion." The fierce reaction to the New Deal produced the modern lobby-ing industry and most of its techniques.

Crawford was a young reporter from the Midwest writing from Washington for liberal publications, including *The Nation* magazine, when he published *The Pressure Boys* in 1939. He made no attempt to hide his sympathy for FDR and the New Deal. In his book the corporate lobbyists are "hirelings of private property interests" working to protect those interests "to the detriment of a growing majority of dispossessed Americans." Crawford used the term "property" to describe those who tried to use the levers of power in Washington to defend their wealth and privileges: "Property has not hesitated to corrupt government when necessary to preserve its precious advantages, and to extend them."

His description of the methods corporate lobbyists used could be written today: "Pressures are applied by (1) leading Congressmen to believe that they can be re-elected only if they support or oppose a given bill or (2) convincing their constituents that the Congressmen should or should not be re-elected." The first form of pressure includes promises of campaign contributions and other forms of electoral support. Crawford described the second as "the newer, now more favored technique. Here the Congressman's constituents themselves are proselytized by various forms of persuasion and propaganda." Even more common was the sort of campaign conducted by the utilities to artificially create the impression of popular support for their position.

In 1935 one of the smartest and most resourceful senators of the twentieth century, Hugo Black of Alabama, led a rigorous investigation of the lobbying by utility companies opposed to the Public Utility Holding Company Act of 1935. This New Deal legislation required electric utilities to be regulated by either the states or the federal government, and limited their involvement in other kinds of businesses.

The industry launched an elaborate lobbying campaign to try to block the legislation, known, for its key sponsors, as the Wheeler-Rayburn Bill. (Burton K. Wheeler was a progressive senator from Montana; Samuel T. Rayburn a legendary House member from Texas who later served as speaker.) When Capitol Hill was blanketed with letters and telegrams opposing the bill that all sounded alike, members became suspicious. Black, a longtime critic of Washington's lobbyists who had pressed for rules requiring them to disclose their salaries, expenses, and clients, launched a formal investigation.

It produced juicy results. One was the testimony of Elmer Danielson, nineteen, a Western Union messenger who delivered telegrams in his hometown of Warren in northwestern Pennsylvania. Danielson told Black's committee that the Associated Gas and Electric Co., a leading opponent of the Wheeler-Rayburn Bill, had paid messengers such as himself to persuade citizens of Warren to send a telegram opposing the bill to their congressman, a Democrat named Denis J. Driscoll. AG&E suggested what we now call talking points that the messengers could use, Danielson testified: Just tell people the bill would put the electric companies into the hands of "big men"—precisely the opposite of the truth. Each telegram was worth three cents to the messenger, Danielson testified.

Driscoll supported the Wheeler-Rayburn Bill. When he received 816 telegrams opposing it in two days—all of them sounding alike, most of them from citizens whose names began with A, B, or C—he became suspicious, and shared his experience with an investigator for Black's committee, who subsequently learned that the utility lobby had spent $4 million ($62 million in today's dollars) on a campaign to try to block the law. The utilities hired numerous expensive Washington lawyers to press their case. Black summoned several of them to testify and to reveal their fees. Thousands of fake telegrams, many signed by names taken from telephone directories, had arrived on Capitol Hill urging members to vote no.

To promote his bill on lobbying, Black gave a stem-winding radio speech on the subject, denouncing the utilities for hiding "behind a mask" concealing their true identity, calling them "high-powered, deceptive, telegram-fixing, letter-framing" and more. He warned Americans that "contrary to tradition, against the public morals, and hostile to good government, the lobby has reached such a position of power that it threatens government itself. Its size, its power, its capacity for evil; its greed, trickery, deception and fraud condemn it to the death it deserves."

This speech and the hearings won Black national acclaim, but his efforts to put new restrictions on lobbyists ultimately failed. Black gave that radio speech shortly before he left the Senate to join the Supreme Court. With his departure from the Senate, his campaign to control and expose lobbying was orphaned. Though versions of the lobbying legislation he proposed had passed both House and Senate, attempts to negotiate a version acceptable to both failed.

Despite the rich history of venality associated with influence peddling in Washington, there has always been more to lobbying than corruption. Americans can wax indignant at perceived abuses or at a system they consider crooked, but they also believe, often fervently, in the right to "petition the government for a redress of grievances," a right forcefully guaranteed in the First Amendment to the Constitution* and in the En-

---

* "Congress shall make no law respecting an establishment of religion, or prohibiting the free exercise thereof; or abridging the freedom of speech, or of the press; or the right of the people peaceably to assemble, and to petition the government for a redress of grievances."

glish common law from which the Constitution grew. To petition for the redress of grievances—to make a formal complaint about a perceived injustice committed by king or governors, and demand action to correct it—is often to do something that can fairly be described as lobbying. Of course lobbying can be corrupt, nefarious, even disgusting—Jack Abramoff demonstrated all of that. But lobbying can also express one of Americans' fundamental rights.

The lobbying profession elicits conflicting responses because it symbolizes a deep conflict of American values. Lobbying is corrupt and deplorable, as the Supreme Court declared in *Trist v. Child*, until one's own ox is gored or threatened, at which point, let the lobbying begin! So chief justices for years have lobbied Congress for higher judicial salaries—never for their personal benefit, naturally, but to serve the national interest. As William H. Rehnquist, then the chief justice, put it in 2002, "Inadequate judicial pay undermines the strength of our judiciary."

There is no evading this very American moral conundrum—a classic dilemma for a society and culture that loves to romanticize its history and avoid facing up to the gulf that so often separates its mythology from the truth. In the matter of lobbying, Americans seem doomed to accept what often feel like contradictory propositions. So, for example, Americans tend to believe that people should not be getting rich by influencing government decisions after contributing money to the people who make them. But many of America's noblest institutions, among them the Red Cross, the United Way, the Kiwanis clubs, and the March of Dimes, pay handsome fees to Washington lobbyists to help them influence government decisions. If Americans enjoy an inalienable right to petition their government, are they not also entitled to some help from an expert who might actually know how the government works, and how its decisions might be influenced?

As a matter of historical fact, Americans have "lobbied" their governments for more than four hundred years, from the earliest days of the Virginia colony. Historians interpret this as evidence that a strong democratic impulse was operating in America long before independence or the founding of the modern republic. Seeking benefits, protection, or just a fair shake from the authorities of the day is an American reflex long taken for granted.

The historical record is compelling. Englishmen began sending petitions to king and Parliament in the thirteenth century, when Edward I invited citizens' formal requests and complaints every time he called a session of Parliament. Over the subsequent three centuries, as Parliament became more democratic and included an increasing number of elected members, the right to petition the authorities evolved into a pillar of the unwritten English constitution.

English settlers began to colonize North America early in the seventeenth century. The royal charters creating the earliest colonies specifically guaranteed that the rights of emigrating Englishmen would be preserved in the new world. By then these explicitly included the right to petition the authorities to redress grievances, and the new colonists quickly took advantage. The records of the initial settlement in Jamestown, Virginia, show that a petition (seeking "Reformatyon" of "certayne [unspecified] preposterous proceedings and inconvenyent Courses") was presented to the governing council of the brand-new colony on June 6, 1607, just two weeks after the first colonists had landed. Four days later the petition was considered and the "Reformatyon" it sought was approved.

When the Virginia colony convened its first representative assembly in 1619, an early item of business was a petition from the residents of the town of Argall asking for relief from certain financial obligations they had incurred. The assembly endorsed the suggestion.

By the end of the seventeenth century the procedure was an important part of governance of the colony. For example, the 1696 assembly considered petitions requesting a change in the town of Accomack's court days, a reduction in the fees set by the clerks of the courts, a ban on Sunday horseracing, specific road improvements, and new bridges. In that session, the assembly passed fourteen laws, nine of them responses to citizens' petitions. Petitions were actually more democratic than the elections of that era, because only propertied white men could vote, while anyone, including a slave, could sign or originate a petition.

In the 1700s petitions became an important means of communication between governed and governors. The authorities relied on them to learn public desires and opinions. Citizens could present them personally, or hire an agent or attorney to take the petition to the assembly. Such agents may have been the first American lobbyists. After independence, the House of Burgesses established committees to investigate and consider citizens' petitions more systematically.

Many of Virginia's petitioners sought economic benefits, including direct state support for their enterprises or tax relief and other subsidies to protect entire industries, like iron production. During the Revolutionary War, John Ballendine and John Reveley petitioned the commonwealth for a loan of £5,000 to help them build a big iron mine and blast furnace on the banks of the James River. Because iron was needed for cannon, shot, and military utensils, they got the money and built the furnace. The project was a failure, never produced much iron, and devoured the state's £5,000. The petitioners never repaid the loan.

On the other hand, petitions from citizens of Virginia prodded their legislators to enact numerous measures that encouraged the economic development of the commonwealth. Petitions led to regulations on the inspection of tobacco and grain exports that improved the quality of Virginia's products and, thereby, their sales. Petitions led to the state charter of an important bank in Alexandria, and to the creation of the first insurance companies. These no doubt benefited individual entrepreneurs, but they helped Virginia develop a thriving economy at the same time. In precisely the same way, building the transcontinental railroads may have corrupted politics and lined the pockets of undeserving schemers, but the country benefited hugely from the railroads themselves.

Ethical ambiguity is the inevitable accompaniment to organized lobbying. The lobbyist is paid, often handsomely, to make something happen that might not have happened without his efforts. The worst of these transactions can be utterly venal, but how should we evaluate the best of them? Was the country well served by the creation, at taxpayers' expense, of a top-flight nutrition research center at Tufts? By the construction of new buildings for two of its best training academies for diplomats?

Cassidy and Schlossberg cast themselves on the side of the angels, helping deserving colleges and universities with the creative use of politics and government money. Happily for them, the work paid well.

CHAPTER 7

EARMARKS BECOME ROUTINE

Looking back years later, after earmarking had become a favorite congressional sport and a broadly accepted way to spend billions of the taxpayers' dollars, those early appropriations for Jean Mayer's projects at Tufts University look historic—and they were. Mayer, a true academic entrepreneur, had found a new way to pay for significant improvements to a fast-developing university. Ken Schlossberg and Gerry Cassidy had stumbled onto a new kind of business, making money by extracting money from the federal Treasury for their fee-paying clients.

But in the late 1970s when all this began, its historic qualities were not noticed. Schlossberg and Cassidy knew they had discovered something fabulous, but they had no interest then in flaunting their discovery. On the contrary, they hoped to continue developing their business in the shadows where, initially at least, few would notice it. Mayer had nothing to gain from publicizing his successes in Washington; it was enough that his Tufts constituency understood and appreciated what was happening. The members of Congress who had helped were happy to accept credit for pushing through the earmarks without mentioning that the whole idea had been Mayer's, or that the tactics used to pursue it had largely been Schlossberg-Cassidy's.

The firm operated successfully for several years with very little publicity or notoriety. One article in the weekly *Chronicle of Higher Education* in 1977 reported the "unusual" grants to Georgetown and Tufts' Fletcher School, and quoted Schlossberg, "a consultant to Tufts," on the broad support for those earmarks in Congress, but no story appeared anywhere explaining what was really going on. Academic administrators gossiped about this new way to pay for buildings, first in the Boston area, where Schlossberg-Cassidy's accomplishments for Tufts led to new contracts with Boston University and Boston College. Both got big earmarks of their own.

Schlossberg remembered going to Mayer after they won the earmark for the Fletcher School's new building and renegotiating their retainer. He was emboldened to ask for a big increase—from $120,000 to $250,000 a year—after reading an article, also in *The Chronicle of Higher Education*, reporting on the fees universities paid to fund-raisers who solicited contributions for them. Schlossberg realized, he said, that Tufts was paying a pittance for the big money they were helping Mayer get from Congress. Mayer was willing to raise the retainer slightly, to $125,000.

One outsider who grasped the potential of the Schlossberg-Cassidy business model was Bill Cloherty, who had worked for Dean Gullion of the Fletcher School in the 1970s and watched how the Tufts earmarks had been acquired. Cloherty recalled Gullion's remark when he first heard the proposal to seek an earmark for Congress to pay for Fletcher's new building: "It had never occurred to me that Congress could pass a law for the benefit of Tufts University!"

Cloherty resembles a fireplug, and words come out of his mouth the way water cascades from a hydrant. He is only about five feet, six inches tall, and looks nearly that wide, an appearance that belies his career in the 1950s as a star running back at Hull High School outside Boston: "I averaged 6.7 yards a carry." Cloherty finds a way to inform a new acquaintance within the first few minutes of meeting that he graduated from Harvard (class of 1962), obviously a proud accomplishment for an Irish kid, oldest of seven in his family, who still speaks with a thick Boston accent. Cloherty is bright, quick, observant, and a lifelong hustler.

In 1977 Cloherty left Tufts to accept a job as an all-purpose assistant to John Silber at Boston University. They became fast friends, but Silber was often exasperated by Cloherty's work habits. "I called him the leprechaun," Silber recounted, "because you never know when he is going to appear, or disappear."

In 1980 Cloherty fulfilled an old ambition by moving to Washington for a government job working on President Jimmy Carter's trade policies. That ended after Reagan defeated Carter, but he liked Washington and wanted to stay. Silber offered him $1,000 a month to be his man in the nation's capital, which Cloherty accepted.

One of Cloherty's Washington pals was Gerry Cassidy, whom he had met while working for Silber, at the time of Silber's testimony before Senator Brooke. These two Irishmen found each other entirely simpatico and became the best of friends. Cloherty said he was impressed by the way Cassidy represented his clients, and within months he told Silber he would get more out of hiring Schlossberg-Cassidy than Cloherty could possibly give him. Silber took this advice and signed a contract with the firm. Boston University would be the firm's client for the next three decades, and Silber and Cassidy would become friends, business partners, and, on one occasion, co-defendants.

After Cloherty had successfully made a match between Silber and Cassidy, it occurred to him that he did not have to stop there. He was a natural salesman, and Schlossberg-Cassidy had a product he could sell. Its appeal, Cloherty thought, was obvious. Every college and university had ambitions for its own development and expansion, dreams that might be converted into earmark requests. Many a college administrator could be tempted by the prospect of finding money in Washington. Members of Congress liked the idea of bringing home bacon. Cassidy and Cloherty began discussing how Cloherty might become part of the operation.

Cloherty remembered a conversation with Cassidy about how to expand his business: "I've got an idea for you. I can do this in a way that will cost you nothing. And Gerry said, 'Oh, tell me about that, I like that idea!' I remember him perking up the way he does. 'How's this going to work?' Well, instead of paying me, just give me 10 percent of the fees in perpetuity. He said we can't do it in perpetuity, because the Magna Carta prohibited contracts in perpetuity. So I said well, ninety-nine years. So he said yeah, we can do it for ninety-nine years." Cloherty laughed loudly as he told this story; he loves to laugh.

Cloherty described his sales technique: "I started systematically reading *Science Times*. It's really how I developed most of the business. On Tuesday, when *The New York Times* had a science section, I read that meticulously. I read the *Times* anyway. . . . I read seven or eight papers every day."

The *Times* reported on particular professors or departments that were pursuing promising research that gave him an opening. "There was one about some astounding breakthrough that was going on at Polytech in Brooklyn [Polytechnic University]. So I would simply call up the fellow. And I would accurately say, 'I'm from Washington, D.C.' Immediately all sorts of sugarplums would go off in their heads. 'I saw your article and I'd like to come up and talk to you about it.' 'Oh, when could you come?' 'This afternoon!' 'Great, okay, come on up.'

"I remember going up to the Polytechnic in Brooklyn, and seeing a terrific guy—this was twenty-five years ago, I can't remember the details, but this was exciting stuff. And I said Well, there's a new business developing in Washington. We don't do research grants, we don't help you get a grant through NIH or something, but if you have a particular need here, for a state-of-the-art facility, I can't make any promises, but there's a chance we can get it funded by Congress. . . . And Polytech signed up."

Like many an Irish storyteller, Cloherty has a gift for embellishment. Could this really have happened? Well, yes, mostly, it did happen. The story was not in the *Times*'s science section, but was buried in Section D, page 23. It reported that Brooklyn Poly was doing unusual work in the realm of imaging sciences that had potential uses in space and on earth. That "terrific guy" was Bernie Bulkin, the vice president of Brooklyn Poly for research, who ran the imaging sciences program. Three decades later he was a venture capitalist and international consultant, and he still remembered Cloherty.

"He was just a character really. He did make enough of an impression that we gave him a hearing, what can I say? I seem to remember that he got my home number and called me at home, the first call. And he came right away, he was very immediate and very persistent. They did sort of feature the hard sell."

The idea of hiring a Washington lobbyist was controversial within the administration of Brooklyn Poly, Bulkin remembered. "In many ways it was not to our liking to do this." They feared alienating civil servants in Washington who had given Poly research grants in the past. "But we were frustrated; we were a small institution, and we saw people who were not as good as us getting money in various ways and we wanted to be part of the game. We thought we would give it a try, basically." They signed on as a Schlossberg-Cassidy client.*

An old friend of Cloherty's, Terry Holcombe, had become the vice president of Columbia University for development—Columbia's chief fund-raiser. Holcombe had recruited Cloherty in the mid-1960s to join ACCION, a private group patterned on the Peace Corps that provided technical assistance to developing South American countries. Cloherty had spent a year with ACCION in Venezuela. Holcombe had previously been the chief fund-raiser at Yale where he raised millions. At Columbia he organized a $500 million fund drive.

It occurred to Cloherty that Columbia's ambitions for that money

---

* Brooklyn Poly never got an earmark, but Schlossberg-Cassidy did help it win some research money from the Pentagon.

might include a project suitable for an earmark. "I got into my little Volkswagen and drove up to New York," he recounted. When he sat down with Holcombe, he got right to the point: "I bet I'm the answer to your prayer—I bet you have something in that mix of projects [to be funded by the $500 million he was pursuing] that is going to be a real ball-buster to try to raise the money for."

Yes he did, Holcombe remembered when asked about this episode more than a quarter-century later—a $30 million reconstruction of Columbia's chemistry laboratories. The university had two old buildings that housed its distinguished chemistry department, but they were overcrowded, dreary, and dilapidated. In one the pipes leaked. For Columbia's president, Michael Sovern, reconstructing the labs into a state-of-the-art chemistry facility had become a symbol of his ambitions. "But we didn't have any alumni that I could find who would give in that range," Holcombe said. It was never easy to find big gifts to renovate existing facilities—big donors wanted their names on new buildings. So the alternative Cloherty proposed—a grant from the federal government—had obvious appeal.

"With Cloherty, you always have to separate myth from reality," Holcombe recalled with a chuckle, so he asked his old friend to arrange a meeting with the people whose services he was trying to sell. Cassidy and Schlossberg came to New York to meet with Holcombe and Cloherty. Holcombe was impressed: "It was real, they really could produce the money."

He also saw the problem: great universities, including Columbia, had long supported the idea that federal money should be dispensed to such institutions only on the basis of "peer review"—the recommendations of independent panels of academic experts, peers of the applicants, who could evaluate competing proposals, usually for research. Columbia had long been a top recipient of research funds allocated by the peer review process.

President Sovern was familiar with Schlossberg-Cassidy's successes: "I knew about Tufts," he said in an interview. He also knew that the federal government, which once provided significant aid to universities for the construction of facilities based on peer review of proposed projects, had gone out of that business. The federal programs involved had run out of money and not been refunded. "At that moment the alternative was not peer review, it was nothing. We were not persuaded to take nothing when we saw real possibilities for important work to be done." After Sovern met personally with Cassidy and Schlossberg, Columbia signed up, agreeing initially to a fee of $10,000 a month. From the first day, Cloherty collected $1,000 a month himself (the number rose in later years after contract renewals raised Columbia's monthly fee first to $17,500, then to $20,000), though he never did any work for Columbia in Washington. That was his 10 percent, the fruit of his original idea.

Cassidy and Schlossberg, on the other hand, worked hard on the Columbia earmark. Always looking for alliances that could help achieve their clients' goals, in this case they combined two of their clients' projects, Columbia's and one for the Catholic University of America.

Catholic, located in Washington, had a new president, Father William Byron, who came to the school from Loyola University in New Orleans. He signed up as a Schlossberg-Cassidy client soon after taking office. He told Cassidy he wanted to build a new facility for the university's vitreous state lab, which studied fiber optics. This sounded like a cousin of the Columbia chemistry labs. Cassidy and Schlossberg saw the possibility of a package deal.

They helped both schools present their proposals in politically appealing ways. Schlossberg suggested to Columbia that it rename its chemistry lab the National Chemical Research Center, and describe it as a response to the "threat" posed to the American chemical industry by competition from Japan and elsewhere. The firm also promoted the idea that because of its location in the New York region, a center of pharmaceutical research and production, its chemistry department had economic significance, not just an academic role.

Cassidy encouraged Father Byron to try to exploit the Reagan administration's recent request for $250 million for a new National Center for Advanced Materials Research at the University of California's Lawrence Berkeley National Laboratory, a pet project of President Reagan's science advisor. Eventually both schools made a regional argument—if California was to get that big center, shouldn't there also be something for the East Coast? Cassidy recounted accompanying Byron to meetings with old friends of his from New Orleans: J. Bennett Johnston, then the senior Democrat on both the Senate Energy and Natural Resources Committee and the energy appropriations subcommittee, and Lindy Boggs, the second-ranking Democrat on the House Appropriations Committee.

New York's congressional delegation took up the Columbia request, led by Charles Rangel, the Harlem Democrat whose district included Columbia. Senators Daniel Patrick Moynihan, a Democrat, and Alfonse

D'Amato, a Republican, and Republican Congressman Bill Green of Manhattan pitched in. Moynihan took up the geographical distribution argument with gusto.

But the projects got caught in a classic congressional spat over committee jurisdiction. "There was a war going on between the House Science Committee and the energy and water appropriations subcommittee over turf," Schlossberg realized, and he and Cassidy had been cultivating the appropriators on behalf of the Catholic and Columbia projects. Congressman Don Fuqua of Florida, the Democratic chairman of the Science Committee, was angry, as was his staff director, Schlossberg recalled. They said they would block the two earmarks unless they were first properly authorized by the Science Committee and then the full House.

Fuqua was not the only problem. The legislation that was drafted to include these earmarks was provocative, because it did something that had been avoided with Schlossberg-Cassidy's earlier academic earmarks: it identified spending programs from which the money for Catholic and Columbia would be taken. In other words, if Catholic and Columbia were to become winners, other entities would have to be losers.

Specifically, the earmark language proposed reducing the first appropriation for the National Center for Advanced Materials at Berkeley by $5 million to make a down payment of that amount on the new $14 million facility at Catholic University. It took $5 million—also a down payment, toward an eventual total of $30 million—for Columbia from several already approved line items, including equipment for high-energy physics projects at the University of Washington, Yale, and several other institutions. Those items had been included in an authorization bill passed by Fuqua's Science Committee, so enacting the earmarks would have the effect of altering or undoing the Science Committee's work.

At the same time, using political clout to win these earmarks at the expense of previously approved grants to others alarmed most of the organized higher education community. Such political logrolling could overwhelm traditional methods of allocating federal support for science and higher education by peer review.

Cassidy and Schlossberg concentrated first on their Fuqua problem. Their best approach, they decided, was through Speaker O'Neill. If Fuqua realized that O'Neill, his party leader, supported the earmarks for Columbia and Catholic, then Fuqua would be less likely to oppose them—this, Schlossberg said, was their reasoning.

Father Byron at Catholic University contacted members of his board of trustees who might help. One was Humberto Cardinal Medeiros of

Boston, O'Neill's local cardinal and friend. Medeiros called the speaker and told him how useful the earmark would be for Catholic University. Archbishop Philip Hannan of New Orleans made a similar call to Representative Boggs.

But the situation called for more than phone calls from Catholic prelates. Cassidy and Schlossberg called in additional chits of a kind that would become more familiar in years to come. First, Schlossberg recounted, they exploited a relationship Cassidy had been cultivating with the speaker's youngest son, Michael O'Neill, the third and least successful of three O'Neill boys. His father worried about him. He had a series of personal problems and was still looking for his place in the world when he joined a Boston insurance agency. Boston University, by then a Schlossberg-Cassidy client, agreed to buy insurance from this agency through Michael O'Neill. Later Tufts and Columbia did the same.

In the spring of 1983, when they were looking for the right way to solve their Fuqua problem, Michael O'Neill was visiting Washington. Schlossberg recalled: "We went out to lunch at L'Enfant Plaza," the hotel adjoining the Schlossberg-Cassidy office. "Michael volunteered to set up a meeting with his father to talk about the trouble we were having with Fuqua. . . . The three of us met the speaker. Gerry asked the speaker to talk to the cardinal [Medeiros] about Catholic [University]. . . . I asked him about Columbia. He was clearly uncomfortable, but he agreed to do it because of Michael. He said he would talk to Fuqua."

Schlossberg-Cassidy did not leave Fuqua entirely to chance either. The congressman's senior aide on the Science Committee blocked Schlossberg's efforts to meet with Fuqua to explain the Columbia and Catholic University projects, so they tried another approach. Using the connections of a newly hired member of their staff, a former aide to Speaker O'Neill named Frank Godfrey, they suggested to a different Fuqua aide that the firm could organize a fund-raising event for the congressman.

Schlossberg remembered the fund-raiser vividly—a breakfast in the L'Enfant Plaza Hotel held on a morning when the space shuttle was blasting off from Cape Canaveral in Fuqua's district. Televisions were set up so the guests could watch the blast-off. Government records show that Cassidy and Schlossberg each made two $500 donations to Fuqua that year. Schlossberg remembered that the event raised thousands more for the congressman from others who attended. Later in the year, "Fuqua was our guest at the big Democratic Congressional Campaign Committee fundraiser at the Washington Hilton," Schlossberg said.

The only contemporaneous news coverage of this episode appeared in *Science*, the weekly magazine of the American Association for the Advancement of Science, in a story by Colin Norman, a staff writer. Norman learned about and reported the roles of the two cardinals who had been recruited to lobby O'Neill and Mrs. Boggs. He reported that Schlossberg-Cassidy represented both universities and had helped organize the "highly unusual" campaign for the earmarks. He reported that O'Neill wrote to Fuqua on April 28, 1983, to say he hoped Fuqua could find money in his authorization bill for the two projects. Norman did not learn about the fund-raising for Fuqua.

When an amendment approving the earmarks came to a vote, the House majority leader, Jim Wright of Texas, spoke in support of it, a signal that the leadership favored the proposal. During the final debate Fuqua said he supported redirecting $5 million authorized in his committee's original bill for other purposes to the Columbia project. When the full House voted, the earmarks were approved by a vote of 261–113 (for Catholic University) and 215–150 (for Columbia).

By the time those votes were recorded on May 12, 1983, Schlossberg-Cassidy's years of relative anonymity had ended. The two partners' days in the shadows were over. The controversy over the Columbia and Catholic University earmarks prompted both men to give extensive interviews to the press for the first time. Schlossberg spoke to Colin Norman of *Science* when he was preparing that first report on the Columbia-Catholic earmarks in the spring of 1983. Their real debut as formal interview subjects occurred in the pages of *Science & Government Report*, a twice-monthly newsletter written by Daniel S. Greenberg, a respected science writer. Greenberg devoted five of the eight pages of his mid-November 1983 issue to the transcript of a conversation with the two lobbyists.

Greenberg began with a brief introduction: "The Washington end of academic politics has been in an uproar since last spring when, without prior discussion, the House suddenly voted rare construction money for laboratories at the Catholic University of America and Columbia University. Inquiry revealed that the coup . . . was the work of two for-hire lobbyists, Kenneth Schlossberg and Gerald S. J. Cassidy."

He began the interview with this rude first question:

"What do you charge a university for your services?"

Cassidy responded coyly. "All I'll give you is a ballpark answer. We work on a retainer, let's say between $25,000 and $120,000 a year." He went on to describe the different services the firm could provide, from guiding university officials around Washington to helping them with their campaigns to raise funds from alumni and other nongovernment sources.

Over the course of the interview the two partners revealed much of their basic technique: helping a client to recognize its own needs and capabilities, then to draw up a specific proposal for an earmark; looking for legislation already passed that might authorize the project being pursued; seeking the right appropriations bill that might fund a particular earmark; contacting members of the Senate and House from the state or district where the client institution is located and encouraging them to sponsor the earmark being sought, and to lobby their colleagues for support; introducing university officials to other members of Congress and their staffs who might be able to help; drawing on friends of the institution who might know key members of the House or Senate—Cardinal Medeiros, for example; helping the institution strengthen its own government relations operation and focusing its attention on the project at hand; organizing a school's alumni on Capitol Hill in hopes that they could help the effort to win an earmark.

They used this interview with Greenberg to respond to their critics from the scientific and academic organizations that had created the "uproar" Greenberg mentioned. These included the National Academy of Sciences, the Association of American Universities (a consortium of fifty leading research institutions), and the National Association of State Universities and Land Grant Colleges. Responding to the earmarks approved for Columbia and Catholic University, all three had formally pronounced their opposition to the allocation of government funding for science by political maneuver, supporting allocation based on competition and peer review instead.

"I don't think there's anything wrong with members of Congress taking an interest in a particular project," Schlossberg said in that interview. "There's nothing that says Congressional activities aren't going to produce as good a result as the peer-review process might produce." He noted the government's embarrassing recent decision to abandon construction of a new nuclear accelerator at the Brookhaven National Laboratory, a failed project he called "a $200 million mistake." A distinguished review panel of physicists had approved the Brookhaven accelerator—it had survived rigorous peer review.

"Many people in the educational associations have an executive branch view of the U.S. government," Schlossberg told Greenberg. "They think all that Congress is supposed to do" is act on requests from executive branch agencies, for or against. That, said Cassidy, left no room for "schools that have ambitions to be better and are willing to commit to the effort." They deserve a chance too, but the existing system, including peer review, favors the institutions already well established. "The 'haves' have," Cassidy observed.

Cassidy added that the earmarks the firm had helped win for its academic clients "hurt . . . no one." They represented "money spent on science that would not have been spent" if these institutions had not sought and received special appropriations. "The economy is only going to be improved by the fact that Columbia has an organic chemistry laboratory, and that right here in Washington there's a new vitreous state laboratory" at Catholic University.

Would the controversy they had generated be bad for business? Would the backlash "put a roadblock in your way?" asked Greenberg.

"I don't think so," Cassidy replied. "I don't even expect that members of the AAU [Association of American Universities] are going to give up their own interest or allow their decisions to be made by anyone else but themselves." In other words, AAU members—Columbia was one—would be seeking their own earmarks despite the organization's opposition to their use.

Greenberg asked if the firm's clients get their money's worth—"[Do] your customers' retainers come back many-fold?"

"In every case, many, many fold," Cassidy replied.

This was good publicity, but Greenberg's readers constituted a relatively small and specialized group of influential scientists and academics. Four months later the firm got a splendid free advertisement from a much more visible publication, *The Wall Street Journal.* Once again the firm cooperated.

Written by Burt Schorr and published on March 5, 1984, the story chronicled the recent academic earmarks. Schlossberg and Cassidy were its central figures. Schlossberg was quoted in the fourth paragraph explaining why the phenomenon was catching on:

"Congress is in business to serve the public. . . . [If members can help] in a way that isn't obnoxious to them—and even serves the public interest—they're delighted to do it." There, in two sentences, was the beauty of the system Schlossberg-Cassidy had almost inadvertently created: it could easily be cloaked in the public interest, and it delighted members of Congress who had to be the key actors to make the system work. Later in the *Journal* article readers learned its other feature that so pleased its authors: the money was awfully good. Schorr reported: Cassidy and Schlossberg "pay themselves 'more than $100,000' a year, Mr. Cassidy says." In fact, by the time his article appeared, they were paying themselves more than $200,000 a year. In 1984, a member of Congress, House or Senate, made $72,600 a year.

Schorr's story in the *Journal* recounted the firm's success winning the earmarks for Columbia and Catholic. It made the firm sound ingenious. It reported that other clients of the firm were "in line for more federal money." Schorr also reported on the controversy over earmarks versus peer review, but in a way that seemed to favor the critics of the old-boy system of peer review that had long directed most federal support for scientific research to a relative handful of institutions. Schorr noted that there had been no federal funds for new buildings on American campuses for more than a decade, and he quoted a Syracuse University professor who had written a book on the subject as saying the universities had huge needs for new and renewed physical infrastructure—at least $40 billion worth. Schlossberg-Cassidy's lobbying "is being used to get money out of Congress to meet some of those needs," Schorr reported. Schlossberg could not have written a more favorable story himself.

Schlossberg-Cassidy had invented a new way to make money in Washington. It was remarkably simple—and clever. Their success depended on one of the fundamental attributes of all democratic legislatures: the perpetual eagerness of their members to please the voters who elected them. Democratic legislatures have the power to initiate new laws and policies for the governments of which they are a part, but their essential nature is reactive. Mostly they respond to the proposals, or petitions, of others. Those others may be an executive branch or a government, or outside institutions, corporations, citizens, or agents hired by citizens and institutions to advance a particular cause. Schlossberg-Cassidy & Associates had established itself as a new kind of agent that specialized in a new kind of fund-raising for academic institutions.

This new business was lucrative, but also labor-intensive. As the stories of the Tufts, Columbia, and Catholic University earmarks suggest, every project was time-consuming; each one required special attention, care, and feeding. In the first years of this kind of earmarking, the lobbyists had to teach the members of Congress how to do it—this indeed was one of Schlossberg-Cassidy's selling points. As Cloherty put it to potential new clients, they "invented the business."

The firm thrived, but the relationship between the partners did not. The two men behaved a little like siblings, moving abruptly from affection to hostility, relying on each other both personally and professionally, but qualifying their respect and affection with sporadic eruptions of anger or suspicion. After Cassidy's unhappy sojourn at the Democratic National Committee and after his auto accident in 1973 that had left him flat on his back, Schlossberg comforted him, then gave him his old job back. Schlossberg acknowledged that he also considered Cassidy "a shoulder to lean on," and thought one reason he may have gone to the hospital and offered to rehire Cassidy was the realization that his own marriage was disintegrating. "I knew I was getting into trouble personally, and I needed someone by my side I could rely on. And we . . . were so close. You know, bad things usually only happen . . . to people who unfortunately are very close."

Schlossberg's marriage did collapse, and Cassidy did provide comfort and support during the bitter divorce fight that ensued. Schlossberg remembered a birthday party Gerry and Loretta threw for him during this period in their modest townhouse in Burke, Virginia, a suburb twenty miles west of Washington. "He praised me to the skies and gave me an expensive set of gold cuff links with little emeralds in them. He was also enormously entertaining, telling hilarious stories of his childhood in Brooklyn."

After they had launched Schlossberg-Cassidy & Associates, Schlossberg fell in love with a beautiful Russian-born widow named Sophia Gorokhova. She recalled that Cassidy treated her with suspicion, as though she was going to distract Schlossberg from his work. But when they decided to marry, Schlossberg asked Cassidy to be his best man. Then when Ken and Sophia announced over dinner that she was pregnant, "Gerry went white," Ken Schlossberg remembered—a baby would be another distraction from the business.

As the firm prospered in the early 1980s, the relationship changed again, and not for the better. Schlossberg grew impatient with Cassidy's abrasive personality. Schlossberg thought his partner treated little people badly, and threw his weight around. He disliked Cassidy's gruff manner on the telephone. "Despite the fact that things were going great, Gerry was causing a ruckus," Schlossberg recalled. "I didn't know how to talk to him about it. . . . Maybe it was my fault. . . . I don't have a good way to deal with those kinds of problems."

Cassidy remembered different difficulties: "As we grew, the tension of having a lot of clients to represent, the pressure, really wore on Ken, and you could see it. He started developing colds all the time, he was home sick all the time." Cassidy felt he did more of the work than his partner, though they always shared the money equally.

Sometime in the early 1980s, Schlossberg said, he finally read the bylaws of their company that Cassidy had drafted in 1975. Schlossberg realized that, technically at least, Gerry and Loretta—two members of a three-member board—could fire him. Schlossberg remembered consulting a lawyer who urged him to build up the business as fast as he could so that if the partnership broke up, it would have a higher value. Schlossberg decided that the firm should grow.

Cassidy, Schlossberg remembered, disliked the idea; another employee would mean a dilution of the profits. But Schlossberg prevailed, and proposed that they hire a Republican. "The town was going Republican" after Reagan won the presidency in 1980, he thought. He suggested that they take on a young Republican named James Fabiani, a staff aide to Silvio Conte, Tip O'Neill's Republican colleague and pal from western Massachusetts. Fabiani had worked in Conte's district before coming to Washington, as a dean at an elite prep school. Schlossberg got to know him working on the Tufts projects, which O'Neill had asked Conte to help promote. Conte had assigned Fabiani to the task. This experience had taught Fabiani how to do earmarks.

Fabiani recalled that Schlossberg first offered him a job in April 1982. At first he said he wasn't eager to leave Conte, the senior Republican on the Appropriations Committee. He was uncertain about becoming a lobbyist. But by June he had decided to accept the offer, which doubled the salary Conte was paying him.

This led to an extraordinary event for the Washington of that time— a reception hosted by a senior member of Congress (Conte) on behalf of a lobbying firm. That wasn't the way it was described; ostensibly Conte was just giving a farewell party for a member of his staff. But he invited Schlossberg-Cassidy to organize the event, and the firm paid for it.

"They printed up invitations, like a wedding invitation," Fabiani remembered. "They invited whoever Ken and Gerry had on their list, whoever I had on my list. It was in the Gold Room of the Rayburn [House Office] Building. . . . Hundreds of people showed up. My parents had come in. Silvio and Gerry and Loretta and Ken and my parents literally stood in a receiving line. Silvio all evening stood in a receiving line, God bless him, and just greeted people. It was a big event." And an advertisement for the lobbying firm whose import was difficult to miss: this outfit had good relations with Silvio Conte.

Schlossberg then set his sights on another potential new hire, Frank Godfrey, an aide to Tip O'Neill whom the speaker (he assumed that title in 1977) had assigned to work on earmarks for Schlossberg-Cassidy's

Massachusetts clients. Godfrey, a big bear of a man, kind and gentle and beloved by many House members, dispensed largesse as a member of O'Neill's staff. His job was to satisfy requests for favors or assistance from the Democratic members—the speaker's constituents. Schlossberg calculated that Godfrey had already helped the firm earn hundreds of thousands of dollars by supporting earmarks for its university clients. But Cassidy and Fabiani were both reluctant to hire Godfrey, another mouth to feed. "I pushed it through," Schlossberg recalled. He was still the president of the company.

This time the host of a big reception for a new Schlossberg-Cassidy employee was the speaker himself. The crowd was even bigger than for Fabiani. Guests passed through a receiving line that included both Cassidy and Schlossberg. Again the message was unmistakable: these guys had clout. "It sure was impressive," Cassidy said.

If Conte or O'Neill had any qualms about personally promoting a lobbying firm, they were never recorded. It seems unlikely that they did. Washington was changing; those receptions were examples of the change. (Conte died in 1991, O'Neill in 1994.)

Schlossberg-Cassidy's tactics were also examples of the new Washington mores—for example, promoting those earmarks for Columbia and Catholic University by helping the speaker's son sell insurance and by raising and contributing money to Congressman Fuqua's re-election campaign. Not that using money and favors to achieve legislative objectives was a new idea—it is as old as the republic. But for the young and evolving lobbying firm of Schlossberg-Cassidy, this was new terrain.

Schlossberg said these maneuvers made him uncomfortable. "I didn't much care for how the whole thing developed and finally went down," he said of those efforts to cultivate O'Neill and Fuqua. "It reeked of quid pro quo and buying influence." He said he feared he could get into serious trouble, even go to jail. "Was what was going on legal? . . . I actually got a copy of the ethics rules governing House members and I discovered that there was no legal prohibition on doing business with children of members. So, I sucked it up."

Electoral politics, Washington lobbying, political fund-raising, and the nature of Congress were all changing in the years when Schlossberg-Cassidy's lobbying business was taking off. Members of Congress were discovering the benefits they could gain by helping the growing new class of lobbyists, which included many others besides Cassidy and Schlossberg. The lobbying business was growing because of the benefits lobbyists could win for clients from members who were realizing that they needed ever-increasing amounts of money to run the campaigns that could keep them in office.

In the early 1980s a new relationship began to develop between lobbyists and their clients "downtown," where a growing number of lobbying firms, trade associations, labor unions, and corporations maintained Washington offices, and "the Hill," Capitol Hill, home of the House and Senate. It was a relationship of mutual dependency. It was just beginning then and has strengthened significantly since, altering the public life of the country.

CHAPTER 8

A GREAT AWAKENING

Ken Schlossberg remembered an event in February 1982 that helped to crystallize his own anxiety about the changing role of money in politics. It was a convention of the Ocean Spray cranberry cooperative held in San Diego. Schlossberg-Cassidy had arranged for Congressman Conte, by then an established friend of the firm, to give a speech to the convention for a $3,000 fee—an "honorarium," as these payments were called. At the time a member of the House could collect in honoraria as much as 40 percent of the $60,662.50 salary paid to members in the early 1980s, and could legally put as much as $2,000 per appearance into his personal bank account. In this case, Conte's financial disclosure form shows, he kept $2,000 and donated the remaining $1,000 to charity. For obvious reasons, lobbyists liked to arrange these appearances. Cassidy had also helped Ocean Spray create a political action committee to make donations to members' re-election campaigns. Cassidy recommended who should get the money; Conte received $4,500 from the PAC in 1982–83.

Another speaker at the convention was Congressman Tony Coelho of California, who in 1981 had become chairman of the Democratic Congressional Campaign Committee, the fund-raising organization of the Democratic majority in the House. Coelho would make a historic contribution in the 1980s by persuading corporate interests of many kinds to show their respect for—by giving campaign contributions to—the Democrats, who controlled the House and wrote important legislation that affected American business. To the exasperation of many Republicans who thought *they* were the natural allies of big business, Coelho raised millions of dollars for House Democrats from business interests.

Years later Cassidy remembered Coelho's speech to the Ocean Spray event: "Essentially he said, Look, you may have your personal politics but issue politics is different, and you should consider that the Democrats can be as much help to you as the Republicans can, and we are not unsympathetic to business." The cranberry farmers and processors in the crowd constituted "a universally Republican audience," Cassidy said, but Coelho "did things very smoothly," and no one present was offended. "I don't remember him saying anything that was heavy-handed," Cassidy said. Cassidy liked Coelho; one of the first contributions the Ocean Spray PAC had made to a politician—in March 1980—was a $200 donation to Tony Coelho's re-election campaign.

Schlossberg was troubled by this event, which seemed to symbolize trends he disliked that involved money, Congress, and his Democrats. "From where I was coming from politically," he said, "the whole thing struck me as strange and queer." The Ocean Spray event aggravated his concern that the firm's activities were getting too close to the line. "My problem was with the quid pro quo aspect" of making donations to politicians, especially "as the amounts became increasingly larger and the actual connection between them and the actions of the members on our projects became closer and closer."

The world Schlossberg lived and worked in was changing fundamentally. Money was the easiest way to measure the change. The first half-dozen years that Schlossberg-Cassidy was in business proved to be, coincidentally, a turning point in the history of campaign spending in America. In those few years, the amount of money expended on political campaigns took off.

In the congressional elections of 1974, the combined campaign spending of every candidate for the House and Senate—in thirty-four Senate and 435 House contests—was $77 million. Just four elections later, in 1982, the combined total was $343 million. In other words, campaign spending rose 450 percent in eight years. By 1982 the average winning campaign in a seriously contested House race—one where the winner had less than 60 percent of the vote—cost $359,000, a dizzying number for members who were first elected in the 1960s and 1970s, when most winning campaigns still cost less than $100,000, and many cost less than $50,000. The winners of close races in the Senate in 1982 spent, on average, $2.3 million; losers of those races spent just as much. Only a few years earlier, Senate campaigns cost a few hundred thousand dollars.

A second profound change in these years was the dramatic growth of PACs. Organized labor had established the first PACs in the 1940s, but the idea did not catch on until after Congress passed campaign finance reforms in 1973 and 1974 that limited the amount individuals could give to campaigns, but authorized the creation of these committees. They gave companies, interest groups of all kinds, and unions a way to solicit their members, employees, and stockholders to give money that would be directed to politicians' campaigns in the name of the organization sponsoring the PAC. This created a legal vehicle that special interests could use to funnel money to politicians, cultivating their gratitude in the process.

In 1974, as PACs were just coming into vogue, there were 608 of them registered with the then new Federal Election Commission. By 1982, 3,371 PACs had registered with the FEC; 1,467 of them were affiliated with corporations. In 1974, all PAC contributions to House and Senate races totaled $12.5 million, or 16 percent of all the money the candidates raised; by 1982 that number had increased nearly 700 percent, to $83.1 million, which was 24 percent of all the money spent by House and Senate candidates that year. PACs favored incumbents and influential members, especially chairmen of committees and subcommittees, many of whom raised more than half the money they spent on their re-election campaigns from PACs.

These numbers record not just a change in degree, but a change in kind. In the course of a few years, campaigns for Congress were transformed. Because campaigns determine the membership of the House and Senate, when they change, Congress also changes. American politics in the twenty-first century still reflect the transformation that occurred in the late 1970s and early 1980s.

The escalating cost of campaigns was one aspect of a great awakening in American politics. The rise of lobbying was another. The proliferation of interest groups trying to influence the political process was a third. All of these were related to each other, and all were related to the realization that government decisions could affect the economic well-being of a large and growing number of Americans. That in turn was a consequence of the evolution of the American government into the modern state of the late twentieth century—the version that still exists today. Though its origins could be found two centuries earlier, its creation was not completed until the 1970s.

During the Gilded Age of the late 1800s, business interests, led by the burgeoning new railroads, discovered the often glorious benefits that could be derived from influencing government decisions. At about the same time, rapacious captains of industry realized they could create vast trusts that dominated key sectors of the economy and earned enormous profits. The wretched excess of that era provoked a wave of reform led first by President Theodore Roosevelt (president from 1901 to 1909), then by Woodrow Wilson (1913 to 1921). Roosevelt was a Republican and Wilson a Democrat, but both were progressives who made the regulation of economic behavior an important government activity. Regulatory legislation enacted during their presidencies ended many of the excesses of the Gilded Age and vastly improved basic working and living conditions for ordinary Americans.

Roosevelt's Square Deal and Wilson's New Freedom—the slogans they used to describe their reforms—created the precedents Franklin Roosevelt drew on in 1933 when he cobbled together a New Deal to try to cope with the Great Depression. FDR further developed the idea that the tools of government could be used to mitigate the impact of raw economic power. So did his successor, Harry Truman, who called his reform program a Fair Deal for working Americans.

Despite all the new laws, new agencies, and new regulations of the first six decades of the twentieth century—rules and institutions that had a huge influence on the American economy—Washington was still a remote political outpost for most of the rest of the country when John F. Kennedy was elected president in 1960. Kennedy famously quipped that the nation's capital was a city of "northern charm and southern efficiency," capturing the city's status at the time as a peculiar place that didn't really fit anywhere in the real America.

Only a handful of business organizations and big corporations had Washington offices or representatives then. Partly this was the result of corporate myopia: very few American businessmen appreciated in 1961 how significant the decisions made in Washington could be for their businesses. But there was also an understandable corporate unease about Washington. The political atmosphere of the 1960s was not friendly to big business, and big business lacked confidence in its own ability to prevail in what fast became a liberal era dominated by Democratic majorities in the House and Senate. Big business was part of the stolid, old-fashioned America that found itself on the defensive in the 1960s, when the war babies and early baby boomers first made their mark on the broad American culture. The young imposed rock 'n' roll on what had been a Bing Crosby society; they discovered marijuana and sex with birth control pills. The 1960s ended a long period of post–World War II stability and squareness, putting the squares at a psychological disadvantage.

In 1965 Ralph Nader published *Unsafe at Any Speed*, a polemical but also thoroughly researched attack on the American automobile business and especially its largest company, General Motors. Nader caught the industry off-guard, exposing shoddy engineering and marketing tactics that put chrome and tail fins far ahead of safety and reliability. He also caught the national mood. His book led to new laws and regulations, beginning with the mandatory installation of seat belts in new cars. More important, it set an example for a new kind of activism in Washington. And when Nader discovered that General Motors had hired private detectives to try to find embarrassing details of his personal life, he sued and won a settlement worth $284,000, which he invested in new efforts on behalf of "consumer rights," as he called his anti-business crusade. In response to Nader, Congress created three traffic safety agencies that were consolidated in 1970 into the National Highway Traffic Safety Administration, a powerful regulatory body.

The spirit of this era was infectious. The Senate's Select Committee on Nutrition and Human Needs was one manifestation of it. So, revealingly, was the presidency of Richard Nixon, who took office in January 1969. Apart from the crimes of Watergate and the other transgressions that led to his resignation, Nixon was a creative chief executive in the tradition of Theodore Roosevelt and Woodrow Wilson who initiated a startling expansion of the federal government's regulatory apparatus. Confronted with fierce inflation, he even tried fixing wages and prices. John Adams Wettergreen, a conservative academic who sternly disapproved of Nixon's proclivity to regulate, called the period from 1970 to 1974 a "regulatory revolution," marked by an escalation in the quantity and reach of federal regulatory agencies more significant even than what occurred in the twenty years of the New Deal and Fair Deal.

As noted earlier, Nixon proposed and Congress created the Environmental Protection Agency and the Occupational Safety and Health Administration. Numerous existing agencies were given broader mandates or new authority. In 1988 Wettergreen claimed that "over 70 percent of the current regulatory apparatus is, in one way or another, the product of the regulatory revolution" of those four years. He offered no explanation of this unprovable calculation, which was almost certainly an exaggeration. But there is no denying that when Nixon left the White House, the American economy was significantly more regulated than it had been before he took office.

As it had in the New Deal era three decades earlier, new regulation encouraged a strong response. The counterreaction of the 1970s was both heralded and stimulated by a memorandum written in August 1971, while Nixon was still president. It was the work of Lewis F. Powell, a Richmond, Virginia, lawyer prominent in legal and corporate circles who was responding to a request from his friend and neighbor Eugene Sydnor, an official of the United States Chamber of Commerce. Powell was not well known when he wrote this memo, which suggested new tactics for the beleaguered Chamber. Two months later Nixon would nominate him to the Supreme Court, where he became an important swing vote on many issues.

Powell's memo got no publicity when it was written, and its significance was not evident for many years afterward. Powell belonged to the boards of directors of eleven American corporations. He was a past president of the American Bar Association, a conservative Virginia Democrat, and an intuitive supporter of a Chamber of Commerce view of the world. He sensed that in politics, the news media, and the country's universities, a tide was running against "the American economic system," by which he meant free market capitalism. He thought that the Americans who shared his outlook had abdicated their responsibility to defend their system.

"No thoughtful person can question that the American economic system is under broad attack," Powell wrote. "We are not dealing with sporadic or isolated attacks from a relatively few extremists. . . . Rather, the assault on the enterprise system is broadly based and consistently pursued. It is gaining momentum and converts."

Those under attack had failed to respond. "The painfully sad truth is that business, including the boards of directors and the top executives of corporations great and small and business organizations at all levels, often have responded—if at all—by appeasement, ineptitude and ignoring the problem."

Though he urged the Chamber of Commerce to act on many fronts, "In the final analysis, the payoff . . . is what government does," Powell wrote. "Business has been the favorite whipping-boy of many politicians for many years. . . . As every business executive knows, few elements of American society today have as little influence in government as the American businessman, the corporation, or even the millions of corporate stockholders. . . . One does not exaggerate to say that, in terms of political influence with respect to the course of legislation and government action, the American business executive is truly the 'forgotten man.' . . . It is evident that most politicians are making the judgment that the public has little sympathy for the businessman or his viewpoint."

Powell's antidote was simple: political power. "Such power must be assiduously cultivated; and when necessary, it must be used aggressively and with determination—without embarrassment and without the reluctance which has been so characteristic of American business. . . . Business and the enterprise system are in deep trouble, and the hour is late."

This document made a powerful impression on the Chamber of Commerce, though the Chamber did not immediately embrace all of Powell's recommendations. But soon after it began circulating among businesspeople, a group of conservative activists seized on the memo as a kind of manifesto. The founders of the Heritage Foundation, the single most effective agitator for conservative ideas in Washington in the post-Nixon years, embraced it. Tracing the impact of such a document is never easy, but Powell's memo resonated. His argument had the force of logic; Nader and his ilk did seem to be in the ascendancy, their obvious target was corporate power and the target was not responding effectively.

The Powell memorandum—perhaps as cause, perhaps as effect, probably as both—was part of the great awakening. Just when it looked as though even Republicans—that is, Nixon—had embraced the progressive ethos of Teddy Roosevelt and all his twentieth-century descendants, from Woodrow Wilson to Lyndon Johnson, seeds were planted that would grow into a new Republican Party, one whose adherents would consider Nixon a blasphemous infidel, at least on domestic policy.

A small group of wealthy individuals and the foundations they created began, in the early 1970s, to fund a variety of new institutions—the Heritage Foundation was a leading example—that would articulate a new conservative political doctrine and alter the course of American politics. These were not traditional "country club" Republicans, but ornery outsiders with an itch to change the world. Joseph Coors, the brewer, was one of the most generous; Richard Mellon Scaife, an heir to Mellon millions and an idiosyncratic misfit among his peers, gave even more.

These men and others of a like mind were creating what became the "New Right," the conservative movement that was born from the wreckage of Barry Goldwater's failed campaign for president in 1964. Johnson trounced Goldwater that year, but Goldwater attracted a legion of conservative enthusiasts who would not accept failure as their permanent fate. Members of that legion were the early New Right agitators, who first got the country's attention in 1976, when Ronald Reagan, the conservatives' hero, challenged and nearly beat President Gerald R. Ford in the contest for the Republican presidential nomination.

The New Right was doing just what Lewis Powell had suggested—fighting back. Its pioneers, backed in many cases by great wealth, began to challenge the prevailing political arrangements in Washington. Initially their cause seemed quixotic. But before long fighting back became a popular cause, and then, for a new class of Washingtonians, a profession.

On the eve of Nixon's election in 1968, seven hundred trade associations, including unions, maintained headquarters in Washington. Ten years later the number was nearly 1,600. The associations themselves became more professional, more engaged in the political process. In the same decade, dozens of big corporations opened or expanded Washington offices. A few corporations had long maintained outposts in the capital, but in the 1970s what had been unusual became typical. Company after company set up shop in Washington. In the 1970s, observed Norman Ornstein, a political scientist who has made Congress his specialty for nearly forty years, most big companies were wary of Washington. "They used to say, stay as far away from there as possible. Now it's a primary arena for corporate America."

This change, first noticeable in the 1970s, was another manifestation of the great awakening. Private interest groups and corporations began to realize how much they had at stake in Washington, which led them to begin paying closer attention. "So many people realized they had issues with the government," said Robert Strauss. Strauss began to develop the lobbying practice in the new Washington office of his Dallas law firm in the 1970s, when others were getting similar ideas. One was William E. Timmons, a Republican aide on Capitol Hill until Nixon appointed him assistant to the president for legislative affairs, the chief White House agent on Capitol Hill. In 1975 he left that job to establish Timmons & Company, the first high-powered lobbying firm in town that operated in the open, without cover of the traditional law firm. Timmons wasn't even a lawyer. He offered the services of his new firm to help companies protect and advance their interests in Washington. The less exalted proprietors of Schlossberg-Cassidy opened their business at almost the same moment, in the spring of 1975.

Nixon's presidency was momentous in other respects. It brought changes to political fund-raising and the organization of Congress that altered the country's politics. The consequences of both are still with us.

The financial excesses of Nixon's two presidential campaigns, revealed in the course of the Watergate affair that ended his presidency, were the stimulus for reform legislation passed in 1974 that created the legal framework that governs—ineffectively—campaign fund-raising and spending today. The 1974 act established an independent body to administer election laws, a goal of reformers for many years. It also set limits on individual contributions to campaigns, and opened the door to political action committees. This combination amounted to an invitation to the country's interest groups to set up a PAC—which meant raising and spending money to try to influence the political process.

Probably even more important, Nixon gave his country a revolution in Congress, one that profoundly altered the nature of the House and colored the way both houses have done business ever since. Nixon's was an unwitting gift whose import was visible only after the fact. It was the consequence of the total unraveling of Nixon's political position as the many sins described by "Watergate" were revealed by newspaper reporters, congressional investigators, and the courts.

It is not easy now to recall the wave of popular disgust that followed Nixon's forced resignation in August 1974. The president, whose approval rating in polls was then barely above 20 percent, faced certain impeachment in the House and conviction in the Senate for his many crimes. To avoid being the first president ever removed from office by impeachment, he chose to be the first president ever to resign.

For Democrats, the timing of his resignation could not have been better. The new president, Gerald Ford, had compounded the Republicans' political problems by formally pardoning Nixon for his crimes, assuring that he would never be prosecuted. The midterm elections came just three months after the resignation and two months after the pardon, when the disgust was fresh and intense. The Grand Old Party paid a heavy price for Nixon's transgressions; Republicans found no arguments that could dissuade voters from exacting revenge. In November 1974, Democrats won a huge majority in the House (291–144) and a dominating position in the Senate (61–38). The House was transformed by the seventy-five new Democratic members, who tended to be more liberal and more inclined to activism than their elders.

Until the "class of '74" arrived on Capitol Hill in January 1975, liberal Democrats in the House had been frustrated for years by an informal alliance of conservative southern Democrats and Republicans. Power in the House was wielded primarily by the chairmen of its committees, and chairmanships were allocated by seniority; the longest-serving member of the majority party on each committee inherited the chairman's autocratic power. Among Democrats, the longest-serving members tended to be southerners, who generally had safe districts and no meaningful opposition. And southerners, with a few exceptions, were among the most conservative members of the Democratic caucus.

The class of '74 had no patience for this traditional arrangement, and it had the votes to change the rules. Starting in 1975, rank-and-file Democratic members could vote to approve or disapprove their leaders' choices for chairmanships. This gave them some influence over the selections. Seniority still counted, but it no longer determined who the chairmen would be. The newcomers wanted power to be shared more widely, which led to a proliferation of subcommittees (and of subcommittee chairmanships, and of subcommittee staff). They resisted authority, so their leaders, including committee and subcommittee chairmen, had to win members' support issue by issue—deference no longer assured that the leadership would get its way.

Before 1975 "you had such strict seniority that chairmen could tell members no," recalled Gerald Cassidy years later. When "no" was still a viable leadership tool, chairmen wielded enormous power, and ordinary members had little. When the class of '74 changed "the distribution of power," as Cassidy put it, chairmen were diminished and individual members were strengthened. This new reality required those who wanted to influence Congress to develop new skills and tactics. In the post-Watergate world, the old system of persuading a few key individuals—the speaker and a few chairmen, typically—to favor a particular bill or provision no longer produced the desired result. Now, individual members of the House had influence and a freedom of maneuver previously known only to their colleagues in the Senate.

A great awakening had occurred, without warning or precedent. Quite suddenly, many more citizens, often acting through the groups they belonged to, and many more corporations, singly and in associations, were joining the political fray to protect or advance their interests. Watergate, one of the great scandals of American history, had energized reformers of many kinds; they in turn energized established power-holders and other targets of the reformers' zeal to fight back. The decentralization of power in Congress made it much easier for all the participants in this new politics to find members who might help them achieve their goals. The new hunger for campaign contributions felt by senators and congressmen running ever more expensive re-election campaigns helped open their doors to those who would try to influence them.

The American genius for creating new service industries when new services were needed came into play. Because of this great awakening, the number of institutions looking for help and guidance in Washington was growing at a rapid pace. This was the category that the thriving class of Washington lobbyists called clients.

CHAPTER 9

A MARRIAGE UNRAVELS

By 1984, Schlossberg-Cassidy & Associates had two actual associates, Fabiani and Godfrey, and a long list of new clients. The firm's successes winning earmarks for universities prompted something of a great awakening in the world of higher education. Tufts, Boston University, Catholic University, and Columbia were soon followed by Atlanta University, Boston College, Brown, Indiana, Northwestern, the Rochester Institute of Technology, the University of Massachusetts, and the University of Southern Mississippi in Hattiesburg, among others. By 1984 there were fifteen university clients looking for earmarks and paying Schlossberg-Cassidy monthly retainers, typically $10,000 a month. A dozen other clients including several big companies were also contributing to the firm's coffers. Schlossberg remembered that by 1984, he and Cassidy "were taking home about $500,000 each" on an annual basis. Ten years earlier they had been making $37,000 (Schlossberg) and $32,000 (Cassidy) as employees of the United States Senate.

Both men loved their new prosperity. Both had homes in McLean, Virginia, a rolling suburb of country lanes and large houses. Cassidy drove a big Mercedes, Schlossberg a Jaguar. Schlossberg recalled with some guilt that Cassidy always encouraged him to spend more money, and he did. When he bought his house in McLean—a big house on a two-acre lot—Cassidy cheered him on: "You want to build yourself a tennis court—do it!" Schlossberg built "my dream tennis court . . . and I loved it!" The Cassidys were living better than they had ever imagined possible.

But Schlossberg was far from content. The anxiety he felt about the way they had cultivated Speaker O'Neill through his son was part of a sense of foreboding about the ways money was changing Washington, he said. Schlossberg had a vivid memory of Cassidy's elation after the Ocean Spray cranberry cooperative had agreed to create a political action committee that Cassidy would help run. "I will never forget how excited he was when we left the meeting with Ocean Spray where the subject first came up. He was bouncing up and down in his seat as he was driving, banging the steering wheel with his hand, going on and on about how great it was." Schlossberg was uncomfortable with the growing demands for political contributions, but he saw that Cassidy wasn't uncomfortable at all—on the contrary.

"I never had a problem with fund-raising or going to fund-raisers," Schlossberg said. "My problem was with the quid pro quo aspect of it as the amounts became increasingly larger and the actual connection between them and the actions of the members on our projects became closer and closer."

And Cassidy's conduct continued to get on his nerves. Schlossberg recalled one "heart-to-heart" conversation with his partner in which he complained about Cassidy's behavior, "treating maître d's in restaurants like crap, and really beating up on little people. He got upset and said 'Hey, we got a good thing going here, don't spoil it.' And I'm thinking to myself, What's the good thing we've got going here? It's a piece of shit now. Why should I want anything to do with it? But you know, he was talking about the money. I don't think Gerry ever thought I could walk away from the money."

Money had come galloping into their lives on a fast horse. Schlossberg concluded that it was more important to Cassidy than it was to him. He and his wife, Sophia, both remember conversations with the Cassidys when they discussed their ambitions for wealth. Sophia said she had lectured them: "It would be so lonely to be rich. . . . What's the point." But Cassidy was determined. She remembered him saying that "rich kids like you, to whom everything was given, just don't understand." (Sophia's father had been a civil engineer, then vice chairman of a chemical combine in the Soviet Union; he provided a privileged upbringing in Soviet terms, but no wealth. Schlossberg enjoyed a comfortable but hardly lavish upbringing in suburban Boston.) Years later, Cassidy said that Sophia enjoyed the money they were making as much as anyone. She never complained that they were getting too rich, he said, and she was always "very resolute" that her husband get his full share of the profits.

Cassidy never hid his appetite for more. Even as they were building up their lobbying business, he was tempted by potentially lucrative opportunities that had nothing to do with lobbying. One was a proposition advanced by a Cuban refugee from Miami who claimed to have an inside track on a large quantity of rare Brazilian hardwoods that could be imported into the United States and sold at a big profit. Schlossberg was tempted too. Cassidy suggested they create a new corporation to exploit the opportunity, which they did. The Cuban came to Washington to meet them; they spent a long day discussing the idea. As Schlossberg recalled it, he and Cassidy were to put up $50,000 or even $100,000 in advance to acquire the hardwood. "I was skeptical about the guy," he remembered. He was about to go to Florida to visit his parents, and offered to meet the Cuban again in his own office in Miami. "He showed me around a suite of almost empty offices. I decided he was queer as a three-dollar bill."

But Cassidy was eager to take the plunge. So, Schlossberg said, was Bill Cloherty, the salesman who was starting to bring new clients to the firm. Schlossberg agreed to put up his share of the cash if the others insisted on going forward, but warned that they might never see the money again. He remembered that he had to travel to Boston for a family Passover celebration, and left Washington with the matter still up in the air. A day or two later Cassidy called him in Boston to say he had asked a relative who was a lawyer in Florida to do a little more checking on the Cuban; he now thought they should drop the plan, it was too risky.

When Schlossberg got back to Washington Cassidy told him his relative thought the Cuban was a faker. "Then he tells me, with a kind of sheepish look on his face," that he and the Cuban had shared drinks and an extended conversation after their original meeting in Washington. "The guy said some stuff about you being Jewish and how he didn't trust you. The guy was kind of an anti-Semite," Schlossberg remembered Cassidy saying. "Gerry held that back from me because he wanted the deal so much. As you can imagine, I was not a happy camper hearing that after the fact," Schlossberg said.

Cassidy, an instinctual hard worker driven by the demons of his childhood, resented his partner's more relaxed approach. This was a recurring source of discord, and also a reflection of the fundamental differences between the two men.

Cloherty described the difference: "Ken was a very amiable guy, very affable, I loved to chat with him. . . . But he was not somebody that would go through the brick wall, necessarily, not somebody who was not going to be denied. . . . The amount of toughness and determination to get the goal accomplished was light-years higher for Gerry Cassidy than for Ken." When Cloherty signed up a new client for Schlossberg-Cassidy, he said, he always recommended that the client ask that Cassidy, not Schlossberg, handle its business.

Schlossberg felt disdain for compulsive workers: "I liked the 1950s—Mom and Pop and the two kids, working five days a week, nine to five, weekends off. It was a very healthy thing." Those who want to work all the time, he said, "put normal people at a terrible disadvantage."

The two men found it difficult to discuss their differences. Schlossberg remembered Cassidy once inviting him to lunch for a serious conversation: "We have a problem. Loretta says we have to talk." Cassidy said he felt Schlossberg was cutting him out of some clients; Schlossberg had the same feeling about the clients Cloherty was bringing in. Schlossberg said Cassidy was doing things he didn't know enough about, particularly using the Ocean Spray PAC money in ways that might affect their other clients. Schlossberg said he told Cassidy that "I didn't want to end up like those Watergate guys going to jail for something I didn't know anything about. He said, 'We'll work things out.' We didn't."

Cassidy said later that as the number of clients, and thus their workload, grew, Schlossberg had trouble handling the stress. Schlossberg often stayed at home when he should have been working, Cassidy said. "I went to his house once to see him about it and told him, we can't go on like this. . . . And he told me he was really going to do better, he committed to the business and so on." Schlossberg said this never happened.

The two partners' accumulated frustrations and resentments came to a head in San Francisco during four days of July 1984. Schlossberg and Cassidy had decided they should establish a presence for the firm at the Democratic National Convention that year, a new custom for lobbyists and trade associations. In the convention setting it was possible to entertain members of Congress at all hours, and, in return for the right-sized contributions, hobnob with various big shots at events organized for that purpose. Schlossberg-Cassidy suggested to its two biggest corporate clients, Ocean Spray and the Pirelli Corporation, that they maintain "hospitality suites" in San Francisco. The idea was to entertain members of Congress who were delegates while introducing the clients to important politicians. "We anteed up big bucks to attend special events" organized by the Democrats to raise money for the campaign, Schlossberg said.

He particularly remembered a lunch event hosted by Speaker O'Neill atop the Bank of America headquarters in San Francisco. Cassidy arranged for Schlossberg to sit at a table with O'Neill, Pamela Harriman, the widow of W. Averell Harriman and an important fund-raiser for the party, Walter Shorenstein, a San Francisco real estate magnate and big

Democratic contributor, and several others. Cassidy would not have been comfortable at such a table, Schlossberg said. "The conversation was fascinating." Schlossberg remembered O'Neill's prediction that Walter Mondale would easily defeat Ronald Reagan in November—"Alice in Wonderland."

But Cassidy, Cloherty, and a young Boston politician named Jimmy Collins, an O'Neill protégé whom the firm brought to San Francisco as a general helper, all had the impression that Schlossberg and Sophia were not particularly interested in working the convention. "Sophia and Ken were out there for a good time," as Collins put it many years later. Collins and Frank Godfrey, the newest and youngest Schlossberg-Cassidy employee, ran around San Francisco for days, Collins recalled. "There was a lot of work to do." He was thrilled when, toward the end of the convention, Cassidy offered him and his wife the chance to take a ride up the Pacific Coast with Loretta Cassidy in one of the two limos the firm had hired for the convention week.

All the parties involved agreed on what happened next. The Schlossbergs had seen an ad on a bulletin board in a San Francisco restaurant offering Brittany spaniel puppies for sale. "Silvio Conte had a couple of Brittanys and they seemed like terrific dogs," Schlossberg said. "So we called and made an appointment to go see the dogs, about an hour north of San Francisco." Meantime, Loretta Cassidy and Jimmy Collins and his wife, Mary, had gone for their drive up the coast. Schlossberg had arranged with Frank Godfrey to use the same limo for the spaniel expedition. At the appointed hour, the limo did not appear to pick up the Schlossbergs at the Fairmont Hotel. "I think I called Frank and he told me that Loretta had the car. Then I called Gerry and asked him what happened. I forget what he said, but Sophia got on the phone and read him the riot act. Sophia doesn't take crap from anybody."

Cassidy remembered this too: "Sophia took the phone away from him [her husband] and was on the phone yelling at me, and I hung up."

When the limo finally returned, Collins remembered, the Schlossbergs were steaming. Sophia "gave a ration of crap to my wife, who was appalled," Collins said. Loretta Cassidy was a witness to the exchange.

The Schlossbergs got their dog nonetheless, but the partnership could not survive the eruption in San Francisco. By his own account, Cloherty provoked the final breakup. "I was the person directly responsible for getting rid of Ken. I played a small but key role."

Cloherty was with Cassidy in San Francisco. After the flap over the limousine, "Gerry got his nose out of joint . . . he got really ripped about this," Cloherty remembered. "There had been other blowups of various types like this. So I took Gerry aside at the Fairmont Hotel and said, 'Do you really want to bring this thing to a conclusion? Take a hard minute here and think about it. Do you really want to end this thing [the partnership with Schlossberg]?'

" 'God Bill, I do, I do,' he answered. And I said then if you really want to end it, I'll get you a lawyer. That's where you put your money on the table, Gerry, you hire a lawyer whose job it is to separate this operation. There's really no going back on that once you really are launched. I asked him two or three times. 'Do it, do it today,' he said." And Cloherty did. He took the assignment of finding "a crackerjack lawyer" to help Cassidy break up Schlossberg-Cassidy & Associates.

His search led to Lester Fant, known to all as Ruff, the son of a law professor at the University of Mississippi whose mellifluous intonations quickly betrayed his origins. Fant was a partner in the Washington office of Sidley & Austin, a huge Chicago-based firm, when Cloherty interviewed him. "I told Gerry, Your lawyer for the corporate divorce here is Ruff Fant from Mississippi. He said, 'You couldn't find me an Irish Catholic lawyer?' I said you'll like this guy. We've got a meeting today. He said, 'You've got it all set up?' And I said yeah, and we had the meeting, and the process started."

Schlossberg had also sensed that after San Francisco the partnership was doomed. "I went to our company attorney and told him I wanted him to inform Gerry that I wanted to split the business. I had in mind that I would keep most of the university business and Gerry could have the corporations and the PACs." The lawyer quickly reported this to Cassidy, who then convened a meeting of the firm's other key employees, Fabiani and Godfrey. (Cloherty remained a "consultant," never a full employee.)

"Gerry explained the situation and said I want to get Ken out before Ken succeeds in getting me out, and I want you guys on my team," Fabiani recalled. "The discussion got right down to changing the locks on the door, having Ken's company car towed away. To this former schoolteacher it sounded pretty drastic," Fabiani said. But he and Godfrey quickly agreed to stick with Cassidy, though Schlossberg had been responsible for hiring both of them. Fabiani said there was no doubt in his mind that Cassidy was the more serious businessman, who offered him the best prospects.

In Fant, Cassidy had found a soul mate, someone who in later years would make an enormous contribution to Cassidy's financial successes. Fant, a small, wiry man with an intense gaze, was in no way a Washington insider. After a brilliant academic career at Harvard Law School, he had come to town to practice tax law. Sidley & Austin lured him to create a tax and corporate practice in its big Washington office, which had none. He mostly represented businesses.

He quickly saw that in the corporate charter Cassidy had originally drafted for Schlossberg-Cassidy, the company had three directors: Gerry, Loretta, and Ken. It didn't take "much of a lawyer" to know how to take advantage of that arrangement, Fant said years later. Though Schlossberg clearly owned 50 percent of the company, Fant thought the other two board members together could still fire him. He drafted a letter for the Cassidys to sign informing Schlossberg that he had been terminated.

Schlossberg hired his own lawyer. He noted that although they had never formally made Sophia a director, she and Loretta had been paid identical $2,000 annual "directors' fees." He filed a lawsuit and told his lawyer "to go to war. . . . I spent $60,000 on legal fees and was fully prepared to litigate our disagreement. I was prepared to leave the business in ashes if necessary. Gerry knew that perfectly well." Schlossberg expected his friends in the news media to assure coverage of the trial, where he planned to hint at scandalous behavior. On the eve of the trial, Cassidy and Schlossberg reached an agreement.

Cassidy would pay Schlossberg a total of $812,600. Schlossberg would also get the company-owned Jaguar and some artwork and office equipment. He would get his retirement money out of a pension plan they had created. Schlossberg thought he would continue on his own as a lobbyist.

"When we finally broke the business up we had twenty-seven clients," Cassidy said. "Two of them were pro bono clients. The pro bono clients and Mead, Johnson & Co. [a pharmaceutical firm] went with Ken, and the other twenty-four clients stayed with me. And our deal—part of getting this done so he would leave—was that we threw open the accounts, we could both try to get them to sign with us. It was really, I thought, stunning to him that none of them went with him. But it was because he had withdrawn from the business so much."

Cassidy's account is accurate; all the paying clients but one stayed with him, Fabiani, and Godfrey. Schlossberg remembered a phone call from John Silber, the Boston University president, whom he considered a personal friend, who told him he would be going with Cassidy. "I said, Okay, just please remember all I did for you," Schlossberg recounted.

Decades later Silber—by then a close friend of Cassidy's—confirmed this story: "I decided that Cassidy was the brains of the outfit, and the dynamic force behind the outfit, and that Schlossberg was something of a dilettante, a very nice, and very pleasant man, a very engaging man who might be a useful rainmaker for the firm but wasn't a guy who could run it."

The formal letter specifying the terms of their agreement was signed on October 17, 1984. Cassidy and Schlossberg, once as close as brothers, once warriors in a liberal crusade to feed the hungry, then inventors of a fabulous new way to make money in Washington, were suddenly just another divorced couple. They never spoke to each other again.

CHAPTER 10

"WOULD THAT BE PROPER?"

Cassidy and Schlossberg had been in business together for nearly ten years, transformative years not only for them. Just twenty days after they dissolved their partnership, Ronald Reagan trounced Walter Mondale, winning 59 percent of the vote and carrying forty-nine states on the way to his second term. In the decade since Schlossberg-Cassidy had begun lobbying, the country's politics had obviously been transformed too.

The clearest early warning of the change to come was Reagan's challenge to Gerald Ford for the Republican presidential nomination in 1976. Reagan was a political descendant of Barry Goldwater's; for the conservative faithful, Reagan's televised address on Goldwater's behalf on October 27, 1964, was a rare and memorable bright spot in that disastrous campaign. Old-fashioned Republicans thought Goldwater's humiliation was proof enough that their party should avoid picking another presidential candidate from its right wing—Reagan was too big a risk. But many newer Republicans, especially from the Sun Belt, who were more conservative than the midwestern and northeastern Republican establishment, adored Reagan for both his politics and his charm. The bumbling Ford, especially after he pardoned Nixon for his crimes, was tainted by the unpopular ancien régime. Ford's embrace of Henry Kissinger's foreign policies alienated numerous conservatives. So Reagan did much better in 1976 than the experts, particularly the guardians of Washington's conventional wisdom, expected. He won twelve of the twenty-seven state primaries that year, and fell just 117 delegates short of beating Ford at the Republican National Convention in Kansas City. This was an omen, little understood at the time.

The next unmistakable sign of political change came from a primary election in California in June 1978, when California voters gleefully embraced Proposition 13, a practical expression of the anti-tax, anti-government sentiment that was percolating across the country. This was a sentiment Reagan had exploited in 1976. Proposition 13, an amendment to the state constitution, sharply reduced local real estate taxes, and made future tax increases extremely difficult to enact. Most of the elected office-holders in California opposed "Prop 13," predicting (entirely accurately, as it turned out) that the results would be bad for California's schools (once the nation's best, now among its worst) and other public services. But the tax-cutters brought droves of new voters to the polls and prevailed by two to one. Politicians of every stripe, including many far beyond California, immediately rushed to embrace tax cutting.

Five months after Prop 13, voters in many parts of the country shrank the Democrats' majorities in both the House (by fifteen seats) and Senate (by three). This result reflected the unpopularity of the Democratic president, Jimmy Carter, and economic strains caused by expensive oil and high inflation. But in time it became clear that more was going on in 1978 than a normal swing of the political pendulum. Elections in several locations across the country that year foretold something more portentous.

One was the Senate race in Iowa, where a liberal Democratic incumbent, Dick Clark, ran confidently against a conservative Republican challenger, Roger Jepsen. Clark's own campaign stopped polling after a survey in early October found that he led Jepsen by 57–27, with the rest undecided. The *Des Moines Register*'s final poll a few days before the election gave Clark a ten-point lead. But on election day the turnout of voters was light, and the winner was Jepsen, with 51 percent of the vote.

The result so shocked Peter Hart, Clark's pollster, that "I didn't get out of my blue bathrobe for three days," he recalled years later.

One source of the shock was a newly organized conservative religious faction that called itself the Pro-Life Action Council. Its issue was abortion, which Jepsen proposed to outlaw. The Supreme Court had legalized most abortions five years earlier, sowing the seeds of a national controversy that has festered ever since. Senator Clark was pro-choice and had voted to allow the use of federal funds to pay for the abortions of some women. The Pro-Life Action Council, an Iowa group consisting largely of people who had never before been active in a political campaign, distributed 300,000 anti-Clark, anti-abortion leaflets to Iowa churchgoers the Sunday before the election.

Clark's brother, who had converted to Catholicism, found the leaflet—which featured a gruesome photo of an aborted fetus—on his windshield after church that Sunday. "He called to warn me I had big trouble," Clark recalled. Catholics constituted the base of the Iowa Democratic Party, but in 1978 they deserted Clark in droves. In five heavily Catholic counties, his support fell 15 to 18 percent below the vote he received when first elected in 1972. This was enough to elect Jepsen.

Robert C. Dopf, an attorney and secretary-treasurer of the Action Council, happily took credit for Clark's defeat. "There is not much argument from anyone about the impact we have had," Dopf said the day after the election. "The handwriting is on the wall for more than Senator Clark. . . . Politicians are going to have to deal with this issue. The network we have here is tremendous. We see it as a foundation for the 1980 presidential campaigns. We are very optimistic."

Another unexpected conservative victory in a Senate race that year illuminated the way television advertising was transforming electoral politics. This was the contest between a thirty-seven-year-old airline pilot named Gordon J. Humphrey, who had moved to New Hampshire in 1974 and decided to run for the Senate in 1978, and Thomas J. McIntyre, an incumbent Democrat, native of the state, former mayor of Laconia, and senator since 1962. McIntyre was an influential, senior member of the Senate Armed Services Committee, a bright and serious senator. He was more than the favorite—no poll gave Humphrey a chance, including one he himself commissioned.

Humphrey had never held elected office or any government job. Humphrey's political background consisted entirely of his active participation in conservative—not Republican—causes. He was chairman of the New Hampshire branch of the Conservative Caucus, created in 1974 as a conservative response to the citizens' lobby Common Cause. Humphrey opposed abortion and—staunchly—communism. Most fervidly, he was a critic of the treaties that returned the Panama Canal to Panamanian control. McIntyre had voted to ratify the treaties, and in the Senate debate on the issue, had criticized the opposition to them from "the bully boys of the radical new right." The Panama Canal became one of Humphrey's two big issues. The second was the fact that McIntyre owned a condominium in Florida but no residence in New Hampshire—proof, Humphrey said, that McIntyre had forgotten where he came from.

There were two Democrats running for statewide office that year, McIntyre and Hugh Gallen, who was challenging Governor Meldrim Thomson, the eccentric right-wing favorite of the Manchester *Union Leader*, a conservative newspaper that dominated the state. In 1978 Thomson was seeking a fourth two-year term. McIntyre and Gallen used the same political consultant to make their 1978 television commercials. In the course of the 1970s most candidates for governor and the Senate and many for the House came to accept the need for such commercials—they worked, however unappealing it was, especially for old-timers like McIntyre, to sell yourself like detergent. Gallen, a former car dealer and state representative, had no qualms about the commercials. Don Madden, the political consultant to both men in 1978, remembered Gallen patiently reshooting one spot more than thirty times to get it just right.

McIntyre, on the other hand, had no patience for Madden's shoots. On one occasion when he wasn't performing very well, Madden asked him to try again, then again. "That's it," McIntyre announced after the third try, though the result hadn't been very good.

Gallen put his commercials on Boston television stations, viewed by the largest portion of the New Hampshire electorate in the southern part of the state. This was expensive and inefficient—most people who saw the ads lived in Massachusetts. Nevertheless, they reached a lot of New Hampshire voters. Governor Thomson declined to spend heavily on commercials on the Boston stations.

Gordon Humphrey did not have a lot of money—he had to loan cash to his own campaign—but he decided he too had to use Boston television stations to broadcast a spot he made ridiculing McIntyre's Florida condo. McIntyre declined to raise or spend money on Boston television. He never spent all the money he'd raised for the race.

Gallen, the Democratic candidate for governor, defeated the conservative Thomson by 10,400 votes. But Humphrey, the conservative candidate for Senate, beat McIntyre by 6,100 votes. The two winners got almost the same number of total votes, more than 133,000 each. Obviously, there was more involved than the two Republican candidates' conservative positions. Humphrey credited an anti-incumbent mood in the state, but advertising on Boston television clinched the deal, he thought. This was costly, but it apparently worked. No statewide candidate in New Hampshire had previously relied on Boston television, but they all have ever since.

Humphrey and Jepsen both benefited from the efforts of the band of self-described "radicals" who proudly called themselves the New Right. They considered 1978 the election that established the conservative ascendancy. Ironically, McIntyre had attacked the New Right by name in his speech in support of the Panama Canal treaties, describing the conservatives as bullies who "justify any means, however coarse and brutish, of imposing [their values and positions] on others." He got their attention; then on election day, they got his.

The New Right was nurtured by a kind of agitprop first used successfully by liberals, but perfected by these determined new conservatives— direct mail. Political leaflets were mailed to the homes of people identified by their own previous activities as conservatives. The leaflets included requests for money, but they were usually many pages long, filled with exhortations, information, and appeals to patriotism. The names and addresses of their recipients most often came from lists first compiled by Richard Viguerie, one of the founding fathers of the New Right. Viguerie is a large figure in modern American history who deserves more fame than he has enjoyed outside the world of conservative activists.

A devout Christian and uncompromising New Right conservative, Viguerie grew up in Texas. In the early 1960s he got to know a number of young conservative activists, eventually moving to New York to work with a New Right pioneer named Marvin Liebman. Liebman organized some of the first New Right organizations, including the Young Americans for Freedom. Viguerie did well, and soon found himself running YAF in Washington as its executive secretary. But in 1965 he quit that job "to concentrate on what I enjoyed doing, and did best—raising money." Viguerie opened his own direct mail business.

To succeed, Viguerie needed the names and addresses of conservative Americans who were prepared to support their politics with money. Liebman gave him his first mailing lists. After the Goldwater debacle, Viguerie personally spent hours in the offices of the clerk of the House of Representatives in the Capitol, writing out in longhand the names and addresses of Americans who had contributed $50 or more to the Goldwater campaign. With the help of a number of volunteers, he harvested the names and addresses of 12,500 Goldwater contributors.

By his own account, it wasn't until 1972 that Viguerie fully appreciated the potential of direct mail. His teacher that year was George McGovern, whose outsider's campaign for the Democratic presidential nomination succeeded "because he understood the new technology," as Viguerie put it in a 1979 interview. "He was a creature of direct mail." The McGovern campaign found supporters by sending mailings to people who had previously given to liberal causes. When recipients replied, the campaign moved quickly to hook them with an "insider's newsletter" and a coupon book that they could clip and send in with a check every month. They also received monthly reminders in the mail. This was hugely successful; it gave the McGovern campaign a steady stream of cash that amounted to $100,000 a month by early 1972. McGovern was practicing what became gospel to Viguerie—that "direct mail is a form of advertising, part of the marketing strategy," not simply a way to solicit contributions.

In 1976, four years after that McGovern campaign, Viguerie was hired to raise money for the third presidential campaign of George Wallace, the former segregationist governor of Alabama. He raised $6.9 million for Wallace from what became a mailing list of nearly a million donors. Under the terms of his contract with Wallace, the names on the list became Viguerie's property. Viguerie scrubbed that list and produced a version with 600,000 names and addresses of people he thought were inclined to support political insurgents from his end of the political spectrum. These 600,000 became the founding foot soldiers of the New Right.

Viguerie was a gifted agitator. He thought of direct mail as "one method of mass commercial communication that the liberals do not control. . . . You can think of direct mail as *our* TV, radio, daily newspaper and weekly news magazine." He helped create new organizations, then shared their membership lists with other groups that were his clients. He kept building his basic mailing list until it contained millions of names. He also became well-to-do himself by charging high fees and demanding payment in advance.

Viguerie had an explanation for why Jepsen and Humphrey won their Senate races in 1978—"single-issue direct mail." He created or supported numerous upstart organizations formed around a single issue like abortion, prayer in the schools, or the Panama Canal. Mail that mobilizes voters who will respond to those issues can move 1 to 5 percent of the electorate in a close race from the Democratic to the Republican candidate, Viguerie has said. "Single-issue direct mail can make that difference."

He also set up or raised money for new organizations invented as conservative versions of liberal groups. His own list of such groups created in the 1970s included the Conservative Caucus where Gordon Humphrey got his start in politics, the Republican Study Committee, the Senate Steering Committee, and the National Conservative Political Action Committee, which helped both Jepsen and Humphrey in 1978.

Viguerie and his cohorts considered 1978 "our critical year." They "consciously thought of *themselves*—not the Republican Party—as the alternative to the Left and the Democrats," Viguerie and David Franke wrote in a 2004 book called *America's Right Turn.* For the leaders of the New Right, the electoral successes in 1978 were evidence not of a Republican revival, but of their own ascendancy. They saw the Republican Party in total disarray after Watergate forced Nixon's resignation. "Politics, like nature, abhors a vacuum, so the conservatives filled that vacuum and provided leadership for the Right in America." Using the political and financial resources that direct mail could provide, Viguerie and his colleagues-in-arms were able to "wrest control of the GOP," all the time working "under the radar" where the national news media rarely noticed them.

Viguerie compared the Republican Party after Nixon's forced resignation to a pilot-less airplane that was "meandering in all directions." This created an opening for the founders and leaders of the New Right. "The cockpit was vacant! So we put down our coffee cups and legal pads, and we had a blast for six or seven years—*flying the plane!*"

For conservatives, the biggest excitement arrived just two years later, when Reagan vanquished Jimmy Carter and became the first unequivocally conservative Republican to win the White House since the 1920s. Democrats lost twelve seats in the Senate, relinquishing control to the Republicans for the first time in twenty-six years. In the House, Democrats lost thirty-five seats; they held a nominal majority of 242–192 (there was one Independent), but because their 242 included dozens of moderates and southern conservatives, President Reagan actually enjoyed a working majority in both House and Senate on most issues.

In 1964 the Republicans had been decimated; in 1974 they were decimated again. Yet here they were six years later in a stronger position than Republicans had enjoyed since the first two years of Dwight D. Eisenhower's first term as president nearly thirty years earlier. It was a breathtaking reversal of fortune.

But these were different Republicans, changed by the new, conservative activists who were more in the mold of Richard Viguerie of Houston, Texas, than of Dwight Eisenhower of Abilene, Kansas. There were still traditional midwestern and northeastern Republicans in the House and Senate—more of them after the 1980 Reagan landslide than before—but the center of gravity in the Republican Party was shifting south and west.

An early harbinger of the change this shift would bring came in the person of an untenured history professor at the University of West Georgia named Newt Gingrich. He first won a seat in the House in 1978, on his third try. He was just thirty-five at the time, and he was impatient for change, first of all in his own party. He had a vision for the Republican Party that had nothing to do with Eisenhower Republicans. He was a fighter, a self-styled visionary, and a determined optimist who sought from his first days as a congressman to build a conservative Republican majority in the House—something that seemed inconceivable at the time.

For Gingrich, the end always seemed more important than the means. He self-consciously patterned himself on revolutionaries from other times and places who set out to accomplish goals others considered hopeless, and the methods he used could offend more fastidious souls.

His third campaign for the House, in 1978, was revealing. His first two attempts against a sitting conservative Democrat, both close calls, were run by amateurs and volunteers. The incumbent retired before the third race, and because both previous elections had been close, the National Republican Congressional Committee decided to invest in Gingrich in 1978. It and other Republican committees gave him $50,000, nearly a quarter of the $219,000 he raised, compared to $135,000 in 1976—an increase of more than 60 percent. The Republican committee encouraged Gingrich to hire a staff of professionals, which he did. His paid consultants made controversial television commercials and conducted an advertising campaign in rural newspapers in Georgia's 6th Congressional District that was downright nasty.

L. H. Carter was Gingrich's campaign manager in 1978; he later turned against his old friend when Gingrich let power "go to his head," as Carter put it. He described a Gingrich television spot he helped make to undermine Gingrich's 1978 opponent, a state senator named Virginia Shapard.

"We found bills in the Georgia Senate with great titles like 'A Bill to Reduce Your Taxes.' It was a terrible bill. It failed like 49 to 1, and of course Virginia voted against it. We had a voice-over saying, 'Virginia Shapard had a chance to reduce your taxes. . . . She knows how she voted. She only hopes you don't.' She was a touch on the heavy side and we had a chunky woman's arm with an iron bracelet come down and stamp a big red 'no' in the middle of the bill," Carter said. "We slaughtered her with that ad. And it was really unfair."

Carter described a newspaper ad that contained a photograph of Gingrich, his wife, and two daughters, and one of Virginia Shapard by herself. The ad said, "Newt will take his family to Washington and keep them together; Virginia will go to Washington and leave her husband and children in the care of a nanny. Newt is deacon of the First Baptist Church of Carrollton; Virginia is a communicant of the Church of the Good Shepherd in Griffin." The use of "communicant" was meant to suggest she was a Catholic, not the most popular religion in South Georgia. (Not long after he was elected, Gingrich visited his wife when she was in a hospital bed being treated for cancer, and announced that they were getting a divorce.)

That Gingrich campaign was consistent with the changing nature of campaigns at the time, when "going negative" became popular, particularly among conservative Republican candidates. Humphrey in New Hampshire and Jepsen in Iowa both relied on negative campaigning to win their races that year.

This was the era of fast-growing campaign costs. The technology of politics was changing, and the newest techniques were expensive. It cost money to take polls, make and broadcast television commercials, send large quantities of direct mail, and hire professional campaign workers. The use of all of these was still rare in House and Senate campaigns in the early 1970s, but was widespread by 1978 and commonplace soon thereafter—and ever since.

One aggressive promoter of negative campaigning was the National Conservative Political Action Committee, one of the organizations for which Viguerie raised money by mail. NCPAC identified six senators it wanted to help defeat in 1980, and conducted its own negative campaigns against each, spending nearly a million dollars. NCPAC was an "independent" committee with no direct ties to the campaigns it was supporting. Like Gingrich, Terry Dolan, the young leader of NCPAC, put ends ahead of means. He invented reasons why voters should reject the senators he had targeted.

In Idaho, for example, a NCPAC television spot showed an empty missile silo while a voice in the background said Senator Frank Church, then the chairman of the Senate Foreign Relations Committee, had "almost always opposed a strong national defense." It turned out the empty silo had housed a Titan missile, an out-of-date model long since replaced by the smaller, more powerful Minuteman, which Church had supported. Other advertisements accused him of voting for a pay increase for senators that he had actually opposed, and of promoting abortion, which he generally opposed.

During the campaign Church's opponent, Congressman Steven Symms, was caught on camera coaching a supporter to ask a question at a campaign rally about the investigation of the Central Intelligence Agency that Church had led in the 1970s. Moments later the supporter raised his hand and asked Symms the question he had suggested: Did the Church investigation weaken the CIA? Symms, who did not realize he had been recorded planting the question, acted surprised by the query and referred it to James McClure, then Idaho's second senator and a conservative

Republican who detested Church. McClure was campaigning that day with Symms.

McClure responded by saying he had talked to Richard Welch, the CIA station chief in Athens at the time of the Church investigation. He quoted Welch as saying that Church's inquiry was "going to get some of our people killed. And two weeks later, that man [Welch] was dead, assassinated." But the Church-led investigation had never mentioned Greece or Welch in its reports or hearings.

Church was deeply hurt by these accusations, and alarmed by the tactics used against him. In an interview with National Public Radio shortly before the election, the four-term senator revealed his anger, his pride, and his self-regard: "They think that their propaganda techniques manipulate public opinion and can win elections regardless of the underlying facts, or even a lifetime of service to a state like Idaho. And this is their avowed objective. And if they prove that to be the case, then I think it's going to be sad not only for this state but for the country, because it could very well be that this crowd, boasting of their corrupt methods, could in fact take over the power structure of the country."

"They" were the New Right, NCPAC, the negative campaigners out to remake first the Republican Party and then the United States in their own image. On election day four of the targets they had picked, liberal Democrats all, were defeated, including Church and George McGovern. The country's changing politics caught up with them in 1980. Their liberal populism came from an earlier era, and their conservative opponents were able to drive a wedge between them and their electorates. Idaho and South Dakota voted overwhelmingly for Reagan that year, a sign that they were moving into a new conservative coalition of southerners and westerners that would become steadily more important over the next twenty years.

The 1980 election marked a sharp turn in the country's politics, though not as sharp as it looked at first blush. Reagan carried forty-four states and won 489 electoral votes; Carter prevailed in just six states and Washington, D.C., accumulating forty-nine electoral votes. But other numbers complicated the picture. Only 52.6 percent of the voting-age population cast a vote in 1980, and Reagan won just 50.7 percent of their ballots. (Independent candidate John Anderson won 5.7 million votes, or 7 percent of the votes cast.) In other words, only 26.7 percent of American adults created the Reagan "landslide."

Of the six Democratic senators NCPAC targeted in 1980, two won easy re-election despite the hundreds of thousands of dollars conservatives spent to beat them. Ten Democratic senators were beaten. But another ten incumbent Democrats were reelected, many of them staunch liberals. This mixed outcome complicated any attempt to draw broad conclusions from the results.

Politicians and pundits like to think that the voters are as conscious of political issues and tactics as the experts are, but the real America is an apolitical country whose citizens mostly participate—or don't—in politics every two or four years on election day. When their biannual decisions surprise the experts, the best explanations can most often be found in deeper currents in the culture that encompass partisan politics but go beyond them. That seemed to be the case in 1980, when public opinion polls revealed a rattled electorate that was scared by the worst inflation in a generation, by the appearance of long lines to buy gasoline, by the Iranian ayatollahs' ability to humiliate the United States, by Jimmy Carter's obvious limitations as a leader in challenging times. Proposition 13 in California had revealed and encouraged anti-tax sentiments that subsequently swept the country. All of this helped Reagan and the Republicans, who naturally benefited from the many votes against the ins, because they were the outs.

But such analysis could not protect Democrats in Congress from the sharp sense of insecurity that the election results induced. They were not prepared for the humiliation the voters inflicted in 1980.

Frank Church's pre-election warning had proved prophetic. "They"—the new breed of rough-and-tumble conservatives who proudly flouted good political manners—had taken giant strides toward taking over "the power structure of the country," as Church had put it.

The exultation among Republicans and the anxiety in Democratic stomachs both contributed to a new politics in Washington. Republicans had been losing races for the House and Senate so persistently for so long that throughout the 1970s and even in 1980 they could not raise as much money as the Democrats.

But that year Republicans closed the gap. And the difference between the ways the two parties raised money in 1980 was revealing. Individual Democratic candidates for House and Senate—mostly incumbents, many with positions of influence—vastly out-raised individual Republican candidates. But the Republicans' House and Senate campaign committees, the umbrella organizations that directed money raised all over the country to challengers and incumbents alike, left their Democratic counterparts in the dust. The National Republican Congressional Committee in the House raised and spent *thirteen times* what the Democratic Congressional

Campaign Committee—the "D Triple C" in the argot of Washington politics—raised and spent: $29 million for the Republican committee, $2.2 million for the DCCC. Just two years earlier the Republican committee had raised only $14 million (though still vastly more than the Democratic committee raised). So the trend added to Democrats' anxieties.

House Democrats therefore took a fateful step when the new Congress convened at the beginning of 1981. They elected Tony Coelho, then a second-term congressman from California, the new chairman of the DCCC.

Every member of Congress is ambitious—only the ambitious would put up with the exhaustion, the frustrations, and the occasional humiliations involved in running for and then serving in the House or Senate. The successful members, the ones who win positions of leadership and leave a mark on their institution, combine ambition with discipline and focus. They get beyond the pleasures of being catered to and bowed to and actually make things happen. One such was Tony Coelho.

Coelho grew up in the little farming town of Dos Palos in California's Central Valley. His father was a not very successful dairy farmer. His grandparents had come to California from the Azores, Portuguese islands southwest of Portugal off the west coast of Africa. His father doubted the utility of higher education, but Coelho was determined to be the first in his family to go to college—Loyola University in Los Angeles, a Catholic school. He entered in September 1960, two months before John F. Kennedy was elected president. Kennedy became a hero to the young Coelho, and Kennedy's assassination in his junior year sent him into a tailspin. Coelho was twenty-one. He decided he had to do something useful with his life. "What I really wanted to do was become a priest."

As he was graduating from Loyola, Coelho's plan was derailed by a doctor. Since an accident in a pickup truck when he was sixteen, Coelho had suffered from occasional blackouts, which he tried to ignore. The doctor told him in June 1964 that he had epilepsy. For his Portuguese family, this was unacceptable: "No son of ours has epilepsy," his parents told him. On the Azores, folklore held that epilepsy was a punishment for past sins in the victim's family. More immediately important, Coelho also learned that the Catholic Church had closed the priesthood to epileptics. He needed a new plan.

A Jesuit priest recommended Coelho to Bob Hope, who needed a clever young man to help with his charitable activities. Coelho took the job, and moved into the Hope household. The comedian took a shine to his young protégé. In one of their many long talks, Hope observed that the desire to help others that once pushed Coelho toward the priesthood might also be satisfied in politics. Hope suggested he go to work for a member of Congress. "You can satisfy your priestly needs and desires," Coelho remembered Hope saying.

This idea appealed to Coelho. Lyndon Johnson had persuaded Congress to help people on a big scale when he became president, particularly after being elected in his own right in 1964. Congress was passing civil rights bills and funding a war on poverty. Congress might indeed be the vehicle Coelho could use to do good works.

He had an uncle who was active in California politics, who got Coelho an interview with Congressman B. F. Sisk, who represented the Central Valley. Sisk offered Coelho an internship in Washington. "I absolutely fell in love with the work," Coelho said later, "the fact that you could really help out people and you could change people's lives." He worked for Sisk for thirteen years. When the congressman announced plans to retire, Coelho decided to run for the seat, and won it easily. At thirty-six, he was a member of Congress.

He was a natural. A small, slim man with an intense manner, he loved physical contact with his colleagues. He was a famously good listener and learned everything he could about every Democratic member. His years with Sisk taught him that the leadership jobs would be the most rewarding, so he set out to win one—first, chairman of the Democratic Congressional Campaign Committee.

Coelho promised his colleagues he could raise at least $5 million for the 1982 elections, and would help them catch up with the Republicans, who had gotten themselves organized as a party. They had built facilities in Washington to help their candidates learn the new technologies of politics, make television commercials, do research on their opponents, and more. Coelho also realized that Republicans—helped by a former partner of Viguerie's, who joined the staff of the Republican National Committee—were using direct mail to build a huge list of small donors, something the Democrats could not equal. Coelho promised to help his party catch up by matching these Republican capabilities. He easily won the chairmanship of the campaign committee.

Coelho's method was straightforward. As he did with the Ocean Spray cranberry cooperative at the event described earlier, he met with as many business groups as he could, particularly those with political action committees. He gave them all the same pitch: Democrats remain in charge of the House; Democrats are not anti-business; those in the business community who cared about the contents of legislation needed to maintain good relations with Democrats; the best way to do that would be to give them money.

Since the mid-1970s Republicans had been encouraging trade associations, companies, and business groups of all kinds to create PACs. Congressman Guy Vander Jagt of Michigan, chairman then of the National Republican Congressional Committee, hoped business PACs would neutralize the labor union PACs that had long been significant supporters of Democratic candidates. Vander Jagt and his colleagues had tangible success—the number of business PACs grew from fewer than eighty in 1975 to more than a thousand in the early 1980s. But to the Republicans' frustration, these new business PACs gave a considerable portion of their money to Democrats—incumbents with influence. Their donations to Republicans never compensated fully for the money labor PACs gave Democrats.

Nevertheless, Coelho realized when he became chairman of the DCCC in 1981 that he had to move quickly, because after the 1980 election the Republicans had momentum. And they were cocky. Vander Jagt and other Republican leaders courted the business PACs with new ardor, promising that with enough money, they could capture the House in 1982.

Luckily for the Democrats, the worst economic recession since the Great Depression of the 1930s began in July 1981. Economists attributed the downturn primarily to the tight monetary policy that Paul Volcker, chairman of the Federal Reserve Board, had instituted late in 1979. Volcker sought an abrupt slowdown of the American economy to control inflation, which was higher than most living Americans had ever experienced. He pushed up the prime lending rate that banks charged to preferred customers until it reached 21.5 percent in June 1981, a level guaranteed to bring credit-sensitive sectors of the economy—particularly housing and automobiles—to a standstill. By September 1981, the unemployment rate had passed 10 percent, a level not seen since the Depression.

The result was political catastrophe for the House Republicans. They lost twenty-seven seats—all but six of those they had gained in 1980. The Democrats again had a working majority that could stymie the Reagan administration. Coelho raised $6.5 million in his first two years as chairman of the DCCC—$1.5 million more than he had rashly promised, and enough to make him the new hero of his party.

This was a startling figure for the Democrats. But the National Republican Congressional Committee continued to do far better, raising

$57.4 million for the 1982 elections. Vander Jagt and his colleagues kept the pressure on the business PACs to increase their contributions. Their optimistic predictions that the GOP could retake the House proved woefully out of step with reality when the votes were counted on November 2. "We were not given realistic assessments," complained the director of the American Medical Association's PAC, who felt burned when he realized that the Democrats would again dominate the House after an election in which his PAC had given too much money to Republicans.

The next two-year election cycle proved to be even more significant. The economy recovered briskly, and so did President Reagan's political fortunes. By November 1984, he was able to dispatch former vice president Mondale, his Democratic challenger, with ease. This time Reagan's victory was an unalloyed landslide—the country enthusiastically wanted him back in the White House. But his coattails were weak. In the House, Republicans could pick up just sixteen seats, leaving the Democrats in firm control with a majority of seventy-one. Reagan carried many more House districts than the Republican House candidates did. In the Senate the Republicans actually lost two seats to the Democrats, though they retained control narrowly, 53–47.

Money was important to the Democrats' ability to minimize losses in 1984, especially in marginal seats. For example, Congressman Robert Mrazek, whose Long Island district contained more Republicans than Democrats, spent $707,000 in 1984, more than twice what he spent in 1982, to hold his seat. Congressman Jim Jones of Tulsa, Oklahoma, raised and spent $1.4 million in 1984, compared to $635,000 two years earlier. Such expensive House races were a new phenomenon, but Democrats could still win them.

Coelho was thrilled. He had increased his collections for the DCCC to $10.4 million, while the Republican committee's fund-raising was stagnant in 1983–84. He could take credit for helping prevent a Republican takeover in Washington and for restoring the morale of his colleagues. The 1984 results obliterated the theory—popular among pundits and, especially, Republicans after the 1980 election—that a great national "realignment" was under way, one that would give Republicans political dominance for years to come. The 1981–82 recession, the new party apparatus Coelho was building, the money Democrats were raising, and the continuing advantages of incumbency all combined to put the Democrats back in the game.

But Coelho's triumph came at a high price. The Democratic Party had moved into new territory. It had voluntarily begun to depend on money from business—from people whom old-line Democrats had traditionally thought of as, well, Republicans. And most of them *were* Republicans—pragmatic Republicans who responded to Coelho's argument that they could do business with Democrats in the House who were not hostile to their interests, and who occupied positions of power.

One of the first things Coelho did as chairman of the DCCC was to establish the Speaker's Club, unabashedly a replica of the Republican National Committee's Eagles Club, created after the 1980 election. Contributors who gave at least $10,000 to the Republican Party became Eagles and received invitations to special events attended by Reagan administration officials and Republican leaders in Congress. Coelho cut the price to $5,000 for membership in the Speaker's Club. A brochure his staff produced described the benefits of membership:

> As a member of the Speaker's Club, you will have many opportunities to meet personally with the Democratic leadership and committee chairmen of the House of Representatives and share with them your interests and concerns. . . . Whether it's playing a round of golf with the Speaker, having dinner with the House leadership or sharing your ideas with other prominent club members, you will be broadening your circle of friends and contacts among the senior members of the House. When you come to Washington you will be assured courteous and direct access to those whom you wish to meet.

These committees were a new kind of animal for Washington. Wealthy individuals and their interests had always found ways to get to the politicians and officials they wanted to see, of course, but now both parties had formalized the procedures. Politics, Coelho liked to say, had become a business. Yes it had, and business was booming.

Did the Speaker's Club emit the unpleasant odor of corruption? Of course it did. But Coelho was ready with a facile response to that accusation: "The thing we've done basically is to provide access, to let people talk to people. Now if somebody wants to talk to me about a bill, and says 'I'll give you X amount of dollars to get a bill through,' I walk away from it, I'm not interested in that. But if they just want to talk to somebody, I'll help them talk to someone. But that's as far as I will go."

If Coelho could draw that line and respect it, other members did not. Reporters in Washington began to find cases where contributions seemed to produce legislative results. Used car dealers persuaded both House and

Senate to vote overwhelmingly to overturn a decision by the Federal Trade Commission that would have required them to put stickers on the cars they sold listing all their known defects. The National Automobile Dealers Association, through its PAC, had given nearly a million dollars to more than three hundred members of Congress in the previous three years. Dairy farmers' contributions appeared to help protect federal subsidies at a time when many similar programs were being cut back. Doctors, dentists, and optometrists persuaded the House to pass a bill barring the FTC from taking any antitrust action against them after they contributed about $2 million to members (the Senate narrowly defeated this legislation).

Senator Bob Dole of Kansas, at the time the chairman of the Senate Finance Committee, must have startled his colleagues in the summer of 1982 by telling Albert R. Hunt of *The Wall Street Journal* the truth about the influence of PACs. "When these political action committees give money," Dole said, "they expect something in return other than good government. It is making it much more difficult to legislate. We may reach a point where if everybody is buying something with PAC money, we can't get anything done." Dole was equally candid about the uneven distribution of benefits that ensued: "Poor people don't make campaign contributions. You might get a different result if there were a 'Poor PAC' up here" on Capitol Hill. Dole's comments appeared in the first of three articles the *Journal* published that summer under the title "Cash Politics."

Coelho had a similar moment of candor with Brooks Jackson, the author of a fine book about him and his fund-raising successes, *Honest Graft*. Sure, the need for scores or hundreds of thousands in campaign contributions every two years has an impact—"it *does* affect legislation," Coelho told Jackson. "You don't have the people [members of Congress] feeling they can be creative," Coelho said. The need to raise big money makes them cautious because "they don't want to turn people off."

He gave a hypothetical example of a member concerned about housing who is under pressure to raise $50,000 for his next campaign. (In the Coelho era this wasn't much—the average winning campaign in a contested district cost more than $400,000 by 1984.) "If you are spending all your time calling up different people . . . to raise $50,000 [a number he picked arbitrarily], you all of a sudden, in your mind, you're in effect saying, 'I'm not going to go out and develop this new housing bill that may get the realtors or may get the builders or may get the unions upset. I have got to raise the $50,000.' . . . That isn't a sellout. It's basically that you're not permitted to go out and do your creativity."

Gerald S. J. Cassidy on a triumphant occasion, the thirtieth birthday party of his firm. (Susan Biddle, *The Washington Post*)

Cassidy survived a traumatic youth dominated by his stepfather's drinking and his family's poverty. His mother repeatedly sent him to live with relatives. He spent second grade in Our Lady of Perpetual Help elementary school in Dallas, where he lived with his sister Mickey. In the class photo above, Cassidy (third from left, center row) towers over most of his classmates, who were a year or two younger. (Courtesy Gerald Cassidy)

Cassidy as a senior at Holy Cross High School in New York City. (Holy Cross yearbook photo)

Above: In 1969, Cassidy was working as an attorney for South Florida Migrant Legal Services, representing poor workers who picked fruit and vegetables in and around Immokalee. That year, he and his colleagues entertained members of the United States Senate's Select Committee on Nutrition and Human Needs. Cassidy, above right, gesturing, briefs Senator George McGovern, the committee chairman. (Courtesy Gerald Cassidy)

Below: Cassidy (in sunglasses) and his wife, Loretta, with two of the migrant workers in Immokalee. (Courtesy Gerald Cassidy)

On the nutrition committee's 1969 field trip to Florida, Senators George McGovern of South Dakota and Jacob Javits of New York visited a family of migrant workers. The next year President Richard Nixon signed amendments to the National School Lunch Act and the Child Nutrition Act, two of the many pieces of social welfare legislation that Nixon approved. (Bettmann Archive; Harry Naltchayan, *The Washington Post*)

Kenneth Schlossberg (seated) and Cassidy pose in their Washington office in 1983 for *Science* magazine, one of the first publications to write about their booming earmark business. (Colin Norman, *Science*)

In 1977, two years after the firm called Schlossberg-Cassidy & Associates was launched, Ken Schlossberg married Sophia Gorokhova, a beautiful Russian émigrée. Cassidy was Schlossberg's best man. Here the newly wed Schlossbergs (far left) are joined by the Cassidys (far right) and other friends. (Courtesy Kenneth Schlossberg)

Above: In 1989, over the objections of several of their colleagues, Cassidy (right) and James Fabiani agreed to pose for a *Washington Post* photographer for a picture that accompanied a revelatory story about their business. Until this time Cassidy had avoided publicity and seldom allowed his picture to be taken. (Frank Johnston, *The Washington Post*)

Middle: Cassidy and his wife, Loretta, in a Washington restaurant in 1992. (Nancy Andrews, *The Washington Post*)

Below: Vincent Versage (right) and Frank Godfrey, two of Cassidy's longtime associates. (Courtesy Vincent Versage)

Above: Lee Atwater was the architect of George H. W. Bush's 1988 presidential campaign, which illuminated the ways that new technologies had altered American politics. With a hollow, issue-free campaign, Bush easily dispatched the hapless Governor Michael Dukakis. On his deathbed two years later, Atwater repudiated his own political tactics. (*The Washington Post*)

Below: Roger Ailes made negative television commercials attacking Dukakis that have entered the lore of American politics. One of those commercials featured a staged "revolving door" of criminals who, the commercial charged, Dukakis had let out of prison in Massachusetts. (*The Washington Post;* Bush campaign commercial)

Before the late 1980s, relations across the aisles in the House and Senate were friendlier than they later became. Congressman Bob Michel of Illinois (left), for fourteen years the House Republican leader, and Speaker Thomas P. "Tip" O'Neill of Massachusetts (right), the Democrats' leader, maintained good personal relations despite political differences. (James K. W. Atherton, *The Washington Post*)

John Stennis, one of the lions of the old Senate, spent less than $5,000 on his first five re-election campaigns. But in 1982, facing a well-funded Republican opponent, Stennis's political consultant told him he needed to raise $2 million, and recommended that the senator solicit contributions from the big defense contractors whose weapons systems Stennis had supported. Stennis, then eighty-one, was taken aback. "Would that be proper?" he asked. (James K. W. Atherton, *The Washington Post*)

In the 1980s, Congressman Tony Coelho of California (left) became the Democrats' star fundraiser, tapping corporate interests for tens of millions of dollars to help his party maintain a majority in the House throughout the Reagan years (1981–89). One beneficiary of Coelho's success was Congressman Jim Wright of Texas (right), who succeeded O'Neill as speaker in 1987. (Harry Naltchayan, *The Washington Post*)

Coelho added, "I think that's bad"—but not legally corrupt. "The press always tries . . . to say that you've been bought out. I don't buy that. I just don't think it's true. I think that the process buys you out. But I don't think that you individually have been bought out, or that you sell out. I think there's a big difference there."

Coelho made a distinction—for him, evidently, an important distinction—between selling your vote outright and allowing the process to buy you out. Selling your vote was "legally wrong." Succumbing to the process was "morally wrong, in effect," according to the man who once planned to become a priest, but it wouldn't put you in jail. As Jackson wrote, Coelho saw himself "as a law-abiding player in an immoral system."

Leon Panetta was another Democratic congressman from California who watched what Coelho was doing with trepidation. Coelho's idea, he recalled, was that the Democrats should compete with the Republicans "for the same money"—the business interests' money. "What it meant was, we were going to sell part of our soul to the Washington power interests for a lot of cash. . . . I told Tony, the more dependent we become on their contributions, the less flexibility we will have on the issues. And he always answered, 'You can't worry about the issues if you're not in power.' "

Panetta was an example of an old-fashioned politician who never got comfortable with the money-driven politics that conquered both parties in the 1980s. There were others who found it difficult to accept the new morality that Coelho embodied, though few spoke out publicly about what was going on.

One who did was Richard Bolling of Missouri, an influential liberal leader in the House for three decades who retired from Congress at the beginning of 1983. Just as Coelho's courtship of business PACs was beginning to bear fruit, Bolling published an article in an academic journal acknowledging "the corrosive, pervasive and too often invisible influence of special interest money" that was "increasingly corroding the integrity of Congress."

The money came in many forms, Bolling noted: campaign contributions, undisclosed lobbying efforts, and the "speaking fees known as honoraria" that allowed interest groups to put money directly into the pockets of members. Bolling, an expert on congressional procedure who worked throughout his career to reform the House, noted that corrupting a committee of Congress isn't so difficult. "Congressional committees are often narrowly divided to begin with, and one or two subservient individuals may make a great difference in the outcome on very important legislation. The system is so fragile and vulnerable that real purity is essential to consistent success for the public interest."

A poignant, unpublicized exchange on this subject occurred early in 1982 between Raymond D. Strother, a spirited and original Democratic political consultant from Louisiana, and Senator John Stennis of Mississippi, one of the most complex and formidable senators of the twentieth century. Stennis was a white Mississippian and no friend of civil rights, but he was also a smart, serious, and thoughtful senator with an expansive view of the Senate's significance and a deep commitment to the institution. He wrote the first Senate ethics code, and in 1964 became the first chairman of the Senate's Select Committee on Standards and Conduct, later known as the Ethics Committee.

Stennis was first elected to the Senate in a special election in 1947. He faced re-election for the sixth time in 1982. He had never raised more than $5,000 for any previous campaign, and since his first victory had never faced a serious opponent. In 1982 a thirty-four-year-old Republican activist named Haley Barbour (later a big Washington lobbyist, chairman of the Republican National Committee, and governor of Mississippi) challenged Stennis. Ronald Reagan had swept Mississippi in 1980, Republicans had taken control of the Senate, and they were eager now to knock off vulnerable Democrats. They put the eighty-one-year-old Stennis in that category.

Stennis's friends among the old bulls in the Senate were nervous about what might happen. Russell Long of Louisiana and Lloyd Bentsen of Texas, who had both used Strother's services in the past, arranged for him to act as Stennis's campaign consultant in 1982. Strother realized that Barbour's campaign would try to convince Mississippians that Stennis was too old and frail to serve another term. Strother's plan was to undermine that argument with TV commercials that would feature testimonials from Stennis's colleagues and carefully made spots featuring the senator himself looking perfectly competent.

This would cost serious money, Strother told the senator when they met one day in his office in the Russell Senate Office Building. The senators' offices there were designed to be imposing—big rooms under ceilings that are seventeen feet high. Strother broke the news to Stennis that he needed to raise $2 million. How, the old man asked, could he do that?

Bentsen and Long had volunteered to raise some of the money, but Stennis would have to help. When Strother talked about this, he wrote later, Stennis "would just wring his hands. Finally, in desperation, I reminded the old senator that he was chairman of [the] Armed Services Committee [at the time he was the ranking Democrat, because Republicans had control—and he served separately on the appropriations subcommittee on defense] and had spent billions of dollars with the defense industry. What about LTV? I asked him. What about McDonnell Douglas [two giant defense contractors]?" In other words, Strother was telling Stennis, it was time to cash in some chits with the corporations that got rich on the Pentagon programs that Stennis had supported.

"Would that be proper?" Stennis asked.

Then he answered the question himself, addressing Strother the way he addressed most grown men, as sir: "I hold life and death over those companies. I don't think it would be proper for me to take money from them."

Personally, Strother agreed, but he told his client that this was "how all the other senators do it." His reassurance "did not salve his feeling that it was wrong," Strother remembered.

Stennis's question "has bothered me for years," Strother said twenty-five years later. "I'll never forget that conversation or the troubled look on his lined face. When I left his office he was looking at his folded hands on the table in his office that had once belonged to Harry Truman. It looked as though he was in prayer. I was very sad. I had just diminished something he held dear. It was obvious he thought I was telling him to sell his vote for campaign money."

The money was raised; the commercials were made and broadcast. Stennis thumped Barbour by nearly two to one. He served out his seventh term and retired in 1989, at eighty-seven.

CHAPTER 11

A MONEY MACHINE

As 1985 began, the directory of tenants at the L'Enfant Plaza office build-ing in southwest Washington changed. Schlossberg-Cassidy & Associates vanished, succeeded by Cassidy & Associates. Gerry Cassidy had arrived. In just a few years in the early 1980s, this tentative but ambitious striver had found his groove. He gained confidence, then stature.

"When I joined the firm in 1982," recalled James Fabiani, "Gerry was emerging." Fabiani saw the qualities that Cloherty had referred to when he told new clients to ask that Cassidy handle their business—the deter-mination, the willingness to do whatever was necessary to achieve the client's objective.

"Ken's bottom line," said Fabiani, "was giving clients good counsel, making them feel comfortable in Washington. But it wasn't going up to the Hill, twisting arms and pushing hard for clients." Cassidy understood that with a maximum effort, clients could achieve a big payoff—$20, $25, even $50 or more in earmarked appropriations for every dollar they paid to their lobbyist. University fund-raisers traditionally calculated that it cost a dollar to raise ten, Fabiani said. Cassidy could point to Tufts, or Boston College, or Columbia and Catholic universities, all of which had returns of forty to one or better on the money they had paid for the firm's lobbying services.

The Cassidy who was emerging in the early 1980s could make a mem-orable impression on others. One such was Terry Holcombe, Cloherty's pal from South America who had been the principal fund-raiser at Yale (his own alma mater) and then at Columbia at the time Columbia hired the firm. Cloherty thought Holcombe should be working for Cassidy &

Associates, and urged Cassidy to hire him. Cassidy invited him to Washington to see the operation.

Holcombe was tempted. He realized that Cassidy's employees were making three or four times what Holcombe made for similar work—in effect, raising money for universities. And he'd been impressed by Cassidy.

"He was a tough Irishman, very smart, very driven, and very focused," Holcombe said years later. "Normal people in that business situation would not have had the *cojones* to stick to the high price" of $10,000 a month originally demanded of Columbia when the firm was first trying to sign up the university. Holcombe thought a lobbying firm might have considered a prestigious institution like Columbia an impressive addition to its list of clients—might even have seen Columbia as a "loss leader," a client you could take at a reduced fee because of its value in marketing the firm's services to others. But Cassidy, he remembered, "made it clear that if you want to play with us you have to play by our rules."

So he traveled down to Washington for a conversation. "I was well met. Cassidy and I had a nice long conversation and a dinner at his house. . . . I ended up impressed, and particularly impressed with him. There's kind of a controlled energy in him. Not seething, but roiling away under the surface. You knew he was going to make things happen. . . . He was one of the most memorable and driven people I've ever met. He was extremely clear about his mission." But Holcombe decided that lobbying was not for him. He later returned to Yale and spent many years as its vice president for development, raising hundreds of millions of dollars.

Once Schlossberg was gone, Fabiani's importance to the firm grew quickly. Schlossberg had hired him and taught him a lot, Fabiani said, but he was soon drawn to Cassidy. "I learned an enormous amount from Gerry," he recalled—"how to get things done, how to stick to it, and be determined, and get creative, dig in and find legislative precedents and so on." He expected Cassidy and the firm to thrive—as they did.

Fabiani loved making things work: "I am anally compulsive about procedure and process," he said. "I'm an organizer. You won't find me in the top quarter of my class at Harvard or anything like that, but when it comes to practically organizing something, to get tasks done, I can do it."

When he first arrived at Schlossberg-Cassidy, Fabiani saw a need for those skills. Success at lobbying, he quickly realized, required attention to detail and follow-through. Winning the support of a member of Congress for a particular earmark, even if it was the chairman of the key subcommittee, did not automatically produce the earmark. Getting a line item into an appropriations bill required persistent attention to detail at every level of the complex legislative process. Often, the congressman and his staff had to be taught how to do it. Then the lobbyist had to stay in touch with the staff members assigned to getting the earmark through the Congress and into the hands of the intended recipient—aka the client.

Not long after he joined the firm, Fabiani recalled, "I went out and bought one of these big wipe-off boards. We had a very small conference room. I put it up on the wall. I put the names of the clients down one side, and across the top I put all of the steps that we needed to accomplish our goal, and at what time points they needed to be accomplished. Then we had the grid, the matrix." The matrix became one of the firm's basic tools. For years to come, the "matrix meeting" would be part of the weekly routine at Cassidy & Associates. Initially neither Schlossberg nor Cassidy had been enthusiastic about the matrix, Fabiani said, but Cassidy came to appreciate it. Eventually Cassidy chaired the firm's weekly matrix meetings, which allowed him to manage the firm by tracking its activities.

Fabiani's second large talent was for marketing—finding new clients. This soon became his primary responsibility for Cassidy & Associates, and he did it brilliantly. First he exploited the Cloherty model. If Cloherty could bring in numerous clients in return for 10 percent of the fees they paid, why couldn't others do the same? "You ought to be able to replicate this the way McDonald's replicates its restaurants," Fabiani remembered thinking. And he did just that—dozens, then scores, then hundreds of times. The first breakthrough came when Fabiani was able to persuade Frank Rose to become a "ten-percenter" for the firm.

Rose was a dynamo who had been the most successful president in the history of the University of Alabama in Tuscaloosa. He held the job from 1958 to 1969, and became nationally famous as a mediating figure when the University of Alabama was integrated by court order in 1963—the notorious occasion when Governor George Wallace "stood in the schoolhouse door" in a vain attempt to block the way of the university's first black students. Rose was a builder and a promoter. He created a new University of Alabama at Birmingham and took advantage of the federal space program's installation in nearby Huntsville to promote astrophysics at Alabama. He had often found ways to attract federal dollars to help his projects.

Fabiani and Rose met soon after Fabiani joined the firm, when he was working on a possible earmark to pay for a new medical library at Tufts. By that time Rose was semiretired and working as a consultant to Georgetown University and its medical school, which was also trying to get federal support for its medical library. Rose was in his sixties and suffering from lung cancer, which would kill him in 1991, but he was still energetic and ambitious, Fabiani said. He spent much of his time on a beautiful farm near Lexington, Kentucky. When Fabiani moved to the lobbying firm, he recalled, Rose made him a proposition: " 'Let me come over and have an office in your place, pay me a percentage and my expenses, give me some help staffing, and I'll get business for you.' That's how we began," Fabiani said.

Rose brought in a partner, Elvis Stahr, another former state university president (West Virginia and Indiana) and secretary of the Army under Robert S. McNamara in the Kennedy administration. Both Rose and Stahr enjoyed good reputations among their peers in higher education. Eventually, they lured three other former university presidents to help out. They became hugely successful ten-percenters for Cassidy & Associates.

Fabiani was awed by Rose's stature: "You went around the country with Frank Rose, there was not one university where we did not meet with the president. Not one." In less than a year, he and Rose visited twenty campuses and signed up nineteen new clients for Cassidy & Associates. "He would take me in the door [of the university president's office] and say . . . 'You've got to listen, these guys have something for you,' " Fabiani recounted. "Then he'd turn on my switch. I would do my thing [pitching the firm's services, emphasizing its record of winning earmarks for its clients]. I would say it costs $20,000 a month. Frank would say, 'It's worth every penny of it,' and you'd have a deal within a couple of weeks."

Eventually the firm had scores of these salesmen on its rolls—more, Fabiani acknowledged, than they could stay in touch with. But he did have at least seventy-five "that you could keep in contact with. . . . And we'd send out a message: Hey, there's going to be an energy bill next year, here's the five companies in your area that we think we might be able to do something for, here's why—we'd give them three bullets. Can any of you get us in the door? Please don't take us in the door at level four. Bring us in the door at level one or maybe level two. . . . Nine times out of ten you try to get to the CEO."

New clients required more lobbyists to "service" them, in the argot of Cassidy & Associates. In the early years after he took control, Cassidy preferred to hire aides from Capitol Hill who knew how bills got written and passed—worker bees without big reputations of their own, people whose heads could be turned by offers to instantly double their Hill salaries. When Cassidy began hiring them after 1985, the revolving door that car-

ried congressional staff assistants downtown to the offices of private lobbyists was still moving slowly and sporadically. Later it would spin at a
dizzying pace, but the first people Cassidy and Fabiani hired were pioneers of a kind, following a path first traversed by Fabiani and Frank
Godfrey.

One was Vincent Versage, a Hawaiian who had come to town to work
for Congressman, later Senator, Daniel K. Akaka. Versage had his own
relationship with Senator Inouye and a number of other important
Hawaiians. He was joined by George Ramonas, an aide to Senator Pete
Domenici, Republican of New Mexico, and a specialist on appropriations
work. Then came Jonathan Orloff, an aide to Senator Ted Kennedy. Then
Richard Pena, who had worked for Jim Wright, the majority leader of the
House at the time. Typically Cassidy nearly doubled their last congressional salary, and paid them handsome year-end bonuses besides. None of
them had come to Washington looking for money, but now they had
stumbled across it. No one complained.

Versage called this group, including Godfrey, the "shoe-leather lobbyists" who actually delivered the goods. They were often frustrated by
the grand promises Cloherty, Fabiani, and some of the ten-percenters
made to potential clients about what could be extracted for them from
Congress, feeling that the salesmen tended to overpromise. But they were
also very proud of their accomplishments.

Beginning in 1985, the business really took off. Two decades later
Fabiani still remembered the figures: total revenues of Schlossberg-
Cassidy in 1982 slightly exceeded $700,000. Five years later, in 1987, Cas-
sidy & Associates' revenue was $17.5 million. Most of the growth came
from clients found by the ten-percenters. How many companies can grow
their business by a multiple of twenty-five in five years? Exploiting Jean
Mayer's original idea and the talents of his new colleagues, Cassidy had
struck gold.

Costs had risen too—new salaries to pay, expenses for the consultants,
and, after 1986, rent on grand new offices at Metropolitan Square, an elegant office building constructed behind a preserved old Beaux Arts facade
on Fifteenth Street, just two blocks from the White House and one block
from the Treasury. The old quarters at L'Enfant Plaza had been crowded
and ordinary; that building was neither fashionable nor well located. It
seemed fitting that the firm's new home should be on the eleventh floor of
a newly developed office complex adjoining the famous old Willard Hotel,
also recently renovated to a sparkling new standard. The 1980s were a

boom time in downtown Washington real estate, part of a transformation of the capital city that had followed Ronald Reagan to town.

Until Schlossberg left the firm, Cassidy had always worked for or with others, but he had long been eager to take responsibility for his own fate. In 1975, when he was preparing to leave the nutrition committee staff with Schlossberg, he had one clear notion: "I never want to be in a job again where I can get fired." Now the only name on the door was his.

This change in Cassidy's status had several revealing consequences. The first reflected not just his new authority, but also the upward arc of the business. Everything was going well in 1985, and Cassidy's early approach to management helped explain why. First with Fabiani, then with others, he seemed intuitively to realize that he could get a great deal out of his employees if he gave them room to run and held them to high expectations. According to Fabiani, for example, Cassidy was delighted with the speedy expansion of the consultants' network, showed his gratitude both personally and financially, and stayed out of Fabiani's way—except to remind Fabiani persistently that he expected still more consultants and, always, more revenue. Make room, and keep the pressure on—this was a pattern that would recur again and again over the years, as Cassidy became seriously rich. He had a knack for exploiting the talents of the people around him.

Being the boss also allowed Cassidy to act out a lifelong ambition to *be* somebody. Philip Costanzo, his best friend from high school, thought Cassidy's mother encouraged this: "His mom wanted him to be famous on some level." When they were teenagers Costanzo jokingly called him "the prince." He said he could see Cassidy practicing to be somebody important when he was still in his twenties, and recalled several visits with Gerry and Loretta to a French restaurant in Washington when Cassidy worked for the nutrition committee: "There were lots of airs. Gerry always treated the waiter as if he deserved to be really well served. . . . He would always send back some dish that didn't meet his specifications." Schlossberg, of course, had seen this trait too.

Costanzo had seen Cassidy's temper when they were in high school. He thought Cassidy was often "fighting demons," presumably from his early childhood. People who have known Cassidy at every stage of his life remember his tantrums. In the offices of Cassidy & Associates in the mid-1980s they became legendary. He warned some of the people he hired then that he could be a hard man to work for. "I can be very volatile," he told Elliott Fiedler, hired in 1987. Cassidy & Associates was essentially a male institution—Versage compared it to a football team. Cassidy was the coach.

But one woman played an important part in the new firm: Carol Casey. Cassidy had befriended this bright and engaging Irish-American political operative in 1973, during Cassidy's brief stint at the Democratic National Committee, where Casey also worked. She had been the first of his friends to learn that Robert Strauss and Barbara Mikulski had fired Cassidy. Later Casey worked as a researcher for the Congressional Research Service at the Library of Congress. Then she worked on the Ted Kennedy presidential campaign in 1980, and on the Gary Hart campaign four years later. In the fall of 1984, not long before Reagan beat Mondale, she and Cassidy had lunch in Washington and he offered her the job of research director, a new position.

Cassidy needed Casey's skills because the firm had just lost its best writer and researcher—Schlossberg. Research and writing had become important to the earmark business. Casey did this work well. Over the years she held several different jobs in the firm. She was personally close to Cassidy and Loretta.

In the office, Casey often bore the brunt of Cassidy's temper. The tantrums could reduce her to tears, but Casey concluded that "I was sort of a release valve. He would call me in and let off steam." After a tantrum he would apologize. "He'd explain, How could you be upset about any of that? You know I didn't mean it. I really think he went into a blackout during those rages, he really didn't know what he was doing. . . . He really is a good and decent man. His goal in life was not to make my life miserable, or anyone else's."

There were always some employees in the firm whom Cassidy never yelled at. "Gerry would test you," said Scott Giles, a Hill aide hired into the firm in 1986. "Part of what you got was how you responded. Gerry's a fighter, and the thing he respects more than anything else is another fighter. . . . If you stand up, he respects you," Giles said.

Fabiani's relationship with Cassidy was particularly complicated. They found themselves colleagues in a Washington lobbying firm that was doing well by influencing the legislative process and the decisions of the executive branch of government, but their association was essentially a business proposition. They had no political affinity, as Schlossberg and Cassidy had; they shared no personal history and had no common friends. Cassidy sometimes yelled at Fabiani, who told friends that Cassidy could remind him of his own father. Their relations were never easy, but the two men shared a powerful mutual interest. Beginning in the mid-1980s, both were making piles of money that neither could have earned without the help of the other.

The two men were eight years apart in age and came from different worlds. Cassidy was always the tough Irishman, the football player, blunt and temperamental. His inability to trust others made easy banter with colleagues difficult. He cultivated a certain remoteness from the people around him. He enjoyed being firm, decisive, and demanding. His custom-tailored suits, the chauffeur who drove him around town, the fancy big house in McLean that he and Loretta bought for $750,000 in 1985 all contributed to the somebody Cassidy was trying to be, and all helped separate him from his employees.

Fabiani was boyish and more open. People around him quickly realized that he was bright, anxious, and eager to please. He was also famously indecisive, sometimes struggling openly with choices that struck his colleagues as easy or insignificant. He liked organizing systems and procedures that simplified decision making.

Fabiani grew up in comfort, a generation removed from the sorts of struggles that Cassidy had known as a boy. Dante Fabiani, his father, was the son of a gardener and the first in his family to go to college—Tri-State University in Angola, Indiana. He was, the son reported proudly, "the first Italian-American to be CEO of a Fortune 100 company." That was the Crane Company, manufacturer of plumbing fixtures. Dante Fabiani could send his son (who had the brains needed) to Phillips Andover Academy and Harvard. Fabiani initially thought he wanted a career in education. He worked as a dean at Deerfield Academy, a snooty Massachusetts prep school, before Conte brought him to Washington to be minority staff director of the House Appropriations Subcommittee on Labor, Health, Education, and Welfare.

When he first joined the firm it was all new to Fabiani, and he was feeling his way. He remembered traveling with Cassidy to Indiana to try to sign up the University of Indiana as a client. They flew into Indianapolis at night and found a Best Western motel. Fabiani volunteered to go in and register. When he returned to their rented car he told Cassidy, "We're in room 42. And Gerry said, 'What do you mean we're in room 42?' And I said, 'You know, there's two beds.' And Gerry said, 'No, we're not sharing a room in a Best Western in Indianapolis, Indiana.' " Telling this story years later, Fabiani said: "I needed some coaching on what you spent money on."

It was also a story about the distribution of power in their relationship. No one who worked with them in the late 1980s, when they were the principal figures in the firm, could have the slightest doubt about the pecking order, including Fabiani. "In the early years," he recalled, "it was Gerry leading the business and my finding a way to carry out those ideas. I got good at that, and Gerry had good or great ideas. Where I think I became valuable was [creating] those structures, particularly marketing, which generated huge amounts of revenue."

Cassidy clearly understood Fabiani's importance to the business. He was paid extremely well—more than $1 million a year in salary and bonus in the fattest years of the late 1980s. In 1985 he too got a chauffeur to drive his company car. But there was no question about his status. Soon after Schlossberg left, Fabiani asked Cassidy about the possibility of adding the name Fabiani to the firm's. Cassidy dismissed the suggestion without real discussion. It was never mentioned again.

Fabiani must have been disappointed, but he was not discouraged. Like Cassidy, he was making more money than had ever seemed possible before they found themselves making it, exploiting a business model that remained exclusively their own. They were in Washington, trying to influence government decisions to improve the fortunes of their clients, but neither man thought he was "in politics." They were in *business*, in what was becoming a go-go era for American entrepreneurs of many kinds. They rode a wave that created a new class of wealthy Americans and the best eighteen years (1982–2000) ever experienced by American stock markets. They were in Washington when Washington was becoming a new American fat city.

The Cassidy & Associates business model became a template—a way to package and sell a project that would maximize the chances of winning an earmarked appropriation for it. In the years when the firm enjoyed what was virtually a corner on the earmark market for universities and hospitals, the method was honed and polished. Its success did not depend on political contributions or free dinners or trips to the NCAA Final Four basketball tournament, though all of those were involved at times. The heart of the Cassidy & Associates method was to support original ideas with thorough, careful, and elegant presentation.

The Cassidy lobbyists who executed the template were proud of their work and of what it accomplished. Scott Giles was typical. When first approached about a job at Cassidy, Giles had worked for four years for Congressman Frank Horton, a moderate Republican from upstate New York. Giles's first contact with the firm came when Fabiani and Versage came to see him in Horton's office to lobby for an earmark for the

Rochester Institute of Technology in Horton's district. Giles had come to work for Horton originally to take a break from graduate school. His intention had been to make a career in higher education, so Cassidy & Associates appealed to him. "It was my sense that they were the only lobbying firm around that had an interest in higher education," Giles said. He accepted the job in 1986, when he was twenty-five.

The key to the firm's success, Giles thought, was not its relationships with members of Congress, though they helped, but "their system, beginning with the 'resource inventory.' " Once a new client had been signed up, "we'd go through a very in-depth process to try to inventory their intellectual and political strengths—and weaknesses." Jean Mayer of Tufts, the godfather of this system, knew when he started that he wanted to build a human nutrition research center, but a more typical new client did not have a specific objective in mind. In these cases, Cassidy lobbyists helped them come up with an idea.

They usually began with three or four days of interviewing on the campus, Giles said. First came a conversation with the school president. Giles would ask the president to choose someone from his administration or faculty as Giles's helper. Giles tried to win that person's enthusiasm by promising to "teach him more about his own campus than anyone else on it knew."

The point was to learn everything that might bear on the school's chances of winning an earmark. In some cases this meant finding something the client was doing extremely well that might deserve federal support. In other cases the key might be a weakness—something the school did not have and could use. Weaknesses often helped mobilize the community where the school was located by identifying a potential new capability that would be good for the school and for its hometown or region. "A weakness could be as useful as a strength." The local congressmen often responded to proposals for new research facilities that could encourage economic development, for example.

"We did exhaustive work on the institution," Giles said. Sometimes their findings embarrassed the school or its administration. "We wanted to learn who the star faculty members were, what government advisory boards they were on. We looked at the list of alumni for members of Congress or staff on the Hill."

The purpose of the inventory and the many conversations that contributed to it was to come up with a "case statement" or "prospectus" for a specific project. This was supposed to be an eloquent argument: why the project was desirable, what benefits it would bring to the school, its community, its state, or the entire country. It was meant to give the hometown member of Congress "a high level of confidence that the project was well conceived" and also a document the member could use to promote the project with his colleagues.

The template called for the creation of "a local advisory committee for the project," Giles said. "It would include interested and affected parties. If it were a new treatment facility for some disease, you might look for a patients' advocate in that disease. Local political leaders too. You'd want a group that would endorse the project as a good thing for the community and its region, people who could come to Washington and help lobby."

"Then," Giles recounted, "we'd work out a political strategy. We'd train the people we were going to use in Washington on how to lobby, how to talk about the project—people from the institution and from the advisory committee."

The lobbyist's role was "procedural," he said. "Back then [in the mid-1980s], if you weren't a member of [an] appropriations [committee] or a senior member of Congress, you probably didn't have a staffer who understood the fine details of the appropriations process. So we explained it. Members are so overwhelmed by what's on their plates, and staff too, that they often need help to deal with new stuff, stuff they are not familiar with. The original Cassidy model was designed to address this need. In effect, we would act as staff for a project that we were pushing."

The first meeting with the member of the House or Senate who represented the state or district where the institution seeking the earmark was located was an important moment. The lobbyists coached the people who would speak for the project on how best to make their pitch. In the meeting the lobbyist often remained silent. Sometimes, Giles said, the member was unfamiliar with earmarks and would ask, Has something like this been done before? The lobbyist had to be ready with a list of precedents—similar projects approved for other schools or institutions.

"We'd give them the case statement, in fact or in effect," Giles said. The lobbyists had created a folder to hand to the staff assistant whom the member designated to deal with the matter once he had heard the pitch; the folder would contain "draft copies of all the documents the staff would need to work the project from beginning to end." This could include a draft letter requesting money for the project to the relevant appropriations subcommittee; a draft of a possible report that could accompany a bill appropriating money for the project; an executive summary of the case statement; and drafts of statements supporting the project that the member could make on the floor of the House or Senate or insert into the *Congressional Record.*

Often, all subsequent business on the earmark would be done with the staff member designated to work on it. Giles and his colleagues offered to help that person in any way they could. "We'd offer to be the support staff. . . . That's how we built a staff relationship." In other words, every earmark produced a new set of earmark-aware staff members who could play the game again someday.

Cassidy lobbyists prided themselves on finding legislative vehicles, as they are called in Congress, that could carry the weight of their earmark projects. This meant identifying laws on the books that might be exploited as authorizing legislation that permitted a certain appropriation, or finding programs created by new bills that might create possibilities for future earmark requests.

Fabiani remembered one of his early successes: "I found a nuclear medicine account in the Department of Energy, and all of a sudden I could do an appropriation for Children's Hospital in Pittsburgh, $15 million in the energy appropriations bill." This paid for two projects, a new entrance to a trauma center and facilities for a bone marrow research program. "You got creative about where the money came from. If you could convince a member that this is going to be easier than doing it in the Labor, Health and Human Services appropriations bill [the standard vehicle for grants to hospitals], and they try it and sonofagun they're successful at it, then you've got another bucket, if you will, that carries you. We were just dogged about it."

Giles also remembered these scouting expeditions: "We read the *Federal Register* [where the government reports proposed or final changes in federal regulations of all kinds] and the *Congressional Record* [which provides a transcript of all debates on the House and Senate floors, plus documents inserted into the *Record* by members] on the lookout for new government interests, programs, and such" that Cassidy clients might try to exploit. The young lobbyists also studied every year's appropriations bills and reports to try to identify every earmark, and to learn what was being funded. "We tried to learn as much about those bills as the people who wrote them." He remembered once identifying rising government interest in genomics—the study of genomes, or the gene sequences of living things—long before the Human Genome Project made this a famous topic. "We actually got some DOE [Department of Energy] and NIH [National Institutes of Health] money for clients for genome research."

Cassidy's business model also included a standard pattern of remuneration. "Ideally," Giles recalled, "you'd sign up a new client in late spring, then work up a concrete proposal by about August, agree on its details by November, do all the necessary paperwork, meet with the member in December or January, and be ready to meet the February-March deadline for members to file appropriations requests with the committee. . . . The second year was devoted to full, aggressive advocacy with the support of the involved member and his colleagues from the same state, region, whatever. We'd look for local editorials to support the project. We'd try to arrange meetings with appropriators [members of the appropriations committees] to explain the project to them. In the third year, the appropriation would be made."

This was the ideal sequence, and could easily be complicated or thrown off by special circumstances. And some big projects were covered by multiple appropriations over a period of years. The great thing was, the client signed up for a fixed fee, usually $10,000 to $20,000 every month for the duration of the effort. A retainer of $20,000 a month means a guaranteed annual income for the firm of $240,000, and there were many of them.

Cassidy was making this money as an intermediary between institutions seeking government grants and Congress, which could make the grants. He found a way to put a toll booth on a very lucrative highway. This has always been one of the best ways to make money in a capitalist economy—every banker in history has understood it.

Not that the work was simple. Cassidy and his associates had to build the highway themselves, then persuade potential clients that they could use it. They were good at both parts of that equation. The cash register kept chiming.

But Cassidy's success offended some, who saw earmarks as a perversion of the public policy process. Among the offended were two brothers from St. Louis, William and John Danforth. In June 1986, just as the reconstituted firm called Cassidy & Associates was breaking into the economic stratosphere, the Danforth brothers collaborated on what became a legislative maneuver that might have ended academic earmarking forever.

CHAPTER 12

DISASTER AVERTED

Ronald Reagan twice campaigned for the White House with promises to control federal expenditures—"guv'ment spending," Reagan called it. His fiery young director of the Office of Management and Budget, David Stockman, considered this the Lord's work, undertook it with determination, and initially achieved considerable success. Ironically, Stockman's successes were good for the earmarking business. By cutting "discretionary domestic spending"—money spent on domestic programs and projects that were discretionary, not the "entitlement" programs like Social Security whose benefits are paid automatically under the law—the administration actually encouraged those who sought special, earmarked appropriations for themselves. When less federal money was available in general, it became more attractive to seek federal money in particular, through earmarks.

Earmarking advertised and promoted itself. The more it happened, the more suppliants appeared who wanted it to happen again—for them. So when universities and hospitals saw that Cassidy's clients were winning direct grants, they naturally wondered how they could acquire such grants themselves. This was the way Cassidy got more clients. It was also the way, over time, competitors to Cassidy came into the marketplace. The realization that the government might fund individual projects like the Columbia University chemistry laboratories spread through the academic community like another sort of great awakening.

The argument ignited by the earmarks for Columbia and Catholic University did not subside. The president of the Association of American Universities, Robert Rosenzweig, led a continuing campaign against academic earmarks. The AAU, which represented about fifty leading research universities, both public and private, included all of the big schools that received most of the federal support for research—the "haves" that Cassidy liked to complain about, while defending his right to represent the "have-nots" that were trying to improve themselves.

William Danforth was a leading figure in the AAU in the 1980s. A cardiologist by training, he had long been an administrator at Washington University in St. Louis, and became its chancellor in 1971. He and his younger brother John were heirs to the Ralston Purina fortune—to the manor born. John was an Episcopal minister who became a politician—first attorney general of Missouri, then in 1977, United States senator. According to both brothers, William Danforth prevailed on John to make an issue of earmarking on the Senate floor. On June 5, 1986, Senator Danforth did just that.

The Senate was debating an "urgent supplemental appropriations act," one of the many mystifying names for legislation used in Congress that can confuse ordinary citizens. An "emergency supplemental" is supposed to be a bill to spend money for purposes beyond those covered in the regular annual appropriations bills, theoretically for pressing and unexpected purposes. In fact, both the executive branch and Congress periodically use emergency supplementals as expedient ways to appropriate money in a hurry, sometimes for controversial purposes that would run into opposition if handled in the conventional manner. Emergency supplemental bills often reach the floor of the House and Senate on a hurry-up, take-it-or-leave-it basis; amendments are unusual.

It was nearly midnight on that June 5 when Senator Danforth rose to propose an amendment. He noted that "the bill before us earmarks $80.6 million in research spending to 10 universities," and the amendment he proposed would eliminate all of that money. He announced that twenty-one other senators had signed on as co-sponsors of his proposal.

The ten earmarks had an unusual legislative history. They had initially been included in a defense appropriations bill passed at the end of 1985, but deviously. The bill itself did not specifically itemize the ten projects, but they were mentioned in the "report" accompanying the bill, a nonbinding document explaining the intentions of the appropriations committees that approved the legislation. "Report language" meant to instruct executive branch agencies on how to spend appropriated money had become a favored method for getting earmarks to their intended recipients. Usually the relevant executive branch agency did what the report language suggested rather than offend Congress, but in this case the Pentagon demurred. None of these projects had been properly studied or authorized, the Defense Department said, and it refused to spend the money as directed.

The Pentagon's reluctance prompted the sponsors of the earmarks—among them Speaker O'Neill and Bob Dole, the majority leader of the Senate—to include them explicitly in the supplemental appropriations bill that the Senate was considering on that June day. The Pentagon's stance had also emboldened the AAU, the National Science Foundation, the National Association of State Universities and Land Grant Colleges, and other critics of earmarking to try to make a stand in opposition to these earmarks. This led to William Danforth's request to his brother to propose what became known as the Danforth Amendment, knocking out all the earmarks.

"The issue before the Senate," Danforth said, "is whether research money to be spent for university research should be earmarked by the Appropriations Committee frankly on the basis of political logrolling . . . or, rather, whether that money should be spent according to a competition process . . . on the basis of merit." He noted that "three of the projects [covered by the earmarks] were never submitted to the Department of Defense," and "in the case of four projects, the Department of Defense, after analyzing the proposals, found that the universities in question were without the research capabilities to justify funding. . . . And in the case of four of the projects, they were for construction for general purpose research buildings. The Department of Defense has a policy against spending such research money for general purpose construction."

Danforth noted the stern opposition to earmarks from the White House and the Department of Defense. He submitted letters from various academic and scientific organizations opposing the ten earmarks.

One, from Frank Press, president of the National Academy of Sciences, accurately summarized the situation. Press noted the huge backlog of unmet needs to rebuild the country's "obsolete research facilities" and the fact that "the Federal government now has virtually no program for funding research facilities." The ten earmarks in the bill "reflect the pressure arising from a widespread need to modernize . . . research facilities at universities and colleges throughout the nation," but they were ill-considered. Congress should support new programs "to provide support for academic facilities that are judged to be scientifically excellent," Press wrote. But he criticized the approach taken in this instance: "Efforts by a few academic institutions and their representatives in Congress to bypass merit review in order to meet their individual needs harbor the potential for enormous damage to the nation's research enterprise. Approval of such earmarking creates incentives for other institutions to seek similar treatment from the Congress."

Senator Lloyd Bentsen of Texas spoke in favor of Danforth's amendment, observing that the earmarks it sought to eliminate were part of "a growing trend toward congressional earmarking of funds for home-State institutions" that was quickly growing out of control. The evaluation of research projects, particularly for purposes of enhancing national defense, should not be left to "535 members of Congress," whom Bentsen described as "a cumbersome and ill-equipped group to make such evaluations."

Jeff Bingaman of New Mexico saw more at stake than just these ten earmarks: "I believe that we face a crossroads. Over the past few years, we have at an accelerating pace been moving toward a log-rolling or pork-barrel approach in the allocation of research funds. I believe that this practice has already damaged the conduct of scientific research, and will ultimately damage the overall scientific and technical capabilities of the Nation. It should be stopped."

Pennsylvania's John Heinz was one of several supporters of the Danforth Amendment to comment on a passage in the report of the appropriations committee that had—sheepishly, it seemed—recommended the earmarks. "It is clear that the committee itself is aware of how its action in earmarking research funds violates all common sense," Heinz said. "The report states that the committee will, and I quote, 'not consider any future requests to earmark DOD research and development funds for specific research projects that have not gone through competitive, merit review processes without specific authorization.' If you detect a guilty tone in that statement, you are on the mark."

It was after midnight, but the defenders of the earmarks had lots to say as well. Dennis DeConcini, a Democrat from Arizona—Arizona State University had a $25 million earmark in the emergency supplemental—made an argument with broad appeal. He held up a map showing that more than half of all federal support for research went to just sixteen states, year after year—all on the East Coast, in the northern tier of the Midwest, or in California. The map, said DeConcini, "shows beyond a shadow of a doubt that unless your university is on the east or west coast, you are picking up the crumbs, if anything, of any Federal research dollars. . . . The heartland of America, from Iowa down to Louisiana and westward to the Arizona-Nevada western border, has been virtually shut off. . . . No one can tell me that the northeastern universities, the elite schools, have cornered the market on research and development. They are good schools, but they also control the peer review. No one can convince me that Iowa, Arizona, Louisiana, the Dakotas, and many more cannot be part of this process. I do not know how else to get them in as part of this process."

DeConcini also noted that according to the National Science Foundation, half of all federal aid to universities for research and development went to sixteen elite schools. "That amounted to $4.2 billion in fiscal year 1984, spread out over sixteen universities." And the biggest recipients were schools that had been allocated major government research institutions years earlier (mostly in the early years of the Cold War) on a noncompetitive basis. He listed their estimated budgets for the 1984 fiscal year: "The University of California Lawrence Laboratories, $690 million; the University of California, Los Alamos Scientific Lab, $424 million; Cal Tech Jet Propulsion Lab, $554 million; Stanford Linear Accelerator Laboratory, $117 million; MIT Lincoln Laboratory, $255 million; Princeton Plasma Physics Laboratory, $132 million; and Brookhaven National Laboratory, $173 million." The government spent this money without any competition or peer review, DeConcini noted.

Alfonse D'Amato of New York, a Republican notoriously proud of his ability to bring federal bacon home to his state, had two earmarks in the supplemental bill: $12 million for Syracuse University and $11.1 million for the Rochester Institute of Technology (a Cassidy client). Speaking against the amendment, D'Amato sought to clarify a fact that Danforth and his allies in the debate had obfuscated: the contested earmarks that Danforth repeatedly described as "research money" in most cases did not fund research, but paid for new facilities in which future research could be conducted. There was no way for any American university to compete for government funds to build research facilities, because "there have been no funds whatsoever set aside for this," D'Amato accurately noted. There could be no "peer review" to allow independent experts to decide the best way to allocate federal dollars, because there was no federal program that provided such money.

Iowa's Tom Harkin, a Democrat, noted that when the Pentagon allocated money for defense-related research at universities, "there is no 'peer review' in the Department of Defense at all." Pentagon officials evaluated different proposals, but no outside experts or peers were involved. "These projects do not go out among a bunch of universities to decide which is best. It is done only within the confines of Department of Defense."

One of the most colorful contributions to the debate came from an old bull, Senator Russell Long of Louisiana. Long, the son of Huey Long, the Kingfish, was first elected to the Senate in 1948; in 1986 he was the ranking Democrat on the Senate Finance Committee. Long was famous for his aphorisms, of which the most famous perhaps was his definition of tax reform: "Don't tax me, don't tax thee, tax that fellow behind the tree." In opposing Danforth, Long spoke for senatorial prerogatives.

"When did we agree," he asked, "that the peers would cut the melon or decide who gets this money? . . . Am I to understand that this is a situation, which is certainly without my knowledge, where Congress said that we are not going to have any say about who gets this money? Are we going to have some peers decide who gets the money? I have been around here for a while. I do not recall that I ever agreed to that. . . .

"The question then is, how do you get to be one of the peers? The answer is, you do not. You just stay where you are. I do not know of anything in here for Louisiana [any earmark for a Louisiana university], and I am not talking about taking anything for Louisiana. But if Louisiana is going to get something, I would rather depend on my colleague on the Appropriations Committee than on one of those peers."

Lowell Weicker of Connecticut, a liberal Republican, echoed Long. To say that the existence of peer review means individual senators cannot "make a case for circumstances within their state, then there is not much point in having an appropriations committee or indeed to act as a U.S. Senator."

Mark Hatfield of Oregon, another liberal Republican, who was the chairman of the appropriations committee that recommended the earmarks, also spoke about senators' authority to spend the government's money. He acknowledged that the earmarks had been made without respecting the ordinary legislative process. "We circumvented the process because we exercised a legislative prerogative. Now you begin to abdicate in one area the legislative prerogative to establish priorities or to establish earmarking, and we have set a precedent." In other words, senators should guard their prerogatives, not squander or surrender them.

Alaska's Ted Stevens, then a veteran of sixteen years on the Appropriations Committee and a gleeful dispenser of federal largesse, first of all to Alaska, made a mischievous contribution to the debate in the form of a list. "Just in case you have not read the list," Stevens said, tweaking his colleagues when he knew that few if any of them had seen such an enumeration, "let me read the list to you" of the "colleges and universities that have been given non-peer-review moneys"—earmarks—in other appropriations bills just in the course of the previous two-year session of Congress, 1983–84:

"Baylor, Boston College,* Boston University,* California South University, Catholic University.* the College of American Samoa, the College of Micronesia, Columbia University,* Florida State University, Gallaudet, Hampshire College, Iowa University, Iowa State, Massachusetts Institute of Technology, Mississippi State, New York University, North Dakota State, Oregon Health Sciences, Oregon State, Pennsylvania State, Purdue University, St. Paul Vocational Technical Institute, Seattle Community Central College, State University of New York, Texas Tech,* Tufts,* University of California at Davis, University of California at Los Angeles, University of Connecticut, University of the District of Columbia, University of Hawaii,* University of Missouri, University of New Hampshire, University of Oregon, University of Rochester, and West Virginia University.*

In other words, Stevens was telling his colleagues, this particular horse had long since fled the barn, regardless of Danforth's high-minded—or sanctimonious, depending on your point of view—effort to now slam the barn door shut.

But shortly after one o'clock on the morning of June 7, 1986, those who cast themselves as the high-minded prevailed. Senator Weicker moved to "table," or kill, the Danforth Amendment, but his motion failed by a vote of 58–40. The Senate then approved the amendment to excise the ten earmarks from the supplemental appropriation bill by acclamation.

Years later, Gerald Cassidy said Danforth's maneuver "was a total surprise." That is probably a faulty memory, since Danforth had been signaling his intentions for several weeks. However, the vote was certainly a shock to Cassidy and his troops, and they quickly grasped its import. Danforth and his allies had cast the issue as a matter of principle that went far beyond the ten earmarks in question. They were trying to kill off earmarks for universities completely.

"This was a great moment of truth, a turning point for the appropriations business," recalled Jonathan Orloff, the former aide to Senator Kennedy who had recently joined Cassidy & Associates. Only two of the earmarks the Senate had removed were to go to Cassidy clients (Rochester

* A Schlossberg-Cassidy client.

Institute of Technology and Arizona State University), but the firm's very lifeblood was suddenly at risk.

Lobbyists working with Cassidy at the time remembered the urgency that suddenly took hold of the office. "There was a scurry," James Fabiani said. The immediate goals were to articulate the case for earmarks persuasively, then contact members to be sure they knew the significance of Danforth's maneuver and the effect it could have on members and their constituents, especially earmark-seeking institutions.

To argue the case, Carol Casey assembled a briefing book and made multiple copies that were bound in black three-ring binders. "Most of it had been prepared already in the event that this came up at some point," Cassidy remembered. "It was put together from materials we had already organized; we were able to get it to people very quickly."

The notebook included direct, not always polite, rebuttals to the arguments advanced in the debate by Danforth and his allies, starting with Danforth's definition of the issue at stake—"Whether the Appropriations Committee should earmark research money to certain specified universities." No, Casey wrote, "the amendment in question did not provide funds for research projects; it provided funds for facilities and equipment."

The book quoted Senator Heinz asking in the debate how he could go home to Pennsylvania and explain to universities there that federal money was now being handed out "not on the basis of quality, but on the basis of senatorial committee assignments," meaning to projects in the states of members of appropriations.

The briefing book asked in turn how Heinz would advise the two senators from Maryland "to explain to the University of Maryland" that $103 million for a new defense software institute had gone to Carnegie Mellon University in Pittsburgh despite the fact that Maryland's proposal "ranked first in the merit competition" conducted by the Pentagon. Carnegie Mellon had prevailed on Heinz and a bevy of outside lobbyists to influence that decision, and Heinz had personally lobbied for it.

The Cassidy briefing book was a shrewd political document. It argued the case that the disputed earmarks would be used to build first-class research facilities, which in turn could attract the first-class scientists who would win peer-reviewed competitions for research funds. The loose-leaf binder included eloquent testimony to this effect from John Silber. Just a year earlier, Silber testified to a House committee on the earmark dispute. He noted that the National Science Foundation Act of 1950, which established the system of federal support for research, explicitly directed the new National Science Foundation to "strengthen research and education in the sciences . . . throughout the United States, and to avoid undue concentration of such research and education."

But as the system had evolved, support went to a relative handful of privileged institutions, leaving most American universities on the sidelines. Silber called the beneficiaries "the haves," and said they "constitute an informal cartel." The only way to break the cartel would be for Congress to "spend funds to establish additional [scientific research] centers, or to upgrade the quality of existing centers," Silber said. "Obviously, such facilities attract outstanding research scientists." He had plans to build one at Boston University—with money from earmarks.

The briefing book contained figures showing how a small number of institutions received most of the peer-reviewed grants to universities for research—twenty schools got 56 percent of the money in 1985, for example. The book contained maps showing the sixteen states where the twenty schools were located. Many of the recipient schools were home to the federally financed research laboratories that Senator DeConcini had named in the first debate on the Danforth Amendment, from the Lawrence Labs at Berkeley to the Lincoln Lab at MIT. One page of the book enumerated the federal research grants given in 1985 to "Historically Black Colleges and Universities"—$3.08 million, or "less than three tenths of one percent" of government funding for research allocated by the peer review system of the National Science Foundation.

"We put together the book as quickly as possible, made individual copies of it," Cassidy recalled two decades later. "We started off with phone calls and asked for meetings. We probably met with at least two dozen senators on the issue. I would bet we met . . . sixty or more senators and staff. We also went after the AAU [Association of American Universities] schools that we thought were weak on the issue. There were a lot of members of AAU then, and now, who are really just honored to be in the company of the elite. If you could explain to them that it was doing them no particular good, and that their interest was in getting their fair share, you could move them on the issue. . . . Some wrote letters, some made private phone calls to their members. They weren't willing to go on the record. . . . Universities all have trustees, mobilizing them was very helpful too. And then reminding members what they had got from the committees was one of the important things. We just researched a period of four or five years to show them what they had gotten through appropriations—was that something they were interested in giving up?"

"What they had gotten through appropriations" was, of course, money for their home states and districts—what the cynics called pork.

The ability to direct federal spending to favored targets and reap the political benefits that often ensued was the key prerogative to which Senator Hatfield referred in the debate. Congress' power to decide where the money went was also enshrined in the Constitution (Article I, Section 9, Clause 7): "No money shall be drawn from the treasury, but in consequence of appropriations made by law."

Fabiani spoke of the importance of "mobilizing our friends on the Hill," including the members of both houses who had helped Cassidy clients win earmarks. One was Ted Kennedy. Orloff spoke to him about helping persuade colleagues to support earmarking. "He had an abiding interest in helping universities," Orloff said—including Boston's Northeastern University, which had a $13.5 million earmark in the disputed supplemental appropriations bill. Kennedy called half a dozen senators looking for votes against the Danforth Amendment, Orloff said.

The Danforth Amendment altered the Senate version of the supplemental spending bill, but the House of Representatives still had a voice in the matter. Its first version of the legislation was different, providing just two earmarks; the differences would have to be worked out in a conference committee, the traditional congressional device for reconciling the bills passed by both houses. Ultimately, both houses must agree on the same version of a bill. The conference committee, composed of members of the House and Senate appropriations committees, became the next target for the earmarkers' lobbying campaign.

It proved to be a soft target. Speaker O'Neill had a personal interest in the $13.5 million earmark for Northeastern University "for engineering research and related purposes"; Senator Dole, the Republican leader, was similarly eager to direct money to two Kansas institutions, Wichita State and Kansas University. Though the Senate had voted against the ten earmarks Danforth had targeted, the Senate appropriators on the conference committee remained sympathetic to them, and agreed to a "compromise" version of the supplemental bill that included nine of the ten. This may look odd—much of the way Congress operates looks odd—but there was (and is) no rule against conference committees' adding provisions that were not in the version of either House. The nine-earmark version went back before the Senate on June 26, 1986.

Danforth began this debate by noting what had happened in the previous three weeks: "The Senate's position was, 'Do not earmark for university research.' The House position was, 'Earmark two projects.' The conferees came back and said, 'We will earmark nine projects for specific spending for university research.' " He continued to insist, inaccurately, that all the money was intended for research.

Now, Danforth said, the Senate had to decide. Would it "stick by its guns? Is the Senate going to stick by the principle which we established on the night of June 5 . . . that research money should be spent according to merit, not according to politics?"

Danforth knew who his enemy was: "There is a lobbyist in town named Mr. Cassidy," he told his colleagues. "This Mr. Cassidy goes around to colleges and universities and says, 'Pay me $2,000 a month for a minimum of two years and I will help you to get government grants.' . . . It is just plain wrong for colleges to be bellying up to the trough of the federal government. If they want research grants to do research for our government, it should be on the basis of their competence and their ability, not on hiring a lobbyist and getting into the pork barrel."

Universities had been transformed, Danforth said, "into organizations that apply to lobbyists, pay lobbyists, lobby the Congress, just like anything else. I think that is wrong."

Cassidy was shocked by the mention of his name. (He was probably also offended by Danforth's unilateral reduction in his fees; no Cassidy client paid as little as $2,000 a month.) But he was also hopeful that senators on his side of the argument were going to prevail.

A succession of senators stood up to defend the earmarks. At least four of them used arguments right out of the Cassidy & Associates briefing book. One was DeConcini of Arizona, who said that the ten earmarks "are not proposals for some kind of research. [In fact several were for research, but most were not.] They are [for] the facilities to do the studying and the research. . . . Developing university research facilities is fundamental to assuring our continued economic vitality and national security. It is our responsibility as Senators to support through appropriations, when necessary, efforts directed toward those goals. There is nothing sinister or wrong about this."

Howell Heflin, an Alabama Democrat, D'Amato, and Kennedy also drew heavily on the Cassidy briefing book.

Said Kennedy: "The issue before the Senate is whether new funds should be specifically appropriated for the construction of research facilities and the purchase of research equipment to academic institutions of established reputation who seek to become competitors for research money in a field dominated by a select group of universities that seek to maintain their privileged position." Kennedy quoted statistics from the

Cassidy book: "In 1985, fifty-six percent of all Federal research funds went to only twenty universities."

(Carol Casey said later: "We provided talking points to a number of people on the Hill, and some of them, as they sometimes do, followed them verbatim. That was their choice.")

Cassidy's efforts were rewarded in a different way by Bob Dole, who told the Senate: "Only a small segment of the academic and scientific community opposes the earmarking of funds. Just this morning I received a telephone call from Dr. Jean Mayer, the president of Tufts University. He firmly believes that Congress has every right to direct where the research money that it appropriates goes. Further, he described the peer review process as an 'old boys network' that feels threatened every time something new happens."

Dole also quoted a letter that the president of Northwestern University, in Evanston, Illinois, had written to Senator Paul Simon, an Illinois Democrat, noting that the federal government had no program for helping universities build new research facilities. Northwestern was an early Cassidy client and an earmark recipient.

Harkin of Iowa came directly to Cassidy's defense: "I was quite astounded . . . to hear the name of an individual for whom I have a high regard who is not a Member of the Senate, but an individual in the private sector, who represents different universities. . . . I could not believe my ears to hear his name and his firm used in a rather pejorative sense. The individual referred to, Mr. Cassidy, does indeed have a firm in Washington in which people are employed to assist universities all over the United States. . . . There are over fifty people employed in this firm in helping universities develop and grow.

"I cannot think of more laudable work [than] to . . . help build the scientific and educational base of this country. . . . I would just point out for the record . . . that in this firm of Cassidy & Associates there is the former president of the University of Alabama, Dr. Frank Rose, fourteen years president of the University of Alabama, a distinguished academician in his own right. He is there in this firm to help other universities develop their programs. Also in this firm is Dr. Elvis Stahr, former president of the University of Indiana. So to speak of this firm as just a bunch of lobbyists I think really is being a little bit disingenuous on the part of the Senator from Missouri when he used Mr. Cassidy's name here on the floor."

As the debate wound down, Danforth's allies were mostly silent. When the vote was taken, the reason why became clear—there were fewer of them. Three weeks previously the Senate supported Danforth and opposed earmarks by 58–40. Now the vote was nearly reversed—fifty-six senators voted for the earmarks and against Danforth; forty-two supported his amendment. The senators who voted for Danforth on June 5 and voted against him on June 26 included Democrats and Republicans, liberals, moderates, and conservatives. Just six of the twenty-nine members of the Senate Appropriations Committee voted for Danforth's amendment.

In retrospect these were historic votes, but at the time they got very little attention. No major newspaper treated the two votes as an important story. Neither the television networks nor the big newspapers even reported the second vote. But something big had happened: the Senate had looked itself in the eye and blinked. When the friends of earmarks made the case that voting against them would amount to relinquishing a choice prerogative—would deny members opportunities to bring home bacon—the opposition shrank. As Cassidy observed, the second vote "pretty much put a cork in the issue."

The anti-earmarking position might conceivably have prevailed if its proponents were in fact the white knights some claimed to be. But Danforth and his allies were compromised by the realities of the system of peer review and competition that they were defending. It *was* loaded in favor of the elite schools that already got the most government money, and had received funding for the huge federal laboratories that attracted the best scientists and most research grants.

But it was hardly more fair to allow the politically best-connected institutions to win the earmarks, whether or not their projects were the most deserving. Jean Mayer or John Silber could defend earmarks as a necessary ingredient of efforts like theirs to turn mediocre schools into something much better, but it was difficult to explain why Tufts and BU got benefits not available to others.

Which side had the better argument? Neither one. Danforth and his high-minded allies defended a principle that in fact did not exist—totally fair competition for government grants. In reality Danforth was defending the status quo, which surely did constitute an old-boys' network, in which "the peers"—scholars at the best, meaning the richest, institutions—decided who most deserved federal grants. Their system protected an elite.

Their opponents, on the other hand, spoke of defending little guys against the big—have-nots against haves—but they were really defending the right of politicians to provide favors to their constituents and friends.

In the end both sides were protecting their own interests, an instinct as old as human politics.

The big immediate winner was the booming lobbying firm of Cassidy & Associates. No university president in America could have missed the import of the Danforth Amendment episode: earmarks were now kosher, and in vogue. New clients kept appearing at Cassidy's door, many brought in by the firm's consultants including Rose and Stahr, others by the firm's growing fame. By 1987, the year after Danforth made his stand, the firm's revenue had grown to $18.8 million. Cassidy took between $3 and $5 million in salary and bonus every year from 1985 until 1990. He sold his Mercedes sedan and bought a Lincoln Town Car, and hired a chauffeur to drive it. He took grand vacations to Ireland and England, collected fine antiques, bought bespoke suits, shirts, and shoes.

As his firm and his income grew, so did Cassidy's confidence. The five years after the firm's name changed were a golden era for him. He had important friends and lucrative clients. As he became seriously wealthy, he cultivated his own charisma with considerable success. He attracted the deference that so often goes to the richest man in the room. The people around him began to take him more seriously.

So did some people from far away. One was Peter Gummer, founder and chief executive officer of a fast-growing British public relations conglomerate, Shandwick. Cassidy recounted what happened.

"In '87 I was on vacation in August, and I got a call that Mr. Peter Gummer was trying to reach me. Peter, later to be Lord Chadlington . . . wanted to buy the company [Cassidy & Associates]. I listened to him, and had a number of conversations with him, and I went to London to see his operation, and I got a very good idea of what he was doing. He had taken his company public on the London exchange, and the stock . . . created a currency for him with which he could buy companies. . . . I really studied what he was doing, and had him make pretty elaborate proposals to me—we made about three runs at this. I did not want to sell, but I wanted to learn."

James Fabiani recounted admiringly that Cassidy had extracted a $1 million deposit from Gummer while their talks continued. Fabiani thought they were close to a deal when Shandwick's stock tumbled on the London stock exchange. The "currency" with which Gummer hoped to buy Cassidy & Associates was suddenly devalued, and the deal fell apart. But Cassidy kept Gummer's million dollars. This episode gave Cassidy a taste of the really big money he had dreamed of for so many years.

Success seemed to stimulate Cassidy's imagination. The same itch that had attracted him to the Cuban refugee's Brazilian hardwood deal led him to Tom Mathews, a charming Irishman who was a partner in the leading Democratic direct mail firm, Craver, Mathews, Smith & Company. This was a Democratic version of Richard Viguerie's Republican direct mail company. Craver, Mathews had solicited money for Congressman Morris Udall's 1976 presidential campaign, Congressman John Anderson's independent presidential run in 1980, the Democratic National Committee, Amnesty International, Planned Parenthood, and many other liberal groups. His firm "raised I don't know how many hundreds of millions of dollars for these organizations by direct mail," Mathews said in a conversation about his relationship with Cassidy.

Mathews thought Cassidy's interest in him "was indicative of Gerry's curiosity and incessant search for new forms for his business. . . . I think Gerry wanted to explore whether or not our experience could be a part of his operation. . . . We engaged in a number of long conversations. And he was very generous about paying consulting fees for this too. Finally we just really discovered that there wasn't a fit. . . . But we became friends, so in that sense it was a success. But I couldn't bring to bear anything that was worth a lot of money. I was an expert in raising a huge amount of money in small amounts from a large number of individuals." Cassidy couldn't figure out how to make that skill profitable for his firm.

Their conversations did lead to a creative attempt to win the Metropolitan Museum of Art in New York City as a Cassidy client. "I suggested it," Mathews recalled, "and Gerry grabbed at it." Cassidy came up with a plan for an earmark of $5–10 million for the museum for an education project that would bring schoolchildren to the Met. The firm produced a loose-leaf notebook describing how the project might work. Cassidy devised a political strategy built around New York City congressmen he hoped would help with the earmark. Mathews had connections that helped get a meeting with Philippe de Montebello, the French-born aristocrat who became director of the Met in 1977. Mathews accompanied Cassidy to the meeting.

"We encountered—I think for the first time in Gerry's experience—an utter disdain for public money from Philippe. He was so aristocratic and so adamant and so dismissive of this idea—he shot it down out of the sky without a miss. The amusing part of it was how startled we all were that this aristocrat would stand up and defy one of the laws of nature!" Mathews remembered "how surprised, and shocked, and really angry Gerry was that he wasn't taken seriously. . . . He was accustomed to being heard and being respected."

Mathews was right about that. Cassidy had found ways to win the allegiance, even the respect, of some important people, and the more success he had, the more he seemed to expect it. Favors and loyalty were his principal currencies, and he was generous with both. "Truly," Mathews said, "he was a genius at discovering the permeable membrane between what a lobbyist could do for a congressman and what a congressman could do for a client without it being in the least bit illegal. . . . All he really did was raise money for congressional figures who could help get through an appropriation."

Mathews described Cassidy's trips to the favor bank for members of Congress with an old Boston expression: "Gerry engaged in activities which, while not nefarious, couldn't stand a frisk." That meant, he explained, that some of the favors Cassidy did were effective because they weren't open to public scrutiny—"the kind of scrutiny that would kill a deal. Nothing serious, nothing felonious in it."

One of the favors Cassidy did for members in the 1980s was take a number of them to the Final Four, the semifinals and finals of the NCAA men's college basketball championship. The 1987 tournament was held in New Orleans. Cassidy arranged for six members of the House Appropriations Committee to attend a "Congressional Forum" in New Orleans from March 27 to March 30, an event sponsored by two of Cassidy's corporate clients, the Ocean Spray cranberry cooperative and the Pirelli company. Both companies had set up political action committees at Cassidy's suggestion, and let him decide how the money should be spent. Creating this forum in New Orleans allowed its sponsors to pay "honoraria" of $2,000 each to the six members, a legal gift at the time. (Such honoraria were banned in 1989.) But the weekend involved no serious work.

The NCAA outings "were great fun," Cassidy said years later. "You could only come if you were a friend of mine. And no lobbying was allowed. We used to play basketball—we'd get there on a Friday night, have a good dinner. We'd play basketball Saturday during the day. The first two games were Saturday night . . . then on Sunday we'd play basketball again. . . . We'd go to the final ball game on Monday night, and we'd go home. We would just have a great time. It would be the guys, and we were all friends, it was just another time, another place where you could have a lot of fun."

This outing suited Cassidy's image of himself as an old jock. Most of the people around him had the impression that he'd been a football player at Villanova, an idea he never seemed to discourage.

The 1988 Final Four outing featured football in an unusual event that is part of Cassidy lore. Robert Livingston, then a congressman from Louisiana and a member of the Appropriations Committee, told the story years later. It was late afternoon and the group gathered in a room in their hotel for cocktails. "We all had a few pops." Cassidy and Congressman Norm Dicks of Washington State, a former football player himself who, like Cassidy, had preserved a lineman's physique, started a "competitive back and forth about who had been tougher on the gridiron." Livingston can't remember which of them said, "Come on, let's get down!," but Dicks and Cassidy went into three-point stances, facing each other. They counted to three. "Norm got a jump and lifted Cassidy up and right into the lap of my wife," Livingston recalled. Drinks spilled in the confusion. Cassidy proposed they "try that again." This time he got the jump, lifted Dicks up and pushed him across the room toward an open window. For a moment Livingston was afraid Cassidy couldn't stop.

"To see him and Norm Dicks just about fly out the window, that was an experience, a trip! I mean, I'm a fraternity boy, *Animal House* was not unusual for me. But at a nice afternoon cocktail party, I haven't seen too many people go at it like that. It was fun, and fortunately, Norm didn't fall out the window."

Vincent Versage used a football analogy to describe the team spirit at Cassidy & Associates during these go-go years. "We loved playing for Cassidy then," Versage said. "We thought of him as our Vince Lombardi. We'd have run through walls for the guy."

This was true despite Cassidy's notorious temper. It could erupt without warning, sometimes ferociously. "Gerry managed by fear," one of his lobbyists said of this era, but this "spurred people into action."

Versage also remembered the boss's capacity for kindness at difficult moments. When Versage's father died, Cassidy had food delivered from a local caterer in Rochester, New York, to the Versage family home so no one had to worry about cooking. "He sent the food for three days!" Versage remembered. That, he thought, was the sign of a boss who knew how to boost team morale.

Of course the steady flow of money—the big salaries and big bonuses year after year—was a critical ingredient in this era of good times. So were generous terms of employment, which included excellent benefits, paid parking, and free drinks at the Old Ebbitt Grill downstairs from the office in Metropolitan Square, where Cassidy & Associates ran a tab for its employees and its friends on Capitol Hill in the easygoing days when such gifts to members and their staff did not violate any rules. (The House and Senate passed a gift ban in 1995, which did away with most such perks.)

Campaign contributions and favors, including honoraria for speeches and appearances, were the price of doing business. "Lobbyists have always been contributors, they always will be," Cassidy explained. "It's like if you lived in a rural community and you wanted to be part of that community, and they had a volunteer fire department and you didn't participate, you wouldn't be very well accepted in the community. And it's as simple as that."

Well, not always as simple as that. When the majority leader of the House, Jim Wright of Texas, published *Reflections of a Public Man,* a book of his speeches and public comments—a paperback of just 113 pages— friends and supporters were encouraged to buy multiple copies. It was a "two-bit book with very little fresh stuff," according to its own publisher, William Carlos Moore, who owned a printing business in Fort Worth, Wright's hometown. Moore was also a political consultant and gregarious Texas backslapper who had been one of Wright's principal supporters for many years. He once spent four months in federal prison for tax evasion.

Wright's book contract with Moore was one any author would envy. The book was to be sold for $5.95, and Wright would receive a royalty of $3.25 per copy. A standard author's contract with a commercial publisher would pay a royalty of 7.5 to 15 percent of the list price of a paperback book; Wright's royalty was 55 percent. But the real purpose of this arrangement was to convey money to Wright. Under House rules, members were limited as to how much they could accept in honoraria, but they could receive unlimited book royalties.

The book wasn't sold in bookstores; it was sold in bulk to Wright's friends and supporters. These sales put cash into his pocket perfectly legally. One of the supporters who bought books was the Ocean Spray cranberry cooperative, whose book purchases were arranged by its lobbyist, Gerald Cassidy. Ocean Spray bought $7,000 worth of Wright's book; Wright's share of that was $3,850.

CHAPTER 13

TRICKS OF THE LOBBYING TRADE

On June 13, 1988, all of Washington learned how Cassidy & Associates actually did business. Until then the firm's reputation had grown on reports of its successes; its critics, including Senator Danforth, had spread the word, intentionally or not, that these lobbyists were effective. Cassidy's clients often got the money they were seeking from Congress. But how?

Dan Morgan, one of the best reporters in Washington for many years, provided a detailed answer to that question in an article that appeared on the front page of *The Washington Post* that Monday morning. Morgan had spent months figuring out how the United States government had become "a silent partner" of the Pirelli Cable Corp., the American subsidiary of the Italian Pirelli Group:

> Since starting U.S. operations in 1978, Pirelli has hired a lobbyist, raised $119,300 from 19 executives for its political action committee, contributed $25,000 toward an academic chair in the name of the ranking member of the House Appropriations Committee, paid for the travel of members of Congress to such destinations as Hawaii and New Orleans, and handed out thousands of dollars in honoraria to members of the House and Senate.
>
> In that same period, Congress has earmarked $4 million toward the cost of Pirelli's $8 million fiber optics research building in South Carolina and funded a futuristic research and development project in Hawaii that ultimately could net Pirelli and others hundreds of millions of dollars in commercial business . . .

The lobbyist Pirelli hired was the firm then still known as Schlossberg-Cassidy & Associates. This was the first big client Fabiani had signed up—in March 1983, soon after he joined the firm. As a lobbyist Fabiani cultivated good relations with his old boss on Capitol Hill, Silvio Conte, the ranking Republican on the House Appropriations Committee. The $25,000 contribution Morgan mentioned for an academic chair was to the University of Massachusetts, to help fund the Silvio Conte Professorship of Polymer Science.

Morgan reported these additional details:

The first government-funded project Pirelli had pursued was a plan to develop an "interconnect cable" that could carry electrical power from the Puna area of Hawaii's Big Island, where ancient volcanoes created good conditions for geothermal power generation, to Maui and Oahu, two more populous islands. But the technical challenges were great. First geothermal generators would have to be built. Then a cable carrying power to Oahu and Maui would have to cross the Alenuihaha Channel, where the Pacific was seven thousand feet deep and turbulent. Hawaii sought federal support. But the Reagan administration had decimated federal programs for alternative energy research and development; only an earmarked appropriation could provide funds for the project.

In August 1983, Pirelli Cable became the lead subcontractor for the development of the Hawaii undersea cable. Senator Inouye, of course, was a leading appropriator. Congressman (later Senator) Dan Akaka was a member of the House Appropriations Committee. Hawaii's other senator, Spark Matsunaga, had a seat on the Energy and Natural Resources Committee. All were popular Democrats. They were able to insert language in both authorizing legislation and appropriations bills to fund the Puna project.

They needed Republican help, because Republicans controlled the Senate. Cassidy told Morgan he helped arrange a meeting between Pirelli officials and Senator Mark Hatfield, Republican of Oregon, who then chaired the Appropriations Committee. When they met, Morgan reported, the Pirelli officials "indicated that the company would probably build a new West Coast plant to make the cable [for Hawaii] when and if the project went commercial. Hatfield staffers said they had the impression that Oregon was the leading candidate as a site for the plant."

In 1984, Pirelli created a political action committee. Over the next four years its executives contributed $119,300 to the PAC—"on a strictly voluntary basis," the company told Morgan. One of the PAC's first contributions was $1,000 to Senator Hatfield.

Another member who could influence the cable program was Congressman Don Fuqua of Florida, chairman of the House Committee on Science and Technology, who had supported the earmarks for Catholic and Columbia universities. Fuqua also got $1,000 from the Pirelli PAC. He and his wife were flown to Hawaii for a week for a "seminar" sponsored by Pirelli. The congressman got a $2,000 honorarium.

Fuqua retired in 1986 and was succeeded as chairman by Robert A. Roe of New Jersey. In the first seven months of his chairmanship, Morgan reported, Roe received a $2,000 honorarium from Pirelli. The Pirelli PAC gave him $1,000, as did the company's general manager. Fourteen employees of Cassidy & Associates contributed an additional $10,500.

While the cable project continued, Pirelli found a second opening in South Carolina. Just before Christmas in 1985, Congress passed a "continuing resolution" for the fiscal year that had begun on October 1, a mammoth spending bill that combined the appropriations bills that thirteen separate appropriations subcommittees had written. It contained a single sentence appropriating $4 million to the Economic Development Administration for a state-of-the-art fiber optics research facility in Lexington County, South Carolina.

The key supporter of this transaction was Senator Ernest F. Hollings, known to all as Fritz, a courtly Democrat from South Carolina. Pirelli had recently opened two new cable factories in Abbeville and Beaufort, South Carolina. The company wanted to open a fiber optics research laboratory as well, and its lobbyists—Fabiani and Frank Godfrey of Cassidy—suggested it might be possible to get a government grant to help finance it. The lobbyists encouraged officials of Lexington County, South Carolina, and the University of South Carolina to support an effort to win a grant for the facility from the Economic Development Administration of the U.S. Department of Commerce.

Hollings was a member of the appropriations subcommittee that controlled the EDA's budget. He proposed a $4 million grant to Pirelli. The chairman of the subcommittee, Warren Rudman of New Hampshire, told Morgan he had agreed to go along out of respect for his friend and colleague Hollings. Such an earmark was unusual for that subcommittee, Rudman said, though he acknowledged why such provisions were popular: "People want to bring home the bacon and represent their district in the Congress."

Fabiani, Morgan reported, organized a breakfast fund-raiser for Rudman in early 1986. Six Pirelli executives each wrote $500 checks to the senator on that occasion.

But EDA dallied, and in October 1986, Hollings inserted firm language in a new appropriations bill directing the agency to proceed on Pirelli's Lexington County research building "without further ado." Construction began soon afterward. The government's contribution to the $8 million project was $3.8 million.

In the same *Post* story Morgan revealed Cassidy's Final Four outings, partly funded by Pirelli.

The cable project in Hawaii was controversial. The Sierra Club opposed it as encroachment on a national park and the Big Island rain forest. Local indigenous peoples considered the territory sacred and also opposed the geothermal project. An engineer from the Massachusetts Institute of Technology had called the project "pork." Morgan asked Cassidy about these complaints. The lobbyist said he thought "most of the good things that are happening in government today are on the Office of Management and Budget's 'pork list.' " He called the criticisms "foolish," adding: "You get me the checkbook, I'll get you the opinion. If it's the idea of calling this pork, the idea of telling us that some guy from MIT doesn't like it, I'll hire another guy from MIT who does like it."

During the 1980s Congress had approved money for the Hawaii project on six different occasions, Morgan found, but few members realized what they had voted for. When Morgan asked Hollings, obviously a Pirelli supporter, about the Hawaiian cable program, he replied: "I never heard of it." Neither the Hawaii project nor any of the electric energy research projects funded in the energy and water appropriations bill were named in the bill itself. One sentence in the committee report accompanying the bill was the only direct reference to it.

"Pirelli appears to have done nothing improper," Morgan wrote. "Rather, congressional sources say, the legislative process has become so big, complex and unaccountable that it increasingly invites members of Congress, contractors and lobbyists to engage in closely held, special-interest deals. As the Reagan administration ax has fallen on broad federal programs, the pressure to carve out obscure pockets of opportunity in the budget has risen. Moreover, as the Pirelli story suggests, closely held projects generate money for the political war chests that help incumbents get reelected."

Cassidy & Associates' latest accomplishment for Pirelli had come just a month before Morgan's story appeared. Congressman Roe, the new chairman of the Science Committee, had sponsored a change in the authorizing language that requested an additional $1 million on top of

$5.2 million previously designated for the Hawaiian cable. Frank Godfrey told Morgan that the language Roe offered to change the bill was actually drafted in the office of Cassidy & Associates. It provided for "$6.2 million in systems research for continuation of the Hawaii Deep Water Cable program, including $1 million for the designer and manufacturer of the deep water test cable." That unnamed "designer and manufacturer" was Pirelli.

If the Hawaii program came to fruition, Morgan reported, "Pirelli would be well-positioned to obtain the commercial contract to supply 269 miles of cable worth at least $400 million." But the program faltered in later years, local opposition grew, and the idea was dropped.

This newspaper story was Cassidy's first experience with an exposé of his firm's activities, and he did not like it. The day after the story appeared, he went up to Capitol Hill to see Congressman Conte, whom he assumed would not have liked the story either. According to an aide to Conte who was in the office at the time, the congressman was furious at the suggestion that he had done something improper for Pirelli. According to this aide, Conte let Cassidy cool his heels in the reception area of his office for the entire day. "At about 6 p.m.," the aide said, "Cassidy stood up, folded his fingers in front of his chest and thanked the staff for their hospitality." The next day, the aide said, Fabiani came to see his old boss, and Conte agreed to meet him. The congressman gave Fabiani "a royal chewing out," the former aide said.

Fabiani said he did not remember the incident nearly twenty years later, but he did remember that Conte liked Pirelli. The company had once taken the congressman to Italy—Fabiani accompanied him—and Conte enjoyed the trip.

Asked about this episode years later, Cassidy said the story was "not true." Yes, he had gone up to Conte's office to try to smooth things over, but he had not been kept waiting. "I was in there [in Conte's office] within five minutes."

Conte's reaction was the only apparent consequence of Morgan's story. There was no other response from the parties involved, and the story had no visible political effect. Perhaps embarrassment contributed to the silence. Perhaps it was old news to the participants in the Washington game that this had become the way things got done on Capitol Hill. Congressmen and senators take money from lobbyists and special interests, then do what the lobbyists and interests want? Yes, that had become commonplace. Was it proper? Some editorial pages and reformers asked such questions, but not members of Congress, who regularly found ways to take the money and do what its donors hoped they would. Was it *normal*? By 1988, yes it was.

Just a year later, Morgan published a second eye-opening article about Cassidy & Associates. He had spent the intervening months reporting and writing about the secretive congressional appropriations process, the dark side of the legislative moon. His reporting had led him to the National Defense Stockpile Transaction Fund.

This was an example of the sort of arcane government office that few citizens know even exists. The fund, established by the Strategic and Critical Materials Stock Piling Revision Act of 1979 (you can look it up!), allows the Department of Defense to trade in strategic metals, minerals, and other materials needed to build its weapons and equipment. It is meant to be a "revolving fund," accumulating money by selling the strategic materials that it also buys. The fund exists to ensure a steady supply of materials such as chrome and titanium. Cassidy & Associates came up with the idea that the fund could also be used as a legislative conduit to direct earmarks to specific universities.

Fabiani explained to Morgan what had happened. The University of Massachusetts, a Cassidy client, wanted to build a new facility to retain scientists who were working on advanced plastics and other exotic materials. These materials could substitute for some rare metals including titanium. Learning this, Cassidy researchers, using computerized compilations of appropriations bills, found a match between the word titanium and the National Defense Stockpile Transaction Fund. A strategy was born.

Again, Congressman Conte played an important part. Amherst, site of the University of Massachusetts, was in Conte's district. He was a member of the appropriations subcommittee responsible for the fund. He put a $9.5 million earmark for the center into an appropriations bill. Paul Laxalt, Republican of Nevada and President Reagan's best friend in the Senate, included the same amount in the Senate version of the bill for a similar facility at the University of Nevada in Reno. Over three years, the University of Massachusetts got a total of $19.5 million for the project. And as Morgan had reported, the Silvio Conte Professorship of Polymer Science was born.

"Under Cassidy's tutelage," Morgan wrote, "the appropriators have come to appreciate the potential of the Stockpile Fund as a vehicle for justifying appropriations for construction of university facilities." When this story was published on June 18, 1989, Cassidy had won grants for four clients this way. Between 1985, when this gambit was first used, and 1989, $78 million had passed through the Stockpile Fund to nine universities.

Some like the University of Massachusetts center were indeed related to strategic materials, others were not. For example, Cassidy & Associates had been retained by Loyola College, the Jesuit school in Baltimore, which needed money for its computer center. Fabiani and Vincent Versage helped Loyola repackage its request; the computer center became a "Center for Advanced Information and Resource Management Studies." When a House Armed Services Committee report soon afterward expressed concern about the management of the Stockpile Transaction Fund, Loyola's lobbyists and supporters said its new center, when operational, could "begin to address these and other federal systems management problems on a government-wide basis." Loyola got $6 million, passed through that Stockpile Transaction Fund.

Despite their unhappiness with the Pirelli story a year earlier, Cassidy and Fabiani had decided to cooperate with Morgan this time. Some of their colleagues disapproved of the idea, believing they should always stay in the shadows. But the firm's two principals gave Morgan interviews and posed for a joint photograph outside their office in Metropolitan Square. Years later Fabiani acknowledged that this had been indiscreet. "Were we trying to give ourselves exposure and credit and profile and so on? Sure."

Morgan's story showed Cassidy violating his own cardinal rule of lobbying: never take credit for the work of members of Congress. He had tried to avoid this in the interview he gave to Morgan by saying: "I applaud the members who are taking the lead [promoting the new materials research centers]. The dollars would not be spent if they were not being pushed through by members who had an interest in seeing technology advanced."

But Morgan's reporting showed that it was really the lobbyists who had taken the lead. The story made clear that Cassidy and Fabiani, not any member of Congress, had come up with the idea of using the Stockpile Transaction Fund in this way. Anyone reading Morgan's article who understood the appropriations process realized that the lobbyists had devised a nifty gimmick that members were delighted to exploit.

Delighted, because these earmarks helped members in at least two important ways. First they helped at home—voters in western Massachusetts, for example, were bound to be impressed that Conte (who got the public credit) could produce $19.5 million in federal dollars for the state university. Second, obtaining the earmarks and working with lobbyists helped them raise the money they all needed more and more of to run their re-election campaigns.

Morgan's story—like the first one a year earlier—pointed out the relation between funds raised for members and the favors that were delivered. He connected the lobbyists' success with "the insatiable demand of members of Congress for ever-larger campaign war chests to ward off challengers. In some cases, Washington lobbyists, law firms and corporate representatives became an extension of the fund-raising operations of congressional offices as those offices were becoming more crucial to the lobbyists" seeking earmarks. He noted that Cassidy and his wife had contributed $50,000 to candidates in the 1987–88 election cycle.

This time Morgan's work did provoke a significant reaction—from just one senator, but an important one. The result was notoriety for Cassidy that both upset and rewarded him.

Six months earlier Robert Byrd of West Virginia, the Democratic leader in the Senate for a dozen years until 1989, had given up that job and became chairman of the Senate Appropriations Committee. Explaining this switch, Byrd, seventy years old at the time, was remarkably candid: "I chose the role . . . that will be best for West Virginia." He promised to use the chairmanship of appropriations "to see that West Virginia receives the share for which it is eligible."

Byrd was perhaps the most unusual man in the Senate. He did not learn until he was seventeen that his given name at birth was Cornelius Calvin Sale Jr. His mother died in the great flu epidemic of 1918 when Byrd was a year old; an aunt and uncle, Vlurma and Titus Byrd, raised and renamed him. He grew up in coal mining country and in poverty. He did not live in a house with running water until he was twenty-one. He won political office—a seat in the West Virginia legislature—before he could afford to go to college, and eventually took classes at four different West Virginia schools. In 1952 he was elected to the U.S. House. For the next ten years, through his election to the Senate in 1958, Byrd studied law at night at the Washington College of Law, completing his degree in 1963, when he was forty-five years old.

Throughout his career Byrd has been tortured by insecurities, the source of vanities that have often driven his colleagues to distraction. Nevertheless, the Democrats picked him to be their leader in January 1977, because he was fair, reliable, smart, and the best parliamentarian in the Senate. His colleagues admired Byrd's reverent devotion to their institution, whose history he knew better than anyone. He regularly gave speeches about the "world's greatest deliberative body," trying to explain its traditions to his fellow senators.

Byrd worked *all* the time—he was famous for never taking a vacation. He knew how to satisfy the political needs of his colleagues, and did not seek the limelight himself—except when he pulled out his fiddle to play country music, which he liked to do while campaigning in West Virginia, and also at Washington political dinners. He "made the trains run on time," as virtually everyone on Capitol Hill observed during the years he was majority, then after 1980 minority, leader.

But he had no real pals in the club. "Truth is, nobody likes the son-ofabitch," a fellow Democratic senator said in 1981. "He's impossible to deal with . . . a man of tremendous insecurity. He's most difficult to be around. . . . He has no friends." He styled his hair in a swept-back pompadour that looked a little like Elvis Presley, at least until it turned white. His manner was self-conscious and awkward.

Lobbying was on Byrd's mind in the spring and early summer of 1989. Congressional investigations had uncovered a scandal at the Department of Housing and Urban Development during the Reagan administration. Republican lobbyists and political consultants had exploited their personal connections to several political appointees at HUD to help real estate developers win big federal contracts to rehabilitate Section 8 housing for low-income renters. One of the most successful of these influence peddlers was James Watt, Reagan's first secretary of the interior. The lobbyists made millions, though many of the projects were of dubious merit. This was the ninth year of Republican control of the executive branch, and the Democrats who controlled Congress were delighted to exploit the scandal.

Lobbying, never popular with the public, was an obvious target for them. Byrd asked his staff to draft legislation that would put new limits on lobbyists and require fuller disclosure of lobbying activities that were intended to sway the executive branch or Congress. And then Morgan's article on the Stockpile Transaction Fund appeared on the front page of the *Post*.

Morgan's story alarmed Byrd, perhaps because he knew two items of recent history that Morgan had not discovered. The first was the story of the National Research Center for Coal and Energy at West Virginia University, funded by $15 million in earmarks, the first approved two years earlier. The university had retained Cassidy & Associates to help with that project. A new employee of the firm, Donald P. Smith, was the lead lobbyist. Cassidy and Fabiani were delighted to hire Smith, who had been a senior staff assistant on the House Appropriations Committee, the first alumnus of that important source of earmarks that the firm had hired. Smith remembered that his last salary on the committee was just over $62,000 a year; Cassidy hired him for $85,000, and gave him a $60,000 bonus after his first year.

Byrd and his staff supported the earmarks for the coal research center and worked with Smith on them. Smith had been present for the groundbreaking ceremony initiating construction of the center in October 1988. On that occasion the president of West Virginia University, Neil Bucklew, made a political blunder that Smith remembered nearly twenty years later with a rueful shake of his head. Smith recalled briefing Bucklew just before the event, reminding him to thank Senator Byrd in his brief speech. Byrd was to be in the audience. But when he rose to speak, Bucklew instead gave elaborate thanks to Elvis Stahr, his predecessor as president of the university, and said nothing about Byrd. Stahr, of course, was a Cassidy ten-percenter. Smith paid close attention that day to the senator's demeanor: "You could see the steam coming out of Byrd's ears," he said.

A few months later Bucklew and Smith went forward with a plan for a second project to be paid for by earmarks, a materials research center to be funded through the National Defense Stockpile Transaction Fund. They met with Byrd's staff, then with Byrd. Indicating his knowledge of what was going on, Byrd asked when this meeting began if there were lobbyists present? Smith nodded affirmatively, and Byrd asked him to leave the room so he could meet with "my constituents."

Smith quickly left, assuming that this was at least partly a response to the snub Bucklew had given Byrd the previous autumn. In the meeting with Bucklew and his colleagues, Byrd embraced the plan and agreed to send a letter to the chairman of the relevant appropriations subcommittee asking for his support. The idea was to seek $18 million over several years for the new project. When the meeting ended, Smith recalled, Byrd came out to the anteroom where he was waiting and shook his hand. You understood that, didn't you? Byrd asked. Sure, Smith replied. He understood, he thought, that Byrd was putting on a show.

This plan had not been publicly divulged, and Morgan had not learned of it when he wrote his story about the fund. But Byrd and his staff must have realized when they read the *Post* story that their own state university had a plan to acquire one of the grants that Morgan described. This could prove embarrassing. Perhaps worse, Morgan's story suggested that the appropriations process was being manipulated by lobbyists at the very moment Byrd, the chairman of Senate Appropriations, was drawing up legislation to both limit and expose lobbying. The chairman was in an awkward spot.

His first known reaction to the Morgan story was to write an angry letter to Bucklew, sharply complaining about the university's use of a lobbyist when it could count on the support of the chairman of the committee, West Virginia's senior senator. Bucklew wrote back apologetically, telling Byrd he had hired Cassidy only to help formulate the proposal, not to win votes for it or to gain access to senators. For pushing the bill through the Senate, Bucklew wrote, he counted on Byrd. "This was the case with the National Research Center for Coal and Energy," Bucklew wrote, referring to the earlier project. "Without question, you were responsible for the successful funding for the Center"—the point he had forgotten to make at the center's groundbreaking ceremony.

On July 24, just five weeks after Morgan's story was published, Byrd surprised both the Senate and Washington's lobbyists by introducing a new legislative provision, quickly named the Byrd Amendment, that appeared to impose significant new rules on lobbyists and their clients. The provision required all recipients of funds from the federal government—grants, loans, or loan guarantees—to file reports to the government agencies that provided the funds disclosing any assistance they had received from lobbyists, how much they paid for it, whom the lobbyists tried to influence, and where the money had come from to pay the lobbyists. Byrd's amendment specifically prohibited using federal funds to pay lobbyists. It was approved by the Appropriations Committee on the day Byrd introduced it, and by the full Senate two days later, an unusually speedy progression.

Speaking in favor of the amendment on the Senate floor that July 26, Byrd cited two justifications for it. First was the HUD scandal, which had revealed "abuses that allowed firms with the 'right' lobbyists to secure loans, and loan guarantees, et cetera, which never should have been granted." Second, Byrd cited "news articles relating to lobbyists . . . who collect exorbitant fees to create projects and have them earmarked in appropriation bills and reports for the benefit of their clients.

"The perception is growing," Byrd continued, "that the merit of a project, grant or contract awarded by the government has fallen into a distant second place to the moxie and clout of lobbyists who help spring the money out of appropriation bills for a fat fee. . . . Inside the Beltway, everyone knows how the game is played. These influence peddlers sell themselves as hired guns to the highest bidder. They claim that they know the password to the backdoors on Capitol Hill. They tout their prowess at being able to deliver the goodies. . . . They are arrogant about their ability to shake the appropriations money tree—for a fat fee. Every Senator in this body ought to be repulsed by the perception that we will dole out the bucks if stroked by the right consultant."

Byrd was obviously talking about Gerald S. J. Cassidy. Two days later, on the afternoon of July 28—a Friday when few members could be found at work—Byrd summoned Morgan to his office to make his point explicitly clear. Byrd startled the reporter by announcing that he was withdrawing his support for an $18 million grant for a materials research center at West Virginia University. Byrd described his surprise when he had learned several months earlier that West Virginia University was a paying client of Cassidy's—though he must have known this (as his staff certainly did) for two years. He told Morgan he had expressed "indignation and anger" to university officials, and had asked them "why do you waste your money on a lobbyist when I'm being paid to be your senator? . . . If I can't do it, nobody can."

Byrd told Morgan, no doubt truthfully, that he had been surprised to read in the paper that the idea of using the Stockpile Transaction Fund had come originally from Cassidy & Associates. He claimed to be surprised as well that $78 million had already been allocated to universities through the fund.

Byrd was full of theatrical indignation. He told Morgan that after reading his story, "I was angry that I was being used by the lobbyists." Most revealingly, he told the reporter: "I don't want that kind of story on my committee." The publicity was the biggest problem for the chairman of the Appropriations Committee. The publicity had revealed how lobbyists had been manipulating the appropriations process over which Byrd presided.

Both houses of Congress passed versions of the Byrd Amendment, but in its final form, a compromise between House and Senate, it was considerably weaker and easier to evade than Byrd had initially made it sound. Its one significant, enduring feature was to require semiannual reports from lobbyists recording who their clients were, and how much they were paid.

But the episode did have an effect on the reputation of Cassidy & Associates. As Cassidy acknowledged years later, his competitors, among others, considered the Byrd Amendment a black mark against his firm's name: "The talk was that it was about us."

Colleagues remember an eruption of the famous Cassidy temper when Morgan's account of the manipulation of the Stockpile Transaction Fund appeared. Cassidy didn't deny that he was upset. "Members of Congress strongly objected to members of this firm talking to Dan [Morgan]," Cassidy said. The story "made it feel like we were getting credit for what was done by them."

First Morgan's stories, then the Byrd Amendment had put Cassidy in a place he did not enjoy—on the receiving end of public criticism. One shot came from *The New York Times*, which published an editorial on August 15 calling for lobbying reform. Noting that Byrd had rushed a reform provision to the Senate floor without even holding hearings, the *Times* wrote that "Senator Byrd was himself embarrassed recently by *The Washington Post*'s report on a lobbying firm, Cassidy & Associates, which earned large fees by peddling projects to prospective clients and then lobbying for the funds. One client was a university in the Senator's home state. Mr. Byrd then withdrew his support for its proposed $18 million research center."

Cassidy decided he needed to respond, and wrote a letter to the editor of the *Times*, which was published on August 25. "We fully support" new rules requiring "more detailed disclosure" of lobbying, Cassidy wrote. His firm already told clients they could not use money from federal grants to pay the lobbying firm, he added.

"Our efforts for clients on university capital projects have been fully documented over the years, and we are proud of our representation," Cassidy wrote, though the only detailed documentation available to the public was in Dan Morgan's stories. "We assist clients in preparing a proposal, work with them on strategies and then help them to receive a full hearing from members of Congress and their staffs. The eventual decision is made on the proposal's merits and its benefits to the national interest.

"Washington is a labyrinth," Cassidy added in a plug for his service, "thronged with thousands of individuals and groups trying to present their messages to Congress and the Administration. . . . I am convinced that the message of an individual or group of citizens is more likely to be heard, in both content and in form, if it is shaped by someone who understands the legislative and regulatory processes."

Others at Cassidy & Associates did not think Morgan's articles were a problem. They saw a boon for the firm. "It was great advertising," Smith said. "If you're good enough to get your name in the paper you must be doing something right." Many in the firm shared that view. Smith recalled an excited telephone call from his mother when the story that included his name was published. He was famous!

Years later Cassidy acknowledged that his colleagues did not see this episode the way he did. "The younger guys in the firm didn't have to go around and talk to the members of Congress about this," he said. They could enjoy their moment in the sun, but he had to go to "two dozen or so senior members and explain to them the circumstance, that we in no way meant to take credit away from them." This was Cassidy's variation on Harry Truman's famous dictum about Washington: "There's no limit to what you accomplish, as long as you do not care who gets the credit." Cassidy realized he shouldn't get credit in public—though he had been tempted to claim it. Better just to get the fees.

In this instance, Cassidy had to give up both credit and fees. Byrd personally told Bucklew, the university president, that he should sever the relationship with Cassidy & Associates, which cost West Virginia University $10,000 a month. "Within a very quick time frame," Bucklew recalled in an interview, "the arrangement we had worked out with Cassidy was dissolved with their full understanding and support."

Generally Cassidy insisted that signed contracts be fulfilled, but in this case he did not complain. There was no percentage in challenging the chairman of the Senate Appropriations Committee. "It was one of the few cases when Cassidy let someone get out of a contract," Smith recalled.

CHAPTER 14

THE NEW TECHNOLOGY OF POLITICS

Robert Byrd was the chairman of the Appropriations Committee because Democrats in the Senate and House had benefited from two good election cycles at the end of the 1980s, when they put the anxieties of the Reagan ascendancy behind them. Reagan's second term, marred by the Iran-contra affair and the scandals at HUD, undid his political magic. Democrats recaptured the Senate in 1986 when they picked up eight seats, an unusually strong showing for the out party in an off-year election. In the House, Democrats gained five more seats in 1986, increasing their majority—once again apparently impregnable—to eighty-one.

Partisan Democrats, Gerald Cassidy included, allowed themselves to daydream of a Democratic sweep in 1988, and for a brief moment in the summer of 1988, that looked likely. Just after the Democratic convention in Atlanta that July, their nominee for president, Governor Michael Dukakis of Massachusetts, led Vice President George H. W. Bush by nearly 20 percentage points, according to several national polls.

That lead did not last out the summer. By running a nasty, tough, creative, and effective campaign, mostly on television, that was based on symbols and emotions almost entirely disconnected from traditional issues, Bush surged. The hapless stumbling of an ineffectual opponent, Dukakis, made success considerably easier than it might have been. Bush won the popular vote by nearly 8 percentage points.

The 1988 Bush campaign was a triumph of the new political technology, which came into its own in the 1980s. Appropriately, Bush's "media consultant," Roger Ailes, the maker of its television commercials, learned how to combine politics and television as a twenty-eight-year-old whiz kid

working on the first high-tech campaign, Richard Nixon's in 1968. Ailes
had learned the techniques of television as the producer of *The Mike Douglas Show*, a daytime talk show popular with housewives. In 1996, the same
Roger Ailes would launch Fox News. For Nixon in 1968, Ailes orchestrated and produced one-hour programs that featured Nixon answering
questions from panels of questioners. In those relatively early years of television, a campaign could buy a one-hour, prime-time slot for such a program. Spooked by the impact of television on his losing campaign against
Kennedy in 1960, Nixon was determined to conquer the new medium in
1968, and Ailes was one of his most important co-conspirators.

Ailes's approach was recorded memorably in Joe McGinniss's book
The Selling of the President 1968, which reprinted internal memos from the
Nixon campaign, including an analysis by Ailes of Nixon's performance in
one of those hour-long programs. Topic A in Ailes's memo was something
he called "The Look." Nixon, he wrote, "looks good on his feet" and conveyed a sense of confidence. "Generally, he has a very 'Presidential' look
and style. . . . We are still working on lightening up his eyes a bit. . . . I may
try slightly whiter makeup on upper eyelids."

In the twenty years that separated Nixon's campaign from Bush's,
technology changed everything about electoral politics in America. The
new technology diminished the role of the Democratic and Republican
parties, because with television as their principal tool, candidates could
win elections as political entrepreneurs—on their own, with the support
of contributors who might have no connection to the party on whose
ticket they ran. Polls—by the 1980s extremely sophisticated and revealing—took much of the guesswork out of political campaigning, allowing
campaigns to find out what voters wanted to hear; then candidates gave
them precisely that. The new technology could reduce or eliminate the
significance of traditional issues by using polling to invent new ones that
would resonate with voters. Ultimately the new technology rewrote the
list of personal traits and qualities needed to win elections, eliminating the
need for candidates to be able to articulate a coherent view of the country
and the world. Instead of a worldview or a personal political philosophy,
candidates needed to be telegenic, articulate, and capable of raising large
quantities of money. Money became the single most important ingredient
of most successful campaigns.

Use of the new technology began with public opinion polling and
"focus groups," gatherings of ten to twenty individuals questioned by an
expert at length to draw out their feelings as well as their opinions. Findings of polls and the insights gained from focus groups helped the consul-

tants who were the key exploiters of the new technology to create "pieces of mail"—letters to be sent to targeted voters—and advertisements for newspapers, radio, and, most of all, television. Often, the consultants who produced these items, especially the commercials for television, would show them to focus groups before putting the ads on the air, to be sure they had the desired effect. By the 1980s television commercials consumed at least half the budget of most campaigns for the White House, the Senate, and the House of Representatives. Those campaigns, as we have seen already, were many times costlier than they had been before television became so important.

In an earlier era of American politics, from the 1960s through the 1980 presidential campaign, most of the political commercials on television were "positive," meaning they emphasized a candidate's purported qualities. But by the late 1980s it was more typical to spend television money on "negative" commercials—mostly thirty-second spots that found fault with the candidate's opponent. The professionals who exploited the new technologies as the politicians' hired guns looked at 1986 as a turning point; that year negative commercials dominated the "air wars"—the candidates' televised commercials—in contests all over the country, and they worked.

Roger Ailes loved negative commercials, and defended them vigorously. "I don't agree with this idea about negative campaigning being so awful," he said after the 1988 election. "Americans learn a lot from these spots." What they "learned" from Ailes-produced spots in that campaign were profoundly misleading descriptions of Governor Dukakis's record in Massachusetts. One Bush commercial asserted that Dukakis had failed to clean up the badly polluted Boston Harbor: "As governor he had the opportunity to do something about it but chose not to." In fact a court decision in Massachusetts had forced Dukakis to set up a new agency and initiate a $6 billion program to clean up the harbor. Bush's commercial featured a picture of a warning sign in the harbor: "Danger Radiation Hazard No Swimming." The sign was decades old, and had been posted near a Navy yard where nuclear submarines had once been repaired. Another Ailes-produced spot showed a stream of mean-looking men wearing prison uniforms walking through a revolving door while an announcer criticized "the Dukakis furlough program" that allowed dangerous criminals to leave prison on weekend passes. The commercial provided exaggerated statistics about a program that had been initiated by a Republican predecessor to Dukakis. The Democrat had actually ended the furlough program.

It was that furlough program that produced the most memorable leading man in an anti-Dukakis commercial, a murderer and rapist named Willie Horton. Massachusetts prison authorities gave Horton a forty-eight-hour furlough in 1986 and he disappeared. Ten months later he was captured in Maryland, where he had terrorized a couple, assaulting the man and repeatedly raping his fiancée. A commercial that went on the air in September 1988 showed a picture of Horton, a black man with a beard, and recounted the story of his crimes and his weekend furlough. It ended: "Weekend prison passes: Dukakis on crime." Bush and his running mate, Senator Dan Quayle, regularly mentioned Horton in their campaign speeches, echoing the commercial.

The spot, however, was not made by Ailes or the Bush campaign. It was the work of a legally "independent" group called Americans for Bush, which gave the Bush campaign some protection from criticisms that the commercial was exploiting racial anxieties by featuring the photograph of Horton. The consultant who made the Horton spot was Larry McCarthy, a former senior vice president of Ailes Communications Inc., Roger Ailes's firm.

Lee Atwater, the aggressive young South Carolinian who was Bush's campaign manager, had learned about Willie Horton from Senator Al Gore, who had accused Dukakis of giving "weekend passes to criminals" during a debate of Democratic candidates the previous April, when Gore was still a candidate for the Democratic nomination. This led Atwater to discover the furlough program, which he quickly perceived as a winning issue for his candidate. "If I can make Willie Horton a household name," he told a Republican group soon afterward, "we'll win the election."

George H. W. Bush ran for president on these issues because they converted uncertain voters into Bush supporters. Ailes and Atwater had discovered their effectiveness the previous May, when half the members of two focus groups they had organized in Paramus, New Jersey, had turned against Dukakis (until then their favored candidate) when they heard the Bush campaign's tendentious account of his past positions on these and several other issues. Ailes's negative commercials (with help from Larry McCarthy's) quickly wiped out Dukakis's lead, which had disappeared by the end of September.

Dukakis never understood why these attacks were effective, and it took him many weeks to respond to them; then he did so ineffectively. He was an apt standard-bearer for a national Democratic Party that had not even begun to recover its bearings after being drubbed by Ronald Reagan.

Dukakis's early lead in the polls probably reflected an appetite in the country for a change after eight years of Reagan, but the assault unleashed by Atwater and Ailes put a quick end to that.

Bush was the ideal candidate for the sort of race Ailes and Atwater wanted to run. He had no positive agenda of his own, no new programs to propose, no strong beliefs that he wanted to propagate. Bush ridiculed the alleged importance of "the vision thing," no doubt because he knew he had no vision himself. Though nominally a Texan, he was really a traditional WASP from Connecticut who wanted to serve his country and be president. He was happy to let Ailes and Atwater tell him how to win the job.

These characteristics made Bush typical of the politicians of his time. After twenty years in the game, the consultants had emerged as probably the most influential group in American politics—more influential, often, than the candidates who hired them. Like the new class of lobbyists so aptly represented by Gerald Cassidy, the consultants had learned how to become wealthy as appendages of the political process. The most successful could make millions. And they could spend millions.

This was a key to understanding the impact the new technology and its practitioners had on our politics. Campaigns dependent on pollsters, consultants, and television commercials were many times more expensive than campaigns in the prehistoric eras before these inventions took hold. When their success became obvious, few candidates thought they could run without them—not just for president, but for the House and Senate as well. The 1988 presidential campaigns were funded by taxpayers under the public funding provision that was then still operative (it broke down after 1992), but there was no public funding for congressional races. So congressmen and senators who used the new technologies—which was most of them—quite suddenly needed much more money than ever before to run for re-election.

This reality is reflected in the history of Cassidy's and his wife's contributions to political campaigns. The Cassidys donated just $3,500 to House and Senate candidates in the 1981–82 election cycle, but in 1985–86 they gave *thirteen times* more—$47,850. They gave a similar amount again in 1987–88. During these years the cost of the campaigns for the House and Senate rose dramatically. For example, incumbent Democrats in relatively close races (who won with less than 60 percent of the vote) spent, on average, $223,000 in 1980, and $689,000 on their

1988 campaigns—their campaign costs more than tripled, which is why they solicited the Cassidys, and thousands of others like them, more aggressively.

Just as Atwater and Ailes determined the content of the 1988 Bush campaign, so pollsters and consultants shaped the campaigns of numerous members of Congress. Even the practitioners of the new political magic were distressed by the change in their status from helper to guru. Peter Hart, a brilliant Democratic pollster who invented many of the poll-taker's most effective tricks, was one: "I got into this business [in the 1960s] when I called everybody 'sir,' " Hart said years later. "I got out of the business when they started calling me 'sir.' " He stopped working with individual candidates after the 1986 elections.

Another disenchanted former practitioner was Douglas Bailey, a moderate Republican consultant who worked in partnership for many years with John Deardorff. They are famous among their colleagues for making brilliant commercials that nearly rescued the presidency of Gerald Ford in 1976, when Jimmy Carter narrowly defeated him in the aftermath of Watergate. They represented numerous candidates for governor and Congress.

Interviewed in 1988, Bailey summarized the impact of the new political technology in a chilling comment to *The Washington Post:* "The biggest problem is that it's no longer necessary for a political candidate to guess what an audience thinks. He can do it with a nightly tracking poll. So it's no longer likely that political leaders are going to lead. Instead, they're going to follow."

The election results of 1988 confirmed the accuracy of Bailey's observation. They showed unmistakably that George Bush was not leading America, but had simply prevailed over his hapless Democratic opponent by pandering to public opinion. At the same time he was winning a convincing victory over Dukakis, Democrats picked up one new seat in the Senate and two in the House. Bush had no coattails. The technology could help him, but not his cause. Indeed, the technology had helped him get elected president *without* a cause.

Even when a candidate did have a cause, the political technicians could often knock it out of him. Bill Bradley, the former Democratic senator and candidate for president, described how this happened:

A good citizen decides to go into politics in hopes of promoting a national health care system, for example. To run, he or she has to rely on the new technicians, especially a pollster, a consultant, and a chief fundraiser. "The candidate says, 'I'm in politics to get national health insurance.' And the consultant says, 'You can't do that.' And the candidate says, 'I don't care—what good is it to be in politics if you can't make big changes?' So the consultant then talks to the fund-raiser. He says, 'You know Joe, he's crazy, he wants to reform health care, he won't win. Believe me, I know, I'm in the business of winning, and that'll be the death knell if he insists.' So the fund-raiser goes to Joe and says, 'Joe, you can't do that.' And Joe says, 'What do you mean, that's why I'm in politics, we talked about it before I got in.' 'Yeah, but the consultant, who knows how to win, says you can't win with that proposal. And Joe, what good are your big ideas if you lose?' So Joe makes the compromise. That's the first thing that happens."

The new political technology was too good to ignore in the years between elections. Once its effectiveness was clear, few politicians were prepared to neglect it or its implications after they had won office. In the days before polling and television commercials, senators assumed they had four or five years between campaigns to do the legislative work of the Senate, without spending much time or energy on campaign politics. House members thought they had at least a year or even eighteen months to concentrate on legislating before they again turned to campaigning. In the 1980s those assumptions were overtaken by new realities. Quite suddenly, the political season was extended—extended indefinitely, so that it never ended. American politics entered the era of the permanent campaign.

The phrase was coined by a young journalist named Sidney Blumenthal, who wrote about politics for the *Boston Phoenix*, an alternative newspaper. Blumenthal published a book in 1980 called *The Permanent Campaign* that was as prescient as it was insightful. "The permanent campaign," he wrote, "is the political ideology of our age. . . . It remakes government into an instrument designed to sustain an elected official's public popularity." Blumenthal thought he was describing a reality that already existed, but in fact, the use of campaign techniques to govern and to build popularity for the governors was in its infancy in 1980. In the years since, this has become the prevailing style of American politics at all levels.

CHAPTER 15

DISORDER IN THE HOUSE

When Gerald Cassidy advised the Ocean Spray cranberry cooperative to spend $7,000 on unneeded copies of Jim Wright's book in 1985, Wright was the firmly entrenched majority leader of the House of Representatives and everyone's favorite to succeed Tip O'Neill, who would retire from Congress at the end of 1986. Wright took the speaker's gavel in January 1987. He was soon the target of an official ethics investigation. The $55,000 in "royalties" that Wright had pocketed in the book deal were one of the subjects being investigated. The special counsel conducting the inquiry summoned Gerry Cassidy to explain Ocean Spray's book purchases in a formal deposition. Cassidy had violated no laws or rules, and the investigation caused him no legal difficulty, just embarrassment.

Wright was not so fortunate: in April 1989, when the Ethics Committee published the damning results of its investigation, he lost the confidence of his colleagues, gave up his job as speaker, then resigned from the House. Wright was a victim of the political warfare that Newt Gingrich had initiated. For Washington, this was a stunning reversal of fortune.

It was one of Cassidy's rules of thumb that Washington is constantly changing, but this was more change than he had bargained for. Wright had long been one of Cassidy & Associates' "champions," the name the firm gave to members who could help win earmarks for its clients. This relationship developed from Wright's friendship with John Silber, a Texan and dean at the University of Texas before he became the president of Boston University. For many years, Silber made political donations to Wright and encouraged friends to do the same. The congressman and the university president became pen pals. When Silber signed on as a Cassidy

client and begin to seek earmarks for Boston University, Wright, as
majority leader, helped get them approved. In 1985, when he was adding
new people to the firm, Cassidy hired one of Wright's principal aides,
Richard Pena. Given this history, it was no surprise that Cassidy would
respond positively when he was solicited to buy copies of the book.

What was a surprise was the open political warfare in the House of
Representatives that followed O'Neill's retirement and Gingrich's rise.
Wright was a casualty of that warfare. His dramatic demise, a triumph for
Gingrich, marked an important moment in the metamorphosis of the
Republican Party.

But in 1989 it was far from clear that Gingrich and his impatient,
bomb-throwing colleagues would soon displace the old Republican establishment in the House, then lead the Republicans to a historic victory in
1994. At the time of Wright's resignation, many Republicans worried that
Gingrich—at forty-five a young man compared to most of his colleagues—had overplayed his hand. Five years later, he would become
Speaker of the House. The story of how this happened illuminates the
changes that were transforming both Washington and the country's politics. It begins in 1981.

The sense of foreboding that had pushed the Democrats toward Tony
Coelho's vision of a majority protected by contributions from business
interests had other consequences as well. One was an aggressive decision
by Tip O'Neill and his lieutenants, including Wright, to allocate the
Democrats more seats on the key House committees in 1981 than their
fifty-seat majority justified. Traditionally, the division of committee seats
reflected the balance of power in the entire House, so by picking up
twenty-seven seats in 1980, Republicans expected closer ratios on the
major committees. But the Democrats barely yielded an inch. On the
Ways and Means Committee, for example, what had been a 24–12 Democratic advantage became, at O'Neill's insistence, a 23–12 Democratic
advantage. For Republicans this was exasperating.

The results of the 1982 House elections demoralized Republicans
further. They lost twenty-six seats to the Democrats, nearly every one
they had gained on Reagan's coattails in 1980. O'Neill and his colleagues
again had a strong liberal majority to frustrate both House Republicans
and the Reagan administration.

If Gingrich was discouraged he did not show it. Instead he organized
the Conservative Opportunity Society, a small band of like-minded
younger members who shared Gingrich's belief that "the Republican

Party could not simply be against," as his colleague Vin Weber put it. "They [Republicans] had to replace what existed with something new."

The most important thing that existed was Democratic control of the House—it had existed since 1955. Gingrich thought his colleagues were mired in the minority because they could not imagine being in the majority. He urged confrontation with the Democrats without concern for good manners or appearances. His aggressive posturing alarmed Congressman Bob Michel of Illinois, the Republican leader, and many other older Republican members, but they could not deter Gingrich. A student of warfare and a lover of military metaphors, he envisioned a multifront war: against cautious, moderate Republicans; against Democrats; and for public support outside of Congress.

In 1979, the year Gingrich came to Washington, C-SPAN began gavel-to-gavel television coverage of the House. Cable television was still young, and the initial audience was tiny, but Gingrich—recently elected with enormous help from slick television commercials—saw a new-age opportunity he thought others were missing. After organizing the COS in 1983, he and his comrades, led by Congressman Bob Walker of Pennsylvania, decided to make a habit of addressing the House after the close of regular business, when their only live audience was likely to be C-SPAN viewers. In fact the House was not their primary audience; they were speaking to the country.

Using this free access to the 17 million households then said to receive C-SPAN on their cable television service, Gingrich and Walker built a following. For months the Democrats paid no attention to these speeches. Then in May 1984 they noticed.

On May 8, after their colleagues had gone home, Gingrich and Walker addressed the empty House chamber together. They took turns reading from a long article, "What's the Matter with Democratic Foreign Policy?," written by a staff member of a conservative group called the Republican Study Committee. The paper lambasted, by name, Democratic members, all described as "radicals." One was Speaker O'Neill's best friend, Edward Boland of Massachusetts. After quoting Boland decrying the Vietnam War in 1971 as "little more than an exercise in futility," the report (this portion read by Gingrich) described the "pattern" of the rhetoric of Boland and others it quoted: "Give the benefit of every doubt to the communists, and doubt every benefit of your own nation. Make mincemeat of any ally dumb enough to fight on the side of the U.S. Trash America, indict the president, and give the benefit of every doubt to Marxist regimes. That's the standard formula." The report went on for thousands of words, ridiculing the past statements of twenty named Democratic members.

When O'Neill learned about this he erupted. He was furious that Gingrich had attacked fellow members by name without warning them that he planned to do so, when they could not respond—this was, in O'Neill's view, a gross violation of House tradition. In response, he ordered that thenceforth, when members gave speeches at the end of the day, the cameras should pan across the empty chamber to show that no one was listening. O'Neill obviously hoped this would make Gingrich and his comrades look foolish.

By rising to their bait, O'Neill had rejected the advice of colleagues who thought the Democrats should stay far away from the intensifying internecine Republican struggle between pro- and anti-Gingrich factions. Congressman Coelho, widely respected for his political acumen, said he had tried to persuade O'Neill to let "the right-wing crazies" hammer the Republican moderates. Coelho realized that many Republicans disapproved of Gingrich's aggressive tactics. "We should not get in the middle of that battle."

But O'Neill was angry. He defended his actions on the House floor on May 14 and criticized Gingrich's "un-American" attack on named colleagues: "A more low thing I have never seen."

When the House convened the next day, Gingrich rose from his desk to claim a "point of personal privilege." He walked to the well of the House, below the high bench on which the presiding officer sits with his gavel. He sharply rejected O'Neill's criticisms, noting that he and Walker had sent a letter to the congressmen named in the Republican report inviting them to join a debate when the two of them read the report into the record. He denied suggesting anyone was un-American. The issue was whether the named and quoted Democrats had good judgment. "It is perfectly American to be wrong . . . to have bad judgment," Gingrich said.

As Gingrich spoke, several Democrats, including Wright, asked him to yield the floor, the standard way to begin a debate. Gingrich refused and kept talking. Finally O'Neill himself came lumbering onto the floor and asked again: "Will the gentleman yield?" This time Gingrich did.

His voice rising, O'Neill shook a finger toward Gingrich and declared: "You deliberately stood . . . before an empty House and challenged these people [the named members], and challenged their Americanism, and it is the lowest thing that I have ever seen in my thirty-two years in Congress."

Trent Lott of Mississippi was then the deputy leader of House Republicans. When O'Neill referred to "the lowest thing I've heard," Lott jumped to his feet and asked the presiding officer to strike the remark from the record—it was "out of order" as a personal attack and should be "taken down," or excised from the *Congressional Record* that recorded all debate. After consulting the parliamentarian, the presiding officer ruled in Lott's favor: O'Neill's personal attack was indeed out of order. No one could remember another example of a speaker's words being "taken down."

Gingrich picked up his papers and walked back to his desk on the Republican side. His colleagues stood and applauded him—not just his conservative allies, but moderates and senior members too. Bob Michel, who occasionally played golf with O'Neill and always prided himself on his good relations with the speaker, was one of the few Republicans who did not applaud Gingrich.

Only later was the significance of that day clear. Until then Gingrich had been "a junior Republican," as *The Washington Post* called him in its report on these events—an outspoken troublemaker who made his elders nervous. His confrontation with O'Neill did not change everyone's assessment of him, but it vastly enhanced his stature in the Republican caucus.

O'Neill did what no Republican could have—he united House Republicans. In 1984 they were a motley gang, ranging from Hamilton Fish Jr., a patrician, liberal Rockefeller Republican from New York, to Gingrich and his right-wing colleagues in the Conservative Opportunity Society. The factions did not hide their misgivings about each other. But that spring Republicans all responded positively to a tape of highlights from House debates assembled by their leadership staff. It featured what they considered O'Neill's imperious behavior, showing the speaker ignoring, bullying, or insulting Republicans. They called the film "Tip's Greatest Hits," and it had a tonic effect. "It just brings everybody on our side together as a team," said Steve Lotterer, a staff assistant to the National Republican Congressional Committee. Many Republican members gave Gingrich the credit for creating—with O'Neill's invaluable help—this new unity.

But it was a unity *against*—against O'Neill—which was not the same as a strategically united party sharing the same political objectives. And it did not lead to electoral success. In 1984 the Republicans were disappointed again; they could pick up only sixteen seats from the Democrats, even as Reagan was swamping Mondale. Michel even criticized Reagan for doing too little to bring House candidates into office with him. The Republican mood was gloomy.

The Democrats, not surprisingly, were feeling cocky. They had survived a second Reagan landslide and held their big majority in the House—more than seventy seats in 1985. To increase that majority by a single seat, they then memorably and momentously overplayed their hand.

At issue was the outcome in Indiana's 8th Congressional District, which held the closest House election in the country in 1984. On election night, the Democratic incumbent, Frank McCloskey, appeared to win by just seventy-two votes. But a subsequently discovered counting error in one county produced a different result: victory for Republican Richard D. McIntyre by thirty-four votes. Indiana's secretary of state certified that result. Democrats demanded a recount, which increased McIntyre's lead to 418 votes; the secretary of state certified McIntyre the winner for a second time.

But the Democrats refused to accept that outcome. They complained about uncounted ballots and other irregularities, though journalists and independent election experts could find no basis for rejecting McIntyre's victory. *The Washington Post* editorialized: "The votes are in. They have been counted twice. The margin of victory is comfortable, and Indiana election officials have twice certified the winner."

Instead the House leadership created a bipartisan "commission" of one Republican and two Democratic members who hired outside election experts and auditors from the Government Accounting Office to conduct their own recount, though this was traditionally considered the states' role. After many complications involving absentee ballots that had been incorrectly counted originally, the final count of the GAO auditors showed McCloskey, the Democrat, ahead by four votes. On this highly disputable basis, the Democrats voted to seat McCloskey. When Republicans moved to declare the seat vacant and ask the governor of Indiana to call a special election, Democrats defeated that idea too, though nineteen Democratic members voted with the Republicans for a new election. The vote was 229–200.

Now the animosity between Republicans and Democrats was fierce. Congressman Bob McEwen, an Ohio Republican, summed up his party's view on the day of that vote: "Mr. Speaker," he said on the House floor, "you know how to win votes the old-fashioned way. You steal them."

Michel, the Republican leader, did not hide his anger. "Might does not make right," he said on the floor. "The McIntrye case is but one example of a consistent abuse and misuse of power by the majority." He and his colleagues recited a long list of horror stories, from pugnacious Democrats like Marty Russo of Illinois picking fights on the floor to Democratic presiding officers miscounting votes to Republicans' disadvantage.

The Republicans' first reaction to the decision to seat McCloskey was obstructionist; the next day they forced the House to adjourn without accomplishing anything. Gingrich, the principal beneficiary of these events, spoke of making some kind of civil disobedience a regular occurrence, but Michel and other cooler heads blocked that idea. Democratic behavior united the Republicans in indignation, but did not produce a unified Republican response. On tactical and ideological issues, the caucus remained sharply divided. Hard-liners, Gingrich the most prominent, thought fulfilling their goal—the end of Democratic control—could justify radical means. The more cautious traditionalists around Michel were not prepared to throw bombs.

By 1985, the two parties in the House were hopelessly divided. They could not even see the same realities. Democrats perceived an aggressive opposition pressing them harder than they had ever been pressed before; they saw Republicans raising more money than they in election after election; they saw a Republican in the White House and Republicans running the Senate. They felt under siege, and vulnerable too. So as long as they had a clear majority in the House, they would use it to advance their interests aggressively.

Republicans saw themselves as permanent victims. In the post-Watergate House, in which Democratic members had insisted on reforms that gave them all more individual influence, the biggest losers were Republicans. After the brief interlude in 1981–83 when Reagan prevailed on many important votes, House Republicans had little to no influence on legislation. So they made campaign commercials personally attacking O'Neill. They tried to force votes on the floor on meaningless but politically sensitive amendments that might embarrass Democrats in their next elections. In speeches and articles the Conservative Opportunity Society members depicted the Democratic majority as corrupt and self-serving.

The only consensus in the House was that it had become an awful place to work. Many of the most ambitious and talented Republicans cried uncle, choosing to retire or run for the Senate, where many of them ended up.

Tip O'Neill was also ready to leave his beloved House. Early in 1985, when he was seventy-two, the speaker announced his intention to retire at the beginning of 1987. Wright prepared to succeed him.

Where O'Neill was an old Irish pol, full of fun and rarely agitated,

Wright was bright and aggressive, an intense, ambitious man who always meant business. Gingrich considered Wright a serious opponent who could become a "great" speaker. "If Wright consolidates his power, he will be a very, very formidable man," Gingrich said at the time. "We [have] to take him on early to prevent that."

Gingrich never hid his desire to bring down the Democratic establishment in the House. He was a careful student of the Washington news media, and prided himself on his ability to get their attention. "The number-one fact about the news media," he said in a speech soon after his fight with O'Neill, "is that they love fights. When you give them confrontations, you get attention. When you get attention, you can educate."

One of Gingrich's favorite arguments was that power had corrupted the Democrats. He had cases to support his point: in the 1980 ABSCAM scandal, one Democratic senator and four Democrats in the House were convicted of accepting bribes from phony Arab sheikhs (really FBI agents running a sting operation). All were forced out of Congress. One Republican was also convicted, but this had no effect on Gingrich's argument that under Democratic control, the House had become corrupt. He picked up the theme again in 1983, when two members, one gay Democrat and one straight Republican, were brought before the House Ethics Committee on charges that they had had sex with seventeen-year-old pages, employees of the House. The Ethics Committee recommended "reprimands" for both, but Gingrich pressed for their expulsion. The House decided to "censure" them, a compromise between reprimand and expulsion. Then the Democrats' refusal to seat the certified winner in the 8th District of Indiana confirmed—at least in Republican eyes—Gingrich's argument: the Democrats were corrupt.

Gingrich targeted Wright. He assigned a member of his staff to read the Texas press for years to find possible dirt on the new speaker. He attacked Wright by name in speeches around the country. He encouraged reporters to investigate the new speaker, and shared files his staff created of stories that raised questions about Wright's ethics. Wright, a habitual corner-cutter who refused to see how some of his friendships and actions looked questionable to others, played right into Gingrich's hands.

One of those friendships was with George Mallick, a real estate developer in Fort Worth, with whom Wright and his wife had gone into business. Texas newspapers reported that Wright had arranged earmarks totaling $30 million that Mallick hoped to draw on to finance a project to redevelop the Fort Worth stockyards. The plan never came to fruition.

Then on September 24, 1987, *The Washington Post* published a long investigative report on Wright's book deal, which included the 55 percent royalty arrangement.

Texas newspapers reported on Wright's intervention with federal regulators on behalf of friends and constituents in the savings and loan business in Texas. He did this just as the savings and loan industry was collapsing, creating a financial crisis that eventually cost taxpayers billions of dollars. When stories describing Wright's intervention appeared, he defended his actions as efforts to ensure that constituents of his were treated fairly, but they were fat cat constituents. One had provided a private plane for Wright's use. Other stories reported that Wright had asked the late Egyptian president Anwar Sadat to help a Texas oilman and Wright business partner.

Editorials questioning Wright's behavior followed. In May 1988, the watchdog group Common Cause formally called upon the House Ethics Committee to investigate the speaker. A week later Gingrich jumped in. The original Conservative Opportunity Society consisted of Gingrich and three colleagues. Now he persuaded nearly half the Republicans in the House, seventy-one of them including all the party's leaders except Bob Michel, to sign a letter asking for an Ethics Committee investigation of these and other accusations against Wright. Gingrich had been hoping for an opportunity to make this move for more than a year, but he pretended that the decision to send the letter was the result of recent newspaper stories. "The more he has been scrutinized by the news media, the more questions about his possible unethical behavior there are to be answered," he said.

Obviously Gingrich's stature was growing. This was formally confirmed ten months later when House Republicans had to choose a new whip, the second-ranking position in their leadership. Gingrich won the job by 87–85, defeating the more moderate alternative whom Michel favored as his deputy. Everyone understood the symbolism—the young revolutionaries were supplanting the old guard. Gingrich was a "junior Republican" no more.

By the spring of 1989, the atmosphere in the House was poisonous, and anxieties among members were high. *The Washington Post* disclosed in March that Gingrich himself had an unusual book deal; twenty-one supporters had contributed $5,000 each to a "partnership" whose purpose was to promote a book that Gingrich, his wife, and a freelance writer had written together trumpeting Gingrich's optimism about the future of

America. Gingrich said the idea was to advertise and promote the book so intensely that it would become a best-seller. "I was naive," he told the *Post*. The fund paid his wife at least $10,000, and spent $70,000 promoting the book, which sold only modestly. Its failure in the marketplace allowed twenty-two "partners" including Mrs. Gingrich to take tax deductions related to the partnership's losses.

While the Ethics Committee labored over the course of a year toward a resolution of the Wright case, the *Post* published another revelation: that Congressman Coelho, by then the majority whip, had been given a financial favor by a California savings and loan executive who was his political supporter. The executive bought a special issue of high-yield junk bonds for Coelho; the congressman then borrowed the purchase price to pay him back, and sold the bonds for a $7,000 profit. Five weeks after the story appeared, Coelho shocked Washington by announcing that he would retire from Congress: "I don't intend to put my family through more turmoil," he said.

Four days later, the Wright investigation came to an end. The speaker's lawyers could not convince the committee of his innocence; a clear majority, including Democrats, was prepared to find that he had broken House rules. On May 31, 1989, before the committee had taken formal action, Wright announced that he would resign as speaker, and as a member of Congress.

Gingrich had set out to destroy the Democrats. Now two of their three House leaders had been driven from office. Gingrich had won a mighty victory. But it came at a mighty cost. The ability to get along and work together—"comity" was the congressional term for it—had been shattered. "There's an evil wind blowing in the halls of Congress today that's reminiscent of the Spanish Inquisition," said one of Wright's staunchest supporters, Congressman Jack Brooks, a cigar-chomping Texas pol. "We've replaced comity and compassion with hatred and malice." Brooks was trying to portray Wright as an innocent victim, a forlorn ploy, but his description of the state of the House was accurate nonetheless. In his speech announcing his resignation Wright pleaded with his fellow members to "bring this mindless cannibalism to an end." He might as well have asked them to stop raising campaign contributions.

These events were revealing on many levels. The transgressions of senior members illuminated the ethical climate at the time—cutting corners was in fashion. The animosities within the Republican Party and across the aisle dividing Democrats from Republicans were omens of a future that was now close at hand—a time when Gingrich would lead a resurgent GOP dominated by aggressive conservative allies, and the warfare would be bloody.

Democrats wanted to blame Gingrich and his allies for the ugliness that had become ubiquitous, but that was much too simple. Gingrich was ferocious, a political assassin absolutely determined to transform the House, but he would never have prevailed without the help Democrats had been giving him for years. Their overbearing tactics since 1981 had played right into his hands.

CHAPTER 16

BECOMING A CONGLOMERATE

The fate of Cassidy & Associates during 1989 was revealing. On one hand this was a year of public embarrassments: *The Washington Post* exposed the firm's modus operandi, the ways it exploited its relationships with members of Congress and greased them with campaign contributions and honoraria. The chairman of the Senate Appropriations Committee and former majority leader, Robert Byrd, had described Cassidy & Associates lobbyists (not by name, but unmistakably) as "influence peddlers" who "sell themselves as hired guns to the highest bidder." And yet, business boomed. Between January and September 1989, the firm signed up thirty new clients. Cassidy expected more than $21 million in revenue for that year. No lobbying firm in the history of Washington had taken in so much money.

This apparent contradiction disconcerted Cassidy, who never enjoyed criticism. He particularly disliked the opening that the *Post*'s articles and Byrd's statements gave to a growing group of competitors, lobbyists who finally caught on to how well Cassidy had done in the earmark business and were entering it themselves. "This is a very competitive city, and for a long time, people who we might be competing with would hand out an article about the Byrd Amendment [to prospective clients]. It went on for several years," Cassidy recalled.

Nevertheless, wasn't this a boom time for the firm?

"It was," Cassidy said. "But it was also a very difficult time. It was a boom time because we didn't stop. There's an old Irish expression, 'It's a great life if you don't weaken'—and we didn't weaken. We just pushed as hard as we could. Personally it was a very difficult time, and very stressful.

In a row we had Dan [Morgan]'s article, the Byrd Amendment, and we had
had the Danforth issue. It was very stressful, and it was a real battle to
overcome it."

That was how Cassidy had seen his world since he was a boy—a constant struggle. In the *Oxford Dictionary of Quotations*, "It's a great life if you
don't weaken" is attributed to John Buchan (1875–1940), a Scottish novelist and politician, but no matter: Cassidy saw it as a statement of his own
credo.

Cassidy's colleagues did not understand this side of their boss, perhaps
because none of them had struggled the way he had. They saw an amazing
business model that churned out profits. They saw dozens of clients, more
every month, eager to tap into the U.S. Treasury for earmarks of their
own. As one of the lobbyists in the firm put it: "Where else could a university president or a hospital board get ten or fifteen million dollars by paying several hundred thousand dollars?" He was comparing a typical grant
won by Cassidy & Associates at the time to the typical retainer a client
paid for its services.

John Silber did the math more precisely. To make his calculation he
used the first federal appropriations Cassidy helped Boston University
get to build a new science and engineering building in the early 1980s.
Congress allocated $27 million for the building. Silber, ever the calculat-
ing university executive, imagined that as a contribution to the BU
endowment.

"If you take $27 million, that would bring in, at 5 percent [interest],
about $1.35 million a year. On average we've always been able to get at
least a 5 percent interest rate on our money [in the university endowment
fund]. So just take that first $27 million and regard it as an endowment.
That endowment generates $1.35 million [5 percent of $27 million] every
year, and Gerry [Cassidy] at that time was billing us about $300,000
[annually—a number that eventually grew to $960,000 in 2007]. So that
first grant, by itself, produced about twice as much as was necessary [to
pay for all of BU's lobbying]. . . . So if you talk about a cost analysis, it's a
damn good investment." Silber's calculation was accurate, even after
counting the rising lobbying fees BU paid Cassidy over the years.

Even better, from the lobbyists' perspective, the work was not oner-
ous. "It's easy money," said Don Smith, the former Appropriations Committee staff man who worked for Cassidy from 1987 to 1994. "I don't
think lobbying is hard work."

Once members of Congress understood the earmarking process, they were delighted to assign their own staff to keep track of a particular earmark proposal and make sure that most of the paperwork and member-to-member explanations and exhortations were taken care of. Persuading members to become advocates for specific projects was rarely difficult. Another former Cassidy lobbyist, Elliott Fiedler, explained: "Frankly it wasn't too hard a sell, once you could go in and see a member with your client"—the hospital director or college president from the congressman's district who was looking for the member's help. "It was almost always great politics for the member," Fielder said, noting how eager recipients of earmarks were to sing the praises of the members who helped get them.

So the money kept pouring in. Cassidy may have felt stress, but he also saw opportunity. The interest in his firm shown by Peter Gummer, the Englishman who had put up the $1 million to explore acquiring his business, had convinced Cassidy that his creation had substantial value. Other approaches from several potential buyers confirmed this. Cassidy wanted to figure out how to extract this value and put it in his own pocket. This too set him apart from his colleagues, who were thrilled to be making so much money, and eager to simply carry on as enormously successful lobbyists. Cassidy dreamed of more.

He had an important collaborator in those dreams: Lester Fant, Cassidy's lawyer since 1984 when Bill Cloherty found him to help dissolve the Schlossberg-Cassidy partnership. From then on, Fant—Ruff to all who knew him—was Cassidy's lawyer. He would become one of the most important figures in the history of Cassidy & Associates, despite the fact that he never signed up a client for the firm or lobbied on Capitol Hill. He was important not to the lobbying operation, but to fulfilling Cassidy's ambition for great wealth.

A compact, handsome man, Fant grew up in Holly Springs, Mississippi, near Oxford, and spoke with a euphonious southern accent. He graduated with honors from Harvard Law School, served three years in the Marines, and won a job at a new tax law firm in Washington. Sidley & Austin, the huge Chicago-based firm, lured him from his tax practice by offering him a partnership to run the corporate and tax practice in its Washington office. "That sounds better than it was because there was none in the Washington office at that time," Fant recounted. "My job was to build one." Cassidy & Associates became an important client.

Years later, long after his association with Cassidy had made him a wealthy man, Fant emphasized his ignorance about lobbying. "I didn't know much about that particular industry. I tell people it's like living in

Detroit and not having anything to do with cars. I've really never had anything to do with the government. One of the reasons I wanted to be a tax lawyer was, there was no politics."

As Cassidy & Associates grew, Cassidy had more work for his lawyer. "I enjoyed working for him," Fant said, though he acknowledged that "some of the people at Sidley & Austin," a white-shoe law firm, wondered why he was representing a lobbyist. "We're working for a *lobbyist*? We work for railroads, and AT&T, and things like that, why are we working for a lobbyist? But I really did think he was an ethical person. The key thing was, would he follow your advice? And I thought he would. I thought it was a good professional relationship."

Cassidy liked it too. He considered Fant "one of the brightest people I've ever known. . . . He had very good ideas about business, he was a great counselor." But he added, "You'll find that a lot of people don't like him." Cassidy knew that Fant was unpopular inside Cassidy & Associates, but it wasn't the lawyer's job to be popular. His job was to make Cassidy rich.

In the late 1980s, Fant recalled, Cassidy "was making a *lot* of money, and he was always worrying about it—you know, will I make a lot of money next year? Should I sell the firm? What can I do to capitalize on what I've created? We had a lot of discussions about that." Fant also had discussions with several potential buyers of the firm, but they all came to naught.

Traditionally, the firm operated on a simple formula: all the money that came in was paid out as salary and bonuses, or to cover expenses. The largest amounts always went to Cassidy himself, but everyone was well paid, and at the end of the year, nothing was left over. "The company did not have a balance sheet," as Fant put it. There were no balances. Apart from his handsome remuneration, Cassidy accumulated no capital.

As a practicing lawyer, Fant had helped other entrepreneurs figure out how to take capital out of the businesses they had created. One device he had used was an employee stock ownership plan (ESOP), which permits the sale of companies—in whole or in part—to a plan that benefits the company's employees.

The godfather of the modern ESOP was Russell Long, Democratic senator from Louisiana and longtime chairman of the Senate Finance Committee. Long revered his father, Huey "The Kingfish" Long, who had hoped, before he was assassinated in 1935, to ride his "Share Our Wealth" campaign into the White House. Russell was seventeen when his father was killed. Thirteen years later the young Long was elected to the Senate, where he served for four decades. He saw ESOPs as a kind of employee capitalism that could fulfill Huey Long's dream: "Every Man a King." Russell Long pushed laws through Congress that created numerous, generous incentives for owners to create an ESOP and sell their business to it.

Ordinarily, a proprietor like Cassidy who had created his own company, controlled its ownership, and wanted to extract some of its value would have to find a buyer to whom he could sell all or part of his business. An ESOP offered a more attractive alternative. By selling at least 30 percent of the company to an ESOP, Cassidy could avoid paying taxes on the proceeds as long as they were invested in stock or bonds issued by other American corporations. Moreover, the company selling part of itself to an ESOP would enjoy its own substantial tax benefits. Yet the owner could retain complete control of the firm.

So with Fant's help, Cassidy created an ESOP, which they set up as a retirement plan. The company would buy 30 percent of the shares in Cassidy & Associates and contribute them to the ESOP. The value of those shares would ultimately be used to fund the retirements of qualifying Cassidy employees.

When Fant explained the ESOP, Cassidy remembered, he realized that "everyone in the company would have a stake in the company, right down to the receptionist." This was "an idea that I liked," Cassidy said. It suited his image of himself as paterfamilias to the entire firm.

But there was one significant complication: because the firm was a private company owned mostly by Gerald and Loretta Cassidy, there was no market for the company's shares. So there was no easy way to establish their fair market value. Nor was there any obvious mechanism for cashing in the ESOP's shares when someone eligible for the plan's benefits retired—a problem for the future.

The law allowed the fair market value question to be resolved by an outside appraiser who would put a value on the company's shares. The appraiser valued the firm at approximately $50 million, concluding that a 30 percent interest was worth $15 million. But the company did not have $15 million on hand—as Fant explained, it had no accumulated capital.

So Cassidy and Fant found Aegon, a Dutch insurance company, that was willing to arrange (with four other insurance companies) a loan of $15 million to Cassidy & Associates, to be repaid out of Cassidy's healthy cash flow. The ESOP used this money to buy the shares. Cassidy & Associates assumed responsibility for the loan; it signed notes that obligated the company to pay nearly $2 million a year until the loan was paid off. Interest was set at 10.5 percent per annum.

The company had a big new debt. But because the law favored ESOP transactions, the stock sale also created generous deductions that reduced the firm's current income taxes and generated—on paper—"net operating losses" that would reduce taxes on future income.

And the sellers of the stock acquired by the ESOP had a windfall—first of all Cassidy and his wife. They owned most of the shares, and they sold $11 million worth to the ESOP. Cassidy had also allocated small ownership positions to Fabiani, Fant, Versage, Godfrey, and a few others. These other shareholders divided $4 million in the ESOP transaction.

Cassidy had "sold" nearly a third of his company and was still in charge. The ESOP shares were "owned" by a bank, acting as a trustee ostensibly representing the interests of the employees enrolled in the ESOP. But the trustee had no influence on the operations of the company. The ESOP shares—and thus the employees' retirement benefits—would have no cash value until the company was sold, suggesting the necessity of a sale sometime in the future.

Employees disagreed about the value of the ESOP. Some liked the idea, many thought it was a scam. It was the only retirement plan the firm offered, and many employees wondered if it would ever be worth anything.

Cassidy had begun accumulating serious capital during the booming late 1980s, when his salary and bonus exceeded $3 million every year. He invested $6 million in mutual funds in those years, the first building blocks of his personal fortune. He then bought corporate bonds with the $11 million he received from the ESOP transaction—U.S. securities that qualified for the ESOP tax exemption, so he never paid any federal income tax on the $11 million. (He did not touch these investments for the next quarter-century; by 2006 they were worth more than $65 million.)

So fourteen years after becoming a lobbyist and five years after pushing Ken Schlossberg out of their firm, Gerald Cassidy's net worth approached $20 million. He bought his first million-dollar real estate, a snazzy new $1.2 million home in Old Town Alexandria, the stylish residential neighborhood of eighteenth- and nineteenth-century houses just blocks from the Potomac River. The kid from Red Hook had done it—the financial security he had craved since childhood was now his. This accomplishment did not remotely satisfy him.

The ESOP deal had "created a currency [shares in the firm] where I could go out and attract people," said Cassidy. He thought the time had come to expand, to explore new lines of work related to lobbying and reduce the firm's dependence on "appropriations," the term Cassidy and his colleagues used to describe their earmarks business. Cassidy was ready to take a few plunges.

"Every five years or so you've got to make changes," Cassidy explained years later, and this is what he did. His comment was an expression of his management philosophy: alterations going on as usual during business. He was never content with the status quo and always had a plan to improve it. Now that he was reliably rich, he could fully indulge his more adventurous impulses.

Of course the status quo was never static. Like the country of which it is the capital, Washington changes constantly. In 1989, the year of the ESOP deal, Cassidy could look back on two decades in Washington that spanned four presidencies, from Richard Nixon to George H. W. Bush, a time of remarkable changes. The national economy had been expanding briskly since 1983. The Reagan era (1981–89) had fostered a new ethos in the land; making money was in fashion. These were the first of the go-go years that would continue until the end of the twentieth century—one of the great boom periods in American history. Washington, never immune from the fashions and enthusiasms of American society, absorbed and then reflected the spirit of the go-go years. Commercial and residential real estate boomed as downtown Washington spread to the east and west of the traditional business districts. New stores and restaurants catered to a wealthy clientele. A building boom of mansion-style suburban housing transformed large sections of Fairfax County, Virginia, and Montgomery County, Maryland, Washington's two wealthiest suburbs.

Cassidy, of course, was hardly alone in his pursuit of serious money. Perhaps his best-known compatriot in that quest was Clark Clifford, an older and grander Washington lobbyist of a different type. Clifford had a better Washington pedigree than Cassidy, having served not only President Truman but also President Lyndon Johnson as secretary of defense. His wavy white hair, double-breasted suits, and operatic baritone became fixtures in Washington over half a century. Though he made a great deal of money representing corporations before various federal agencies and Congress, Clifford never deigned to register as a lobbyist. He was a lawyer and a counselor—in his own mind, anyway.

But he also had a big appetite for dollars. Clifford surprised his friends in 1978 by becoming a banker. Then he was swept up in one of the biggest banking scandals of the go-go era when it became known that his First American Bank, headquartered in Washington, had been secretly and illegally acquired by the Bank of Credit and Commerce International, a

Pakistani-owned institution. BCCI was a cesspool of fraud, forced to close in 1991 by the bank regulators of seven different countries. Clifford was indicted on charges of lying to banking regulators, accepting bribes, and falsifying bank records. He was eighty-five at the time, and was spared a trial on these charges because of failing health. It was, as *The New York Times* later wrote, an "inglorious end" to Clifford's career. Clifford's demise was also a fitting morality tale for the times.

Cassidy never tried banking. His next big idea was to create a one-stop, multiservice organization that could serve clients who needed lobbying, public relations, grassroots support, and public opinion polling.

"My thinking had developed about where the business was going," Cassidy said. "You could see the changes happening in the Congress. . . . More and more I was seeing big issues needed to be influenced by public opinion, so I wanted to create a public affairs firm."

His analysis was accurate. Fifteen years had passed since the Class of 1974 had begun to transform the House of Representatives, decentralizing the institution and empowering individual members. The speaker and the committee chairmen could no longer determine outcomes as they had previously. At the beginning of the 1970s reforms in the Senate had similarly diffused power once held by committee chairmen to newly empowered subcommittee chairs. These changes in both houses made it impossible for a lobbyist (or a president) to achieve an objective in Congress by winning over just a handful of powerful leaders. Instead, as Cassidy suggested, special pleaders had to convince individual members—often a majority of them—to support their cause, one at a time. This was easiest to do when the members thought public opinion supported the desired outcome. So it made sense, as Cassidy said, for a lobbyist to want to be able to influence public opinion.

By the time Cassidy decided he needed a public relations arm, PR had become an integral part of American politics, though its role and significance were rarely acknowledged, particularly by politicians. Calvin Coolidge was the first president to consult a public relations man, and he picked a good one: Edward L. Bernays, the Vienna-born nephew of Sigmund Freud and the "father" of modern American PR. Coolidge, a former governor of Massachusetts little known in the country, had become president in 1923 when Warren Harding suddenly died in office. "Silent Cal" was a cold, remote person. His aides wanted to warm up his image in preparation for the 1924 election, when he would seek the presidency in his own right. Bernays proposed an early "media event": a breakfast at the

White House where Coolidge would eat pancakes with the great Al Jolson and thirty other vaudeville performers—all Republicans, who took the opportunity to announce their support for the president. The newspapers loved the story. "Actors Eat Cakes with the Coolidges," was the front-page headline in *The New York Times.* "President Nearly Laughs."

Bernays (1891–1995) was one of the most important figures in twentieth-century America, though his fame has spread only to a limited circle of specialists and aficionados of the profession he helped invent. Brilliant, original, and—as an immigrant from Central Europe— unencumbered by romantic American patriotism, Bernays unabashedly endorsed the manipulation of public opinion as a service to his adopted homeland and to democracy. In 1928 he wrote an article he titled "Manipulating Public Opinion," arguing the desirability of using modern techniques to shape and guide public thinking. Bernays liked to use prominent people whom he called "group leaders and opinion molders" to do that. To improve American society, he argued in that article, public attitudes sometimes had to be modified to overcome "the inertia of established traditions and prejudices."

Bernays criticized American leaders who relied on "hunches and insight" to influence their countrymen when they could use a panoply of modern techniques and devices that would be much more effective. Among them were polling and other forms of market research. One of his favorite phrases was "The Engineering of Consent," which he used as the title of a 1947 essay. He defined the term as "the application of scientific practices . . . to the task of getting people to support ideas and programs." The tools needed by the political engineers who pursued "consent" were readily available, he argued: market research, polls, and symbols—like Al Jolson. Compared to a good piece of research, a hunch was relatively worthless, Bernays believed. "Unless you know what the people want and what their attitudes are, you can't move ahead," he said. Modern political consultants are Bernays's descendants.

Cassidy and Fabiani decided in 1989 that they should develop a public relations capacity themselves. This decision led Cassidy to the first and only genuine Washington celebrity he ever hired, a man who would become his friend and in odd ways his role model: Jody Powell.

Powell, press secretary to Jimmy Carter from the beginning of Carter's campaign for governor of Georgia in 1970 until he left the White House in 1981, was a large personality. He liked to fool people by acting the part he was born to—aw-shucks hillbilly from South Georgia. Behind the thick southern accent and the cloud of cigarette smoke that surrounded him for years lurked a smart, resourceful, and charming person. He was a popular figure in Washington, and widely admired.

Powell and Ruff Fant were neighbors in a leafy section of northwest Washington and had become friends. Fant had arranged for Powell and Cassidy to have lunch a few years earlier, when Powell was running the Washington office of Ogilvy Public Relations, a big New York–based company. "Lobbying firms were a good source of business for us," Powell recalled, "so I was happy to have lunch." He and Cassidy talked about the role public relations could play in lobbying.

Powell was surprised, a year or so later, to read in the paper that Cassidy had hired Sheila Tate, former press secretary to Nancy Reagan and spokesperson for the 1988 Bush campaign for president, and Jonathan Jessar, another Republican PR veteran, to create a public relations arm of Cassidy & Associates. "I thought he'd hire us," Powell recalled years later, chewing his nicotine gum through his good-ole-boy grin. "But instead he created a competitor."

Hiring Tate had been Fabiani's idea. She was a friend of his wife's and the godmother to one of his daughters. Tate and Jessar got off to a slow start at Cassidy & Associates, then Jessar suddenly died. Fabiani urged that they make an approach to Powell. He and Fant had lunch with Powell to discuss it. The timing was fortuitous—Ogilvy had just been sold, and Powell disliked the new owners.

When Powell sat down with Cassidy, the proprietor touted his new ESOP as a reason for Powell to come aboard. Powell liked the notion of sharing in ownership. At Cassidy & Associates, "you could create value, and share the value you created, which is very hard to do at most companies," he said. Cassidy was promising Powell the first serious money he had ever been able to accumulate—millions of dollars over time.

Powell agreed to establish, with Tate, a new public relations firm called Powell Tate as an affiliate of Cassidy & Associates. He started work on September 1, 1991. "I told Gerry he needed to start at the top, hire some good PR people," Powell recalled. Cassidy remembered this too: "I gave Jody a blank check to hire people," he said.

Powell quickly signed up half a dozen senior PR professionals, including former Ogilvy colleagues. Initially, they cost a lot more money than they brought in. Within about a month Powell Tate was $600,000 in the hole. "But we turned it around quickly," Powell remembered with a glint in his eye. Powell Tate was profitable at the end of its first year, and did very well for several years thereafter.

"Cassidy encouraged the creation of a first-class PR operation," recalled Dale Leibach, one of Powell's original hires, "and he didn't try to micromanage." The Powell Tate name was soon well known, and the firm's reputation was excellent. Public relations was not as profitable as lobbying—PR agencies couldn't work on fat retainers, they had to charge for actual work done. And they had a great deal of competition, which held rates down. But Powell Tate thrived.

The launch of Powell Tate coincided with another momentous step: the leasing of new office space. Cassidy had outgrown its posh quarters in Metropolitan Square. The last people hired into the firm while it still occupied that space had to sit at desks in corridors. There was no room to expand there, so Cassidy and Fabiani picked a two-year-old office building two long blocks to the east, closer to the Capitol, at 700 Thirteenth Street N.W., just north of G Street. They leased an entire floor of 21,000 square feet and created a spacious new headquarters.

Fabiani fancied himself something of an interior designer, and Cassidy gave him an important role in decorating the new offices. A believer in the power of first impressions, Fabiani wanted a space that would give visitors—especially potential clients—a sense of wealth and power. He ended up with a suite of offices that he hoped would remind people of a white-shoe law firm. He bought a number of fine, Federal period antiques for the public spaces. On the walls they hung a compelling Audubon print of a bald eagle, English prints including cartoons from *Punch* that Cassidy had collected, and etchings from *Harper's Weekly*.

Cassidy and Fabiani occupied corner offices. Individual lobbyists had offices along the outer walls (all four sides of the building had windows, an unusual feature); secretaries sat in wide interior corridors decorated with statues and busts. For his office Cassidy bought the copy of a Gilbert Stuart portrait of George Washington. The offices and hallways were decorated with crown moldings and wood paneling that was painted in a yellowish beige. A plush carpet of the same color was laid wall to wall almost everywhere, though not in Cassidy's own office, where hardwood floors were partially covered with oriental carpets, including a fine, ivory Agra from India.

If interior decor could speak, these offices would have said money, stability, tradition, and perhaps money again. No Washington law office had finer digs. Cassidy & Associates, a $50 million firm if the ESOP numbers were to be believed, now had entirely suitable quarters.

CHAPTER 17

INFLUENCING POLICY FOR PROFIT

As Cassidy & Associates grew and prospered, Gerald Cassidy yearned to become a bigger player in Washington debates on policy. Earmarked appropriations were his firm's meat, potatoes, and gravy, but the field was getting crowded, the rewards diminishing. As more lobbyists and members discovered earmarking and the number of earmarks grew, their size steadily declined. In the glory days Cassidy could help a university get $10, $15, even $20 million and more for a single project. By 1990 that was no longer realistic.

Lobbyists known for their ability to influence policy decisions had higher status in Washington than simple favor-seekers or pursuers of earmarks. The most famous lobbyists made less money than Cassidy did, but they had more stature. Someone like William Timmons of Timmons & Company, founded the same year as Schlossberg-Cassidy, moved in different circles than Cassidy. Timmons had been in charge of congressional relations—lobbying, in effect—for the White House for five years under Nixon and Ford. That job allowed him to make friends with senior members of Congress, cabinet members, Nixon's and Ford's confidants, and the influential people from outside the government who always hover around the White House. His political and social skills had made Timmons a favorite among important Washingtonians. His lobbying business was immediately successful. He could limit the number of corporate clients his small firm would represent at any one time, and he kept a waiting list of companies that hoped to retain him. Clients such as Anheuser-Busch, Chrysler, and the American Medical Association hired Timmons not just to win favors or influence legislation, but to provide strategic political advice. Cassidy knew he wasn't in Timmons's class, but he knew he was smart, and he wanted more chances to show his stuff.

Cassidy's favorite early client was the Ocean Spray cranberry cooperative, whose interests got him into a series of fights over policy. In the first of them, he had loved going up against the Coca-Cola Company, owner of Minute Maid orange juice, on behalf of Ocean Spray in a dispute over whether cranberry juice could be served as part of the government's school lunch and breakfast programs.

Disputes over policy brought out the strategist in Cassidy. He loved to plot a lobbying campaign based on his own or his client's relationships with government officials and members of Congress and his knowledge of how the system worked. He loved trying to convince officials that what his client wanted was precisely what these officials wanted to do.

Cassidy likes to tell the story of how he helped head off a proposed new regulation from the Food and Drug Administration in 1981 that would have required Ocean Spray to reveal in large type on its labels how much actual fruit juice was in its juice products. Such labels would have acknowledged that a typical Ocean Spray product contained 75 percent water. Orange juice makers would have been able to say their product was 100 percent juice. Cranberry juice producers "would have got killed in the breakfast market," Cassidy said. "So what we did was develop a demonstration where we took a can of [frozen] orange juice and a jug and we went around mixing it with three cans of water and made orange juice. Then we took a can of cranberries, threw it in, added three cans of water, mixed it, and said now, this one is 75 percent water and this is a hundred percent juice. Now, how is that fair?"

Congressman Conte, as an established friend of Ocean Spray and recipient of honoraria from the company, helped get Cassidy and his client a meeting with Vice President Bush, whom President Reagan had appointed chairman of a regulatory reform commission in 1981. "We did the demonstration," Cassidy said. "They actually had fun with it . . . and thought [the proposed rule] made no sense, and sure enough, the regulation got changed."

But the idea for this labeling change would not die. The FDA returned to it again near the end of Reagan's second term. This time Ocean Spray and its lobbyists turned to Congress to head it off. In October 1988, they persuaded a few key members of the House and Senate appropriations committees to insert one sentence in the report of a

House-Senate conference committee on a big annual appropriations bill. As noted earlier, it is a conference committee's job to produce a single bill from the House and Senate versions, which can differ significantly.

The inserted sentence prohibited the FDA from proceeding with a new version of the regulation requiring juice makers to disclose on their labels the actual juice content of their products. Neither the House nor Senate had approved this prohibition, it just materialized in the conference committee report. Ocean Spray had blocked the FDA's proposal for years with the help of members from the states that grow cranberries, primarily Massachusetts, New Jersey, Wisconsin, and Oregon. Again, Ocean Spray argued that the special characteristics of cranberries would make such labels misleading.

The Boston Globe caught on to what was happening and published a good story about it. Cranberries are a local story for the *Globe* since Massachusetts is the leading producer. Cassidy told the *Globe* he had advised Ocean Spray to pay $2,000 honoraria to an unspecified number of members, and to contribute through its PAC to numerous campaigns. The *Globe* reported that these contributions totaled "more than $50,000"; in fact, the Ocean Spray PAC made contributions of more than $375,000 between 1982 and the end of 1988. When asked about the contributions, Cassidy told the *Globe:* "That's the way Washington works."

The newspaper discovered that Senator Robert Kasten of Wisconsin was the key actor in this little drama. Kasten, the recent recipient of a $2,000 Ocean Spray honorarium, had inserted language drafted by Cassidy & Associates into the Senate version of the bill. He then persuaded Jamie Whitten of Mississippi, chairman of the House Appropriations Committee and himself the recipient of at least $4,000 in honoraria from Ocean Spray, to go along. Whitten's staff, the *Globe* reported, did the editing that cut the passage barring the regulation to a single sentence. (Ocean Spray and Cassidy were able to hold off that FDA regulation until 1994, when it finally came into force, without having a big impact on the juice business.)

Cranberry issues were fun, but inconsequential outside the small world of fruit juice. In February 1992, Cassidy got the chance to take on a much bigger policy issue for a much bigger client. It would lead, by his own account, to one of the most satisfying experiences of his career.

The client this time was the General Dynamics Corporation, one of the country's biggest defense contractors. In January 1992, President Bush had surprised and terrified the company by announcing plans for a "recision" of $2.8 billion from funds already appropriated by Congress to build two Seawolf attack submarines. The Seawolf could be sacrificed, Bush and his Defense Department argued, and the money saved could be used for better purposes.

The idea had a certain logic. The Seawolf was designed to hunt down and kill the most advanced Soviet subs—a priority mission in 1989, when Congress had approved construction of three Seawolfs with the expectation that twenty-six more would be added over ten years. But in 1991 the Soviet Union crumbled, ending the Cold War. Why not save the money it would cost to build this gigantic ship for nearly $2 billion each?

From the perspective of the Bush White House, the politics of this idea weren't so bad either. The Seawolf was built in Connecticut and Rhode Island, Democratic states with three Democratic senators. Canceling it would probably help the Newport News Shipbuilding and Drydock Company, the one serious competitor of General Dynamics' Electric Boat division. Newport News was located in Republican Virginia

Lester Crown, patriarch of the Crown family of Chicago, which owned the largest share of General Dynamics, saw a potential disaster. Electric Boat, the first and biggest contractor of the nuclear submarine era, builder of most of the U.S. fleet of missile-carrying and attack submarines, had no other contracts to build new ships. Without Seawolf, its survival was at risk. Crown decided to fight Bush.

General Dynamics was an unusual sort of family company. Crown's father, Henry, the son of Jewish immigrants from Lithuania, dropped out of school in the eighth grade, then accumulated a fortune of about $2 billion. He merged his original sand and gravel company into General Dynamics, then became its biggest stockholder and chairman. His son Lester had assumed both roles.

Lester Crown had friendly relations with Senator Inouye, whom he had met through their shared enthusiasm for Israel. Crown gave money to pro-Israel causes, and Inouye was one of Israel's strongest backers in Congress. Crown and his relatives had also given tens of thousands of dollars in political contributions to Inouye, often in "bundles" delivered on the same day. As chairman of the Defense Appropriations Subcommittee, Inouye would have an important role in deciding the Seawolf's fate.

So Crown went to see him. Inouye recalled their meeting: "I said, you're a big CEO, you can't do everything by yourself, you should get some sort of assistance. There are many who can provide that. But you should be very careful about who you select, because there are some who just open doors, and there are some who make it a point to study your case." Inouye said he "suggested a few names" of Washington lobbyists who might be able to help Crown, "and he apparently picked Gerry" Cassidy.

Crown declined to talk about these events, but he surely knew that Inouye had a good reason for recommending Cassidy: Inouye's longtime associate and dear friend Henry Giugni had become vice president for business development of Cassidy & Associates at the end of 1990. This was also a good reason for Crown to retain Cassidy's services, which he quickly did—$60,000 a month for lobbying, and a like amount or more for the services of Powell Tate to do public relations for the Seawolf.

The story of Cassidy & Associates, General Dynamics, and the Seawolf submarine is an only-in-Washington extravaganza. The plotline was complicated, the actors were numerous, and they all have their own unique accounts of what happened. In the end the Seawolf, Electric Boat, and perhaps General Dynamics as well were all saved from extinction.

For Cassidy & Associates, this was a big victory that afforded boundless bragging rights. The firm has used the Seawolf episode as evidence of its effectiveness ever since. On the firm's Web site nearly two decades later, on a page headed "Achievements," Cassidy boasts of helping develop "an integrated, D.C. and nationwide grassroots, public relations and government relations campaign to save a critical nuclear submarine program from being cut from the federal budget." Cassidy calls it one of his two best lobbying campaigns ever and a source of great pride. Vincent Versage, Cassidy's "team captain" for the Seawolf effort, called it "absolutely, amazingly effective. . . . We worked it for two full years and beat the president."

Fifteen years later, Cassidy still loved to talk about the Seawolf campaign, the first big effort by the firm to take full advantage of Powell Tate's capabilities. "The strategy was developed by myself," Cassidy said, a formulation that several of his colleagues considered a little too exclusive, even as they gave the boss credit for important contributions. "You had to really demonstrate that the policy [killing the Seawolf] had major flaws," Cassidy explained, "that there were really strategic risks to the policy.

"The team was divided into two basic roles: Powell Tate, which I developed the strategy for, and . . . a team here [at Cassidy & Associates]. . . . We located the subcontractors, organized them by districts. . . . Hundreds of them. We located the ones we thought were in the most important congressional districts. . . . Obviously the most important states were Connecticut, Rhode Island, and Massachusetts [where 21,500 Electric

Boat workers lived], but we also found important suppliers in Arizona. There were something like thirty states that had a role in building this ship. We were able to bring well over a hundred subcontractors to town for a number of visits on the Hill. They went from office to office. . . .

"You had two kinds of allies—sometimes they overlapped—those on a policy basis, and those whose congressional districts were going to be economically hurt. . . . We recruited a group of retired flag officers, submarine officers, and a number of strategic thinkers about defense issues, from think tanks and academia, to go on the road. . . . We did media training by Powell Tate. We had film interviews. . . . And we'd send the tape out to local television stations where they could do the introduction and the interview as if it was theirs. . . . We had [the retired officers and experts they recruited] do editorial board meetings in a lot of places. . . . We really got a lot of pretty good editorials. We were successful with [think tanks] like the American Enterprise Institute and the CSIS [Center for Strategic and International Studies] in taking a similar position.

"We then developed a strategy to start working with the Clinton [presidential] campaign. The Clinton campaign needed a position to be stronger than the [Bush] administration in the defense area. So they started criticizing the president's decision and citing the support of admirals and so forth on this, and made it an issue. . . . That was effective. We were building strong support on the Hill, strong support on the Republican side. A number of columnists joined in this."

All of this really happened. Perhaps the most enduring contribution the campaign made was creating the Submarine Industrial Base Council, an organization of companies that had contracts to make parts or provide services for the construction of subs. The organization was still active fifteen years after the Seawolf fight. "A lot of these smaller companies, this was about all they did, because nobody else needs the things they do," Jody Powell said. "So it was life or death for them too." Powell said the council was the idea of his colleague Jerry Ray of Powell Tate.

Jim Turner, the president of Electric Boat at the time, said Cassidy & Associates had been helpful. He recalled a meeting in the Capitol soon after the firm was hired that was attended by Cassidy, Inouye, and a number of General Dynamics and Electric Boat officials. "There was a feeling we could go through the legislative process and save the program, but help would be needed to orchestrate it," Turner said. "That's where Cassidy & Associates came into it."

Turner had never before worked with a Washington lobbying firm. "Cassidy himself, when [I saw] him somewhere in a public meeting, was fine, but I didn't have any observation of him being engaged in the specifics of what was going on," said Turner. "But his people were on top of what was happening, they kept us advised, and the information they had was accurate. It certainly wasn't a bad experience. . . . It was pretty straightforward and aboveboard. The people worked hard." He praised Powell Tate's training of company officials to speak before Congress and the media and the organization of the Submarine Industrial Base Council.

Cassidy and his colleagues described a creative, energetic lobbying campaign that succeeded. But their description does not cover all that really happened to save the Seawolf. A fuller account illuminates some large truths about lobbying in modern Washington.

On May 6, 1992, the Senate held a yea or nay vote on the Pentagon's proposed recision. (The submarine enjoyed more support in the House than in the Senate.) The vote offered a clear choice: build the second Seawolf and leave open the possibility of building a third, or kill the program after completion of the first ship. Fifty-two voted to save the program, forty-six to kill it. The Seawolf was saved.

As senators will tell anyone who asks, they vote as they do on contentious issues out of a combination of their best judgment on the issue, political self-interest, and the obligations they perceive they have to others, first of all colleagues. Senators (and House members) are constantly making deals for votes with each other. When a member sees political self-interest involved in a particular vote, that usually becomes the most important influence on his or her decision. At the same time, a member rarely admits, even to himself, that on an issue of great importance to his constituents, the voters might be wrong. So, for example, farm state members nearly always support and defend farm subsidies.

In the case of the Seawolf, there were four senators whose constituents included thousands of people for whom Seawolf was a critical matter—the senators from Connecticut and Rhode Island, where Electric Boat had its facilities and built submarines. Three of them took the lead in the defense of the Seawolf: Christopher Dodd and Joseph Lieberman, both Democrats from Connecticut, and John Chafee of Rhode Island, a moderate Republican who had been a successful secretary of the navy for three years in the Nixon administration. The other Rhode Island senator, Democrat Claiborne Pell, was in his sixth and final term as a senator; he was elderly and ineffectual (reporters and staff members sometimes called him Stillborn Pell).

Chafee, Dodd, and Lieberman agreed on the importance of building at least the second and third Seawolfs—for their states, but also for the good of the Navy, and the country. This was not another case of farm state senators supporting price supports for corn; all three showed every sign of strong personal conviction about the Seawolf. And despite the indisputable fact that the Seawolf had been designed to counter an enemy that no longer existed, there really were serious arguments against eliminating it as President Bush and his secretary of defense, Dick Cheney, had proposed.

The heart of the matter was the submarine itself, a formidable weapon. Since World War II, American submarines had assured United States domination of the seas. Submarines powered by nuclear reactors that could operate below the surface for months without needing fuel or maintenance dramatically enhanced the submarine's utility. Then, when engineers figured out how to put intercontinental missiles carrying thermonuclear warheads into submarines that could fire them from underwater, the nuclear-powered, missile-bearing sub became the most important ship in the Navy. It was the least vulnerable element in the triad of nuclear weapons—bombers, land-based missiles, and submarine-launched ballistic missiles—that secured the United States.

The Seawolf was the most advanced sub ever designed. It was an attack submarine, whose original mission was to track and kill the Soviet Union's missile-carrying subs if that ever became necessary. It was huge (353 feet long) and fast (underwater speeds of 35 knots, or about 40 miles per hour) and expensive (original cost: nearly $2 billion each). Like all the nuclear-powered submarines that Electric Boat had built since the first, the *Nautilus*, launched in 1954,* it was a finely honed piece of machinery built to the most exacting specifications. Every part in a nuclear sub had to be reliable for a predictable life span.

The makers of those parts constituted the industrial base that the Navy and its supporters in Congress were eager to protect. They included subcontractors who specialized in individual parts, and also highly trained workers who had unique skills and experience. Perhaps the most talented were the welders who had to put the subs together. The sea puts fantastic pressure on the shell of a submarine sailing hundreds of feet below the surface; a faulty weld could not survive that pressure. It took ten years to fully train a submarine welder at Electric Boat.

If adopted, the recision of the Seawolf would have left the United

---

* Senator Thomas Dodd of Connecticut attended the ceremony when the *Nautilus* was launched. He brought along his ten-year-old son, Chris, that day.

States without any new submarine under construction. The Navy had proposed a follow-on ship, the Virginia class sub, but the design was not complete and the contractor had not been chosen. If the Seawolf were abandoned there would be no work for those welders, or for any participant in the industrial base. There was a "real possibility," Dodd said years later, "of losing the capacity to build submarines." The subcontractors might not survive without an active program. The skilled workers would find jobs elsewhere in the civilian economy and their invaluable skills would melt away. Chafee had made the industrial base argument the year before, in 1991, when Senator John McCain, a former Navy aviator and the son of an admiral, had offered the first serious proposal to kill the Seawolf program on the Senate floor, arguing that it was no longer needed or a sensible use of money. McCain's amendment was defeated 90–10 at the time.

President Bush announced his plan to kill the Seawolf in his last State of the Union speech, in January 1992. Dodd and Chafee had only several hours' advance notice. They immediately began organizing their response. Robert Gillcash, a former professor of national security at the Air Force Academy, had just gone to work for Senator Dodd as an advisor on military issues. He recalled their first moves: Dodd called Lieberman and Congressman Sam Gejdenson, who represented the eastern Connecticut district that included Electric Boat. Dodd had represented the same district from 1975 to 1981, before entering the Senate. Dodd asked Gillcash to call the leaders of the unions in New London, Connecticut, that represented Electric Boat's workers to tell them not to despair, he planned a huge fight to save the ship.

In Chafee's office the military affairs aide was Chris Dachi. He began organizing regular meetings—at least one a week—of the four senators, and separate meetings of their assistants working on the Seawolf. Chafee was fighting his Yale friend and classmate George H. W. Bush on the issue, but that hardly deterred him. His credibility as a former secretary of the navy served their cause well, Dachi said.

Chafee, Dodd, and Lieberman all lobbied their colleagues one at a time. "It was really going almost door-to-door" in the three Senate office buildings "to make the case," Dodd said. They visited most of their fellow senators.

Lieberman recalled being impressed by an example set by Senator Byrd of West Virginia, who personally lobbied against a clean air provision that he thought would be bad for West Virginia's coal industry. Byrd called Lieberman and asked to meet with him. A new senator two decades younger than Byrd, Lieberman offered to come to the older man's office. Byrd would hear none of it, "he insisted on coming to see me." He came twice. "This impressed me," Lieberman said, and he copied the tactic. "This was Dodd and I going mano a mano" with their Democratic colleagues, he said. While senators lobbied senators, aides lobbied aides. "We had a humble message," said Gillcash: "We think a mistake has been made, can we talk to you for a few minutes?" Dachi said the goal was to lobby staff members in all one hundred senatorial offices.

About ten weeks after they began their campaign, Chafee, Dodd, and Lieberman discovered that they had an invaluable ally inside the Pentagon, where their problem had originated. This was Admiral Bruce DeMars, director of nuclear propulsion for the Navy, the job held for decades by Admiral Hyman G. Rickover, "father" of the nuclear Navy. This billet gave its occupant unusual independence; DeMars actually had a fixed term of office—eight years. At a hearing of the Senate Armed Services Committee on April 1, 1992, Sam Nunn of Georgia asked DeMars a direct question: If you were a senator, how would you vote on the proposal to kill the Seawolf? Offering "a personal opinion," DeMars said: "I would vote not to sustain [the proposed recision]."

The issue that concerned him most, DeMars testified, was suspending the construction of all new submarines until at least 1998—part of Bush's plan. "A hiatus in submarine construction would surely put the final nail in the coffin of the U.S. submarine construction capability, after ninety years of being the pre-eminent builder in the world."

Did he have his civilian bosses' permission to dispute their policy? He did not. Nevertheless, he produced a 120-page report arguing the importance of preserving the capability to build submarines. "I tried to pull together the best possible story I could," DeMars said years later. "I got that into play," he said, using a euphemism for leaking the report to the Hill and to the press. "It gained us breathing room."

Chafee, Dodd, and Lieberman now had an independent voice of authority on their side of the argument. "He was terrific," Dodd said, noting how rare it was for a uniformed officer to say that the civilians in charge were "really doing the wrong thing. . . . That was really a critical moment." As Dodd pointed out, a senator seeking colleagues' support for a home state project would like to invoke some large reason for supporting his request, which was just what DeMars gave them. Dodd recalled the pitch he used with colleagues: "I don't want you to make the decision because you think this is somehow going to impact us politically," speaking of Lieberman and himself. Instead the question he posed was "whether or not, at the end of the day, we're going to look back and ask why did we give up something this valuable—the industrial base being so valuable—what do we gain from it?" This was a genteel expression of senatorial etiquette; surely some senators who heard Dodd's spiel discounted his disclaimer that he and Lieberman weren't worried about their own political fortunes, but Dodd could now avoid ever making such a crass statement.

Chafee, Dodd, and Lieberman also explicitly accepted the Pentagon's view that, in the longer term, the Seawolf should be abandoned in favor of a simpler, cheaper new sub. They only sought money to complete a second and perhaps a third ship until construction could begin on the next generation, Virginia class submarines.

DeMars's willingness to defy the Pentagon emboldened officers in the Navy's submarine service. According to Dachi, officers from the Navy's Office of Legislative Affairs, its own lobbyists on Capitol Hill, visited all one hundred senators' offices, arguing quietly but forcefully against the stated policies of their civilian superiors.

As with many big votes in the House and Senate, there were respectable arguments on both sides of this question. This allowed members who had no obvious self-interest at risk to weigh their choice against extraneous considerations. In other words, if a senator felt he could vote either for or against the Seawolf at no serious political cost to himself, he had an opportunity to make a deal. Colleagues like Chafee, Dodd, and Lieberman who perceived a great deal at stake personally were likely to listen to all serious propositions.

So Senator Arlen Specter of Pennsylvania told Chafee he could vote to save Seawolf if Chafee would vote to save the Philadelphia Navy Yard, which the Pentagon was threatening to close down. Specter did vote for the Seawolf, and the Navy Yard stayed open for another four years. Both Dodd and Chafee provided crucial votes later to save the B-1 bomber, a vote of great importance to different senators. Dachi thought those votes were trades for the Seawolf.

Lieberman recalled a moment when the reality of senatorial swaps— I'll support your critical vote if you'll support mine—became vividly clear. "I can remember a Democratic caucus [a meeting of all the Democratic senators] when we were talking about this," he said. "Dodd and I were making the case, and some colleagues were asking some pretty tough questions. And David Pryor [an Arkansas Democrat, former governor of his state and a gifted politician] said, 'I've just heard a couple of our colleagues ask tough questions of Chris and Joe. They're interesting questions, they're reasonable questions, but this Seawolf submarine is really important to our two colleagues, and let me'—in that wonderful, quiet David Pryor way—'let me just remind each of us here that we all have or will have our own Seawolfs.' That was a great legislative moment. 'We will all have our own Seawolfs.' In other words, unless you think this is really crazy, I think our colleagues have made a good argument here, it's obviously important to them." Lieberman remembered that moment vividly more than fifteen years later.

So relationships among senators were, as always, very important. One relationship may have been more important than all the others: Chris Dodd's with Daniel Inouye, chairman, of course, of the Senate appropriations subcommittee on defense. It is difficult to imagine the Seawolf surviving if Inouye had decided to support the recision.

Inouye came to the Senate in 1963, where he befriended Chris Dodd's father, Thomas Dodd, who had been elected senator in 1958. In 1967, after revelations published by columnist Drew Pearson, the Senate Committee on Standards and Conduct found that Thomas Dodd had diverted $116,000 in campaign contributions to his personal use. On the basis of this finding the Senate voted to censure him. Dodd suffered a heart attack soon afterward and chose not to run for re-election in 1970. He died in 1971 at age sixty-four.

Inouye was one of Dodd's staunchest defenders at the time. The son, who revered his father, knew this history. When he arrived in the Senate in 1981, he cultivated Inouye, who was pleased to help him out. "I happened to get along very well with father Dodd and son Dodd," Inouye said, acknowledging that he was inclined all along to support the Seawolf as a favor to Chris Dodd, and did so as soon as he determined that this was in the national interest. "We're always trying to help each other in shoring up our constituencies' economy," he said.

"Danny was so critical to us," Dodd said, "very helpful."

When the vote was taken, forty-five Democrats and seven Republicans voted to save the Seawolf; forty-six senators, including thirty-six Republicans, voted to kill it. This was a kind of political role reversal; in the 1980s, Republicans tended to support big weapons programs, while Democrats (including Dodd) often voted against them. Obviously, many of the Democrats voting to save the Seawolf were, like Senator Pryor, trying to help two popular colleagues.

Senators Chafee, Dodd, and Lieberman deserved most of the credit for the result. Admiral DeMars, his fellow Navy dissidents, and Senator

Inouye were also instrumental. But how important was Cassidy's lobbying campaign?

"I don't recall the Cassidy involvement," Dodd replied when asked that question. "I've tried to think about it. It doesn't mean they weren't involved at all . . . they may have been working this thing and talking to people at the same time, but I don't recall any coordination." The issue was too important to rely on any outsiders, he said. "I never would have relied on someone else to . . . make a case."

Lieberman had a briefer reply: "I have no recollection of interacting with Gerry Cassidy or anybody from that firm" on the Seawolf.

Chafee died in 1999; his assistant, Dachi, said he could not remember Chafee ever meeting with anyone from Cassidy & Associates on the Seawolf. He discounted the significance of the lobbying campaign. The lobbyists were "completely outside the legislative arena," he said, and "did their own thing." Dachi quoted one official in General Dynamics' Washington office as saying that hiring Cassidy had been forced on them by "corporate headquarters." Dachi said he thought hiring the firm was a favor to Inouye, because Inouye's old friend Giugni had gone to work there.

But the lobbying was not just a waste of General Dynamics' money. In the words of William Bonvillian, Lieberman's senior legislative assistant at the time, the lobbyists "helped create a good atmosphere for the vote." Editorials in favor of the Seawolf in hometown papers, visits from workers back home who would suffer if the ship were canceled, appearances on local television of retired admirals sympathetic to the submarine—all these helped a member who wanted to vote for the Seawolf but felt a need for political cover.

And the General Dynamics and Electric Boat executives who worked with Cassidy and his associates were reassured by the experience. The lobbyists gave them useful information about the legislative process, gave them confidence in their own ability to make the case for the Seawolf, and, by creating the Submarine Industrial Base Council, provided a powerful lobbying tool whose utility long outlasted the Seawolf fight.

And for a company fighting for its very existence, the cost of hiring Cassidy and Powell Tate was trivial. General Dynamics reported revenues of $8.8 billion and profits of $374 million for 1991, the year before the Seawolf fight took place. It paid Cassidy & Associates and Powell Tate a total of $120,000 a month—an insignificant sum in comparison.

Yet $120,000 a month probably made General Dynamics Cassidy's best-paying client.

This contrast is a key to understanding the fantastic growth of Washington lobbying in recent times. Typically, the decision to hire a lobbyist is made by a corporate manager who sees an opportunity or faces a problem in the capital. The biggest corporations usually hire multiple lobbyists, sometimes so many they can't keep track of them. When the stakes are high and the costs relatively low, and failure could cost the responsible corporate executive his job or even the company its existence, why not?

"You could spend a long time trying to find a corporate vice president for government relations [the generic title of the executives who usually hire lobbyists for corporations] who got fired for hiring too many lobbyists," one Washington lobbyist said. "But you won't find him." By hiring lobbyists those vice presidents were succumbing to the bureaucratic instinct military officers refer to as "cover your ass." The temptation to succumb is strong, and helps explain the lobbying boom in modern Washington.

Cassidy recalled the years before the breakup of Ma Bell, the old AT&T, when Cassidy & Associates was one of many lobbyists the company had retained. "By the end of it there wasn't a conference room in Washington that they could fit all of their lobbyists into. I mean it was like a fraternity meeting—I'd go there and see everybody I ever knew." But this army could not save AT&T. The company didn't listen to advice, and provided no coordination, Cassidy said. "AT&T lost in a glorious fashion."

In the end, all the participants in the Seawolf extravaganza were winners—another fact that helps explain why lobbying has boomed so. Electric Boat shrank but survived, and is now sharing the contracts to build Virginia class submarines with Newport News. General Dynamics has thrived. The Navy got three Seawolf submarines, still the most advanced underwater platform in the world. The third, the *Jimmy Carter*, is an intelligence-gathering craft whose capabilities and equipment are all highly classified secrets. "The Navy was thrilled" to get the third sub, according to Senator Lieberman, a member of the Armed Services Committee. "They wish they had more of them."

Lieberman, Dodd, Chafee, Pell, and Congressman Gejdenson all enjoyed the political benefits of saving Electric Boat. Dodd handily won re-election later that year; Gejdenson was reelected too. President Bush lost Connecticut and Rhode Island in 1992, but he lost a lot of other states too, and the Seawolf was not an issue anywhere.

For Cassidy & Associates and Powell Tate, the outcome was a triumph. They enjoyed the benefits that inevitably come to lobbyists who end up on the winning side of a big fight. They looked good, and they had something new to brag about. Winning an issue like Seawolf helps bring in more business. "You can market yourself on that for years to come," said Victoria Leon Monroe, a former lobbyist for the Cassidy firm. "It gave you street cred for other big corporations."

In September 1993, fourteen months after the Senate saved the Seawolf, *The Washington Post* carried an item about Cassidy that read like a free advertisement: "The Washington lobbying firm of Cassidy and Associates Inc. is a comer as far as Getting the Job Done in the defense business," the story began. Saving the Seawolf was the evidence cited. The firm got all the credit.

In June 1993, the McDonnell Douglas Corp. hired the firm to try to save its C-17 military transport plane. Business boomed.

The Seawolf campaign was one of Gerald Cassidy's two all-time favorites; the other was the firm's work for the Republic of China on Taiwan. This proved even more lucrative than the Seawolf campaign, but its appeal to Cassidy went beyond the money. Representing Taiwan put the kid from Red Hook into the company of a country's president and made him a player in a high-stakes diplomatic game. And it produced more than $10 million in fees for the "Cassidy companies," as the Cassidy empire of the mid-1990s was called.

By then it included Beckel Cowan, an early "grassroots" lobbying firm Cassidy acquired in 1992. It specialized in generating what looked like popular enthusiasm for specific policy ideas or pieces of legislation from the grassroots. This became known as "Astroturf" lobbying, since the grassroots sentiments being propagated were not entirely natural. Another addition was Frederick Schneiders Research, a polling firm. Cassidy purchased both these companies with tax-free ESOP shares in his firm. He was still trying to fulfill his plan to create a one-stop service center to help clients in multiple ways.

As was the case with General Dynamics, the Taiwan business came to Cassidy via a Washington back door. This time the key figure directing business in Cassidy's direction was Colin Mathews, an inconspicuous lawyer and lobbyist who is the son of Cassidy's friend Tom Mathews, the Democratic direct mail specialist. Colin Mathews had worked on Capitol Hill for Democrats, was Congressman Morris Udall's press secretary in his 1976 presidential campaign, and had worked as a lobbyist in the Washington office of a Houston law firm. In 1994 he was a freelance Washington operator looking for a break, working out of a borrowed office in

Cassidy's building on Thirteenth Street, hoping that Cassidy might hire him into the firm.

That spring Mathews got a phone call from an old friend, Jerrold Schecter, who said he had "a matter of the utmost sensitivity" to discuss. A former correspondent and editor for *Time* magazine, Schecter had left journalism to work in the Carter White House as a spokesman for the National Security Council. When Reagan defeated Carter he joined the Occidental Petroleum Company as its spokesman. When he placed that call to Mathews, Schecter too was a freelance operator, writing books and looking for promising situations.

When they met soon afterward, Schecter told Mathews he had been approached by a Taiwanese living in Washington who was close to Lee Teng-hui, the president of Taiwan. Lee was a democratic reformer who was transforming Taiwan's authoritarian regime into a thriving, sometimes chaotic, democracy. He had organized the first free elections to Taiwan's parliament, and hoped to become the first elected president (he did so in 1996). The first native Taiwanese leader of the Republic of China, Lee was a proud man. That April he had been insulted when the United States government refused to receive him formally on a brief stopover in Hawaii, a reminder that since 1979, when the United States gave full diplomatic recognition to mainland China, Washington had treated Taiwan as a second- or third-class entity with less than full status as a nation.

Lee had a Ph.D. from Cornell University in agricultural economics and he loved the United States. But American policy was to deny Taiwanese officials permission to visit the United States. Relations between the United States and Taiwan were conducted by quasi-governmental organizations created to placate mainland China, which considered Taiwan a province of China, albeit one that was behaving like an independent nation.

After the incident in Hawaii, Lee wanted to explore the possibility of changing U.S. policy. Someone in Taiwan knew that Schecter had a personal connection to Strobe Talbott, who had been a classmate and pal of President Bill Clinton's at Oxford University. Several months before Taiwan contacted Schecter, Talbott was appointed deputy secretary of state. That was a good credential. But the Taiwanese also asked Schecter to help them find a lobbyist who would work on changing American policy to give Lee and Taiwan more respect.

Schecter and Mathews had socialized together since the 1970s, when Mathews's wife and Schecter were colleagues at the National Security Council. Schecter asked Mathews to recommend a lobbyist to help Taiwan. He made it clear that he hoped for a finder's fee from whoever became Taiwan's lobbyist. Mathews thought Cassidy might be a good choice, and asked him if he would be interested. Cassidy was. Schecter reacted skeptically to Mathews's suggestion, but met with Cassidy and "was charmed," as Mathews put it.

So Schecter proposed Cassidy to the Taiwanese, who invited the lobbyist to Taipei. Schecter insisted on coming along. The Taiwanese let Cassidy wait for two days in a Taipei hotel before inviting him to meet with Lee, a delay that sat poorly with the orderly Cassidy. Finally they were summoned.

"They have this ceremonial room with the traditional high-backed Chinese chairs and enormous coffee table," Cassidy remembered. "We waited first in an anteroom and then in that room, to meet with him. He came in with a secretary to take notes and I later found out that the secretary was the head of their intelligence service. There was gracious conversation about our mutual experiences at Cornell. He had been there when I was there. . . . We talked about that for a while, what a cold place it was and so forth. Then we talked some about his visit to Hawaii and America's position on Taiwan and my views about that. My views about China and U.S. relations."

The meeting lasted fifteen minutes. "It was like a royal audience," said a Cassidy associate who accompanied him to Taiwan. Cassidy made his pitch, carefully planned in advance: the goal should be to persuade the White House to grant Lee a visa to visit the United States and give a lecture at Cornell. This could be portrayed as unofficial, but would also break the embargo on visits by senior Taiwanese, and make Lee a hero at home. The State Department would oppose them, but Congress could be influenced to force the White House to change the policy anyway. Taiwan, they said, had many friends in Washington, while Beijing had very few—Cassidy & Associates would mobilize the friends and pressure the White House to grant the visa.

Cassidy argued that "America had a basic sense of fairness." Americans admired a country that had turned itself into a democracy, and would fight the idea that Beijing should be able to influence U.S. foreign policy on a matter like this. "Like so many foreign leaders, Lee failed to understand the American system," especially "the power of Congress," Cassidy said. So he explained that Congress had the power to force the administration's hand.

The Taiwanese proposed that the client of record be something called the Taiwan Research Institute, ostensibly a think tank funded by Taiwan's ruling political party, the Kuomintang. According to Natale Bellocchi, the senior American diplomat in Taiwan at the time, this was "just for show." Everyone understood that the real client was President Lee, Bellocchi said.

The Taiwanese signed a three-year contract, agreeing to pay Cassidy $1.5 million a year, a big number that impressed Cassidy's colleagues. One remembered a comment he made at the time: "Nobody's going to pay you thirty thousand a month if you ask for ten. You have to believe in yourself and your product." Taiwan's retainer—the equivalent of $125,000 a month—was twice the handsome fee General Dynamics paid the firm.

Taiwan also satisfied Cassidy's desire to diversify his firm's business. Symbolically, nothing could have been farther from "appropriations" work—lobbying for earmarks—than helping a foreign government change U.S. policy. A certain cachet came to lobbyists who represented foreign powers—even small powers. And the Taiwan issue was a challenge that appealed to Cassidy's sense of himself as someone who ought to be an important player in Washington, a sense strengthened by the Seawolf campaign.

The challenge also appealed to Gerald Felix Warburg, a descendant of the banking Warburgs who had worked from 1976 to 1988 as a foreign policy aide to Senator Alan Cranston of California, deputy leader of the Senate's Democrats from 1977 to 1991. Cassidy had hired Warburg in 1990 to try to develop an international practice for Cassidy & Associates; landing Taiwan was a milestone.

Cassidy and Warburg were the principal strategists. Warburg sent regular reports on their activities to the Taiwan Research Institute, and TRI sent checks to Cassidy & Associates. The Taiwanese played no direct role.

The lobbyists decided to try to persuade President Clinton personally to override State Department concerns that granting a visa to Lee to make a speech at Cornell would anger Beijing and damage Sino-American relations.

Years later Cassidy described his plan of attack:

We started raising the question of why America was kowtowing— we deliberately used that expression all the time—to China regarding its relationship on Taiwan. [We asked] why on matters so small as whether President Lee could visit this country, we could be so influenced by China, and was this not in fact weakening our standing with China? And did this meet America's principles regarding our support of democracy around the world? Did it strike people as fair to allow a small, emerging democracy that had accomplished so much . . . to be abused by a giant like China? . . . We were able to set up a number of editorial board meetings. . . . We eventually got fifty-five editorials [from American newspapers] in our favor, all of which got well circulated on the Hill. We had dozens and dozens of individual meetings with members about this issue. . . .

We also worked with friends in several state legislatures. . . . Massachusetts, New York, Illinois, Washington, California [passed] sense-of-the-legislature votes that were communicated directly to [Clinton's] office. They were quite forceful.

The idea here, Warburg elaborated, was to elevate Lee's visa above the level of the diplomats at the State Department and convert it into a political issue.

Warburg described his mode of operations as a lobbyist: "I go to my opponents and tell them what I'm going to do, and tell them I hope it changes their point of view, and then I do it. But I like to let them know in advance most of the time what we're going to try to do." In this case the immediate goal was to "get a resolution through [Congress] supporting a visit" by Lee. That would be the most important signal to Clinton that he had to change the State Department's mind—but not the only signal. "You don't want to have the target of your lobbying hear about it from one source," Warburg explained. "It's got to be coming from four or five different places."

In this case Warburg was dealing with old friends and colleagues, Democrats in the Clinton administration with whom he had worked as an aide to Senator Cranston. "We tried to warn them," Warburg said of the State Department officials who opposed a Lee visit. "[We said] 'We're going to try to bring some really strong pressure on you guys so keep your flexibility, you may want to change your position.' "

But, typically, the State Department could not imagine losing control of the issue to politicians. This is one of the oldest story lines in Washington: myopic bureaucrats who are certain they understand why their political bosses should do what they want them to do are often surprised to discover that their reasoning is not universally admired or accepted. Diplomats, particularly, seem susceptible to the delusion that their expertise will prevail over the views of mere politicians.

But in 1995, when this issue came to a head, the diplomats' view that a Lee visit would unnecessarily roil the Chinese government in Beijing was

After years of obscurity, Gerald Cassidy gained a certain notoriety in the late 1980s, thanks to two senators, John Danforth of Missouri, a moderate Republican (above), and Robert C. Byrd of West Virginia, chairman of the Appropriations Committee (below). Danforth sought to amend an appropriations bill to eliminate earmarks, or special appropriations, for ten named universities at a time when these provisions had become the lucrative specialty of Cassidy & Associates. Cassidy and his allies defeated Danforth's effort in 1986. Three years later, embarrassed by a news story that showed how Cassidy & Associates used appropriations bills to win approval of earmarks for universities, Senator Byrd offered an amendment that appeared to put significant new restrictions on such lobbying. Cassidy & Associates was its obvious target. (Frank Johnston, *The Washington Post;* Harry Naltchayan, *The Washington Post*)

In 1992 the Pentagon tried to kill one of the Navy's biggest procurement programs, the Seawolf submarine. The contractor, General Dynamics, hired Cassidy & Associates to help save the program. Three key players in that drama were Senator Daniel Inouye of Hawaii, chairman of the appropriations subcommittee on defense (above left); his friend and longtime aide, Henry Giugni (above right), who had gone to work for Cassidy & Associates; and Admiral Bruce DeMars (below), the Navy's director of nuclear propulsion, who defied his superiors and defended the Seawolf. (Rich Lipski, *The Washington Post*; Susan Biddle, *The Washington Post*; Associated Press)

On January 4, 1995, his first day in the speaker's chair, Congressman Newt Gingrich of Georgia (above left) fondles his gavel. Gingrich's colleagues in the new Republican leadership of the House were Majority Leader Dick Armey (above right), and majority whip Tom DeLay (below). (Larry Morris, *The Washington Post*; Keith Jenkins, *The Washington Post*; James A. Parcell, *The Washington Post*)

On May 17, 2005, Gerald Cassidy invited more than one thousand people to celebrate the thirtieth anniversary of his lobbying firm at a reception on the roof of a Washington office building that overlooked the United States Capitol. The guests included Senator Robert C. Byrd of West Virginia (above left), once a Cassidy nemesis, George McGovern (above middle), and Congressman Tom DeLay of Texas, pictured at left below with two of the Republicans in the Cassidy firm, chief executive officer Gregg Hartley, center, and lobbyist Arthur Mason. (Susan Biddle, *The Washington Post*)

John Silber (above left), the former president of Boston University, a leading Cassidy client for decades, flew to Washington for the party. Congressman Roy Blunt (above right, with Cassidy), then House majority whip and Hartley's former boss, also made an appearance. Below are pictured Congressman Edward Markey of Massachusetts (left) and his former colleague Marty Russo, a Cassidy lobbyist. (Susan Biddle, *The Washington Post*)

Jack Abramoff (with his lawyer, Abbe Lowell, seated) takes an oath at a Senate hearing into what became the scandal named for him. The oath committed Abramoff to tell the truth, but in fact he invoked his Fifth Amendment privilege against self-incrimination and refused to answer any questions. (*The Washington Post*)

Robert Strauss, who fired Cassidy from a staff job at the Democratic National Committee in 1973, then went on to become a fabulously successful Washington lobbyist himself. Asked to explain the boom in Washington lobbying during his lifetime, Strauss pondered for a moment, then replied, "There's just so damn much money in it." (Ray Lustig, *The Washington Post*)

Gerry Cassidy at ease: hunting wild turkey on Maryland's Eastern Shore with his friend and employee Jody Powell; at a Washington Nationals game with Bill Cloherty, longtime salesman for Cassidy & Associates; and eating lunch with his wife, Loretta, at Charlie Palmer Steak, the Washington restaurant in which Cassidy was a major investor. (Susan Biddle, *The Washington Post*)

Cassidy in his Washington office, and an aerial view of the Cassidys' $8 million estate, a copy of a nineteenth-century farmhouse on 165 acres beside the Chesapeake Bay. (Susan Biddle, *The Washington Post*)

ineffectual. The politicians didn't care whether Beijing was roiled or not. Cassidy's arguments were much closer to congressional sentiment. Democratic Congressman Gejdenson of Connecticut, a key player in the Seawolf fight, summarized that sentiment in a hearing of the House Committee on International Affairs in February 1995: "I think many of us feel that especially with the progress that's gone on in Taiwan . . . that it seems illogical not to allow President Lee in [to the United States] on a private basis to go back to his alma mater—not just that it's the right thing to do because of all the progress that's occurred in Taiwan, but I think it's also an excellent message to [send to] China."

The public discussion was similarly one-sided. In six days of May 1995, *The Washington Post, The Wall Street Journal, The New York Times,* and *The Washington Times* all published editorials favoring granting the visa to Lee—four of the fifty-five editorials that Cassidy mentioned.

The Republicans had won control of Congress five months earlier, and many of them strongly supported Taiwan. The new Speaker of the House, Newt Gingrich, even proposed that Taiwan be admitted to the United Nations—an utterly undiplomatic idea that would have reopened a matter settled by Richard Nixon years earlier when the United States agreed that Beijing was the legitimate representative of China in the United Nations. In fact, in the entire United States Congress, House and Senate, there was only one man who would take Beijing's side of this argument.* When the legally nonbinding but politically potent resolutions favoring granting a visa to President Lee came up for votes, the House passed its version by 396–0. In the Senate the vote was 97–1.

Weeks after those votes, Clinton met with four moderate Democratic senators to ask for their help in several impending legislative fights. One was Charles Robb of Virginia, an old friend of Clinton's from the time Robb was governor of Virginia and Clinton was governor of Arkansas. As governors, the two men had traveled to Taiwan with their wives; both had a soft spot for the island republic. (Clinton visited Taiwan four times as governor of Arkansas to promote trade.) Robb told Clinton that allowing China to influence his decision and denying a visa to Lee was a mistake. He warned Clinton that Congress seemed ready to pass a law granting the visa if the administration refused to do so. The three other senators†

---

* The lone Senate dissenter was Bennett Johnston, Democrat from Louisiana. He retired from the Senate in 1997 and became a lobbyist. Many of his clients did business with China.

† They were John Breaux of Louisiana, Joseph Lieberman of Connecticut, and Sam Nunn of Georgia.

agreed with Robb. Clinton consulted two aides who were present and said he would give Lee the visa. Cassidy and Warburg had done an effective job. Warburg had good sources on the Hill and in the administration; one friend in the executive branch had tipped him off in advance to Clinton's meeting with Robb and the others. "We visited with each of those senators, and said, Gosh, this is a festering problem, can you bring it up with Bill Clinton?" Robb telephoned Warburg soon after that White House meeting broke up to report the good news. Warburg was thrilled. He also remembered one of the iron laws of Washington: no issue is ever definitively resolved; the losers of bureaucratic battles can always refuse to accept defeat, even when it comes in the form of a presidential decision. Fearing that the State Department might still try to change Clinton's mind, Warburg leaked word of Clinton's decision to the Taiwanese press to get the news into print right away.

Secretary of State Warren Christopher understood the futility of fighting any further. Though he had personally encouraged China's foreign minister to believe that the visa would not be granted just weeks earlier, Christopher now gave up.

Some of the diplomats involved in this episode developed a theory of Cassidy's manipulative omnipotence to explain what had happened. "I was flabbergasted," said Peter Tomsen, who was the deputy assistant secretary of state for East Asian and Pacific affairs at the time. "It was really spectacular how [Cassidy & Associates] maneuvered and got done what Lee Teng-hui wanted."

This was just the impression Cassidy wanted to create. Nothing serves a lobbyist better than the belief that he has spectacular and mysterious abilities to achieve his objectives. Cassidy often told his colleagues that when talking to clients, they should cultivate the notion that the firm had trade secrets that could never be fully revealed. One Cassidy lobbyist remembered the boss's advice: "Never let a client behind the magic curtain. That's your stock-in-trade, knowing what's behind that curtain. Don't give it away."

Tomsen's boss, Winston Lord, then the assistant secretary of state for East Asian and Pacific affairs, was not flabbergasted. "This [granting the visa] would have happened in any event," he said. The lobbying operation was effective, Lord said, "but there was no question that the congressional pressures to let Lee visit were going to be there whether or not Cassidy got involved." He called it an issue of "basic fairness." Congress overwhelmingly supported democratic Taiwan against the Chinese communists, Lord observed.

Cassidy's biggest contribution was framing the issue so shrewdly. Once Congress confronted a choice between granting the visa and succumbing to Beijing's pressure, the outcome was probably settled. The rest of the lobbying campaign probably made a bigger impression on the Taiwanese than it did on any Americans. Leon Panetta, who was Clinton's chief of staff when these events occurred, understood that Clinton had no practical alternative to granting the visa. He remembered telling that to Clinton shortly before the decision was made. As for Cassidy's role, Panetta described the situation as "a lobbyist's wet dream. . . . You've got an issue that from a policy point of view was bound to go your way, you do your campaign with bells and whistles, you win, and you take credit for the result."

Or, as another Washington lawyer-lobbyist tells his colleagues, never be shy about claiming responsibility when things go your way. As this practitioner puts it: "When it rains, dance!"

Colin Mathews and Jerrold Schecter were well remunerated for their contributions to the Cassidy-Taiwan relationship. Mathews received a $75,000 a year finder's fee until 2000, though he never did any work for Taiwan or Cassidy. Schecter, who did work as a consultant on the Taiwan contract from time to time, was paid $125,000 a year.

Lee's appearance at Cornell provoked an angry reaction in Beijing, and contributed to the deterioration of relations between Taiwan and the mainland. Later in 1995 and again in 1996, the Chinese fired missiles into the Taiwan Strait separating China from Taiwan. The last of these missile tests was apparently intended to scare Taiwanese from voting for President Lee's re-election. Instead it provoked the United States to send two aircraft carriers into the strait, signaling a crisis in Sino-American relations. Lee easily won re-election, but the Taiwanese stock market lost a third of its value. This was more excitement than Washington lobbyists usually provoke.

Cassidy and Warburg weren't fazed by these events. They went on representing Taiwan, winning a series of smaller American concessions for Taiwan until Lee Teng-hui left office in 2000. This work earned them about $10 million.

Then they signed lucrative contracts with representatives of the successor regime led by Chen Shui-bian, a fiery nationalist from the main opposition party, but Cassidy and Warburg could never find a way to work with Chen, and the relationship soon ended. Cassidy said his efforts to help Chen understand the United States were fruitless. In the end, Cassidy acknowledged, Chen and his colleagues, who hired three of the Cassidy companies, did not get much for the $5.5 million they had paid.

One of Cassidy's basic instincts as a lobbyist was to look for ways to create a demand for his services based on new developments in Washington. He loved identifying a possible client who might be affected by some new legislation or regulation—proposed or enacted—then signing that client up so that Cassidy & Associates could address the newly discovered problem on the client's behalf. Cassidy is hardly the only Washington lobbyist to do this; many market such services aggressively. Some do so disingenuously. "You can dig a hole," one practitioner explained, "then sell your unique ability to fill the hole." This is the lobbyist's version of featherbedding or makework, and it isn't rare.

In 1993, the American pharmaceutical industry faced a very real new problem: President Clinton's announced intention to reform the country's health care system, including new controls on spending for drugs. As early as the summer of 1992, some in the drug industry had begun worrying about Clinton's campaign promises on these subjects. Kurt Furst, then a Washington lobbyist for the G. D. Searle Company, a Chicago-based pharmaceutical firm, recalled that Searle had hired "a lobbyist in Little Rock" in the summer of 1992, while the presidential campaign was going on, to try to get an inside track on the Clintons' thinking.

When Clinton won the election, Cassidy saw an opportunity. The drug industry "was in a lot of trouble," he recalled. The Pharmaceutical Manufacturers Association could not agree on a response to the threat of new government action on drug prices, so did little. "We were able— I actually did the recruiting—to go out and get ten pharmaceutical companies to band together to conduct a public affairs campaign," Cassidy said. He was describing RX Partners, a consortium of drug companies that paid Powell Tate a $3 million fee to organize that public relations campaign. Searle took the lead role, paying about half that sum, Furst remembered.

Like representing a defense contractor and a foreign country, this was a new kind of venture for Cassidy, and a sign of his growing capabilities and confidence. He and his colleagues came up with the idea for RX Partners themselves and executed it. A key contact was made by Marty Russo. He had just joined Cassidy after losing his House seat in Chicago's suburbs in 1992. Searle's headquarters were in Chicago, and Russo made the first contact with the company's president, according to Furst.

The public relations campaign had two important elements. Powell

Tate organized media tours around the country for the executives of the drug companies participating in RX Partners, setting up television interviews and meetings with editorial boards. "They'd fly one of the executives into a city to sell the idea that the drug companies are the good guys who did good work for everyone. We weren't talking about the Clinton plan so much, but about what we were doing to help people," Furst said. The executives enjoyed these trips enormously.

The second element of the campaign was to organize numerous disease advocacy groups, as they are known in the health care world—organizations of people concerned about a particular disease, often because it afflicted a family member—to make visits to members of the House and Senate. Typically, the advocates from Texas would pay calls on members from Texas; Californians on members from California. Over the course of six months, every member of the House and Senate received at least one of these delegations, Furst said. The visits were financed by the drug companies. "They'd come in for a nice dinner the night before, then we'd take them up [to Capitol Hill]. They were on their own, not with the drug company lobbyists," Furst said. Members were impressed by these visits.

The RX Partners campaign "was another big, big item," Cassidy said—a significant contribution to his effort to change his firm's image by doing high-visibility work in new territory.

But according to Furst of Searle, Cassidy overplayed his victorious hand in that episode. He invited representatives of the RX Partners companies to a victory lunch in his elegant Washington offices. "The drug guys wanted to celebrate their victory," Furst said, "but Cassidy wanted to sign them up for another $3 million. We didn't even have time to have a cocktail and mingle. We went straight to the pitch. And it was an extremely long pitch about a very specific project. They wanted us to continue what we were doing, although the legislation had died. They wanted to keep RX Partners going."

The drug companies weren't interested, and RX Partners died quietly. "Cassidy was greedy," Furst said.

CHAPTER 18

PUBLIC SERVICE, PRIVATE REWARDS

Cassidy & Associates' big corporate clients in the early 1990s—General Dynamics, McDonnell Douglas, RX Partners—and Taiwan were all evidence that the firm was, once again, adapting to a changing Washington. "The environment changes around you," Cassidy explained, so the business "can't stay constant." Not only was the firm attracting big new clients whose needs went way beyond earmarks, but Cassidy was also hiring a different kind of person. He had begun offering jobs to people with reputations of their own, including famous ones like Sheila Tate and Jody Powell. Another was General P. X. Kelley, former commandant of the Marine Corps, who agreed to use his contacts in the American business community to help Cassidy find new clients. Kelley insisted that his contract with Cassidy state explicitly that he would not lobby the Pentagon or Congress. Kelley did help Cassidy create an "advisory board," persuading five substantial businesspeople to join this panel. One was a former dean of the Wharton School of Business; another had been chairman of the New York Stock Exchange. The panel's purpose was to introduce the firm to potential clients. Its members were paid to attend occasional meetings.

In 1993, when he hired Russo, Cassidy succumbed to what had become quite a fashion among Washington lobbyists—hiring prominent former members of Congress. A lawyer by training, Russo had represented his suburban Chicago district in the House for eighteen years. Jim Fabiani remembered that "Frank came forward one day, first to Gerry, and said, 'You want to hire a guy everybody likes? Let's hire Marty Russo.'"

Frank Godfrey, the former aide to Tip O'Neill who had been

Schlossberg-Cassidy's second hire a decade earlier, knew Russo from his time in the House. In addition to being popular with fellow members of the class of '74, the big Chicagoan was a favorite of the leadership. O'Neill liked him, and Congressman Dan Rostenkowski was his mentor. Rostenkowski, also a Chicagoan, was "Mr. Chairman"—chair of the Ways and Means Committee, considered the most powerful committee of the House because of its jurisdiction: money. Ways and Means controlled, among others, all tax legislation, Social Security, welfare, and trade issues. Its members had the easiest time of any in the House raising money for re-election because so many generous special interests were eager to cultivate them. Russo had also become one of the House whips who counted and tried to win votes for the leadership. He was a jock—a golfer and a regular at the House gym.

Cassidy met Russo but concluded he was determined to join a Chicago law firm. Godfrey persisted. He introduced Russo to Fabiani, who was impressed. He and Godfrey then persuaded Cassidy to offer Russo a job.

Russo was not shy about his demands. Not only did he want to live in Chicago (as he did throughout his career in the House) and commute home every weekend, just like a member of Congress, he also wanted Cassidy to open a Chicago office where he could work. He wanted Cassidy & Associates to hire his longtime chief of staff, Robert Macari. He wanted the firm to buy a townhouse on Capitol Hill that Russo would live in. Cassidy gave him all of those and a base salary of more than $300,000 a year. The firm paid $6,000 a month in rent for Russo's townhouse—which was bought for $452,000 by Cassidy, Fabiani, Versage, and Godfrey.

"On the street," Washington slang for unconfirmed gossip, the word went out that Cassidy was paying Russo half a million dollars. This sent a jolt through the lobbying community. "Everybody was gasping because Cassidy paid him $500,000," said the proprietor of a competing firm, "and everybody worried that every congressman who came downtown henceforth would demand Russo-like numbers."

When asked about this figure, Russo said it was an exaggeration. In fact, this number included salaries for Russo and his chief of staff. But it was in no one's interest to deny the rumors, which buzzed on.

Cassidy was delighted with his new hire. "Marty was somebody who had major attributes: number one, he was enormously popular with Republicans and Democrats. Very social guy, fabulous golfer, great friends with the conservatives on the Democratic side, had lived with the guys who were just a legend up there [Russo's famous roommates]. And also very smart. . . . He zipped through college and law school so that he was out by the time he was twenty-three. Now everybody, because of his style, a South Side of Chicago Italian, sort of underestimates how smart he is."

Russo and Cassidy hit it off immediately. Russo and his other new colleagues were a more complicated story. Russo was eager to win his way into Cassidy's favor, and was soon famous at Cassidy & Associates for his apple polishing. Others in the firm thought their new colleague was a lot more interested in golf (an obsession with Russo) than work.

But everyone understood what Russo brought to his new job: relationships. Many members of the House get lost when they come to Washington. They arrive thinking that they must be terribly important—they have been elected to the United States Congress, after all. Then they discover that they are just one of 435 members, and among their peers they enjoy no special status. But Russo was not one of these; thanks to Rostenkowski first and the other elders he learned to please as a young member (he was just thirty when first elected), he became a significant player. Thanks to his gregarious nature and enthusiasm for sports of many kinds, he became a pal to many of his colleagues. He was indeed a very social guy. So when he became a lobbyist, Russo had easy access to every important Democrat in the House, and to many Republicans as well.

For lobbyists, access is a salable commodity, and former members had it. Not surprisingly, a congressman or senator who first made friends with his colleagues as a peer had a big advantage over mere mortals if he returned to the House or Senate as a lobbyist trying to introduce his clients to important people and persuade those important people to pass legislative provisions for the clients' benefit. This reality has been described by former senator George Smathers, a Florida Democrat who was John F. Kennedy's best friend in the House and Senate. Smathers, tall and handsome, was elected to the House in 1946 and the Senate in 1950. When he retired in 1968, he hung out a shingle offering his services as a lobbyist. He was one of the first prominent members after World War II to do so. In an oral history interview with the Senate historian twenty years later, Smathers explained a former member's advantages with spectacular candor:

> When I first got out [of the Senate], it was really a lot of fun. Obviously the mere fact that I could go back to the Senate, and still could go on the floor, I still could park in the Senate garage. You could eat in the Senate Dining Room. You had all those priv-

ileges and perquisites that you had when you were a senator. So I could make a big impression on a couple of clients, let's say from Ohio or from California or somewhere. I'd say, "Come on, I'm going to take you to the Senate for lunch." Then I'd see all of my friends and I'd introduce them. By God, these guys would go back and say, "That Smathers is really something. He knows everybody over there." I could send them a big bill, and hell, they'd be happy to pay it. And actually you could get a good deal done. . . . I was always aware that if you've been a senator you can get in to see the senators a lot more quickly than you can if you're just a normal lobbyist.

Smathers provided this vivid description long after he had given up his lobbying career and become an orange grove magnate in Florida. He was revealing trade secrets. In the years when he was exploiting the advantages he described, few other former members were lobbyists. Though defeated or retired senators and congressmen had often shown up as Washington lobbyists in earlier eras, this was highly unusual in the post–New Deal "good government" era, when high-mindedness was in fashion (even if low-minded behavior was still quite common). For several decades, appearances mattered—which is why, for example, Senator John Stennis worried that raising money from corporations affected by the decisions of his Armed Services Committee might not be proper. Former members as lobbyists were still rare in 1977, when former congressman James O'Hara of Michigan joined a law firm with a big lobbying practice. O'Hara was a talented liberal Democrat who had lost a Democratic primary for a Senate seat in Michigan in 1976. That defeat left him with five sons, two daughters, and no job. He accepted an offer to join the law firm of Patton, Boggs & Blow, which had a large and growing lobbying practice.

O'Hara paid a price for becoming a lobbyist with a number of his former colleagues. Leon Panetta, then a congressman from California and a liberal who had admired O'Hara, remembered the discomfort when O'Hara exploited his former member's privileges to appear on the floor of the House as a lobbyist for private interests. Members gossiped disapprovingly among themselves, Panetta said; in the late 1970s, this still seemed untoward. O'Hara's apostasy was a subject for judgmental conversation among reporters too.

But fifteen years later, when Marty Russo trod the path from Capitol Hill to K Street, it was well worn. Both members and aides from the staffs of senators and congressmen had preceded him in substantial numbers. The great lobbying boom of the 1980s, which made Gerald Cassidy a wealthy man, had undermined, then washed away the old taboos that once made a trip through the "revolving door" from government service to lobbying look unseemly. Russo's decision to become a lobbyist raised no eyebrows and provoked no public comment. It certainly did not bother Russo, who was thrilled to find himself suddenly in the money. He was one of 122 members of both houses who left Congress at the end of 1992; at least fifteen of them immediately became lobbyists. Scores more would follow.

Russo recalled a moment of particular pride: "After I got my first income tax return after I'd been at Cassidy one year, in which I made quite a bit of money—by those standards; I make more today—I actually turned to my father and showed it to him. I said, 'Just look, Pop, this is what you did.' That's when I was really happy."

Another former member who might have made a fortune lobbying was Tony Coelho. When he suddenly resigned from the House in 1989, Coelho could easily have joined the growing army of lobbyists, but he declined all such offers.

Years later Coelho said he thought it was wrong to cash in on one's public service for personal gain. "I'm old-fashioned I guess. I just felt that you shouldn't use what you were given by the voters for your own personal advantage." Instead, he moved to New York and took a job in investment banking. He accumulated a tidy fortune before moving back to Washington to devote himself to organizations that help the disabled.

Coelho is an unlikely spokesman for ethics in Washington, but he formulated the issue in a provocative way. Russo and thousands of other one-time public servants—members of Congress, their aides, and members of the executive branch—have indeed exploited their government service for personal benefit. Like George Smathers, they have found ways to take advantage of relationships forged and experience acquired on the public payroll to create lucrative lobbying careers, most often on behalf of money-eyed private interests. Whether this was just resourceful entrepreneurship or evidence of moral and political decadence, it was indisputably a commonplace occurrence by the time Russo accepted Cassidy's job offer in 1993. It was, by then, the way Washington worked.

The lobbying firm that Russo joined continued to prosper. Business was good. Henry Giugni proved an effective rainmaker who brought in new clients, including companies with business at the Pentagon, where his friend and mentor Dan Inouye's influence was great. The big corporate clients like General Dynamics and RX Partners were paying the firm a million dollars a year or more for a combination of lobbying and public relations services. The appropriations business also continued to thrive. In the early 1990s, thanks largely to Giugni's ties to Inouye and the firm's good relations with Congressman John Murtha, the Pennsylvania Democrat who was Inouye's counterpart in the House, the firm was able to place earmarks for educational clients in each year's Defense Appropriations Bill, the big piece of legislation that came out of the subcommittee Inouye chaired.

If the lobbying business was now well established, so was Cassidy's career as an investor. In 1990 he earned more than $3 million by selling a company he had helped start up four years earlier in Costa Rica. This was Cassidy Aviel Manufacturing, created to take advantage of a then new law sponsored by Cassidy's ally Jim Wright of Texas, the House majority leader at the time. This Caribbean Basin Initiative allowed goods manufactured in Costa Rica to be imported into the United States duty-free. With an investment of $1 million Cassidy helped create this company, which made computer circuit boards for export to the United States. He sold his interest in 1990 for $4.5 million.

Cassidy loved exploiting his status as an attentive spectator of the Washington carnival to find such moneymaking opportunities tied to the government's public policy decisions. Another example was cellular telephones, a new industry that grew under the government's guidance. Cassidy joined with some friends to acquire a government license to build out an early cell phone system in North Carolina; his original investment of just over $200,000 was converted in 1993 into shares of a company that bought out his little venture, Telephone and Data Systems, Inc. Cassidy eventually sold those shares for more than $3 million.

"I made a lot of money without Cassidy & Associates," Cassidy said proudly in one interview.

And he made money with Cassidy & Associates as well. In March 1994 he negotiated a second round of stock sales to the employee stock ownership plan that he and Fant had created in 1989. The Dutch insurance company Aegon was again willing to loan the money needed to finance the transaction—this time $18 million on top of the $15 million it had loaned Cassidy & Associates in 1989. For this second loan Aegon asked for limited personal guarantees of repayment from the principals, Cassidy, Powell, and Fabiani

The details of this 1994 transaction—made public in a document subsequently filed with the Securities and Exchange Commission—indicated that several years after the transaction was complete, the ESOP owned 32 percent of the firm. In the two ESOP deals, in other words, $33 million (the total of the two Aegon loans) had bought roughly a third of the company. Was Cassidy's empire really worth $100 million? There was no way to confirm it, since there was still no open market for Cassidy.

Cassidy and the favored employees to whom he had allocated shares in the company were able to sell shares to the ESOP. This time Cassidy received $4 million. Fabiani and Powell received about $5 million each, Russo somewhat less. Thirty-eight other employees got much smaller amounts. By exploiting the ESOP and tax laws to convert profits into tax losses, pretax earnings of $3.1 million in 1994 became losses of $12.9 million for tax purposes. These were paper losses, of course.

The ESOP transactions did entail real costs: the Aegon loans had to be repaid out of the firm's earnings. When both loans were being repaid, it took about $3.5 million a year to service them. This soon contributed to a strain on the firm's finances.

The ESOP became a source of tension inside the firm. Some employees felt the ESOP was a generous way to share the firm's success with the staff. Powell, for example, remained an enthusiast. But others were skeptical. One who suspected that the ESOP deal was dubious was Vincent Versage, who complained about it to colleagues. Another was Douglass Bobbitt, a former appropriations committee aide and executive branch official who joined the firm in 1991. "The stock was worthless," Bobbitt said, because it could not be sold to anyone outside the firm. "You only got real value for the stock if you sold the company." A stepbrother who understood high finance had explained to Bobbitt the big tax benefits that Cassidy reaped by creating the ESOP. He was one of many who wondered why the firm did not offer a more conventional retirement plan or 401(k).

This second ESOP deal completed the transformation of Cassidy & Associates. What had started two decades earlier as a two-man operation was now a burgeoning business with more than two hundred employees. Its four principal executives—Cassidy, Fabiani, Powell, and Russo—were all wealthy men. Fabiani had grown up in comfortable circumstances, but for Powell and Russo personal wealth was a new development.

Powell had never dreamed of having millions in the bank. By his own account he could never have made so much money elsewhere. "What Gerry understood was that the way to get rich was to generously give other people a slice of the pie," Powell said. The money changed Powell's life. He became a gentleman farmer on Maryland's Eastern Shore, where he could pursue his passion for hunting. He became famous as Jimmy Carter's press secretary, but he became rich by working for Gerry Cassidy. Powell too had found a way to convert a reputation and connections acquired from public service into personal wealth.

Personal relationships in the enlarged Cassidy firm were complicated. Over the years Cassidy had developed a mythic stature inside the company. "The firm was probably misnamed—'Cassidy & Associates' gives people the wrong idea," said one senior executive. "Really it was just *Cassidy*. It was a company he built as an extension of himself." Everyone had to live by Cassidy's rules: dress well in the office, and keep your jacket on for clients, for example. Or never carry a Styrofoam cup of coffee in the hallways (use the fancy firm china instead) or a can of Diet Coke (pour the beverage into a crystal glass, also provided). The boss's mercurial temper affected everyone in the office.

Money contributed to the complications. Cassidy and Fabiani kept tight control of the payroll, deciding personally what salaries and bonuses would be. There was no system, no way for employees to know how these decisions were made. "You had a wealthy, controlling, authoritarian father who knew that his ultimate leverage was doling out your allowance," said one former executive. "And it was done without normal paperwork or documentation, but informally, the way a parent would with a child."

This was sometimes a source of resentment. But it was also the basis for gratitude from employees who realized that they were earning more at Cassidy & Associates than they had ever imagined possible. Ambivalence, even confusion were typical. Everyone on the staff had personal experiences of or had heard stories about Cassidy's generosity, particularly when a colleague had a family problem or a crisis. But the employees could also be frustrated by the arbitrary way money was dispensed and the unpredictability of their remuneration. Controversy over the ESOP contributed to the belief of some employees that while they were doing well, a few people were doing unconscionably better.

On the other hand, a senior figure who came into the firm in the early 1990s was struck by the presumptuousness of some of the lobbyists who had quickly gotten accustomed to big, six-figure incomes, which, in this man's view, they hardly deserved. "Gerry Cassidy has made a lot of fools very rich," was his judgment.

Cassidy acknowledged feeling some resentment himself over complaints that he hadn't been fair with employees. "I was very generous to people here," he said, attributing this to "my experience as a kid. I believed that you shouldn't be selfish, and that workers ought to be treated well, because in my experience the workers in my family got treated like dirt. So I treated the workers well." He told friends that too many of the former congressional aides he had hired lacked the maturity to understand the empire he was building. They wanted to preserve the firm of the late 1980s, when the money poured in and life was simple. They couldn't see the need for change, or the consequences of the firm's growth.

At the same time, Cassidy sometimes did make grand promises to some of the lobbyists about their future wealth if they stayed with the firm that were never met. Versage and Godfrey both thought they had been given assurances that millions were in their future because of the ESOP.

One problem was too fundamental to solve: the peculiar combination of idiosyncratic personalities that made up Cassidy & Associates created a tense, unhappy workplace. Cassidy and Fabiani had an extremely complicated relationship—"like a marriage," in the words of one former colleague. Cassidy managed Fabiani by withholding praise or approval, leaving Fabiani constantly "on guard," as one colleague put it. Fabiani then treated others similarly. Dan Tate Sr., an experienced lobbyist who had worked with Jody Powell in the Carter White House, came into the firm in 1992 and was taken aback by the atmosphere at the weekly matrix meeting, when the lobbyists reviewed the status of all the jobs they were working on. Fabiani, then Vincent Versage, ran this meeting, and Tate disliked the way they did it. "I hated the way they berated people at those meetings," he said.

Since at least the days of Sam Ward in the nineteenth century, the archetypal Washington lobbyist has been a gregarious, backslapping people person with charm. Gerald Cassidy is not one of them. His demons hobbled him. He never learned to schmooze. Tate, a Georgian with an endless supply of anecdotes and a lovable ability to tease and be teased, fit the archetype. Tate thought Cassidy enjoyed accompanying him to Capitol Hill to watch him exchange affectionate jabs with senators who were his pals (there were many).

As the firm and Cassidy's net worth both grew, the boss chose to cultivate his status as a big man in the tribe of Washington lobbyists. As the rich often do, he began self-consciously to develop the charisma of a big chief. He bought a Rolls-Royce but soon sold it—friends said Loretta didn't like it. He rented castles in Ireland for his summer vacations and bought a place in Naples, Florida. He grew the short white beard that gave him the appearance of an archbishop or cardinal in a Renaissance painting.

Doug Bobbitt, who worked in the firm in the 1990s, first met Cassidy a decade earlier, when Bobbitt worked on the staff of the House Appropriations Committee and Cassidy struck a different pose. "I can remember when Gerry came up to the Appropriations Committee to lobby on one thing and another wearing corduroys and a tweed jacket. He walked around sort of hunched over. He was a different guy. I guess that was before he went to charm school."

But a large part of what set Cassidy apart was not deliberate or considered; it was just who he was. Cassidy was moody and unpredictable, and held a great deal in. He went to mass nearly every day; even people who thought they knew him were not sure why. His good friend Bill Cloherty recalled once running into Cassidy at St. Patrick's in the oldest parish in Washington when Cassidy was there for mass. "Gerry said, 'If I didn't do this I'd really be a sonofabitch,' " Cloherty recalled.

Cloherty developed his own tactic for avoiding confronting Cassidy on his darker days. "When I go see Gerry Cassidy I always go in and chat a little bit and measure the temperature," he said. "If I think that Gerry is in one of our black Irish moods, I never bring up what I came to talk to him about. I just talk to him about football games or something and then I leave. I always wait until the mood is right before I present my business to him."

Fraser Baron was a quirky fellow who for years was the research director of Cassidy & Associates. Earlier in his career he had worked in the war on poverty for Sargent Shriver, President Kennedy's brother-in-law. Cassidy liked him for his idiosyncratic independence—Baron wasn't often infected by the conventional wisdom. "He was just a delightful guy, but very different," Cassidy remembered.

Baron was a careful student of politics and elections, and in 1994 he had come to a startling conclusion. "In June he came to me and said we, meaning the Democrats, we're going to lose the House and Senate," Cassidy recalled. "He said this is going to be sixty seats in the House and a majority in the Senate. He sat me down and showed it to me race by race." Cassidy was shaken. As long as he had been in Washington (and for fifteen years before he arrived), Democrats had controlled the House. Republicans had held the Senate for six years, from 1981 to 1987, but the upper house had been safely back in Democratic hands since.

Cassidy took Baron's analysis to a couple of Democratic members, who refused to believe it. "But I took him seriously," Cassidy said. "It said to me that we had a serious problem that we had to plan for." He had a few

Republicans in the office, but Cassidy & Associates was known as a Democratic firm. The time had come to diversify.

He opened negotiations with a small Republican lobbying firm called Boland & Madigan. Its partners had worked for Republicans on the Hill and in the executive branch, and had a thriving "boutique" lobbying business. Cassidy offered to "double the considerable money we were paying ourselves," Peter Madigan recalled, and offered tax-free ESOP shares in the firm. In October they reached an agreement on a merger.

On November 8, Fraser Baron was proved a prophet. Republicans won fifty-four House and eight Senate seats from the Democrats, putting them in control of both houses. This would be the first Republican Congress since 1954.

"People were impressed!" remembered Dale Leibach, then an executive in the firm. "Gerry had in his drawer the most brilliant insurance policy! Boland & Madigan were players, and they were very smart."

And Cassidy? Didn't the decision to woo Boland & Madigan make him feel pretty smart? "Yeah, I was pretty pleased with that."

CHAPTER 19

RADICAL ENDS, RADICAL MEANS

The key to the Republican sweep in 1994, Gerald Cassidy said, "was that the Republicans had nationalized the congressional race. They had turned it into something you never see, a national election about Congress." This was exactly right.

Newt Gingrich and his allies had been campaigning against the corrupt Democratic Congress for years. In 1994 the cumulative impact of their arguments did in the majority party. The Democrats, of course, had been giving Gingrich a great deal of help for years. A combination of scandals and ineffectual legislative flailing had reduced the country's opinion of Congress to historic lows. Two weeks before the 1994 election, just 18 percent of Americans approved of the way Congress was "doing its job." Gingrich deserved much of the credit for the collapse of public support. He was something new in American politics, a relentless propagandist. He took advantage of every scandal in Washington to press home his theme: Democrats were terminally corrupt and had to go. And his skillful exploitation of the news media's fondness for conflict amplified the message.

Gingrich was a careful student of the arts of propaganda. One of the most revealing documents of the Gingrich era was a memo he wrote in 1990 for his political action committee, GOPAC, which distributed it to hundreds of Republican candidates for elected office. He called the memo "Language, A Key Mechanism of Control." It contained a list of loaded words to be used to praise conservative proposals and politicians, and a second list to denounce liberal ideas and personalities. "This list is prepared so that you might have a directory of words to use in writing literature and mail, in preparing speeches, and in producing electronic media. The words and phrases are powerful. Read them. Memorize as many as possible," the memo said.

First came the "optimistic, positive governing words." They included: active, candid, change, commitment, common sense, courage, duty, fair, humane, initiative, lead, moral, opportunity, passionate, pride, principled, prosperity, strength, success, tough, truth, vision. Then came the "contrasting words" to describe the Democrats and their ideas, among them: abuse of power, betray, cheat, corrupt, decay, destroy, disgrace, greed, incompetent, insensitive, intolerant, liberal, pathetic, pessimistic, selfish, shallow, sick, stagnation, taxes, traitors, unionized, waste, welfare.

The words on these lists had been field-tested with focus groups— Gingrich was advancing the new technologies of politics. His ambition was remarkable; he really did want to lead a revolution. Personal ambition was a big part of what drove him, but so was his absolute confidence in the rightness of his own ideas and the wrongheadedness of the Democrats' view of government as a positive force that could be used to help people. In Gingrich's dream, all that would be replaced by the "conservative opportunity society," a society in which government's importance radically diminished and individual initiative thrived.

As this memorandum about language suggested, Gingrich believed that the end—his revolution—justified means that were radical and new to American politics. He accepted none of the traditional bromides—that politics is the art of the possible, for example, or that compromise is good. He had no interest in bipartisanship or even collegiality in the House. He believed in demonizing his enemies and he wanted to fight them to the death. He gave a copy of the "Mechanism of Control" memorandum to every Republican elected to the House in 1994, and many, perhaps most of them, seemed to embrace the vocabulary it recommended.

With Gingrich installed as speaker, Dick Armey of Texas, the new majority leader, and Tom DeLay of Texas, the new majority whip, the House of Representatives was quickly turned upside down. This leadership and the entire Republican caucus in the House after the 1994 election was considerably more conservative and dramatically more aggressive than any of their predecessors in the post–World War II era. When they took over in 1995, it really was payback time. The Republicans had been out of power for so long, and had felt so helpless in the old House so crudely dominated by Democrats, that they saw no reason to contain their revolutionary enthusiasm.

The new Republican majority in the House changed American politics profoundly, establishing new patterns of behavior that have endured ever since. The first of these was the product of a characteristic burst of Gingrich enthusiasm that erupted prior to the election, in April 1994, when he concluded that his dream was about to come true—that the Democrats could be beaten in November. Polls showing the declining standing of Congress and the accumulating political woes of the Clinton administration, whose health care proposals had collapsed ignominiously in Congress, reinforced Gingrich's confidence.

But one important ingredient was missing: money. Ironically, the National Republican Congressional Committee, the fund-raising arm of the House Republicans, had entered this historic election year in terrible financial condition. Early in 1993 the NRCC was $4.5 million in debt. Representative Bill Paxon of New York had agreed to try to revive its fortunes and took over the committee in the spring of 1993; with the help of corporate lobbyists who joined a new NRCC steering committee, he was able to eliminate the debt. But the situation remained grim. Paxon discovered that the NRCC's mailing lists were out of date and unproductive. The party's fund-raising machinery was rusty.

Gingrich's springtime certainty that this was going to be the Republicans' year would be realized only if his candidates had enough cash to fund competitive campaigns. He would have to help Paxon himself, and he began writing fund-raising appeals for the NRCC's mass mailings, promising potential donors that if the Republicans could raise enough money, they would win a majority. The committee's direct mail specialists worried openly that this was overpromising. Gingrich insisted, and his letters proved effective.

He also enlisted his colleagues, meeting individually with more than 150 of the 176 House Republicans that summer to assign them fund-raising goals and tasks. Incumbents with easy races were asked to raise $50,000 for challengers and for colleagues who faced tougher opposition. He asked for even more from the senior members who were in line to become committee chairmen if the GOP won control. With this effort the Republicans finally wiped out the fund-raising advantage that Tony Coelho and his successors had helped the Democrats sustain for years. By November, Republicans had raised so much money that their challengers running against Democratic incumbents in competitive districts had, on average, nearly $100,000 more to spend than the sitting congressman. Republicans also enjoyed a financial advantage over Democrats competing for open seats where there was no incumbent.

Six weeks before the election Gingrich and his allies introduced the

"Contract With America," a menu of congressional reforms and conservative policy initiatives that they promised to implement if the voters gave them control of the House. This was an unprecedented gesture, more like a platform in Europe's parliamentary elections than anything seen in the United States. Polling after the election showed that most voters never heard of the contract, and those affected by it were as likely to have voted against Republicans as for them because of it. But the contract's policy provisions—a constitutional amendment requiring a balanced budget, tax reductions, strict new limits on welfare, and limits on government regulations among them—appealed to corporate interests and their lobbyists, and helped the Republican fund-raising effort.

Gingrich's success finding funds for his Republican candidates was an apt prelude to what quickly became the most remarkable fund-raising binge that Washington had ever seen. After their big victory, Gingrich, Armey, and DeLay vented their pent-up frustration with the lobbyists and trade associations that had succumbed to Coelho's arguments that, regardless of their personal politics, it only made sense to contribute to the party that controlled the House, the Democrats. The new team in charge demanded compensation for these past transgressions, and in a hurry.

Thanks to a front-page story in *The Washington Post* in November 1995, everyone in Washington learned about DeLay's "book"—really a plastic-covered folder—in which he kept the records of donations made over the previous two years to Democrats and Republicans in the House by the four hundred largest PACs. In DeLay's book any corporate lobbyist could see at once whether his company, industry, or association was rated "Friendly" or "Unfriendly," based on the amounts donated to each party. Early in the year DeLay put the folder on a table in the anteroom of his Capitol office, just off the House floor. Any visitor could see it.

There was nothing subtle about the majority whip's use of this document. He would agree to meet with representatives of the friendlies; the others could take a hike—no meetings. A story began to circulate that DeLay required visiting lobbyists to initial the statistics in his book when they came to his office, the way a parent signs a report card to confirm that she has seen it. This story was spurious, but it gained such wide currency that a DeLay aide once asked him if they should do something to squelch it. Delay grinned and said no, "Let it get bigger." The bigger the myth, the easier it was to extort contributions.

Perhaps extortion was the wrong word, since most of the PACs and lobbyists who responded to DeLay's strong-arm tactics sympathized with his goals. The new Republican majority was unabashedly pro-business, anti-government, and, especially, anti–government regulation. On this basis, both donors and recipients could pretend that corporate America's contributions to the House Republicans that began to pour in in 1995 did not constitute an illegal quid pro quo, despite the fact that the House Republicans quickly delivered a series of new bills that did exactly what their enthusiastic new donors wanted: weaken environmental rules, weaken regulations on workplace safety, limit the legal liability of corporations, and more.

By 1995, Senator Russell Long's observation two decades earlier that there was only "a hairline's difference" between a campaign contribution and a bribe was thoroughly out of date. Both parties had long since tacitly agreed that in an era when campaigns had become so expensive, both would accept contributions from parties that had obvious interests in the legislation that Congress passed, and neither would make accusations of bribery.

The new Republican majority found numerous ways to turn the screws on potential donors. Before 1994 the standard "requested contribution" for a political fund-raiser in Washington—that is, the price of admission charged to lobbyists and PAC officials who attended these dreary but inescapable events—was $250. Overnight, the Republicans raised it to $1,000. The leadership encouraged Republican members to hire professional fund-raising consultants and event-planners to organize their money-raising receptions, golf tournaments, and similar events. Tony Coelho's Speaker's Club was open to donors of $5,000 or more. The new Republican majority created the House Council for PACs and corporations that gave them more than $5,000 and quickly had 250 members. But they were the pikers. More generous donors who gave $15,000 to $25,000 were inducted into something called the Congressional Forum; 150 joined up.

Cozying up to the new Republican leadership was well worth the money. DeLay made this clear in the first days after he became majority whip, when he invited lobbyists to write a new bill to impose a "regulatory moratorium," a thirteen-month pause in the enforcement of regulations while the Congress considered sweeping legislation to roll back environmental and workplace rules. DeLay encouraged the lobbyists interested in this legislation to create Project Relief, which became a coalition of 350 corporations that contributed $500,000 to a "communications"—public relations—budget. Members of the group lobbied for passage of the regulatory legislation, some warning members that decisions on future campaign contributions would be based on their attitude toward this bill. Lobbyists and executives from Project Relief acted as extra staff to DeLay and his allies who were pushing the bill. It passed the House by 276–146, with the support of fifty-one Democrats. (It never became law, however; the Senate declined to go along.)

DeLay's cozy relationship with the business lobbyists involved in Project Relief had begun a year earlier. Early in 1994 he had organized a regular Tuesday lunch attended by several dozen lobbyists interested in regulatory reform. This had been DeLay's favorite issue since long before he came to Congress in 1985. When he worked as an exterminator, he decided that the government's bans on DDT and other tools of his trade were ridiculous.

DeLay cultivated the lobbyists who attended his weekly lunches, using them as fund-raising allies in his campaign for the whip's job. In the 1994 election cycle, with help from those lobbyists, DeLay raised more than $2 million for Republican candidates, many of whom won in November, then supported him for whip. In other words, the pattern of doing business that Washington saw so vividly when the Republicans took control of the House had been established well in advance.

From the moment they won power, Gingrich, Armey, DeLay, and other leaders of the new majority worried about holding on to their new majority. Fear of losing it drove their compulsive fund-raising. DeLay's intensity in the pursuit of dollars was one of the traits that colleagues had in mind when they nicknamed him "The Hammer."

He worked over his targets without subtlety. For example, one of the new Republican members, Randy Tate of Washington State, scheduled a fund-raiser early in 1995. DeLay sent a letter to most of the business PACs in Washington noting the exact amount each had given to the campaign of the Democratic incumbent whom Tate had beaten in November. DeLay wrote that he was "surprised to see you opposed Randy Tate," but offered them now "the opportunity to work toward a positive future relationship." Was that clear? In case it wasn't, DeLay spelled it out: "Your immediate support for Randy Tate is personally important to me and the House Republican leadership team."

The letter "had great impact," DeLay bragged later. In the fortnight after he sent it, Tate raised $57,000, more than he had taken in during the previous five months. "We know who we sent the letters to," DeLay said later, "and who we got checks from."

In the course of 1995, individual House Republicans raised almost $60 million; their National Republican Congressional Committee harvested an additional $34.6 million. These numbers broke all previous records. Equally unprecedented was the brazenness of the Republicans' pursuit of dollars—another case of the end justifying the means.

Most brazen of all was the "K Street Strategy," later known as the "K Street Project." This was the brainchild of Grover Norquist, the brass-knuckled conservative operator and friend of Jack Abramoff's. Norquist proposed, and DeLay quickly embraced, the idea that trade associations, lobby shops, law firms, and corporate offices in Washington should be run by Republicans. In cases where Democrats held the jobs, the new majority began to apply pressure to have them replaced by friendly Republicans. DeLay personally told corporate executives not to send Democrats to try to lobby him.

"We're just following the old adage of punish your enemies and reward your friends," DeLay told *The Washington Post* unapologetically. "There are just a lot of people down on K Street who gained their prominence by being Democrat and supporting the Democrat cause, and they can't regain their prominence unless they get us [Republicans] out of here." But lobbyists who supported Democrats were unwelcome at the revolution. "We don't like to deal with people who are trying to kill the revolution," the whip said. "We know who they are. The word is out." Headhunters—employment agencies paid to find new lobbyists for companies and associations—began to call DeLay's office asking for recommendations. Over time, Republicans organized a system to recommend people for K Street jobs. This led to a mass migration of Republicans from jobs as aides on Capitol Hill to lucrative new positions downtown, as lobbyists. Over the course of the next decade, twenty-nine men and women who worked on DeLay's staff moved from Capitol Hill to lobbying jobs.

After forty years of Democratic domination, the 1994 elections established a new reality: Republicans could control the House too. Now every biennial election would be a contest for all the marbles. Instead of presumed stability based on the enduring Democratic majority, both parties would fight each election as though power itself depended on the outcome—which it did.

This reality helped explain the far-reaching changes in the political culture of Washington that followed the Republican victory in 1994. As the Republicans quickly came to appreciate during 1995, being in the majority was ever so much better than life in the minority. Members of the majority were chairmen of subcommittees and committees; they organized hearings and committee meetings; they bossed around large staffs; they drafted bills and worked out differences with senators to shape the final legislation that Congress enacted. They were *powerful*. Interest groups catered to them, flattered them, gave them money and other forms of support. After 1995 no Republican wanted to give back the power, and no Democrat was happy without it. Staying in the majority became Gingrich's obsession.

He, Armey, DeLay, and their colleagues realized that nurturing their alliance with the lobbyists, PACs, and trade associations could be the key to holding power. Each of the Republican leaders established a "leadership PAC"—a committee each could use to solicit contributions from interest groups and dispense it to the members whose votes could keep them in their leadership jobs, and to challengers who hoped to win new Republican seats. This worked well, no doubt because donors thought that a contribution to, for example, Monday Morning, the name of Gingrich's leadership PAC, might do them more good than individual contributions to less powerful members. Why give to the rank and file when the speaker himself was asking for money?

The Republicans created the Thursday Group to institutionalize relations with the donor community of lobbyists and Washington representatives. Every week John Boehner of Ohio, then the fourth-ranking member of the leadership, hosted a strategy session with favored members of this group. Boehner asked for their ideas, and for their help in persuading members to vote with the leadership. Boehner could take their requests and suggestions back to Gingrich, DeLay, and his other colleagues. Favors produced money; money produced favors. The Republicans were eager to help special interests achieve their goals, because then the interests would help the Republicans achieve their goal—remaining in power. With a House leadership that was predisposed to grant favors, lobbying boomed as never before. It was no coincidence that Jack Abramoff decided to become a lobbyist in 1995.

The compulsion to stay in power had ripple effects. One was to heighten party discipline and strengthen senior leadership. There were seventy-three new Republican members of the House in 1995, a huge delegation of freshmen. Many felt special gratitude to Gingrich or DeLay for helping them raise the campaign money they needed. The new members who had won seats in traditionally Democratic districts were the most vulnerable Republicans, and got special attention.

Gingrich believed that strength would follow from unity, and urged, even demanded, that his troops stick together. To an uncanny degree, the House Republicans voted in a bloc, something Democrats had never even tried to accomplish. This unity was easier to achieve after 1994 because so many of the new Republican members shared similar conservative views. The Republican Party, once rooted in the Northeast and Midwest, was now overwhelmingly a Sunbelt party, a fact reflected by the House leadership, consisting of a Georgian and two Texans. Moderate Republicans were, from 1995 onward, a disappearing breed; within a dozen years they were virtually extinct. Many of the new Republicans had defeated moderate-to-conservative southern Democrats, so House Democrats were also becoming more homogenously northern and liberal.

This process of ideological purification was aided by the decisions of numerous state legislatures after the censuses of 1980 and 1990 (and again after 2000) to redraw their House districts to create more safe seats for incumbents and more ideologically consistent constituencies. A House that was once dominated by the political center lost its center as moderates were displaced by conservatives and liberals. After 1994 the House was more sharply divided ideologically than it had been since the New Deal.

During the twelve years that Reagan and George H. W. Bush occupied the White House (1981–93), Democrats in Congress had become more disciplined and more unified, but Gingrich's new Republican majority in the House took the concept of party discipline to a new level. Gingrich's revolutionaries formed a like-minded, tightly organized, and well-disciplined machine. This meant, of course, that those who imposed the discipline had most of the power. Gingrich and DeLay quickly began to reverse the decentralizing trend that had continued in the Democratic House over the previous twenty years, initiated by the Watergate class elected in 1974. Quite suddenly, individual members, subcommittee chairmen, even committee chairmen were subject to a degree of party discipline that hadn't been seen in the House for decades.

Gingrich had strong views about how his colleagues should conduct themselves. He urged the new members to maintain their principal residence at home, to stay in close touch with their constituents, and to avoid any future accusation that they had succumbed to the charms of Washington and forgotten where they came from. Republicans knew this to be an effective election year argument because they had used it to good effect themselves. Rick Santorum, one of the stars of the conservative wing of the party, won his House seat in Pittsburgh in 1990 with a television ad campaign that featured the suburban Washington home of his competitor, a seven-term Democrat named Douglas Walgren. Santorum lambasted Walgren for spending too little time in Pittsburgh. (Santorum won a Senate seat in 1994.)

To make it easier to live at home, Gingrich promised to maintain a shortened workweek. Usually, members could come to Washington on Tuesday morning and leave on Thursday afternoon. Once, members of Congress had constituted a subculture of Washington society; once, as we've seen, it had been common for members to become friends, to dine in each other's Washington homes, and cheer for their kids playing sports for Washington-area schools without regard for party affiliation. By 1995 that was all ancient history. The tide of partisanship that had been rising in Washington since the 1980 election now swept away most of the remnants of those friendlier times.

Vladimir Lenin famously summarized the ethos of revolution after seizing power in Russia in 1917: If you're not with us, Lenin said repeatedly, you are against us, you are our enemy. This became the mentality of the House of Representatives once partisan differences became so sharp. Douglas Bereuter, a moderate Republican member from Nebraska from 1979 to 2004, recalled how the atmosphere changed when members stopped living in Washington. "Members stopped having friendships across the aisle," he said. "I remember younger Republican colleagues telling me the only Democrats they knew were ones they served with on subcommittees, and they weren't friends but opponents. How could they make friends if they were only here from Tuesday to Thursday?"

For Gingrich, the student of war who loved martial metaphors, the struggle to consolidate his revolution constituted political warfare. To fight it, weapons could be used that on their own might not look reputable or appropriate. One such turned out to be the earmarked appropriation. It wasn't long after moving into the majority that Republicans realized the full value of bringing home the bacon—particularly for vulnerable new members who hadn't built a strong reputation with their constituents.

Balancing the budget and reducing government spending were, as noted, important planks in the "Contract With America." Republicans took over the House Appropriations Committee determined to cut the government down to size. Their ambitions were soon compromised. Jim Dyer, the staff director of the committee under Congressman Bob Livingston of Louisiana, who became chairman of Appropriations in 1995, recalled what happened. Gingrich initially supported Livingston's efforts to impose discipline on spending, Dyer recounted, but in the face of perceived political necessity, the leadership wavered. Cutting spending was good, but Gingrich, Armey, DeLay, and others quickly realized that "we have another aspect to our existence here, which is that we must use the

Appropriations Committee as a resource to protect our vulnerables, because once we got into power, we wanted to stay in power."

Dyer recalled meetings with leadership staff. "They'd have lists. They'd have what they called 55-percenters. If you won your seat with under 55 percent you're vulnerable. We've got to do what it takes to bring you back. Sometimes we've got to do stuff we don't want to do." The result was that the committee was "trying to cut the budget, and we're trying to add to the budget. So we're a little schizophrenic along the way, trying to do both. . . . We kept trying to take care of folks." That meant appropriating money for home district projects that vulnerable members could brag about, to help them win re-election.

The relentless fund-raising, cultivation of donors, party discipline, use of earmarks to protect "vulnerables"—all of this was part of the permanent campaign that preoccupied Republicans and Democrats alike. Once there had been "a vital and irreducible difference" between campaigning and governing, in the words of Hugh Heclo, an insightful political scientist. "Warriors [Heclo's term for campaigners, a usage Gingrich would appreciate] and navigators [what he calls the governors] do not have the same ends in view." But in the modern era, those distinctions evaporated. The navigators became warriors themselves, and governing became a way to continue campaigning.

In both the House and Senate the permanent campaign prevailed. In the course of the 1990s playing for political advantage became the main game, governing a secondary concern. This is surely why the House and Senate both gave up so much time and energy to the ultimately fruitless attempt to impeach Bill Clinton, for example, or why in the House, Republicans spent so much effort trying to enact provisions of the "Contract With America," most of which was blocked by Clinton or the Senate.

The demands of the permanent campaign explained why members thought they had to go home every weekend, or why they could not squander time befriending colleagues across the aisle. Instead they had to spend many hours on the telephone, "dialing for dollars." The law prohibits members of Congress from using their offices or official telephones to make fund-raising calls, so they use special facilities set up by the House and Senate campaign committees. No one liked to brag about how much time he or she spent on this dreary work, but it required many hours every week. Mike Kopetski, a Democratic member from Oregon, burned out as a congressman in 1993 and announced he would not run for re-election the next year. "I increased the time available to me to work on legislation by 25 percent once I announced my retirement," Kopetski recalled. Others spent even more time on the phone, begging.

The House Republicans' permanent campaign after 1994 achieved its primary objective: the Republicans retained control of the House in 1996, and again in 1998—barely. The amounts of money raised in those two cycles were staggering: Republican candidates and party committees, including the Republican National Committee, raised just over a billion dollars during those four years; Democrats raised $600 million. Republican House candidates' efforts were rewarded with contributions that totaled $486 million during those two election cycles; Democrats raised $412 million.

The money came from many sources, but one pattern was well established: lobbyists and their clients' PACs provided a great deal of it. Many members of Congress, both Republicans and Democrats, asked lobbyists to be their finance chairmen. Though Gingrich and DeLay had been eager to curry favor with business interests, they obviously expected favors in return in the form of contributions. The mutual dependence between Capitol Hill and K Street was now firmly established.

Newt Gingrich seized on the idea of impeaching Bill Clinton for his "perjury" in denying that he had sexual relations with Monica Lewinsky, a proposal much favored in opinion polls by partisan Republicans but overwhelmingly opposed by Democrats and Independents. Republicans took no formal action on impeachment before the off-year congressional elections on November 3, 1998, but a week before voters went to the polls Gingrich authorized the broadcast of three television commercials that tried to exploit the scandal to improve Republicans' chances.

This episode illuminated the ways the new technologies of electoral politics had transformed America's political culture. Gingrich began planning these commercials a month before election day. One spot was a direct denunciation of President Clinton for lying about his affair. The second depicted two suburban mothers discussing how to talk to their children about the Lewinsky scandal. The third used the famous film clip of Clinton wagging a finger and denying that he had "sexual relations with that woman." None had anything to do with the House and Senate elections. Republicans knew they were playing with fire, but felt they had to invigorate their base of conservative voters—the end justified the means.

Before they were broadcast, Republican operatives showed the commercials to more than three dozen focus groups of voters to assess their impact. "We tested and tested and honed and honed until we got to the point we felt our base understood the message we were trying to get to them," said Rich Galen, one of Gingrich's political advisors. The idea was to show the commercials in a few carefully selected areas of the country where Republicans feared their loyal followers lacked the enthusiasm needed to get them out to vote on November 3.

But Republicans lost control of their story. The commercials became a media event, replayed on television news shows and debated in the press in the days before the election. In all likelihood they did more to motivate angry Democrats than to invigorate the Republican base Gingrich had targeted. On election day Democrats picked up five House seats, narrowing the Republican majority to eleven. It was the first time since Andrew Jackson was president that the party of a sitting president picked up House seats midway through the president's second term of office.

The result humiliated Gingrich, whose warfare with House Democrats and Clinton had made him the most disliked figure in American politics. He had beaten back one coup attempt in 1997 from displeased Republican conservatives who judged his speakership a failure, but now he realized he could not survive. Three days after the election and hours after four of his Republican colleagues had announced their intention to challenge him for the party's leadership, Gingrich said he would resign as speaker and quit Congress entirely.

His revolution was over, but the damage he had done to American public life would endure.

CHAPTER 20

CASH COW ON THE POTOMAC

Gerald Cassidy's hedge against the possibility of a Republican victory in 1994, the deal to acquire Boland & Madigan, proved to be a shrewd move. Boland & Madigan brought in $2.3 million in new revenue in 1995, and $3.4 million in 1996. Nearly half this revenue was pure profit. But Boland & Madigan could not compensate for all the problems created for Cassidy & Associates when its Democratic friends lost control of Congress. For twenty years the firm had traded on political connections that had suddenly lost much of their value. No lobbyist in Washington had any experience with a Congress controlled by Republicans—the last one left office in 1955—but a Democratic firm like Cassidy's entered this new world at an obvious disadvantage.

The institutions and businesses that hire Washington lobbyists can be fickle. Many choose whom they hire for their relationships. The new faces in powerful places on Capitol Hill at the beginning of 1995 took a toll on Cassidy's business. So did intensifying competition from the growing ranks of lobbying competitors, many offering to do the work Cassidy did for considerably smaller fees. James Fabiani, then the chief operating officer of the firm, recalled the departures of numerous clients in late 1994—clients who had contributed $6 million in annual revenue.

These losses came at a difficult time. It was in March 1994 that the firm had borrowed another $18 million from Aegon, the Dutch insurance company, to buy more stock for the employee stock ownership plan. Repaying the total of $33 million borrowed from Aegon required the firm to divert nearly $3.5 million from its cash flow every year from 1994 onward. That money could have gone to salaries and bonuses.

Strains on the firm led to "a lot of hand-wringing . . . and a pretty substantial reorganization, including layoffs," Fabiani remembered. Particularly difficult was "one forty-eight-hour period when we had to decide to fire twenty-seven people." In a company that then had somewhat more than two hundred employees, this was a painful reduction. Cassidy and Fabiani reduced their own compensation. Fabiani remembered that they both gave up their salaries and bonuses for a year; Cassidy said his salary was cut in half. Some of the ten-percenters who received guaranteed salaries as well as their percentage of business brought into the firm lost their salaries.

The air got thin for a time, and some in the firm worried about its survival. But the three principals, Cassidy, Fabiani, and Powell, were all scrappers, and they persevered. At first, Boland & Madigan and Powell Tate were able to make up the slack. Powell Tate's revenue reached $12.6 million in 1995, a timely success. New clients were found—as many as left the firm.

This was largely Fabiani's contribution. By 1995 he had been marketing the firm's services for a dozen years, and he had it down to an art. Like all good salesmen, he was incapable of shyness or embarrassment. He explained his technique.

"If I thought in Sacramento we ought to have four clients, I'd go find three marketing consultants, ten-percenters, in Sacramento. One might be a lawyer in a small firm, another might be a lobbyist, another might be somebody at the Chamber of Commerce. I'd bring them into Washington for a day, I'd say here's what we do, here's how we'll compensate you." These new consultants would then provide leads in their neighborhood, often acting on specific proposals from Fabiani.

This kind of creative marketing—seeking business from companies and institutions that had not previously considered hiring a Washington lobbyist or thought they needed one—became the firm's hallmark. And it was Fabiani's creation.

Geoff Gonella learned marketing at Fabiani's knee, and spent much of the 1990s running the Cassidy marketing operation under his direction. "It was his structure, his process, his vision, and his drive that were largely responsible for the growth in the business," Gonella said of Fabiani. "Jim's a tremendous salesperson and marketer in every aspect." Gonella left the firm in 2002 to found his own lobbying business.

One of the firm's goals in the 1990s was diversification. "We tried to diversify the issues we were lobbying," Gonella said, because more lobbyists were offering help getting earmarks, often for smaller fees than Cassidy demanded. "We made efforts to build up tax and trade, technology and aerospace," Gonella said, using categories that described various specialties that the firm was trying to develop. In other words, he looked for potential clients who had tax issues that might be addressed in Congress, or trade issues that might be lobbied on the Hill or in the executive branch, or technology and aerospace companies whose isssues tended to arise in the same congressional committees and executive branch or regulatory offices. "Being proactive was a key."

"It was the god-damnedest marketing apparatus I've ever seen," said Dan Tate, the old hand who joined the firm in 1993. Tate was particularly impressed by the written material the firm produced. "They would write pitches for clients, a loose-leaf folder, with tabulations, and it wasn't just boilerplate, but very good writing. A prospective client couldn't help being not just impressed, but awed."

Fabiani was most often the closer on a contract with a new client, Gonella said, and he was very good at sealing the deal. Fabiani agreed that the close "became my thing. I really liked doing it. I thought if you could present your capabilities you were halfway there to convincing somebody that you've got skills they ought to hire."

Occasionally Fabiani's enthusiasm got the firm into difficulty. Doug Bobbitt, one of the House Appropriations Committee aides hired to do the shoe-leather lobbying on earmark requests, recalled situations where a client expected to get more money in an earmark than was realistically possible, because Fabiani had mentioned the higher amount when he made his pitch. "I can remember being in marketing meetings with Fabiani and thinking, Don't say that stuff," Bobbitt said. "Sometimes he overpromised."

The aggressive marketing in 1995 reflected the proprietor's compulsion to keep the numbers up. Cassidy wanted to have the biggest lobbying firm in town, which meant the one with the most revenue. Once, recalled Elliott Fiedler, the first former House Appropriations Committee staff member hired into the firm in 1987, Cassidy & Associates could accurately boast that they had never failed a client—they always got the earmark, though it sometimes took longer than the client hoped. In the 1990s that standard died. "You had to accept that you'd fail for some clients, but you could always replace them with new clients," Fiedler said. "The firm started doing just what we always said only the *other* firms did, churning clients." Finding new clients became paramount. "The company went from, Work hard, do good work for good people, to just greed," Fiedler said.

What had been a rather small, narrowly focused lobbying firm turned into a big business, with a big payroll, big debts, a big list of clients, and a big "revenue number," to use the favored term of the lobbying industry. This transformation reflected Cassidy's ambitions, and also the spirit of the times. The national economic boom that began in the 1980s was—after a brief downturn in 1992—intensifying again. Technological wizards, many of them in northern California, had given birth to a thriving new high-tech sector, and were getting rich by selling newly minted companies to the public through IPOs, initial public offerings. The average income of working-class families had barely risen since the early 1970s, when inflation was taken into account, but the most prosperous Americans were flying high. The accumulation of wealth in big metropolitan areas had set off a real estate boom in the 1980s that subsided for several years in the early 1990s, then resumed. Well-off consumers financed a restaurant boom, a golf boom, a second-home boom. Being rich was a realistic option for a large and growing fraction of the population.

Old Washingtonians were surprised to find their city caught up in this new burst of accumulation and consumption. Real estate became a favorite dinner party topic, often supplanting even politics. Second homes became the fashion. Real estate values soared in communities from Rehoboth Beach, Delaware, three hours by car east from the capital, to the Shenandoah Mountains of Virginia and West Virginia, two to three hours to the west. A favorite second-home locale for lobbyists was the Eastern Shore of Maryland, an alluvial plain between the Chesapeake Bay and the Atlantic Ocean famous for its hunting and fishing.

A new wealthy contingent began to emerge in Washington's northern Virginia suburbs, the birthplace (in 1989) of America Online. Soon this was a leading East Coast center of the high-tech economy. In suburban Maryland, the National Institutes of Health spawned dozens of biotechnology firms, some of them extremely successful. In the late twentieth century, private sector jobs in the Washington metropolitan region outnumbered government positions for the first time in history.

Most unexpectedly, a new private equity fund, the Carlyle Group, chose Washington as its corporate home in 1987. Carlyle built a hugely successful global business around a group of high-energy overachievers who met one another while working for the government. One of the company's founders was David Rubenstein, a wonkish lawyer who was deputy assistant to President Jimmy Carter for domestic policy. One of its early chief executives was Frank Carlucci, who held numerous senior government positions, the last as secretary of defense at the end of the Reagan administration. Rubenstein and Carlucci were, by the 1990s, seriously wealthy men, managing billions of dollars and overseeing investment funds that bought and sold companies all over the globe.

Other Washingtonians looked enviously at Carlyle's success. Gerry Cassidy was one of them. If people like Rubenstein and Carlucci—*Washington* people, not New York moneymen or Silicon Valley wizards—could turn themselves into masters of the universe, why couldn't Cassidy? This question or one close to it was put to Cassidy in 1994 by David Ifshin, a charismatic Washington lawyer and operator who had good connections in both Jewish and Democratic Party circles. Ifshin persuaded Cassidy and Fant that they should establish their own investment banking operation. Cassidy agreed to pay the salaries and expenses of Ifshin and several associates, who set up an office on the eleventh floor of the building at 700 Thirteenth Street N.W. that also housed Powell Tate and Cassidy & Associates. They called the new venture Galway Partners LLC. Initially, Cassidy said, Cassidy & Associates owned 60 percent of Galway; Ifshin, Fant, and the other principals owned 40 percent. By 1998 the firm's share had declined to 43 percent.

"Gerry was very intrigued [by Galway]," Ruff Fant recalled. "Lobbying is a cyclical business. When there was a downturn, Gerry had to bring money from home to finance the business. . . . [He] would end up having to guarantee millions [of dollars] of loans, if it was a slow quarter. So he was very keen on something that would result in the company having some assets that it could own. The Galway idea was a way—this was the late 1990s, when everybody had made a fortune doing this." Fant was referring to the years when the stock market soared and new companies sprang up like mushrooms after an autumn rain—a historical moment made famous by two words used in December 1996 by Alan Greenspan of the Federal Reserve Board, who spoke of "irrational exuberance" in the markets.

One of Galway's first gambits turned into an embarrassment for Cassidy. It involved a California physician and entrepreneur named Harvey Eisenberg, who was launching a company to make and market new scanning technology to allow doctors to "see" inside the thorax to diagnose heart and lung ailments. Galway struck a deal with Eisenberg that gave it a 10 percent stake in a new company formed to market this technology in return for "strategic investment advice." If Galway's advice helped Eisenberg succeed, its stake would rise to 20 percent.

At the same time, a unit of Eisenberg's new company signed a lobbying contract with Cassidy & Associates to help gain access to federal officials and members of Congress who could support the thoracic scanner.

Eisenberg hoped that government agencies would buy the device; Cassidy proposed to try to win earmarks to achieve this goal.

In July 1994, Cassidy and Eisenberg met with Senator Inouye to discuss this possibility. *The Wall Street Journal* learned about this meeting, and about the agreements between Cassidy and Eisenberg, and published a detailed story on October 12. In the course of reporting the story, the *Journal* asked Inouye if he had realized that Cassidy owned a piece of the company for which he had come to lobby in July. "That I'm not privy to," Inouye replied. "You can rest assured that I'm going to look into it now."

Given Inouye and Cassidy's relationship, this was embarrassing. Cassidy lobbyists heard from Inouye's staff that their boss was furious. More than two decades later, Inouye said he did not remember this episode.

Galway never made any money from its arrangement with Eisenberg, but that was only a small part of the new firm's woes. According to Fant, Galway never made money from *any* of its activities. Though it remained in business for five years, it lost more than $5 million. Galway was a total bust.

Ifshin's idea for the business was half-baked. "He thought that we know so many important . . . and rich people—through Gerry, we're one phone call away from everyone on the planet. There ought to be a way we can make some money on this," Fant said years later. Ifshin imagined cultivating rich people and then identifying promising young businesses; Galway would introduce potential investors to the entrepreneurs behind these ventures, and receive a stake in their new businesses in return. The plan was vague but they pursued it. Fant became one of the managing partners of Galway. When Ifshin died suddenly of renal cancer in 1996 (Bill Clinton and John McCain both spoke at his memorial service), Fant gave up his partnership at Sidley & Austin to join Cassidy and run Galway full-time.

"I'm not sure that was the smartest decision ever made," Fant said a decade later. "You know, you have to put your head back into the late 1990s or the middle 1990s to understand it. . . . We were in the era of up, up, up."

Cassidy loved Galway. "He loved to have meetings about it," Fant recalled, "he wanted us to come down [from their offices on the eleventh floor] to tell him what we were doing all the time." Cassidy's colleagues did not share his enthusiasm. Many thought it was a distraction and a diversion of the firm's assets. Fabiani was particularly concerned about it.

The problem, he thought, was that the firm's revenues financed Galway. Cassidy & Associates paid the handsome salaries of Galway's executives, paid their expenses, paid the rent on their offices. Fabiani called

Galway "a sinkhole." He also questioned the propriety of using firm revenues to support an outside activity that brought no benefit to the firm.

When Galway was launched, Fabiani said, Cassidy asked him to put up half a million dollars of his own money to help get it going. Fabiani reluctantly did so, he said, but never had much hope of getting the money back. (He didn't.) As the chief operating officer, Fabiani was helping to manage the firm at the time. He recalled a meeting with Cassidy, Fant, and several others to go over financial statements. He saw that the money being advanced to Galway was being described as "contributions or loans to affiliates." He expressed concern that this was not proper.

Fant had never been popular in the firm; skepticism about the ESOP and Galway made him actively unpopular. "He was Gerry's evil twin," one executive of the firm said; "the consigliere," said another. "That Fant was one smart lawyer," said Glenn Cowan, who worked for Cassidy from 1991 to 1998. "But he was Gerry Cassidy's lawyer. Nobody ever thought he was the *firm's* lawyer, though that was his title."

Cassidy thought his colleagues—particularly those who had been with him the longest—were jealous of Fant, the smooth, Harvard-trained lawyer. "He was smarter than they were," Cassidy said. "There was great resentment of that. Ruff is much more cultured than they are, there's a class resentment, and a resentment of his doing things they didn't understand."

Those things were, often, Cassidy's projects to make more money. Fant was involved in most of them. Over the years they worked together, Cassidy helped make Fant a wealthy man. He gave the lawyer stock in the firm so he could benefit from the ESOP deals, for example. The old-timers in the firm saw themselves as lobbyists who were making a lot of money, but Cassidy saw himself as an entrepreneur who happened to be in the lobbying business, and who wanted to get rich. Fant, who was intrigued by wealth himself, was happy to help.

The issue of the money going to Galway came to a head at a heated meeting involving Fabiani, Cassidy, and Fant. "I didn't know if it was illegal, but I did believe it was a breach of our contract with our employees through the ESOP to take that much cash out of the firm. . . . And so much cash had gone to Galway that we couldn't maintain what had been the pattern of bonuses across the business" after the Democrats lost control of the House, Fabiani said. Fabiani eventually hired a partner in a big Washington firm to advise him on the propriety of the Galway arrangements. Fabiani brought this lawyer to a meeting with Cassidy to register his concern. Cassidy was furious.

"Jim just travels with fear, it's there all the time," Cassidy said years later. "So if we did something out of his experience, his reaction was always 'Uh-oh, we're going to get in trouble.' . . . Jim was always very unsophisticated about business."

As to the propriety of using firm money for Galway, "we knew it was legal, we knew it was okay, but Jim had this incredible suspicion of Ruff," Cassidy said. "Part of it was that Ruff had invaded his space. He was the person with a good relationship with me, now Ruff had that relationship. I think that's what it was about."

A breach had opened between the two men who had built Cassidy & Associates into a hugely successful business. It would never be healed.

Galway was one of the many fliers Cassidy took in the 1990s, the fruits of his restless appetite for bigger triumphs. "There was always this urge to drift off into other businesses," said Bob Beckel, founder of a "grassroots" lobbying firm that Cassidy bought in 1992, the same year Jody Powell launched Powell Tate. Beckel and his partner, Glenn Cowan, had created a business that generated expressions of public support for, or opposition to, pieces of legislation in Congress or policy proposals from executive branch agencies. Cassidy bought them out with money from the first ESOP loan. In 1996 Cassidy added the public opinion research firm of Greg Schneiders, who had been a pollster in Jimmy Carter's White House, working with Powell. "Cassidy had embarked on this grand scheme to create a one-stop-shop public affairs operation," Schneiders said. This conglomerate would be able to offer clients a broad range of services, while encouraging the various branches of his burgeoning empire to refer clients to each other. "Synergy" was the goal. At first this looked brilliant; Cassidy's competitors spoke enviously of his creativity. But it never produced the hoped-for bonanza. Collaboration between the lobbyists and Powell Tate was the most productive alliance.

Another idea was to "globalize" the lobbying business by opening a string of offices far from Washington. The model for this was a Boston office opened in the 1980s when so many of the early clients were educational institutions in the Boston area. Jack Brennan, former majority leader of the Massachusetts state senate, made a financial success of this office by combining local lobbying in Massachusetts with services for New England–based clients of the Washington firm. When Russo was hired at the end of 1992 he was supposed to create a comparable outpost in Chicago. He did open an office, but it was never very successful. Offices were also opened in Philadelphia, Sacramento, and Dallas, then in Brussels to try to cultivate European business. None panned out. Another gambit was to open a New York office of Powell Tate; it too was a flop.

Cassidy was perpetually on the lookout for people he might bring into the firm. By the late 1990s his early reluctance to hire people with independent reputations had been supplanted by a willingness to make grand offers to some big names. One was Congressman Bob Livingston of Louisiana.

Livingston was the chairman of the House Appropriations Committee and had already been chosen to succeed Newt Gingrich as Speaker of the House when, at Tom DeLay's insistence, House Republicans formally moved to impeach Bill Clinton in December 1998, weeks after they had lost seats in the midterm election. Livingston first released a statement confessing infidelities in his own marriage, then announced that he too would quit Congress. Because of his experience, intelligence, popularity among colleagues, and effectiveness as a legislator, Livingston was an attractive candidate to become a lobbyist.

Cassidy and Fabiani quickly offered him a job, but he declined. "I had to question my sanity, because they made me a pretty nice offer, but I just wanted to have my own deal." Livingston opened his own lobbying firm instead.

A year earlier, at the end of 1997, Cassidy asked Stan Ebner, a lawyer, former White House official, and original member of the Timmons & Company lobbying firm who had run McDonnell Douglas Corp.'s Washington office, if he would like to be the new president of Cassidy & Associates. Ebner was offered a big salary and stock in the firm, but he declined.

In December 1997, Jody Powell suffered a heart attack, alarming his colleagues. They began to think about strengthening Powell Tate with new hires. Powell persuaded Tom Griscom, who had spent many years as the spokesman for Howard Baker, first in the Senate and then in the Reagan White House when Baker was chief of staff, to join Powell Tate in April 1998. Griscom quickly realized that Powell Tate, like its parent company, was going through "a time of tension and uncertainty." Powell and Griscom tried to recruit Mike McCurry, who had been Bill Clinton's press secretary and had often been compared to Powell as a smart, friendly White House spokesman. McCurry was tempted; there were discussions about renaming the company to Powell-Tate-McCurry-Griscom. McCurry backed out of the plan at the last minute. "I just didn't want to run a PR firm," he said afterward. Powell Tate also approached Michael Deaver, Ronald Reagan's legendary image-counselor. He wasn't interested either.

The firm did not need these big names to keep growing. Revenues exceeded $41 million in 1996, the first year *Legal Times*, a weekly newspaper aimed at lawyers, ranked Washington's lobbying firms. Cassidy & Associates ranked first, with the highest revenue number. But Cassidy wanted more—$200 million more, which he thought was possible if he made the right acquisitions.

"I saw us doing what I thought would be a major departure," he said, speaking of 1997 and 1998, when he got ready for another big play. The list of acquisitions he wanted to make included a firm "that was doing really topflight 'grass tops,' " meaning lobbying of state and local leaders and opinion-makers to win them over to some client's cause; several radio stations; a publication of some kind; one or more advertising firms with experience working for candidates in political campaigns that would do "public affairs advertising to complement lobbying"; and finally, "some of the other premier lobbying operations in town, perhaps a couple of the very best." He and Fant began talking to firms they might try to buy; several expressed interest.

All Cassidy needed to pursue this plan was an enormous amount of money—he thought $40 to $60 million would do. He and Fant came up with an audacious idea for where to get it: they would sell Cassidy & Associates to the public for at least $50 million.

One could argue that this was the third time Cassidy proposed to sell his firm—twice to its employees in the two ESOP transactions, now to the public in an IPO. Thousands of entrepreneurial companies in the 1990s were offering to sell their stock to investors, including many technology firms that made no profits. They were part of what became known, after it burst in 2000, as the high-tech bubble, but in 1998 new stock issues were gobbled up by avid investors who thought the markets could only travel up. So why not be the first lobbying firm in history to go public?

Cassidy and Fant accepted a proposal from a northern Virginia merchant bank, Friedman, Billings, Ramsey, to handle the deal. Fant spent months preparing the detailed S-1 that, under federal securities law, has to be filed with the Securities and Exchange Commission. The S-1 must provide a thorough accounting of the company's past earnings and future potential. It is supposed to contain all relevant warnings about what might go wrong for the company in the future. Investors reading it should be able to understand the company and its prospects. Fant took these requirements seriously. Cassidy's S-1, filed on July 21, 1998, was so thorough that competitors could (and later did) use it as a guide to help them borrow from the successful Cassidy template.

For example, the S-1 revealed the precise extent of the firm's reliance

on its ten-percenters—grandly described as "marketing consultants"—
who numbered twenty-three in 1998:

> Revenues from retainer contracts that were signed as a result of
> leads generated by such marketing consultants for the years ended
> December 31, 1995, 1996 and 1997 were $11.6 million, $11.3
> million and $12.4 million, respectively.

That meant that nearly 60 percent of the firm's business came from
the ten-percenters (who, in those years, would have received $3.5 million
in commissions on those contracts).

The S-1 revealed the Fabiani method for identifying potential new
clients. The language is dense, but the detailed information must have
astounded the competitors who read it:

> The first step in [the] business development process involves se-
> nior professional staff and research staff identifying the key issues,
> pending legislation, regulatory proposals and policy debates that
> are slated for Congressional or Executive Branch consideration
> and action during a given year. The group's professionals then . . .
> determine the sectors of the economy and the specific industries
> that may be affected favorably or adversely. Once specific indus-
> tries are identified, the Government Relations Group, through its
> senior professional staff and its network of consultants, identifies
> the leading businesses or institutions within the affected industry.
> Further research is conducted and then a determination is made
> regarding the proper steps for achieving an introductory meeting
> with the potential client's senior management. . . . The profes-
> sionals from the Government Relations Group [then] meet with
> the leadership of the potential client to discuss the advantages of
> Washington representation, the federal government issues that
> may impact the potential client's activities or objectives over the
> next 24 months and the process of representing a client in Wash-
> ington. When such discussions and presentations are successful,
> fees, terms of engagement, and negotiation on the scope and
> breadth of the relationship are then negotiated and a written con-
> tract executed.

The document even revealed the extent of the firm's aggressive marketing efforts: "In 1997, C&A made presentations to 220 potential clients,

of which fifty-one, or 23.2% resulted in revenue-producing engage-ments."

The S-1 explained why the success rate was so high, under the heading "Client Engagements":

> The first step in a new client engagement is an in-depth discussion about the objectives of the engagement. The Government Relations Group's professionals then work with the client to develop a detailed strategy to accomplish the client's objectives. The Government Relations Group's professionals bring to this effort an understanding of the substance of the applicable law affecting the client and its business as well as an understanding of the goals and objectives of the various Congressional and Executive Branch personnel and units which are likely to be involved in the decision-making process. Typically, a crucial part of any successful strategy is to identify the public policy objectives that can themselves be advanced when the client's goals are achieved.

In other words, wrap the client's cause in the flag; make it look like a manifestation of the national interest, not a narrow, selfish interest.

Then the S-1 offered an explanation of how the work was done:

> The Government Relations Group's professionals then focus on implementing the strategy. This effort frequently involves communicating the client's issues and goals to decision makers by person-to-person meetings with members of Congress, their staff, the members of the Executive Branch and other groups taking part in the decision-making process to gain their support for the client's position. The goal of this communication process is to ensure that decision makers are aware of the relationship among the client's objectives, national policies and the interests of the public.

The document was candid about the uncertainties of the lobbying business, noting that "The loss of any senior lobbyist could have a material adverse effect on the company's business." But it was also bullish on its record and on the future:

> In its 23-year history, [Cassidy] has represented over 1,100 clients, including twenty-four of the Fortune fifty corporations; coalitions and associations; public and private utilities; universi-

ties and colleges; financial institutions; health care providers; state, city and county governments; international businesses; foreign governments and other entities.

Here the candor was less than complete. Nowhere did the S-1 point out that most of Cassidy's business still came from earmarks.

The market for the Company's services is growing. As Congress deals with an increasing number of issues, the number of people and institutions affected by government decisions also grows, creating more conflicts over policy among groups with competing interests. As a result, the demand for experienced government relations professionals who can guide clients through the policy-making process has increased.

So the lobbying and public relations businesses had bright futures. Cassidy's revenues and earnings were rising every year, the document reported, and contracts already signed would provide a minimum of $26.8 million in future revenues.

The pitch was impressive, but the response was limp. Friedman, Billings, Ramsey could never find buyers for the shares Cassidy proposed to sell. They could not interest the stockbrokers and banks that often buy blocks of IPO shares. Cassidy and Fant blamed the timing for their failure; the stock market fell about 17 percent in the two months after the S-1 was filed (though it bounced back nicely in the next few months). "We could have been very successful, maybe if it were two years earlier or something," Fant said.

The failed IPO damaged morale in the firm—not because Cassidy failed to go public, but because the S-1 had revealed the salaries of senior executives, numbers that until then had always been tightly held. According to the S-1, Cassidy himself took home $877,320 in the previous year, 1997; Fabiani made $851,552; Fant $569,996; Powell $589,712; and Russo $476,004. The S-1 also disclosed that Russo had a special rent subsidy of another $72,000 a year.

The other employees thought these were big numbers. Russo's package particularly aggravated the many employees who found him an overbearing, distracted, and clumsy colleague. In fact, Cassidy had lowered these salaries "significantly," including his own, to prepare for the public offering—to make the company's costs look lean to potential investors.

When the IPO collapsed, "I pushed the salaries back up," Cassidy said. And they were secret again too.

Many of the employees were flabbergasted that Cassidy had decided to go public. As often happened inside the posh Cassidy offices, rumors spread in the absence of hard information and full explanations. Some thought Cassidy's hand had been forced by the ESOP—without a big infusion of cash, they reckoned, the firm could never redeem the shares in the ESOP retirement plan at the high values they were supposed to be worth. Selling all the stock to the public, including the shares held by the ESOP, would solve that problem by producing cash for the retirement plan. Fant later acknowledged that this would have become a problem years later, when a significant number of ESOP beneficiaries began to retire, but he insisted it was not an immediate issue in 1999.

Employees were surprised that Cassidy and Fant had decided, after years of opaque operations, to make public so many details about the firm. "A secretive guy who always operated in the shadows wanted to go public? To disclose all those facts about his business? It was weird," said one Powell Tate executive.

But Cassidy and Fant were actually true to their own ambitions, which others in the firm neither shared nor, often, understood. They knew that eventually they would have to sell the firm to make good on the implicit commitments of the ESOP, which they had promoted to their colleagues as a retirement plan. The shares in the ESOP couldn't finance anyone's retirement, obviously, unless they were somehow converted to cash. Cassidy and Fant were also looking for a big financial play, a way to use the go-go stock market to leverage their own wealth. Most of the others in the firm were focused on lobbying or public relations.

The IPO's failure led Fant and Cassidy to Donaldson, Lufkin & Jenrette, one of Wall Street's best firms. "They were very smart," Fant recalled. They saw three choices: complete the IPO, find a big company that would acquire Cassidy's business, or "stay the way we were."

DLJ told Fant and Cassidy that it could complete the IPO and find buyers for the stock, but Fant was struck by what they said next: " 'People on Wall Street'—this is a direct quote—'are very lazy and very greedy. That extends to analysts. An analyst will not write a report on a single company, it's too hard.' " And because theirs would be the only lobbying firm traded on the stock market, Cassidy's stock would soon be orphaned, they cautioned. As Fant remembered the warning, "They said . . . you'll be a public company, but your stock will do nothing but go down. It will languish." When they heard this presentation, Cassidy and Fant decided that

DLJ should abandon the IPO and try to sell the firm instead. DLJ predicted they would get a good price.

DLJ prepared a "Confidential Information Memorandum" on what it called "Cassidy Companies, Inc." to try to attract buyers. The thirty-nine-page document made Cassidy sound irresistible.

In the S-1, Fant had described the business as "a leading provider of government relations services, public affairs communications and opinion research." DLJ found a much richer vocabulary:

> Cassidy . . . is the nation's premier communications firm in providing expertise in government relations and public affairs. The company is the largest government relations firm and one of the largest independent public affairs firms in the United States [and] . . . the only communications firm that has successfully integrated its government relations and public affairs businesses. . . . The company commands premium compensation for its services relative to its peers . . . [and has enjoyed] outstanding profitability growth. . . . It [is] well positioned to acquire other government relations and public affairs businesses.

If the timing was bad for an IPO, it was better for an outright sale. This was a time of consolidation and fierce competition in the world of public relations and advertising. Giant, global firms were eagerly acquiring small ones to try to stay near the front of the pack. "All firms went through this big macho search in the 1980s and 1990s for who's the biggest," said Paul Costello, a former public relations executive and veteran of these wars. In this environment, businesses in Washington became very attractive.

"Washington was seen as a potential bonanaza of untapped dollars," said Costello. "Everyone wanted Washington, because no matter who you were or what your business was, you had Washington issues. . . . Washington could be a cash cow. People started saying, 'What are we, idiots? We could make a bunch off this place.' "

DLJ's booklet on the Cassidy companies caught the attention of the New York office of Shandwick International, where Costello was then an executive vice president. Shandwick was a global firm based in London. Stephen R. Conafay, who ran the New York office, realized that Cassidy's revenues, if added to Shandwick's, would make it one of the top public relations firms in the United States.

Conafay's boss was Michael J. Petruzzello, head of Shandwick North

America, and he was enthusiastic about the possibility of acquiring Cassidy & Associates. Shandwick had itself been acquired in 1998 by the Interpublic Group, IPG, a giant global conglomerate. When the DLJ proposal reached them, "We were on a heavy acquisition charge," Petruzzello remembered. At the time, companies like theirs believed new acquisitions would push up the value of their stock. "At board meetings they always wanted to hear that we had more acquisition deals working."

Shandwick liked Cassidy's ideas for future expansion and wanted him to pursue them. He was encouraged to make new acquisitions both in the United States and overseas. With this support, Cassidy thought he would be able to pursue the ambitions that originally motivated his decision to try to take his firm public. So everyone wanted the deal, and they reached an agreement. No purchase price was announced, but "sources" told reporters that it was $70 to $80 million. That stunned other lobbying firms in Washington. Were their businesses really so valuable?

They were valuable, but not *that* valuable. In fact the IPG deal was worth closer to $60 million, though Cassidy still insists it was more. Sixty million dollars was a big figure, but considerably less than the $100 million valuation that the second ESOP transaction in 1994 suggested the firm was worth, despite the fact that revenues had grown substantially in the intervening five years. Moreover, one reason the price was as high as it was involved $14 million in accumulated tax "losses" on Cassidy & Associates' books, the result of complicated accounting rules involving the ESOP. Shandwick was able to use those losses to deduct $14 million from its own tax liabilities immediately after the transaction was completed.

The acquisition took effect at the end of 1999. It was another big payday for Cassidy—his share was $11.8 million. Much of it was in the stock of Shandwick's corporate owner, the Interpublic Group of Companies, and the stock was rising. Cassidy sold his shares quickly in a complicated transaction that brought him more than $15 million. (Soon afterward, the price of IPG shares plummeted—Cassidy luck.) So altogether, from the two ESOP stock sales and then this transaction, Cassidy had taken more than $30 million out of his and Schlossberg's creation.

Paul Costello was right: Washington really could be a cash cow.

CHAPTER 21

ELECTIONS BOUGHT AND SOLD

By the beginning of the new millennium, Washington was famous for cash of a different sort—campaign contributions. In the 2000 elections, the campaigns of all the candidates for president, the House, and the Senate cost $2.8 *billion*—three times what was spent in the 1976 elections, even after adjusting for inflation. In 2004, the total was $4.2 billion. This steady increase appears now to be a permanent fixture of our politics.

The escalation of the cost of politics has had many repercussions, altering the public life of the country and the political culture in Washington. Higher campaign costs contributed, for example, to a steadily rising number of wealthy men and women sitting in the House and Senate, as "self-funded" candidates exploited their natural advantages in electoral politics. John Corzine, a retired investment banker and a Democrat, spent $62 million of his own money in 2000 to win a Senate seat from New Jersey—the most ever spent on a Senate campaign. (What would the founding fathers, so suspicious of inherited wealth and power, have made of *that?*) As spending on campaigns grew, campaign consultants and pollsters—recipients of a lion's share of the money—became more important in Washington, and a lot more rich. A new kind of political technician entered the game, the fund-raising consultant. By the late 1990s most candidates for the House and Senate employed professionals who helped them raise money, for a fee or a percentage of the money raised. Another new elite in the capital consisted of PAC directors—the people who ran the political action committees that gave steadily increasing amounts to campaigns. Most PACs were connected to corporations, trade associations, and labor unions. Their contributions to congressional campaigns grew from $55 million for the election of 1980 to $363 million in the 2006 election cycle. PAC contributions rose by more than 600 percent in a quarter century.

The most significant repercussion has been on Congress itself. Today's members of the House and Senate lead lives that their predecessors of a generation or two ago would not recognize, because so much of their time is devoted to the search for money. "Most members hate fundraising," Gerald Cassidy observed. "It's the most frequent complaint you hear from members. . . . Lobbyists complain about it, the members complain about it. It just goes back to this trap they're in, that campaign funding has created. . . . No one will disarm. No one will stop fund-raising because it could end their career. They raise money out of fear."

The more important money became to the politicians, the more important its donors became to them. This was a boon to Cassidy and all his colleagues and competitors. "The lobbyists are in the driver's seat," observed Leon Panetta. "They basically know that the members have nowhere else to turn" for money. This was not literally true, because the PACs were so big and so numerous, but lobbyists often told the PACs where to give their money (as Cassidy had with the Ocean Spray cranberry cooperative's PAC for many years). Panetta's remark precisely captured a fundamental truth about modern Washington, however: lobbyists had become indispensable to politicians. They served as advisors, fundraisers, even finance chairmen of their campaigns.

Senator Chuck Hagel of Nebraska, a Republican, explained the reality: "We let the lobbyists run it all because we have these big fund-raising dinners, for example. Democrats and Republicans. And we raise $20 million, $25 million at these things [for the House and Senate campaign committees]. Who do we go to to make sure that we get $20 to $25 million? I've run these dinners so I know what I'm talking about. You go to a committee of twenty-five lobbyists, a steering committee. And you say, Okay, you guys each have to come up with a million dollars. . . . So we go to them for that fast money."

For Gerald Cassidy, giving money to politicians was a fundamental aspect of his job. "It's something everybody in government relations does," Cassidy said, using the lobbyists' favorite euphemism for their trade. "We've always done it."

The history of Cassidy's own giving to candidates illustrates the growing role of money in politics over the nearly four decades he has been a lobbyist. In the early years he gave relatively little, because candidates asked for and needed very little. In the 1981–82 election cycle, Cassidy and his wife together gave just $3,500 to politicians. Ten years later, in the 1991–92 cycle, they gave ten times more, $38,400. By 2005–06, they reached $170,700. Total contributions from the two Cassidys from 1979 through 2007: $1,334,786. Cassidy's employees similarly gave generously. Federal Election Commission records show that from 1979 (the first year for which the statistics are available) through the first half of 2008, Cassidy & Associates employees donated more than $6.2 million to political campaigns.

The people who worked for Cassidy understood that giving was part of their job. In the words of Douglass Bobbitt, a Cassidy lobbyist in the 1990s: "It's kind of the way the world works." Added Don Smith, another former colleague: "Contributions were an absolute key to the business." Geoff Gonella, who worked at the firm from 1992 to 2002, said, "Cassidy realized that the way to get things done . . . was to be a huge financial resource for members of Congress." Cassidy insisted that the main purpose was not to get specific things done, but to build and reinforce relationships: "Certainly you support members where you have an interest. You encourage your clients to contribute because it's part of the political process. And you support people because you believe in them."

By the 1990s political giving at Cassidy & Associates was elaborately organized. Cassidy designated two employees, one Democrat and one Republican, to be responsible for the firm's fund-raising for members from their parties. Sometimes a member or his political staff would contact the firm to ask if it could give a fund-raiser; on other occasions the firm would volunteer to host an event. Cassidy himself always had the last word, and according to numerous colleagues, it was usually yes. Some of his colleagues thought he could be too willing to raise money for members who asked, whether or not they could actually help Cassidy clients.

Employees of the firm were never instructed to make specific contributions, but they knew that they were expected to pony up. "It was clearly understood that we were to give about half of our annual bonus to politicians," Smith recalled. By the 1990s, every lobbyist in the firm received multiple invitations every week to fund-raising events in Washington. Often, many lobbyists in the firm were invited to the same fund-raiser. When Carol Casey was at the firm from 1992 to 2000, she often acted as an informal social director, recommending which Cassidy lobbyists should attend which events.

But everyone realized that the firm would make a bigger impression by hosting its own fund-raiser for a member it wanted to cultivate, so these were common. The typical Cassidy fund-raiser was an 8 a.m. breakfast in one of the two conference rooms in the grand offices on Thirteenth Street.

In busy seasons there were two to three a week. As in all matters that he cared about, Cassidy had a firm idea of how these events should proceed.

First he was careful to tell the guest for whom a fund-raiser would be held what the likely pot would be. "If he offered a member an event to raise $10,000," recalled Larry Grossman, who was responsible for Democratic fund-raisers when he worked at the firm, "Gerry always tried to make it $12,000 in fact. And he tried to make sure that every seat at the table was filled—always a full house. So if there were twelve guests and fourteen chairs, he'd even ask two secretaries to come in, or have two chairs removed. Making the right impression on the guest was critically important." Typically the employees who attended these events wrote checks to the member's campaign for sums between $250 and $1,000.

The food wasn't much. Cassidy liked bagels and lox, which was always on the menu. But the conversation could be interesting. The lobbyists typically flattered the member by asking him to recount his recent activities, describe his plans for the future—in other words, talk about himself, the politician's favorite pastime. Several Cassidy employees said they enjoyed the opportunity to hear influential members discussing their work in a relaxed setting.

The Federal Election Commission collects contribution reports from every candidate for Congress; since 1979 the records have been computerized. The FEC system is imperfect, because it relies on the individual campaigns to provide accurate information about their donors and there is no real enforcement. Lobbyists and their family members are supposed to identify their professional affiliations but they do not always do so. The reporting can be sloppy, and the same donation can be registered more than once. The available figures show the patterns of Cassidy's personal, and his firm's collective, contributions, but the numbers they provide are not precise.

Nor are they surprising. Cassidy and his colleagues have given the most to Cassidy's favorites, and to two categories of congressmen who can be helpful to them: members of the House and Senate leadership, and members of the appropriations committees. As of 2007, these were the top recipients of donations from individuals with an easily identifiable connection to Cassidy & Associates. They are listed in descending order by the amount they received:

- Congressman John Murtha of Pennsylvania, senior Democrat on the defense appropriations subcommittee in the House and an unabashed supporter of earmarks and pork-barrel spending.

• Senator Ted Kennedy of Massachusetts, a Cassidy favorite and supporter of earmarks for Massachusetts educational institutions.

• Congressman Steny Hoyer of Maryland, an appropriator and avid earmarker, who was elected Democratic majority leader after the election of 2006. Hoyer is also a Cassidy favorite.

• Congressman Jerry Lewis of California, the last Republican chairman of the House Appropriations Committee before the 2006 elections and before that chairman of the defense appropriations subcommittee. Lewis was the subject of numerous investigations and journalistic exposés because of his close relationships with lobbyists and beneficiaries of earmarks he supported who then became financial supporters of his. A federal grand jury was investigating him in 2008.

• Senator Daniel Inouye of Hawaii.

• Senator Tom Daschle of South Dakota, whom Cassidy has known since the early 1970s, when Daschle was an aide to Senator James Abourezk of South Dakota and Cassidy worked for the state's senior senator, George McGovern. Daschle was Senate minority leader until 2001, when he became majority leader for two years. He was defeated in 2004.

• Congressman Ray LaHood of Illinois, a centrist Republican and member of the Appropriations Committee.

• Senator Arlen Specter of Pennsylvania, also a moderate Republican, also an appropriator and a supporter of earmarks. He and Cassidy had friendly relations.

• Senator Tom Harkin of Iowa, Cassidy's pal and an appropriator. Cassidy was a fund-raiser for Harkin when he ran for president in 1992.

• Congressman James Walsh of upstate New York, a moderate Republican and member of Appropriations, who brought home a great deal of bacon in the form of earmarks.

The largest recipients of the personal contributions of Gerald and Loretta Cassidy were largely the same Democrats, plus several others. No Republicans made a list of the Cassidys' top ten. Besides the Democrats on the preceding list, the Cassidys' favorites included:

• Senator Harry Reid of Nevada, majority leader of the Senate after the 2006 elections, minority leader before then.

• Senator John Kerry, another Cassidy favorite from Massachusetts, a member of the Finance and Commerce committees, and a supporter especially of Boston University, Cassidy's biggest university client for years.

• Congressman Ed Markey of Massachusetts, a protégé of Tip O'Neill's, like O'Neill a graduate of Boston College, another Cassidy client, and a supporter of earmarks for it and other Massachusetts institutions.

• Congressman David Obey of Wisconsin, Democratic leader on the House Appropriations Committee, and since 2007 its chairman.

• Congressman Dick Gephardt, the leader of House Democrats from 1995 to 2003, and the majority leader, or second-ranking Democrat, from 1989 to 1995, under Speakers Wright and Tom Foley. He left the House in 2005.

• Senator Hillary Clinton of New York, a Cassidy favorite: "She is so damned impressive."

These lists included all of the members with whom Cassidy had meaningful personal connections, and a few with whom he had no personal relationship, like Clinton and Kerry. The small number of his significant relationships in Congress was a function of his shyness, and of his general mode of operation. Cassidy the big-time lobbyist did not do very much face-to-face lobbying, according to numerous colleagues.

"Money is the great equalizer for lobbyists," observed Jonathan Orloff, a former Cassidy employee. "Even if you are not very smart or charming, money makes up for a lot."

Daschle came at the top of the Cassidys' list because of two checks totaling $9,000 from Gerald and Loretta that were donated on June 7, 2001, to the annual fund-raising gala of Dedicated Americans for the Senate and the House (DASH), Daschle's leadership PAC.

The timing of the Cassidys' gift to Daschle is intriguing. Just two weeks earlier, on May 24, 2001, Senator James Jeffords of Vermont, a lifelong Republican, announced that he would vote henceforth with Senate Democrats. When he said that, the Senate was divided 50–50, so Vice President Dick Cheney's tie-breaking vote gave the Republicans the majority, and the chairmanships of all committees. Jeffords's change of heart suddenly made the Democrats the majority party—and Tom Daschle the majority leader.

Asked later about this timing, Cassidy replied with a big laugh. Daschle, he said, was an old personal friend whom he had known for decades. "The whole time Tom was in the Senate," Cassidy said, "I only lobbied him once." In other words, that $9,000 was just support for an old pal, unrelated to Daschle's new power and stature.

There was no way to test Cassidy's assertion. His motives might have been utterly benign, or thoroughly corrupt—who could tell the difference? This was the beauty (for him) of the system that had evolved, the system that made politicians and lobbyists dependent on each other. By 2001, when Cassidy made this $9,000 donation, such gifts were commonplace. DASHPAC reported raising $204,500 at that gala, twice what a similar event raised a year earlier. Much of the money came from lobbyists. As Cassidy had said, giving was part of the job; in the same spirit, *taking* was part of the job of nearly every senator and congressman. How could something so ordinary be wrong? Cassidy had a plausible rationale for making an unusually large donation to Daschle a fortnight after he became Senate majority leader—and that was all he needed, both to satisfy his own sense of appearances, and also to answer anyone who asked about it.

The amounts given to individual members of Congress were actually modest, because these big totals were contributed over more than a quarter century. For example, Murtha received about $90,000 from the Cassidys and their employees over nearly three decades, but no more than $20,500 in any one two-year election cycle. Throughout the 1990s Murtha raised $500,000 to $900,000 per two-year cycle, and from 2002 onward he took in more than $2 million per cycle.

Cassidy observed that in the twenty-first century, senators typically "spend ten, twenty million dollars on their campaigns. I don't believe our small contributions would sway them in any direction."

But if the money won't sway them, why give so much of it, and why give to so many different recipients? Because, as Cassidy said, the goal of these donations is usually not to achieve any particular objective, but rather to reinforce established connections: "A lot of money is given because of long-term relationships and friendships." Much of the money donated to politicians is Washington's version of frankincense and myrrh—symbolic tribute, meant to signal fealty and respect. When they gave money to Murtha, for example, Cassidy and the other Democrats in his firm demonstrated their loyalty to the tribe of Murtha, an old-time politician who lived by the rules and customs of the Washington favor bank.

Cassidy lived by those rules also. For him, as we've seen, nothing was more important than loyalty. In Cassidy's world, giving money is a meaningful expression of loyalty.

An honest lobbyist will acknowledge how their contributions help them function. "Why do lobbyists give so much money to politicians?" Dan Tate Sr., the former Cassidy lobbyist, once asked, rhetorically. "What's the purpose? Well, it isn't good government. It's to thank friends, and to make new friends. It opens up channels of communication."

Without access to members and their staffs, lobbyists have no hope of achieving their goals or impressing their clients. Everyone on Capitol Hill knows giving money leads to access. From time to time a member of Congress blurts out the truth. Congressman Romano Mazzoli, a Democrat from Kentucky from 1971 to 1995, did so soon after he retired from the House: "People who contribute get the ear of the member," he said. "They have the access, and access is it. Access is power. Access is clout. That's how this thing works."

Access can also provide the path to a client's heart. To raise money, as we have seen, speakers of the house from O'Neill onward, White Houses, Senate leaderships have all created special opportunities for big donors to hobnob with the powerful. George Smathers impressed clients by taking them to lunch in the Senate Dining Room. This wasn't a privilege that every lobbyist could match, of course, but any big contributor could get invited to special events where members would be present and approachable.

Those events have often taken place around the quadrennial political conventions of both parties. Larry Grossman, the former Cassidy lobbyist who organized the firm's fund-raising efforts for Democrats in the 1990s, remembered the "epiphany" he experienced at the Democratic National Convention in Chicago in 1996, when he suddenly realized that "the big donors got treated best" by the organizers of the convention, first of all by being invited to the best parties.

Lobbyists can rely on more than their own bank accounts to direct money to politicians' campaigns. Clients can be donors too. Cassidy always encouraged his clients to "participate," to use a word he often employed to describe giving contributions. Fund-raising for members was a selling point for Cassidy when trying to persuade a potential client to sign on. "He talked about it from the very first meeting with a new prospective client," remembered one former colleague. "He'd explain why he did it. He'd say he never met a person who, if you asked them to give you a buck, they'd just give it. That person needs a reason to give."

Said Cassidy, "You encourage your clients to contribute because it's part of the political process." Some needed no prodding. As we've seen, Cassidy persuaded two clients, the Ocean Spray cranberry cooperative and the Pirelli Corporation, to create PACs, and then guided their contributions. Ocean Spray's totaled about $1.5 million over this period, Pirelli's about $170,000 in the seven years that it existed (1984–91). Ocean Spray added another $1.4 million in corporate "soft money" contributions to various Democratic and Republican Party committees. In the favor bank, Cassidy and the firm got credit for these. He also "bundled"—raised money for politicians from friends, acquaintances, clients, whomever. "I raise a lot of money from friends who have not a damn thing to do with what goes on here [in Washington]," Cassidy said. Typically, he raised several times more than he gave himself.

The law gave Cassidy some protection from money-hungry politicians. Until 2002, individual donors were legally limited to $25,000 a year in gifts to candidates for federal office, PACs, and party committees. The McCain-Feingold reform bill enacted that year raised the limit, then adjusted it for inflation every two years. It was $108,500 in the 2008 cycle. However, the old limit did not cover donations to party committees and PACs; the new one does. Under both standards, the Cassidys, and most big Washington lobbyists, routinely "maxed out"—a revealing term that describes giving to the legal limit. Fund-raisers in Washington get used to hearing the same excuse for someone not giving: "Sorry, I'm maxed out."

"If we contributed to every single candidate who asked us for money," said one former Cassidy employee, "everybody would have been broke."

Cassidy has little patience with complaints that lobbyists corrupt the system with their contributions. The lobbyists don't initiate these transactions. When they give they are responding to requests from members. "Gerry used to say, 'It's not as if we're cramming checks down people's throats,' " recalled Carol Casey, who worked closely with Cassidy on his and the firm's contributions. "We are the ones who are asked to give. It's not as though we're calling to ask 'Please will you accept our money?' . . . Your profession is politics; if you're a player people expect you to make political contributions."

Soon after the firm became Cassidy & Associates in 1985, Cassidy asked his lawyers to give regular "ethics seminars" to his employees explaining the law and warning them about ethical pitfalls.

"The lawyer tried to scare us," remembered Don Smith. "He showed us slides including photos of news stories about politicians caught in embarrassing situations. His main point was, Never let an appearance arise of a connection between a contribution and a legislative act. . . . The seminars were well done. They scared the bejeezus out of us—for a couple of weeks." Smith remembered one specific instruction: if a member's assistant ushering them out of an important meeting mentioned an upcoming fund-raiser, the lobbyist was to say, "We don't want to connect that with this meeting, so I will get back to you about it later." Smith and others remembered instances when something like this actually happened.

The lawyer who conducted these seminars for many years was Michael A. Nemeroff, who succeeded Fant as the Sidley & Austin partner in Washington who represented Cassidy & Associates. He provided a PowerPoint presentation that was part of the 2005 ethics seminar and that included these warnings:

"Your actions affect the whole firm. . . . Be open internally; be silent externally. . . . You are a professional, act accordingly. . . . Separate political contributions and requests for official action. . . . Avoid bringing unwanted attention to the firm."

One slide in the presentation began with a question: *Can I volunteer to raise money for a member?* Nemeroff's answer was yes. He suggested the lobbyists "obtain a letter appointing you a 'volunteer fund-raiser' " from the member, and handed out a draft of such a letter. He also instructed the lobbyists to "make up business time spent fund-raising." If they used regular work time for this purpose, it could be considered a contribution from the Cassidy firm to the candidate, which would be illegal. The firm's PAC could make contributions, but not the company itself.

Ethics seminars could not alter the fundamental nature of the money-driven relationship between lobbyists and members. Leon Panetta captured its essence when he described the endless round of cocktail parties around Washington—fund-raising events considered dreary but inevitable by most who attended them: "The lobbyists go from reception to reception with checks in their breast pockets, handing them out to the potential favor-givers, with the latter fully understanding that the time will come when a favor will be sought."

As Cassidy noted, few participants in the money chase enjoyed it, but all took it for granted. When asked, Cassidy said he would favor "public financing" of congressional elections—allocating money from the Federal Treasury to both incumbents and challengers, so neither would have to solicit or accept contributions. This would eliminate corruption and appearances of corruption, Cassidy said. But he added, "there isn't a chance in the world that during my lifetime, I will see public financing. I don't think you'll see public financing in the next fifty years."

If Cassidy is right, the politicians' dependence on campaign contributions will continue to grow, and the culture of money and politics that developed in the years he had been a lobbyist will continue to thrive. To participants, this seems like a safe bet.

"Money drives everything today on Capitol Hill," observed Douglas Bereuter, the Nebraska Republican, who retired from the House in 2004. "Far too often things are done or not done because of money." The issues debated are often those pushed by the donors, he explained, "not because . . . strong consideration is given to the public interest."

This was the point Coelho had made years earlier when he noted that members dependent on contributions from the wealthy and the corporate sector could not be "creative" as legislators, because "they don't want to turn people off." By "people" of course he meant donors. It's the point Bob Dole made when he observed that, "We may reach a point where if everybody is buying something with PAC money, we can't get anything done." Coelho and Dole made those comments in the early 1980s.

Cassidy agreed that the weak and the poor "have less representation" in modern Washington. He also agreed that moneyed interests can set a legislative agenda that flouts the public interest but serves their narrow purposes. He has a favorite example of this, one that brought out the old 1960s liberal that sometimes lurked beneath Cassidy's $4,000 suits: the Bankruptcy Abuse Prevention and Consumer Protection Act of 2005, a project of the banking and credit card industries.

Enacted in April 2005, the act made it more difficult for consumers to evade paying their debts by declaring personal bankruptcy. Consumer groups and academic experts argued that the law would create unfair new burdens for families forced into bankruptcy by unexpected medical expenses or the loss of a job, but the proponents were not deterred. Indeed, the final version of the law forced debtors to repay their credit card debt before they paid child support or alimony.

Cassidy thought it was "the single worst piece of legislation from a public policy point of view that passed in recent years. . . . Here you have a group of people that are essentially unrepresented—those who might go into bankruptcy—and you have the banks, the credit card companies, driving the whole issue. They came up with a system that essentially turns people into paupers. That it could pass with the margins it passed by [302–126 in the House, 74–25 in the Senate, with lots of Democratic support] is absolutely stunning. You look at the amounts of money that were spent on that, it was enormous."

The Center for Responsive Politics in Washington, an independent group that studies politics and money, calculated that banks and credit card companies gave $40 million to the campaigns of members to promote the new law over fifteen years. During the five years before the vote, the eighteen Senate Democrats who voted for the bankruptcy bill received, on average, $51,200 in campaign contributions from banks and credit card companies. Democratic senators who voted against the bill had received an average of $20,200.

CHAPTER 22

POLITICS, THEN GOVERNMENT

In the early years of the new century, many thoughtful students of Washington's ways, people who paid attention to Congress and the executive branch and to the relations between them, understood that the government of the United States was broken.

The breakdown was heralded in the early months of 2004 by two prominent former officials who blew very loud whistles, both trying to warn their countrymen that they had a dysfunctional government. Most dramatically, President George W. Bush's first secretary of the treasury, a practical-minded businessman from Pittsburgh named Paul O'Neill whom Bush had fired in December 2002, revealed how politics determined policy in the Bush White House. O'Neill was fired for opposing a third round of tax cuts in 2003, after the first two reductions proposed by Bush and approved by Congress had converted the budget surplus inherited from Bill Clinton into a large and growing deficit. O'Neill quoted a remark made to him by Vice President Dick Cheney: "Reagan proved deficits don't matter. We won the midterms [the 2002 off-year elections, when Republicans increased their majorities in House and Senate]. This is our due." O'Neill described Bush as indifferent to facts, especially facts that conflicted with his predilections. The president presided over cabinet meetings "like a blind man in a roomful of deaf people," O'Neill said.

Weeks later Richard Clarke, a nonpolitical civil servant who had worked in the White House under both Clinton and Bush on terrorism issues, revealed secrets of White House deliberations before, on, and after September 11, 2001. Clarke said Bush asked him personally to find a connection between Saddam Hussein of Iraq and the 9/11 attacks on the United States. Instead Clarke wrote a highly classified report, signed by all relevant government agencies, concluding there was no such connection.

The White House and its allies responded furiously to these apostasies, but they made no attempt to disprove the facts that O'Neill and Clarke alleged. Instead the White House portrayed both men as disgruntled opponents of administration policy. Bush's spokesman, Scott McClellan, told reporters that O'Neill's criticism "appears to be more about trying to justify personal views and opinion than it does about looking at the results we are achieving on behalf of the American people."

This non sequitur was what reporters call a nondenial denial. The Treasury Department announced it was investigating whether O'Neill had disclosed classified secrets. When Clarke's book appeared, McClellan dismissed him as a friend of another former White House terrorism specialist who had recently gone to work for Senator John Kerry—suggesting that Clarke must be a political opponent of Bush.

This was the style of governance from 2001 through 2006, when Republicans controlled both the White House and Congress for the longest stretch since the 1920s. By the time O'Neill and Clarke spoke out, Bush and his team knew they could avoid concrete replies to such criticisms and spin their way out of whatever apparent embarrassment they had caused for one simple reason: the only institution with the standing and the legal authority to investigate accusations like O'Neill's and Clarke's would do nothing. This was the Congress, which from 2001 to 2007 abandoned the traditional function called oversight, and asked almost no challenging questions of the administration. Instead, the Republican leaders of the House and Senate rallied 'round the president, defended him at all costs, and dismissed his critics as politically motivated. The House of Representatives never tried to discover why the war in Iraq had gone so badly, or how the country's intelligence agencies could have been so wrong about Saddam Hussein's weapons of mass destruction, or why the response to Hurricane Katrina had been so botched. The Senate was hardly better. So the broken government was never formally called to account.

On fiscal matters, politicians who called themselves conservative Republicans cut taxes and increased government spending with abandon, adding nearly $2.5 *trillion* to the national debt by the end of 2008. In 2000, the last year of Bill Clinton's presidency, austerity policies embraced by both parties had produced a budget surplus of $86 billion. In the first decade of the new century Congress spent nearly $1 trillion on wars in

Afghanistan and Iraq without raising a single dollar to pay for them, despite the fact that the federal budget was already in the red. This was the first time in American history that war had been waged without *any* special taxes being levied to help pay for it. So these were the first wars whose costs were passed entirely to future generations.

Washington in the early twenty-first century was loudly acrimonious, defiantly partisan, apparently indifferent to the long-term consequences of its acts, and profoundly negligent. The partisan combatants could agree on nothing—not even descriptions of the problems they faced, or basic facts about contentious issues. In this atmosphere, the fact that the government wasn't working very well was treated as a partisan argument. Only the 2006 elections, which put the Democrats back in control of Congress, forced the Republicans to abandon their fantasies, though even then they could not bring themselves to abandon a president who had become as unpopular as any in modern history.

Curiously, in the aftermath of 9/11, public confidence in the government had soared. Polls showed that in the year following the attacks on the Pentagon and World Trade Center, the public's trust in government jumped to levels not seen since before the Watergate scandal of the early 1970s. Roughly four in five Americans told the Gallup Poll in 2002 that they trusted their government to handle foreign and domestic problems. But this result was wishful thinking, perhaps induced by fear. Osama bin Laden's greatest success was to scare Americans, a new phenomenon in the country's politics, one understood and exploited better by Karl Rove and his boss, George W. Bush, than any of their critics. This was most obvious in the off-year elections of 2002, when Republicans picked up six seats in the House and two in the Senate against all historical precedent. They did so by following Rove's publicly delivered advice to use the 9/11 attacks and subsequent "war on terror" as campaign issues in 2002. "We can go to the country on this issue," Rove told the Republican National Committee in January 2002, "because they trust the Republican Party to do a better job of protecting . . . America."

The least attractive example of these tactics came in Georgia, where a Republican congressman, Saxby Chambliss, ran commercials with photographs of Saddam Hussein and bin Laden that questioned the "courage to lead" of the incumbent Democrat, Max Cleland. Cleland, a Vietnam veteran, lost one arm and two legs in the war. His fellow Vietnam veterans in the Senate, Republicans John McCain of Arizona and Chuck Hagel of Nebraska, both denounced Chambliss's commercial. McCain called it "worse than disgraceful, it's reprehensible." It helped Chambliss win, however.

The best members of Congress knew the truth too: the system was fractured. In an interview in January 2004, the independent-minded Hagel observed that "we have two assets as a society: a free press and the counterbalance that the founders always intended as a check and balance—the Congress." Only Congress can prevent a president from becoming "a democratic dictator," Hagel thought. "Unaccountable power is dangerous. . . . A president must be accountable, and that's the responsibility of the Congress." But with Republicans in both the House and Senate acting as cheerleaders for the Bush administration, "Congress has abdicated much of its responsibility," Hagel said. "Politics are almost overrunning the interests of Congress. . . . There has been a very clear weakening of Congress as an institution, and I don't think that's good for the long-term interests of our country."

One of the brightest and hardest-working members of the House was David Obey of Wisconsin, a Democrat who was first elected in 1968. Throughout the years of Republican control, Obey was the senior Democrat on the House Appropriations Committee (he became its chairman in 2007). He was an old-school legislator who loved every aspect of the legislative process, from gathering information and discovering needs that Congress could satisfy to writing and passing appropriations bills. He took his job seriously.

Early in 2004 Obey recalled what happened right after the 9/11 attacks, when the anthrax scare closed down Capitol Hill. "When we were boxed out of the House by anthrax, I called Bill Young [a Florida Republican who was then chairman of Appropriations] and said, as long as we can't do anything useful in our offices, why don't we go around to all the security agencies to find out exactly what it is they think they need that they don't have?"

Young agreed. They spent a week visiting the agencies involved in the response to 9/11, including the FBI, the CIA, and the Centers for Disease Control. "We got a list of items that those agencies thought they needed immediately. We put that together, asked to see the White House—after telling the staff to cut the list in half, so there wasn't any crap in it. We went down [to the White House] expecting to have a discussion. Bush walked into the Cabinet Room accompanied by Karl Rove, but not by representatives of any of the security agencies, and said, I understand some of you want to spend more on homeland security than my friend Mitch Daniels [then director of the Office of Management and Budget] says we need to spend, so I want you to know that if you appropriate one dollar more than that, I will veto the bill. Then he said he had time to listen to four or five comments."

Senator Ted Stevens, another Alaska Republican, who was chairman of the Senate Appropriations Committee, and Robert Byrd of West Virginia, the ranking or senior Democrat, were present. "Byrd blew up," Obey recalled. "He said it was the first time in thirty years a president had closed off discussion in advance." Obey, famous for his temper, was also angry. "I said, I want to tell you about four installations that were vulnerable [to terrorists]," installations the members had been briefed on by his own security agencies. "I asked if he had been briefed on them." Bush did not reply, and Obey was certain the president knew nothing of these four, still classified examples. Stevens was also upset; he pointed out to Bush that whatever legislation they passed would allow the president to "knock off ideas you don't approve of." Bush did not respond. "I said, I can't believe we'll have an argument about this," Obey continued. "Essentially he stiffed us and walked out of the meeting.

"When I came to Congress in 1969, people saw Congress as a separate branch of government; now it's just two parties at war," Obey said. "If the Congress is turned into a jellyfish, there are no checks and there are no balances." Governing effectively was no one's concern.

Smart lobbyists understood this too. In 2006, Gerald Cassidy offered his own description of the problem:

"The House is a dysfunctional body. . . . They do not function as an oversight body. They give the executive much more power than was ever intended. Authorizing committees seldom legislate, and when they do, the leadership has far too great a role in the development of the legislation. The members as a body aren't here [because of the three-day workweek that then was the norm] so they don't get to participate in the legislation. So you have a much smaller group of people [involved in decision making] and . . . you get legislation drawn up by a few people whose sole role is to stay in the majority."

Staying in the majority was the imperative; anything that served this goal was an appropriate tactic. This was the prevailing ethos of Tom DeLay's House of Representatives. And it *was* DeLay's House. He had orchestrated the election of Dennis Hastert of Illinois to be the new speaker when Bob Livingston suddenly resigned in 1998. Hastert was a former high school wrestling coach, a big bear of a man who was friendly, easygoing, and not particularly bright. He had never dreamed of becoming speaker, but was willing to take the job. He proved to be the ideal front man for DeLay, because he could get along with people better than DeLay could. His plodding manner defused tense situations.

DeLay, the majority leader, dominated the Republican caucus. He was both the party's strategic field marshal and its chief tactician. He cultivated the relationships with lobbyists, partly by encouraging his own people to become lobbyists themselves. Money was critical to maintaining control, and the Republican lobbying community was the key to raising it. DeLay remained eager to reciprocate by giving corporate lobbyists and trade associations the legislation they wanted whenever he could.

DeLay and Hastert turned the House Republicans into a disciplined political machine. After George W. Bush moved into the White House in 2001, Congress began to resemble the parliament of a European democracy that fell in line behind its prime minister. Obey's "independent branch of government" effectively disappeared. John Feehery, press spokesman for Hastert, explained the House leadership's attitude in January 2004: "We tend to work very closely with this president because a) we agree with him, and b) because we find having political disagreements is a waste of time."

Feehery was speaking for Hastert, but also for DeLay and all the Republican leaders. Hastert and DeLay had created a unified "leadership staff" as a device to help them maintain centralized control. They required the committee chairmen to fall into line on all controversial matters that they designated as "leadership issues." Key staff assistants—most notoriously Scott Palmer, Hastert's chief of staff, who shared a Washington townhouse with the speaker and spoke for him on virtually all matters—had more influence than most Republican members, who resented them as a result. A handful of elected leaders and a handful of powerful staff totally dominated the House. What had been under the Democrats an increasingly decentralized body (a great boon to lobbyists, who then had many targets of possible influence) became more centralized than anyone could remember it being. Just as Cassidy said, "a few people" ran the show.

Barney Frank of Massachusetts, an outspoken liberal Democrat first elected to the House in 1980, recalled hearing Speaker O'Neill once say, "I am powerless to tell a member how to vote." But DeLay told his members how to vote, and intimidated them into following his instructions. Benefits of all kinds were available only to loyalists. The small remaining band of moderate Republicans, mostly from the Northeast and Midwest, were particularly vulnerable to threats from DeLay and other conservatives who could support challenges to them from more conservative

Republicans. Such challenges were mounted with the support of conservative groups such as the Club for Growth, and though few succeeded, they generally intimidated moderates. One, Marge Roukema of New Jersey, beat back two right-wing challenges sponsored by the Club for Growth, then retired in 2002 rather than face a third. Similarly, Jim Kolbe of Arizona, a moderate and gay Republican, retired in 2005 after a conservative challenger won 40 percent of the vote against him in 2004. Frank reported that moderate Republicans had said to him "more than once" that they would support him on a particular issue "after the filing deadline has passed"—the deadline by which a conservative challenger had to announce plans to run against that incumbent moderate.

Hagel described "another element" involved in the unusually high degree of party discipline on the Republican side—"the tremendous influence of money and politics in this business of governing." Lobbyists and the money they commanded were tools to be used to assure loyalty to the party line, he thought. "The sophistication, the amount of money, the amount of lobbying in this town for whatever the cause is—gun control, environmentalism, you name the cause—they've all got high-powered lobbyists, high-powered lawyers, a lot of money, a lot of focus. This influences things up here. When you then lock that in a tandem effort with a governing party that controls the White House, and Congress, and [controls] that money and influence, that affects all of us." Hagel was particularly sensitive to efforts made in Nebraska by various interest groups and conservative Republicans to discredit him at home because of his independence in Washington. "Almost at any given time, there's a radio or a TV ad or a newspaper article coming after somebody."

DeLay's K Street Project "represented the formalization of what I am talking about here," Hagel said. He recalled regular appearances at the Republican senators' weekly policy lunch by Rick Santorum of Pennsylvania, one of the conservative senators who came out of Gingrich's House and brought some of the Gingrich-DeLay partisan energy to the Senate. Santorum and DeLay became the proprietors of the project, and met regularly with the lobbyists who supported them. "They wanted to build a triad: the White House, K Street and business, and Congress, and just lock up the issues," Hagel said. "Our role, the Republican Congress, was to do the bidding of the Republican business community as represented on K Street. That K Street Project was about as blatant as anything I've ever seen."

The single most dramatic display of DeLay's and Hastert's muscle came in the early hours of November 23, 2003, at the end of a long debate on a proposal to extend a drug benefit to senior citizens on Medicare. This legislation demonstrated how far the Gingrich-led "revolution" had strayed from its roots. The idea behind it was to win votes to help Republicans retain the White House and their majorities in Congress in 2004. This would mean strengthening one of the most popular and successful big entitlement programs, Medicare—the crowning achievement of Lyndon Johnson's unabashedly liberal Great Society—by adding coverage of drug costs to its benefits.

The cost of this coverage would be immense—more than a trillion dollars over ten years—but the Republicans proposed no new source of revenue to pay for it. The Bush administration actually hid its own estimates of the full cost of the program until after the House and Senate had approved it.

Hastert and Delay, with Bill Frist of Tennessee, the Republican leader of the Senate and a doctor himself, were determined to enact a Medicare drug benefit before Congress adjourned at the end of 2003. They insisted on a more generous plan than the Bush White House originally endorsed—an example of congressional independence from the administration, which did appear from time to time, usually when congressional Republicans feared that a particular White House initiative would hurt them politically. In this case a more generous program had strong support from the pharmaceutical industry, since better benefits would mean greater sales of drugs. According to Congressman Walter Jones, an independent North Carolina Republican, "the pharmaceutical lobbyists wrote the bill."

The legislative process that led to the floor vote in the House on November 23 was messy, like so much of the work of the Congresses of the early twenty-first century. The Republicans adopted unconventional procedures based on partisan hostility. After the House and Senate had passed different versions of a drug benefit in the early summer (the House by just one vote), the two houses appointed conferees to work out their differences. But the leadership allowed only Republicans and a handful of favored Democrats to participate in the conference. Even then, the conferees could not agree on a compromise plan. Finally, Frist and Hastert stepped in with their own plan and forced the conferees to accept it— a strong-arm maneuver that illustrated the way a few members of the leadership controlled the Congress in these years.

Despite the leadership's best efforts, when the Hastert-Frist plan came up for a vote in the House, a group of about two dozen Republican members continued to resist this proposal to expand "big government."

Hastert, DeLay, and DeLay's big whip organization—designed to keep members in line—went into action.

Since the House began to vote using an electronic voting system in 1973, the standard procedure was to allow fifteen minutes for a vote. This gave members time to travel from their offices in the three House office buildings across Independence Avenue, several hundred yards south of the Capitol, reach the floor, and insert their voting cards into devices that kept a running tally. Just once, in 1987, Speaker Jim Wright had kept a vote "open" for an extra fifteen minutes to find the single vote needed to pass a bill he favored, a departure from standard procedure that infuriated Republicans at the time.

This history did not deter Hastert early in the morning of November 23. When the traditional voting period ended at 3:15 a.m., twenty-two Republicans had voted against the bill and no Democrats supported it, so the proposal was going down to defeat. But Hastert refused to accept this outcome. The whips kept whipping. Hastert and DeLay personally began cajoling wayward Republicans to support the bill. One holdout, Nick Smith of Michigan, had announced plans to retire from the House and was hoping his son would be elected in his place. DeLay threatened to withhold $100,000 in campaign contributions from Smith's son—money from the National Republican Congressional Committee—unless Smith would change his vote. He still refused.

Finally, at 5:53 a.m., after a number of votes of members from both parties had switched back and forth, DeLay announced that he had persuaded two Republican dissidents to return to the fold. This produced a tally of 220 in favor, 215 against. The gavel finally fell, ending the vote after nearly three hours. In the words of Thomas E. Mann and Norman J. Ornstein, two respected scholars of Congress, this was "one of the most breathtaking breaches of the legislative process in the modern history of the House."

Hastert defended his handling of this vote in a speech soon afterward. He described his goal as leader: "You will see us take effective action to get the job done. Sometimes, we have a hard time convincing the majority of the House to vote like a majority of the House, so sometimes you will see votes stay open longer than usual. But the hallmark of an effective leadership is one that can deliver the votes. And we have been an effective leadership." No previous speaker had ever used such language, but Hastert seemed oblivious to the implications of his remarks. The end justified the means.

Some of the House conservatives never came to terms with the outcome of this episode, and were embarrassed that their side had suddenly created a huge new government entitlement for 40 million senior citizens without paying for it. But Bush and a great many other Republicans happily used the Medicare drug benefit as a reason for voters to reelect them the following year. And, as always, many of the interest groups that benefited from the new program thanked the Republicans in the currency they liked best—cash money.

For example, the pharmaceutical industry probably benefited most from the Medicare drug benefit. Not only did it give millions of seniors more money to buy drugs, but Republicans in Congress explicitly rejected amendments that would have allowed Americans to import drugs from Canada (where they are generally sold more cheaply than in the United States) and would have authorized the government to negotiate the prices for drugs to be charged under the plan, the way, for instance, the Veterans Administration has long negotiated the price of drugs used in its hospitals. Drug companies opposed both these provisions, not surprisingly; both were killed.

In the 2002 election cycle, before the drug benefit was enacted, drug company executives and PACs gave $7.7 million to Republican candidates and committees. In the 2004 cycle, after the drug benefit was in place, this number rose to $12 million.

The Republican leaders of the House and Senate used sticks and carrots to maintain discipline. Most of the carrots involved money, much of it the taxpayers' money.

In 1995, Gingrich and DeLay had discovered the use of earmarks as a way to defend potentially vulnerable members of their new majority. But after 2001, with Republicans in control everywhere in Washington and no serious challengers on the horizon, the stream of earmarks that began to flow in 1995 became a flood. This defied past Republican rhetoric. Gingrich, for example, declared in 1992 that he was "totally committed to hunting down every appropriation that we can find . . . that is some politician taking care of himself," a good definition of politically motivated earmarks. But instead of hunting them down, Gingrich and then his successors promoted earmarks to a status they had never previously enjoyed.

Congress has discovered many legislative vehicles, as individual pieces of legislation, or bills, are known on Capitol Hill, to deliver financial favors to preferred recipients. A narrowly targeted tax break can qualify as an earmark; so can a provision in the gigantic highway bill that Congress passes every few years. But the most common version of an earmark comes in one of the annual appropriations bills or—easiest of all to manipulate—in an "omnibus spending bill" in years when the system fails to work properly, and all twelve appropriations bills are wrapped up in one huge appropriation.* This happened nearly every year the Republicans controlled the House.

One vivid example of what happened is the Labor–Health and Human Services appropriation. Like each of these twelve bills, Labor–HHS was the domain of one subcommittee; from 1978 until his death in 1994, a legendary legislator from Kentucky, William Natcher, was its chairman. He opposed nearly all earmarks on principle. In the last bill he managed, for fiscal year 1995, there were none at all.

The next year the Republicans were in charge, and they approved $33 million in earmarks for fiscal 1996. In subsequent years the amount spent on earmarks kept rising. By 2002 the number of individual earmarks reached 1,700; their value was $1 billion.

In the splendid old days, when Schlossberg-Cassidy first perfected its system for promoting earmarks in these appropriations bills, it was possible to get large allocations—for example, the $20 million appropriated for the very first one, the Human Nutrition Research Center on Aging at Tufts University. By the time the House Republican leadership had built its earmark machine to help its members bring home electorally appealing bacon, competition for earmarks was fierce, so many members wanted them. As a result, the average size of individual earmarks shrank significantly as the overall number shot up. The 2005 bill, for example, was filled with earmarks like these:

- Amigo de los Ríos, Los Angeles, for an environmental career training program for at-risk youth: $100,000.

- Central State University, Wilberforce, Ohio, to implement a world-class modular automation training system: $200,000.

* Congress has divided "discretionary" government spending—the spending not mandated by "entitlements" like Social Security and Medicare—into these twelve categories: Agriculture; Commerce, Justice and Science; Defense; Energy and Water; Financial Services; Homeland Security; Interior and Environment; Labor, Health and Human Services and Education; Legislative Branch; Military Construction and the Veterans Administration; State Department and Foreign Operations; Transportation and Housing and Urban Development. A separate appropriations subcommittee handles each one.

- Milwaukee Area Technical College in Wisconsin, for developing skills standards: $450,000.

- Mississippi State University, Starkville, Robotics and Automated Systems for Nursery Industry: $500,000.

- Center for Health Workforce Development, Tennessee Hospital Education and Research Foundation, Nashville, for programs to address shortages of nursing faculty and other health professionals: $150,000.

None of these was the subject of a congressional hearing or any serious fact finding by the appropriations committees. Once they were blessed by the leadership, they slipped right through.

Not all of the earmarks were projects supported by Republicans. The appropriations committees in both House and Senate had long-standing traditions of bipartisan collaboration—in the House, Appropriations was the only committee in which bipartisanship survived the political warfare of the 1980s and 1990s. Roughly 40 percent of the earmarks were given to Democratic members, so everyone was in this game together. This was an expression of the survival instincts of incumbents in both parties. It was also a demonstration of the corrupting power of the earmark culture that had grown up since the late 1970s.

Gingrich had picked Bob Livingston of Louisiana to be the chairman of Appropriations in 1995, jumping him ahead of five colleagues who had more seniority on the committee. Gingrich blew up the old seniority system and chose chairmen for his own, sometimes arbitrary, reasons. One consequence of this was that when Gingrich asked Livingston for a favor, Livingston was inclined to grant it. And "the leadership was always trying to help people," as Livingston put it. Gingrich and DeLay repeatedly instructed him to include earmarks in spending bills to help at-risk Republican members.

Livingston's last appropriations bills covered fiscal 1999, a year earmarks grew dramatically. (He retired in May 1999.) "The process wasn't working," he said years later. Gingrich and DeLay were ordering up earmarks to help their members. "Newt would say, 'You've got to give it to him,' " speaking of some at-risk member with an earmark request. "When I was directed, 'You have to do this,' I would do it."

With the proliferation of earmarks came new procedures systematizing them. They became a routine part of congressional business. Appropriations subcommittees required members to submit paperwork for every request, to rank their requests by importance to the member, and so on. As members discovered the joys of giving and constituents learned that money was available, the quest for earmarks became a consuming enterprise.

Scott Lilly, who was the minority (Democratic) staff director of the House Appropriations Committee from 1994 to 2004, explained what a distraction earmarks became.

"Can you imagine the amount of effort it took to put that [annual earmark] list together? There were probably six to ten requests for every entry on the list—each prepared in written form in members' offices. Members probably got three or four times as many requests from their districts as they passed on to the committees. Each one of those requests probably involved numerous communications with mayors, superintendents of schools, college presidents, representatives of community organizations—and of course lobbyists. We are talking about thousands of hours of meetings in each office. Then personal office staff call committee staff regularly to check on where their requests stand and to advise of changes in the priorities they assign to each potential project. Committee staff are completely overwhelmed simply by the job of logging in these thousands of proposals.

"Meanwhile of course Congress didn't have a clue about how the Labor Department was handing out tax dollars, or what the rules of engagement were for contract security personnel in Iraq, or whether we really had a shot at holding together a government in Afghanistan. Members of Congress became so obsessed with how to direct the expenditure of one percent of the discretionary budget [the money spent on earmarks] that they completely lost track of what was happening to the other 99 percent."

Earmarks were one of many distractions that consumed the time and energy of members who were avoiding their traditional duty to keep an eye on the operations of the government. Old-fashioned legislators who loved the process and believed in its importance grew disillusioned as they saw the Congress become less and less effective. One such was Livingston, who first came to Congress in 1977. He liked that era, with its fraternization between members off-duty as well as on. As a young member Livingston earned a reputation for intelligence and diligence. Because he worked well with his colleagues, he was an influential member even during the long years he spent in the minority. He was thrilled by the chance to become chairman of Appropriations in 1995, but then dismayed by what followed.

Livingston is an open, friendly, and voluble man. He discussed the evolution—he would call it the devolution—of Congress since the late 1990s while sitting in his sleek Capitol Hill office, with a view of the Capitol out his big windows. As befits the times, Livingston decided to become a lobbyist when he left the House. Now he competes with Gerry Cassidy and is making his own fortune. But he can still get himself worked up discussing his favorite subject.

The first source of trouble in Congress was the ascendance of political considerations over all others: "One of Newt's biggest mistakes was to tell members to leave their families at home. I think that so many of the problems today stem from that effort. Once they started doing that, they wanted to stay home not only on Saturday and Sunday, but on Mondays and Fridays, and then Mondays and Tuesdays and Fridays. They'd come into Washington Tuesday night, work Wednesday, and leave Thursday. . . . So what you had was ninety subcommittees, and all of the political committees, and all of the leadership committees, all meeting Wednesday morning between nine and twelve. You can't run the Congress like that. You can't run any institution like that. And the institution broke down."

Gingrich considered committee assignments political benefits, Livingston said. "He believed that the more committees and subcommittees a person can be on, the more attractions they can acquire to present to contributors and to voters, to say 'Look what I'm doing for you.' The problem is, they don't know anything about anything that's going on in any of those committees, because they can't be in more than one place at one time. . . . Newt said, 'Well, so-and-so's got a tough district, he's got to be on Armed Services, and then he's got to have Agriculture, and by the way, he's got a lot of bankers, so let's put him on Financial Services as well.' Each of those has got three or four subcommittees, he's on all of them. That's insane."

Insane, and ineffectual too: "They've got themselves hog-tied," Livingston said. "Government doesn't work. The reason the executive branch doesn't work is that Congress has abdicated its responsibility by not providing oversight to make it work. When Congress broke down, the executive branch broke down. . . . They didn't have any oversight for six years on this administration. They deserved plenty of oversight."

Oversight requires experience and skill. "The skill is lost," Livingston said, part of a general decline in capabilities of Congress. "Members don't show up, and you have staff writing the bills. And I will tell you, committee chairmen don't even know what's in the bills, let alone the members. It just drives me nuts!

"They only come to the floor for the fifteen-minute votes," Livingston said. "They pal around with the same people day in and day out—I mean, it must be insufferably boring. They come to the damn floor and their attitude is, well, I don't know you, and you don't know me, and you're not going to trust me, and I'm not going to trust you. It's not that Republicans don't know Democrats, or Democrats don't know Republicans. *Republicans* don't know Republicans. Democrats don't know Democrats. They're so busy with the news media, the twenty-four-hour news services, and their fund-raising that they are literally not doing their business, and they don't know their colleagues. They couldn't work out a compromise if they had to.

"I really think the quality has declined," Livingston said. As a loyal House man, he thought the problem was more obvious in the Senate: "The Senate guys just pontificate endlessly. . . . You've got a few great ones, but not many."

Livingston's view is surprisingly common in Washington, particularly among old hands who knew the city and its politicians before the era of the permanent campaign. Ask several dozen such people if they think the quality of Congress has risen or fallen over the last generation and it turns out that Livingston could be a spokesman for all of them.

Peter Hart, the Democratic pollster, was certain about it: "The quality of people that I started out with and the quality of people today is just so vastly different. Because in part they come from a different background with a different set of ideas. So in 1969 when you were working for a Phil Hart [a much admired and beloved senator from Michigan], or 1970 when you're working for a Hubert Humphrey [a liberal Democrat from Minnesota, Lyndon Johnson's vice president from 1965 to 1969], or a Warren Magnuson [senator from Washington], Scoop Jackson [Henry M. Jackson, also a Washington State Democrat], Frank Church [the Idaho Democrat], Lloyd Bentsen [the Texas Democrat]—all of those were my clients—a big group of those individuals across the country who were really lions [had] a great sense of not only the United States Senate, but also a great sense of history. They appreciated the system and they appreciated the gravity of what they were doing and what their responsibilities were. . . . All of these people were huge figures, not only within the institution of the United States Senate, but within the country."

Hart had fond memories of Republicans too: "You have to be equally positive about a Jake Javits [Jacob Javits of New York], a Chuck Percy [of Illinois], a John Chafee [of Rhode Island]. There were a lot of people from both sides of the aisle who brought a worldview to their job." Hart praised "the civility with which they worked with one another, and the respect . . . and the ability to reach a compromise. They came out of a different era with a bigger, broader understanding."

Hart realized that the new political technology, his own industry, had helped change the nature of the people who were attracted to politics. Polls and the political consultants who depended on them shaped what the clients should say, even what language they should use to say it. "The political process and what's involved today creates smaller people, people who are much more afraid and nervous." The objective was not to govern effectively, not to lead, but to win. "We've figured out how *not* to reach a compromise," Hart said, speaking of the political technocrats who ran modern campaigns. "We ask, what can you do to stir your base? What can you do to demonize the other side? We do it exceptionally well. And it is so dangerous, so bad."

Chuck Hagel agreed. "The political operatives in this business have become so sophisticated and so smart and so clever, politics is now almost scientific. And politicians shoot for the lowest common denominator—say as little as you have to say, play all the games to avoid ever really taking a position. I've known senators who have said, If it takes you more than ten seconds to explain it, then you better get a different issue, or you better get somebody to write something for you. And that's what they do. I mean when's the last time you saw any spontaneity in any of this?"

Hagel was a rarity in twenty-first-century politics: he read books, wrote his own speeches, traveled the world to meet with leaders and experts so he could come to his own conclusions about important issues. He spoke out, criticized his colleagues and his party's leaders, including President Bush. He behaved like one of those "lions" Hart referred to. And in 2007 he gave up, announced his retirement from the Senate and from politics. He told friends that his enthusiasm for the job had expired.

Gerry Cassidy saw the situation much the way Hart and Hagel did. He agreed that in the age of modern political technology, the system did not value people who thought for themselves or wrote their own speeches.

"Everybody talks about lobbyists and what a problem they are," Cassidy said. "But as big or a bigger problem are the campaign consultants and the way they have transformed campaigns into these negative blood-fests. . . . They have made things so mean, and they have spent so much money, and they demand so much money—it is one of the terrible things that's happened. I think it has changed the nature of the people who are attracted to politics."

Cassidy's desire to shift responsibility to the consultants was understandable—he wasn't a consultant. The truth of the matter was more complicated: a system had evolved that had indeed attracted a different kind of person to run for national office. More fundamentally, it had changed the nature of our national politics. But it was a complicated system with many participants. The pollsters and consultants certainly did create a demand for expensive services; their ability to win campaigns only increased the demand. To pay for those services, politicians had to raise ever-greater amounts of money or spend ever-greater quantities of their own wealth. The permanent campaign turned politics into a relentless struggle for power. It was a tactical struggle; posturing for political advantage was more important than solving the country's problems. The losers in this system were numerous, beginning with the citizens of the United States. The winners were few, but influential: they included the technicians who ran the permanent campaign, the politicians who prevailed, and the providers of the lucre that fueled the system, especially the lobbyists like Cassidy and the interests that the lobbyists represented. The politicians had a permanent interest in pleasing the interest groups and the lobbyists, and both sides knew it.

As Dale Leibach, a public relations man who worked for Cassidy for nearly a decade, once put it, the high cost of campaigns and the politicians' dependence on contributions established an inescapable reality: "The Hill [Congress] can't exist without downtown [the lobbyists], and downtown can't exist without the Hill. It's the largest, most democratic bazaar in the world. And it's all about money, going in both directions."

CHAPTER 23

HARD TIMES

Like many a romantic quest, Shandwick's courtship of Cassidy & Associates failed to produce the marriage both parties had dreamed of. On the contrary, the merger in 2000 of Cassidy's lobbying and public relations operations into the global advertising and PR conglomerate Shandwick International "was disastrous."

This was Gerald Cassidy's description, and it was indisputably accurate. Shandwick itself was soon Weber-Shandwick, a new global monster created by the Interpublic Group of Companies, which owned everyone involved, and it was in constant turmoil. None of the executives who worked on the acquisition of Cassidy still worked for the company two years later. The hoped-for "synergy"—Weber-Shandwick clients coming to Cassidy for Washington representation, Cassidy clients using Weber-Shandwick for public relations work all over the world—never materialized. Cassidy's decision to give the unpopular Marty Russo more executive authority in the firm drove away several of his top lobbyists; others left for their own reasons, several to create new lobbying firms to compete with Cassidy. By the end of 2001, more than three dozen lobbyists who worked for Cassidy in 1998 had moved on. Many of Powell Tate's key people also departed.

IPG was a fast-growing conglomerate that had acquired more than 185 companies between 1999 and 2001, using its own shares to buy them. The deal to buy Cassidy was struck just as the dot-com bubble was about to burst, at a moment when IPG stock had been soaring. IPG shares doubled in value from the beginning of 1998 to the end of 1999, reaching an all-time high of $55 that December, weeks before the Cassidy acquisition was formally completed. The IPG share price remained above $50 into 2000. At first Cassidy was optimistic that he would be allowed to use IPG's high-flying shares to acquire public affairs and lobbying firms in Washington and elsewhere, in pursuit of his big dream. But almost immediately the stock plummeted, to $34 by late September. The high-tech bubble in the stock market was bursting. The idea of Cassidy acquiring more companies died with it.

Instead Cassidy & Associates and Powell Tate struggled to try to hold on to their business. Powell Tate had the bigger problems, because Weber-Shandwick had no idea how to merge its Washington public relations company with it. Jody Powell described the two years that followed the merger as the worst of his life.

According to David Whitmore, the Shandwick financial officer assigned to make the merger work, "It should be a Harvard [Business School] case study of how to screw up a merger." The Washington offices of Shandwick and Powell Tate were comparable—each had about seventy employees and annual revenues of about $14 million. Two years after the merger, the combined firm had seventy employees and revenue of about $14 million.

The situation at Cassidy & Associates was "incredibly volatile," according to a senior executive of the firm at the time. "We were losing staff and churning clients. I didn't see how we could meet a business plan when the place was just roiling on a daily basis." The Cassidy firm once prided itself on its retention of clients; traditionally, 80 to 90 percent continued the relationship year after year. Suddenly clients were leaving in droves. "It was hemorrhaging. The joke was, it wasn't a lobbying firm anymore, it was a marketing firm, because so much energy had to be spent drumming up new clients."

This was an awful time for Gerry Cassidy. Fant, who in his law practice had helped numerous entrepreneurs sell the companies they created, recognized familiar signs of stress. After selling their baby, such men often lost their bearings, at least for a time. It didn't help that under its new owners, Cassidy's business quickly ran into trouble.

According to Stephen Conafay, one of the Shandwick executives responsible for the deal, "It was apparent right away that numbers weren't going to be met." Conafay referred to the revenue and profit targets that Cassidy had to reach to collect millions of dollars in "earn-out" payments in the original sale agreement. The biggest immediate problem was Powell Tate; its costs, particularly salaries, were too high, and revenues too low, Conafay said.

Whitmore of Shandwick suggested to Cassidy that Jody Powell might not be the best person to manage the merger. But Powell was Cassidy's favorite colleague. To the amazement of many colleagues and old friends, Cassidy had taken up fishing and hunting, two of Powell's favorite pastimes, so they could enjoy the outdoors together. When Whitmore raised the possibility of perhaps replacing Powell in a meeting with Cassidy and James Fabiani (whom Cassidy had assigned to work on the merger with Whitmore), the famous Cassidy temper erupted. Cassidy hurled a water glass in Whitmore's direction; it smashed into a wall behind the chair in which Whitmore was sitting, sprinkling shards of glass into his hair.*

Several of the Shandwick executives who had engineered the merger developed serious cases of buyer's remorse. "Gerry's just a tough old Irishman," Conafay said. "He was going to have things his way. . . . And there was a lot of concern about whether we wanted someone that difficult to work with." Conafay and others who heard about the glass-throwing incident urged Whitmore to report it to IPG headquarters in New York, and he did so. The company sent a human resources official to talk to Whitmore, Fabiani, and Cassidy. The first two provided similar accounts of what had happened. Cassidy said he refused to talk to the envoy from corporate headquarters.

Cassidy's recalcitrance contrasted with Fabiani's willing cooperation with the Shandwick executives. Ever the orderly and organized executive, Fabiani enjoyed the challenge of working things out. Cassidy, by contrast, was determined to give up as little control to the new owners as possible. Fabiani admired his stubbornness, even as he tried to be a conciliatory figure. Cassidy's position, Fabiani said, was simple: "Nobody's going to tell me what to do, nobody's going to take my business. I may have sold it, but I'm sure as hell not going to give it to them. That was really his whole attitude."

Fabiani received regular phone calls from IPG corporate headquarters in New York complaining that the Cassidy companies were not meeting their revenue and profit targets, and he received regular instructions from Cassidy not to give in to New York. "For example, as part of the deal we were required to turn over payroll operations and salary setting to IPG," Fabiani said. New York wanted to limit raises and reduce payroll costs. "Gerry didn't want it to happen, and it never did." Asked about this,

---

* When asked about this episode, Cassidy said he had slammed his fist on the table on which a water pitcher sat, bouncing it onto the floor, where it shattered.

Cassidy remembered that the deal with IPG gave him authority over the payroll.

Several exasperated Shandwick executives began to discuss the possibility of forcing Cassidy out of the firm and putting Fabiani in charge. They discussed the idea with Fabiani, who did not discourage them. The issue, Conafay said, was effective management: Fabiani knew how to run the company, while Cassidy stubbornly refused to satisfy his new owners' demands.

This plot collapsed after Shandwick became Weber-Shandwick at the beginning of 2001, and its new boss, Larry Weber, rejected the idea of replacing Cassidy with Fabiani. Cassidy got wind of the scheming. He thought trying to preserve Cassidy & Associates without Cassidy was a preposterous idea: "The company has my name on the door. The flag outside the building has my name on it. I don't think there's a firm in town that is more dependent on one name." The story of this attempted coup was kept secret at the time; many members of the firm never heard about it. Fant, who left Cassidy when IPG took over at the beginning of 2000, said the idea that Fabiani could fill Cassidy's shoes was "ridiculous."

Fabiani knew he had been losing Cassidy's confidence over the months he tried to maintain good relations between the firm in Washington and the new owners in New York. This effectively ended their nineteen-year collaboration. Fabiani had played a critical part in building the business, and Cassidy had made him wealthy—he had taken at least $10 million out of Cassidy & Associates. Now Cassidy let him twist for a while in the Washington wind.

"I just waited to take action, and when the time was right, I did," Cassidy said. In early December 2001, the few publications that followed the lobbying business reported that Fabiani was leaving Cassidy & Associates to launch his own firm. No one reported that he had been fired. Cassidy issued a friendly statement thanking Fabiani: "He's helped me to build a company that is well prepared for the future." A few months later, after Fabiani had acquired elegant office space overlooking Pennsylvania Avenue and antique furniture even grander than the pieces assembled years earlier for Cassidy's floor of offices on Thirteenth Street, Fabiani opened Fabiani & Company, a new "government affairs" firm.

The sale to Shandwick was followed by a difficult period in Cassidy's personal life. After nearly forty years of marriage, he took up with another woman. This was a shock to his friends and colleagues. "Gerry worshipped Loretta," said one longtime associate who knew both Cassidys well. "If Loretta did it, it *had* to be okay. Until that girlfriend came along, I thought he was the most uxorious person I had ever known."

By the summer of 2000 Cassidy was openly squiring his new lady friend to Washington functions. In June—five months after he had ceased to be the owner of his own firm—he bought a grand house on Q Street in Georgetown for $2.9 million; the woman moved in. He began to transfer wine from his seven-thousand-bottle collection stored in his and Loretta's Virginia house to Q Street. Sometime later that year, he called senior associates of the firm into his office, one at a time, to announce that he was going to divorce Loretta and marry his new companion. He asked his colleagues to treat both women with respect.

"If I hadn't heard it as a real fact I never would have believed it," said Carol Casey, who had left the firm by then. "I was really shocked." So were professional associates when they learned that Cassidy had broken his habit of attending daily mass.

Cassidy asked several friends to go out to dinner with him and his new companion, creating some uncomfortable moments. Loretta Cassidy hired a divorce lawyer. She bought a new house in McLean, the exclusive Virginia suburb just across the Potomac, sold the couple's retreat in Naples, Florida, and bought a new place in Key West.

But then, after months of separation, the couple reconciled. In August 2001, Cassidy sold the house in Georgetown (for $300,000 less than he paid for it) and moved into the new house in McLean. The couple's friends were relieved.

In December 2001, Cassidy's temper erupted again in an episode that took on legendary proportions in the small world of Cassidy & Associates. This was the end of the firm's second year under new ownership. With aggressive marketing Cassidy & Associates had been able to maintain overall revenues at a high level, but the firm was still losing its traditional clients. On December 12, Texas Tech University announced its intention to drop Cassidy after years as a loyal and lucrative customer. The lobbyist who worked most closely with Texas Tech was Vincent Versage, who left Cassidy & Associates at the end of 2000 to establish the National Group, a rival lobbying operation. Versage was one of the senior employees who felt Cassidy had promised him much more money than he had received, and when the sale to IPG confirmed this, he decided to leave. Cassidy was angry and upset, Versage remembered, but finally gave him a going-away party, where the boss "broke down openly in tears. Even at the party he was still trying to convince me not to leave."

Versage had signed the standard Cassidy employment contract with a "noncompete" provision barring him from representing any Cassidy clients for a year after leaving the firm. His lawyers told Versage that this did not prevent him from inviting his old clients to come with him when the year was up. Versage did this with Texas Tech, offering to represent the university in its quest for congressional earmarks for a fee of $240,000 a year. Texas Tech had paid Cassidy $580,000 to pursue earmarks in 2001. The university signed up with the National Group.

Frank Godfrey was one of Versage's best friends. Versage had invited him to join the National Group, but Godfrey decided to remain at Cassidy, where he had made a lot of money over nearly twenty years. Colleagues remembered that the money mattered a great deal to Godfrey, who had been earning less than $35,000 a year on Capitol Hill when he joined Schlossberg-Cassidy. By 2000 Godfrey and his wife (who had inherited some money and property herself) owned retreats in Florida and on Maryland's Eastern Shore.

After Versage left Cassidy, Texas Tech had become Godfrey's client. He knew from university officials that Versage was going to bid low to try to induce Texas Tech to move to the National Group. According to his wife, Godfrey suggested to Marty Russo, then the chief operating officer of Cassidy & Associates, that they also offer a reduced rate to try to keep the client. Russo rejected the idea. Then on December 12 word arrived that Texas Tech was moving its business.

That evening, a Cassidy & Associates fund-raiser was scheduled to honor Congressman Ray LaHood of Illinois, a popular moderate Republican. Arthur Mason, the firm's top Republican at the time, had organized the event, and a secretary at Cassidy offered her Capitol Hill townhouse as a venue for what amounted to an office cocktail party. Federal Election Commission records show that the event raised $7,500 for LaHood from fourteen employees of the firm.

Fabiani, then still at Cassidy & Associates, recalled riding in his chauffeured limousine from the Thirteenth Street office to the reception on Capitol Hill with Marty Russo. Russo talked angrily about the loss of Texas Tech, and blamed it on Godfrey. "Marty was talking about how Frank had screwed up Texas Tech, how they were firing the firm because Frank had handled the account badly," Fabiani remembered. "I said, 'Marty, that's not what happened at all.' He wanted to pin the thing on Frank."

Fabiani, Versage, and Godfrey all disliked Russo. They thought he was threatened by their long-standing relationships with Cassidy. They had been at the firm for years when Russo came aboard, and they thought

Russo was constantly trying to ingratiate himself with Cassidy at their expense. So for Fabiani, this attempt to finger Godfrey as the culprit in losing Texas Tech was typical. Fabiani knew that Versage had a close personal relationship with the president of Texas Tech, and he wasn't surprised by the decision to go to the National Group.

Cassidy had arrived at the fund-raiser before Fabiani and Russo got there. "Marty goes right to the kitchen area, grabs Gerry by the arm and works Gerry over verbally," Fabiani said. He was giving Cassidy the news about Texas Tech. "Gerry exploded. He banged into me coming around a corner," charging toward the front of the small house where Godfrey was chatting with others.

Jean Davis, owner of the townhouse, was in the hallway that led from the kitchen. She was startled to see Cassidy "charging full speed ahead toward me, screaming obscenities. I got out of his way." Congressman LaHood was standing near Godfrey, astonished by what he was seeing, but his presence had no effect on Cassidy, who grabbed Godfrey's necktie by its knot and—according to Steve Whitaker, another lobbyist in the firm who walked in the front door just at this moment—pushed Godfrey hard up against the wall once, and then again. Russo and several others quickly pulled Cassidy away from Godfrey. Russo hustled him out the front door and into a limo waiting at the curb outside.*

Cassidy thought Godfrey was secretly helping Versage steal clients. Versage was indeed trying to persuade clients he had worked for to come to his new firm; he eventually persuaded ten of twelve to do so. But he insisted that as long as Godfrey worked for Cassidy he did nothing to help Versage.

In the days that followed, lawyers who represented the firm came to the offices of employees who had been at the party with a written statement purporting to describe what had happened. The lawyers asked the employees to sign the statement as if it were their own. According to Whitaker, "it was a bullshit version" that gave no hint of any physical contact between Cassidy and Godfrey. Whitaker was furious that the firm's

---

* In an interview, Cassidy denied that this had happened. He said he had led Godfrey out of the house to give him a talking-to, and had just touched his necktie. He said the person who saw it all was Russo, who would confirm his account. But in a separate interview Russo did not do so; he acknowledged that he had pulled Cassidy away from Godfrey and led him outside. He said he did not remember Cassidy shoving Godfrey against the wall, though several other eyewitnesses described this. Russo also said he did not remember riding to the party with Fabiani. Godfrey died suddenly in 2005 from a heart attack.

lawyers were obviously representing Cassidy's personal interests. He was one of several who refused to sign the document. Jean Davis was another.*

This was a time of high tension at Cassidy & Associates. Bonuses shrank for 2001, a reflection of the firm's difficulties. "We all knew that the future of the firm was in doubt," said Whitaker, "though few would . . . say it." The pressure to generate more income was intense. One of the senior lobbyists who decided to leave the firm after IPG took it over said departing was a great relief. "I thought Cassidy & Associates was the most money-grubbing place I had ever been in," he said. "I hated it."

This was one of many employees whom Russo alienated after he became chief operating officer in 1999. He drove at least half a dozen good lobbyists out of the firm. He was the subject of constant, backbiting gossip in the office. Cassidy knew he was unpopular, but his loyalty to Russo never flagged. "He's not an easy chew," Cassidy acknowledged. "Marty doesn't sugarcoat things. He will say what he means, and that's not always true in this town. . . . Marty is a great lobbyist. He expects people to do their job. If they don't, he tells them they're not doing their job. . . . I've always thought that people resent people that they can't really compete with, and none of them were as good as Marty was. . . . They harbored their resentments, which were pure jealousy."

When Fabiani left the firm at the end of 2001, Russo moved into his big corner office and took over his chauffeur-driven limousine. "Keeping chauffeurs for Cassidy and Russo cost multiple hundreds of thousands per year," said someone who regularly saw statements of the firm's expenses at the time. "You had to lease two cars; two parking spots by the door of the garage in the building, $700 each; a dispatcher, a couple of drivers for each to cover nights and weekends as well as days—at $60,000 to 70,000 each when you count in all the benefits and so on. And Marty's entertainment tabs were just legendary. He could spend $25,000 a month on golf, lunches, and dinners. There was a lot of wanton and wasteful spending." Russo loved the firm's box at the MCI Center, later the Verizon Center, home of Washington's professional hockey and basketball teams, and used it often. It cost about $300,000 a year. The firm's distinctive logo could be seen from across the arena.

---

* Godfrey at first thought he could stay at Cassidy after this incident. The next day he made a scheduled business trip to visit a client in New Jersey. But his friends and his wife persuaded him that he could not remain at the firm. He agreed to consult a Washington lawyer, who prepared legal action against Cassidy. A settlement was reached. Godfrey was paid $800,000. He then went to work for Versage at the National Group.

Asked about criticism of his expenses, Russo called it "baloney. . . . If you could justify what you were doing, if it was for business development, and it's doing what you need to be doing for the business, it's justified. I think it's just a shot at me because some people, for whatever reason, didn't like that I came to the firm."

The revenue targets set in the takeover agreement were never met; Cassidy lost millions in potential payments because Powell Tate could not come anywhere near the financial goals set forth by the terms of the deal. But the lobbying operation did continue to increase revenue in the first years after the merger. The firm may have been churning clients, but aggressive marketing brought in enough new ones to keep the numbers up in 2000 and 2001. The reported totals were $20.5 million for 1999, $27.2 million for 2000, and $32.2 million for 2001, a remarkable increase of 57 percent over just two years. Thanks to the business development system instituted by Fabiani and run by Geoff Gonella, Cassidy remained comfortably in first place among all Washington lobbying firms.

Cassidy's insistence on multiyear contracts helped keep the totals up. A typical three-year contract signed in 1999 would have remained in force into 2002. And the marketing efforts remained impressive. "The focus was on revenue," said one former employee who worked in the firm's marketing department, which in 2001 consisted of half a dozen full-time employees; as many as twenty ten-percenters, called consultants, were trying to drum up business as well. "It was a churn and burn environment," he said, a departure from the old Cassidy firm's focus on maintaining long-term relationships with clients.

In 1998 Cassidy and Fabiani made a deal with Al Gordon, a former state official from New York, to help find clients. Gordon had created a group called National Strategies that had affiliates among state-government lobbyists all over the country. Gordon and his colleagues became consultants for Cassidy and moved their offices to the Cassidy building on Thirteenth Street. According to Gordon, National Strategies brought $24 million in revenues to Cassidy between 1998 and 2002, when they had an angry falling-out. (Gordon asked Cassidy for commissions he thought he was owed; Cassidy responded with a lawsuit against Gordon. Gordon said he never got the money.)

Cassidy & Associates "could have really gone down" after the IPG takeover, Gordon said. "But they didn't. They survived and thrived. . . . Every time there was a downturn, Gerry found people who could right the ship." Cassidy's ability to do this time and again was certainly key to his success.

Another way to enhance the revenue number was to make fee-splitting deals with the former Cassidy lobbyists who left the firm and wanted to take clients with them. Cassidy agreed to several; he got half the fee while his partner in the deal, his former employee, did all of the work.

The Boeing Corporation, one of Cassidy's most prominent clients, thought the firm was keeping its revenue number up by exaggerating it. In April 2002, Rudy DeLeon, the head of Boeing's Washington office, read in the *National Journal*, a magazine for Washington insiders, that according to Cassidy & Associates, Boeing had paid the firm $1.2 million in lobbying fees in the previous year. This number appeared in a table listing the biggest clients of the top lobbying firms. It came right from Cassidy's filing with the clerk of the Senate, required under the Lobbying Disclosure Act. And according to an annoyed Rudy DeLeon, "it was a misrepresentation."

By DeLeon's calculation, Cassidy had exaggerated its lobbying revenue from Boeing one-hundred-fold. DeLeon called the young Cassidy lobbyist who had worked on the Boeing account, Larry Grossman, to ask him where this number came from. Grossman said he had no idea. DeLeon calculated that Boeing had paid Cassidy just $12,500 for "traditional lobbying" in Washington in 2001 (he had taken over the Washington office in the middle of the year). The rest of the $502,000 retainer Boeing paid Cassidy that year was for efforts by Cassidy lobbyists to win international customers for Boeing aircraft, DeLeon said—an activity not covered by the Lobbying Disclosure Act's reporting requirements. When he searched his company's files DeLeon discovered that Boeing had paid $598,000 to Cassidy affiliates for public relations work in 2001. DeLeon said this was not lobbying. Under the law, all such work aimed at the public, as most is, does not qualify as lobbying, which is defined as efforts to influence government officials.

But those numbers—the retainer for lobbying plus the PR fees—did add up to $1.1 million, nearly what Cassidy had reported. Asked about this years later, Cassidy was adamant: "We never overstated our numbers. Never." But he did acknowledge including all the public relations costs in the reported lobbying revenue number. "In the spirit of the law," he said, "we report all of our activities that are in any way related to our lobbying work." Operating "in the spirit of the law" is easy; no government authority enforces the Lobbying Disclosure Act, and there are no criminal penalties for violating it.

In 2002, three years after the merger, all this scrambling for clients fell short. As the exodus of lobbyists and traditional clients continued, Cassidy

& Associates' reported revenue fell more than 10 percent to $28.9 million. It fell to $27.9 million in 2003, putting Cassidy in a thoroughly unfamiliar position, second place. A big law firm, Patton Boggs, was number one.

Its managing partner was Thomas Hale Boggs Jr., son of a former Democratic majority leader of the House and a prominent lobbyist for many years. Boggs was a famous Washingtonian, widely known and often quoted. Cassidy, un-famous and un-prominent, had long taken comfort from the fact that his firm made more money lobbying than Patton Boggs did. No longer. Cassidy thought law firms had an unfair advantage in the rankings, because they could juggle legal and lobbying revenue. "Once it became important for law firms to get business by being number one," he said later, alluding to one of his own favorite marketing tactics, "suddenly their fees grew overnight to be astronomical." This comment more accurately reflected Cassidy's frustration than it described the facts: actually, Patton Boggs's lobbying revenue had been growing steadily for years.

Cassidy knew he had a problem. Washington was now in Republican hands, and he presided over a lobbying business that, though it included several Republicans, still had a reputation as a Democratic firm, dominated by the staunch Democrat Cassidy. His own personal connections meant less than they once did; his most influential friends were mostly gone, and those who remained in Congress were now in the minority in both the House and Senate. This was the heyday of Tom DeLay's K Street Project, when Republicans in Congress were going out of their way to help the Republican lobbyists and the Washington representatives of big corporations who would help them.

Cassidy & Associates did not have close personal relationships with the Republican leadership in Congress. The firm's Republicans were moderates like Arthur Mason—no admirer of the Gingrich revolution, though he made it a point to get along with everybody. Cassidy and his colleagues had looked on as dozens of men and women who had worked on the staffs of leading Republicans came downtown to join corporate and trade association offices or existing lobbying firms, or to set up their own lobby shops to exploit their connections. Cassidy was exasperated with competition based entirely on someone's connections; he had no respect for "people who have staked their career on knowing Joe" without really understanding the issues or Congress. "When Joe's not here anymore, what do you know?" he once asked rhetorically. "And are you going to be making this big living that you've been accustomed to making?"

Nevertheless, Cassidy and his colleagues understood that knowing the right Joes was important. And many of their competitors had better

connections with the Republican leaders in Congress than they did. So
when *Roll Call*, one of the aggressive, small newspapers that cover Congress, reported in April 2003 that Gregg Hartley, the longtime right-hand
man to Congressman Roy Blunt of Missouri, had decided to leave his job,
Arthur Mason noticed.

Roy Blunt was fast becoming one of the most important people in
Washington. Though a relative newcomer, he was a leading candidate to
be the next Speaker of the House. And Hartley "was Blunt's alter ego," as
one lobbyist put it. "He'd go to big events representing Blunt—aides usually don't do that." Hartley had been working with Blunt since the 1970s,
when Blunt was the clerk of Greene County in southwestern Missouri.
Hartley ran Blunt's successful campaign for Congress in 1996, and came
to Washington to be his chief of staff in 1997.

Blunt personified the House Republican leadership's intimate working relationship with the business community and its lobbyists. DeLay
took Blunt under his wing soon after he arrived in the House, and
appointed him deputy majority whip in 1999, just two years after he
became a congressman. DeLay asked the new deputy to formalize the
House leadership's relationships with the city's Republican lobbyists. The
idea was to use the lobbyists as adjuncts to the leadership's whip operation
by exploiting their good relations with members, often built on campaign
contributions and other forms of political support. Blunt's extended whip
organization would help Hastert and DeLay maintain discipline among
Republican members and win important votes. Blunt worked hard and
successfully to add the lobbyists' muscle to the leadership's arsenal of tools
to maintain Republican members' discipline. His success contributed to
his elevation to majority whip at the end of 2002 by a unanimous vote of
his Republican colleagues. That capped an extraordinary ascent for such a
newcomer to Congress.

Blunt's courtship of the lobbying community even included courtship.
He became romantically involved with Abigail Perlman, chief Washing-
ton lobbyist for Altria, the corporate parent of the Philip Morris Tobacco
Company. In 2003 he divorced his wife of thirty-five years and married
Perlman. Blunt's romance led to a public embarrassment. *The Washington
Post* reported in June 2003 that the previous November, just hours after he
became whip, Blunt had instructed aides to slip a provision sought by
Philip Morris into the bill creating the Department of Homeland Secu-
rity. The provision would have cracked down on the sale of stolen ciga-
rettes and made tobacco sales over the Internet more difficult, both Philip
Morris objectives. Blunt acted without the approval of DeLay and

Hastert; when Scott Palmer, Hastert's powerful aide, learned about the amendment, he quickly had it removed. The episode was hushed up at the time, but someone leaked the story to the *Post* eight months after it happened. If the leaker was hoping to damage Blunt, the gambit failed. Blunt remained DeLay's trusted and intimate associate.

Gregg Hartley ran the lobbyist-based whip organization for Blunt. As a member of the House Republican leadership staff, Hartley was a regular participant in DeLay's and Hastert's strategy sessions. He had good personal relations with his bosses and his colleagues, and he was an unpretentious, likable person. In other words, Hartley had exactly the personal qualities, connections, and credentials that would make him a valuable lobbyist.

He also had what he considered good reasons to move from Blunt's staff to "the private sector." His salary in Congress was about $150,000 a year. He had two teenage children planning to go to college, and he was surrounded by friends and acquaintances—former Republican staff in Congress—who were making big money downtown.

"Blunt and I both concluded that I could still be a valuable part of his team, and there was no reason for us not to continue our personal relationship and our political relationship. And indeed, not being on the government payroll probably allows me to do some things in support of him that I couldn't do as a government employee"—give and raise money, for instance.

"I was fortunate in the sense that, being fifty years old instead of thirty-five, having spent seven years on the Hill . . . virtually all of it on leaderships staff, having worked for a guy who had built a pretty good reputation in this town and moved up rather quickly, [all that] gave me lots of opportunities that the average staffer leaving the Hill doesn't have." Hartley soon found himself talking to some of America's biggest corporations and the city's best lobbying firms about possible employment.

Not surprisingly, Cassidy's Republican sources weren't good enough to tip him off to Hartley's plans. The *Roll Call* story in April 2003 did that. Its implicit suggestion that Hartley was in the market prompted Mason and Steve Seale, another Republican then working for Cassidy, to place a phone call. Telling this story in his affable midwestern twang, Hartley recounted what happened.

"They gave me a call and said, Read in *Roll Call* you're leaving, wonder if you want to talk? I said not really, I've already narrowed my choices, I've had a plethora of choices [of possible employers]. . . . I knew them [Mason and Seale] both, both had lobbied me. They said, Would you . . .

do us the honor of coming in this week? All that bull. . . . I said I really don't have any time except this afternoon. They said, 'Can you come over this afternoon?' I came over . . . and visited with Steve and Arthur a few minutes. Arthur walked me down the hallway, walked into Gerry Cassidy's office, he and Marty Russo were sitting there. I sat and talked to them for probably thirty minutes. Gerry Cassidy said, What does it take to get you to change your mind about where you're headed and get you to come here instead? I told him what it took, and he said, 'Will you give me forty-eight hours to get back to you with an offer?' Forty-eight hours later he had made an offer."

Cassidy had been liberated by new managers at IPG, who had renegotiated the terms of their takeover of his firm, separating the fate of Cassidy & Associates from that of Powell Tate. IPG had gone through its own time of troubles; its stock price had continued to tumble from the 50s at the time of the acquisition of Cassidy to $8.45 in March 2003. A series of accounting scandals had forced the new managers to restate earnings and write off losses several times. IPG invited Cassidy to write off the costs of severance packages for any employees he wanted to cut loose, an offer Cassidy exploited. "It gave us a lot of space in our budget to go out and hire people," Cassidy said.

So Cassidy offered Hartley a starting salary of just less than $1 million a year plus a substantial percentage of the lobbying fees paid by whatever clients Hartley could bring to the firm. In 2003, this was a very rich package. Hartley also liked the fact that Cassidy offered him the opportunity to run the lobbying firm as its chief operating officer, with wide latitude to make changes. On the basis of that half-hour conversation and the recommendations of his colleagues, Cassidy was offering to put the firm's future into Hartley's hands.

Cassidy, Russo, and Hartley had met each other just once before, two months earlier, when Blunt and Hartley had come to one of Cassidy & Associates' regular breakfast fund-raisers, this one for Blunt. "I met Marty [Russo] there briefly," Hartley remembered. "Gerry Cassidy sat across the table from me." That was it. No matter; Cassidy was ready to roll the dice once again.

This was consistent with his history of reaching for brass rings, but it also reflected the fact that he was sixty-three years old. He had fewer mountains to conquer. Even before the sale to IPG, colleagues in the firm realized that the boss was pulling back somewhat from the day-to-day business, leaving Russo more room to operate as CEO. The Cassidys were building a spectacular, seven-thousand-square-foot house on 165 acres of

Maryland's Eastern Shore, right on the Chesapeake Bay. The house was an up-to-date copy of an 1840s farmhouse, featuring reclaimed hand-hewed timber beams, hand-hammered iron door hinges, antique heart-of-pine flooring in random widths, and French doors facing out on the bay. It was just a few minutes from Jody Powell's place. Friends reported that both Cassidys were excited about their new country life.

Hartley had been negotiating with a small, bipartisan firm that was prepared to offer him an important management role and a lot of money, but it could not match Cassidy's offer. A party to the negotiations said it was clear that Cassidy was determined to win any bidding war for Hartley. Cassidy's colleagues at the firm had the same impression. As one former Cassidy executive put it, "Gerry had to get Hartley and he knew it."

When he did get him, Cassidy was thrilled. He thought hiring Hartley fundamentally changed the firm: "What Gregg has done is, he's a highly identifiable and respected Republican at a level different than a lot of people," Cassidy said in 2006. "I mean he is a Republican strategist. He is one of the people who really has shaped the Republican policy in the House. . . . He is a gifted administrator. He has a very strong background in policy issues and has brought a good deal of policy work to the firm. He's helped us diversify and to bring on staff."

Hartley arrived at a demoralized Cassidy & Associates in June 2003. Then, in the course of two years, it brought on two dozen new lobbyists, predominantly Republicans. Nearly all were former congressional aides or executive branch officials. One was a popular, moderate Republican ex-member who had represented a Democratic district in Buffalo, New York, for twelve years, Jack Quinn. By the beginning of 2007 Cassidy's Democratic roots had been overwhelmed; of the forty lobbyists in the firm, twenty-seven were Republicans, thirteen were Democrats. "I'm running a Republican lobbying firm," Cassidy sheepishly admitted to an old friend.

This hadn't bothered Cassidy in the spring of 2004 when he proposed the arrangement with Jack Abramoff. In the gossip spread constantly by rival lobbyists, Hartley was depicted as a prime mover in the job offer to Abramoff, whom he had befriended because of Abramoff's ties to the House leadership. But Cassidy and Hartley both denied this, and said the idea was Cassidy's.

Under Hartley, the firm acquired scores of new clients, including many of the big corporations that Cassidy had long coveted. Hartley personally brought in three big telecoms that were heavy contributors to Blunt's campaigns and committees: BellSouth, SBC Communications (the two later merged into "the new AT&T"), and Verizon. He also signed contracts with Freddie Mac, American Airlines, Miliken and Company, Univision, and the Walt Disney Company, among others. These were his personal clients.

Altogether, between mid-2003 and September 2008, the firm signed up 203 new clients. They included universities and medical centers looking for earmarks, but nearly three-fourths of the business that came to the firm after Hartley took it over were "nonappropriations" clients—institutions looking for something other than an earmark, including Hartley's access to the House Republican leadership. The new clients included the Business Roundtable, the National Broadcasting Company and its parent, General Electric, the News Corporation, Swift & Company, Viacom, Deutsche Telekom, Fidelity Investments, Lucent Technologies, Wal-Mart Stores, Norfolk Southern railroad, Expedia Incorporated, and the Whirlpool Corporation. Finally, Cassidy & Associates had a roster of clients that looked as good as their snazziest rivals' on K Street.

Hartley reorganized the firm from top to bottom. He was the boss of all day-to-day business. "Everything that relates to servicing clients reports up through me," he explained. "So all the lobbyists other than Gerry and Marty [Russo] report up through me, and I am responsible for the quality of services that we provide to all of our clients. . . . That's my managerial role. . . . I [try] to make sure we have the systems and processes in place that ensure that we have responsible, knowledgeable lobbyists leading teams of people . . . that I am conversant with them about what they're doing and how they're doing it, that I'm available to them to support their needs."

Hartley's system revolved around teams, usually four or five lobbyists working together to service their own clients. Hartley also expected the teams to bring in new clients. He did away with the old marketing system that had made Cassidy rich. The old firm "used to have a handful of people who brought in the bulk of the business and everybody else serviced," he said. Now "I expect all senior people here to market their team and encourage young people to develop their abilities as a lobbyist by marketing as well."

Hartley believed in diffusing responsibility. He abolished the weekly matrix meeting that Cassidy, Fabiani, and other, earlier managers had used to keep close tabs on the troops and their work—for more than two decades the basic management tool at Cassidy & Associates. This was more suitable when the firm was relatively small and focused primarily on appropriations, Hartley said.

He was looking for new practice areas. He was proud of the new energy and environment practice created by a new hire who had previously worked for Harry Reid of Nevada, the Senate Democratic leader. He was enthusiastic about the two young lobbyists who had worked for Jack Abramoff who had come to Cassidy when the deal was struck with Abramoff in 2004. They were building "a commerce practice representing companies with a variety of commercial and industrial issues on the Hill—large employer issues."

Hartley was also interested in a growth area in Washington lobbying, "federal marketing." Its practitioners used their knowledge of government procurement practices and their personal connections in the procuring agencies to help companies sell goods and services to Uncle Sam.

Hartley liked his new life. "I enjoy 80 percent of [the work]" and the hours were delightful. "When I worked for Roy I worked seventy hours a week," he said, but at Cassidy it was 9 a.m. to 6 p.m., with a few evening hours devoted to attending fund-raisers and other functions. He never worked on weekends. He expanded his house in Arlington, Virginia, and bought and remodeled a place on the Chesapeake Bay, near Annapolis.

And he stayed close to Roy Blunt, raising money for him, donating $47,000 himself (with his wife) to Blunt, his leadership PAC, and the House Republican campaign committee. When he came to Cassidy & Associates in 2003 Hartley had good reason to expect his old friend and boss to keep rising in the House hierarchy. The notion that one day he might be the best friend of the Speaker of the House was tantalizing.

Politicking was Hartley's favorite avocation—he was a classic product of the era of the permanent campaign. "I didn't grow up wanting to run government, I came from the political side of the equation. I like campaigns, I like politics. I only worked in government because that's what paid your way to do the political side." Hartley grew up as a Democrat, started his professional life as an administrator of legal aid programs in southwestern Missouri, and fell in love with politics. "I quickly learned there wasn't much potential in Democratic politics in southwestern Missouri," he said, so he became a Republican. That decision was "as much practical as philosophical. It's hard to be impactful when you're in a minority—[I] learned that lesson early."

As so often happens in Washington, Hartley grew into the role of fierce partisan for the team that brought him to town and gave him a taste of power. Unlike DeLay and many of his colleagues, however, Hartley's partisanship never had a hard edge, a fact that helped him on the Hill, and as a lobbyist. But he was committed to the House Republican leadership and its cause. He continued to participate in meetings called by DeLay and Blunt to plan strategy and tactics.

He was an avid fan of the system of fund-raising that had come to dominate American politics: "I *love* fund-raising! I think it's an important part of the political process. I think a measure of a good campaign and how successful it's going to be is its ability to raise money." And the need for money was obvious: "There's a lot of things that candidates and elected officeholders need to do to keep their political operations going and strong and vibrant, and it takes money in today's world." In the first five years that Hartley was a lobbyist (2003–07), he and his wife contributed $230,000 to political campaigns.

What about reformers who complain that the system is corrupt, or appears to be? What about Fred Wertheimer, the former president of Common Cause and founder of a group called Democracy 21, an advocate of reform who had criticized DeLay's tactics for years?

"Fred is full of shit," Hartley replied, softening the message with his friendly grin. Raising money was part of the game, part of the "helter-skelter of it . . . the rough-and-tumble of it. . . . The American public is intrigued by politics and campaigning and the routes to power," he said. "They want to know about it, and on the other hand they go, 'Ohmigod, isn't it distasteful?' . . . I think politics works. I think most of what people deride in politics is because people don't understand it."

Hartley is not troubled by the relationship between lobbyists and members of Congress, and he won't accept the formulation that the Hill now depends on downtown, and downtown depends on the Hill. Instead he sees more complicated interactions: "A lot of people on the Hill are a new breed. They've come up through more aggressive political times, and more aggressive campaigns," he said, "and they understand there's lots of things you do that interrelate with government." In other words, you can help people who need something from the government, and you can accept their help in return, and that's fine. "There's a lot of things that interrelate there, whether it's the giving of personal time or the giving of money or the giving of ideas, and money is just one form of interaction.

"Most people in the lobbying business contribute [money] so that they're seen as active participants in the process. And if you're seen as an active participant, does that sort of move you into a different realm than people who aren't? Yeah. . . . I would presume that lobbyists who participate heavily in the political process are probably more successful by and large." But giving money "is not compulsory," he emphasizes. "I can't possibly give money to everybody I know on the Hill. It's impossible. But people I don't give money to still see me and talk to me and work with me on my clients."

Hartley's star was tied to his patrons in the House, especially Blunt and DeLay. This was fine through the triumphant election of 2004 and its aftermath. It was in May 2005 that DeLay, Blunt, and other Hartley pals had helped make Cassidy & Associates' thirtieth birthday party such a success. But beginning late in 2005, triumph gave way to tribulation. DeLay got into trouble over the ferocious campaign he waged to persuade the Texas legislature to redraw the boundaries of the state's congressional districts to increase the number of Republican members. In September 2005, a Texas grand jury indicted him for conspiring to violate Texas election law; DeLay had to give up the majority leadership temporarily.

On January 3, 2006 (the beginning of a bad year for Hartley), Jack Abramoff pleaded guilty to conspiracy, fraud, and tax evasion, and Republicans began to panic about the spreading lobbying scandal. It was a Republican scandal, and it tainted DeLay, who had spoken warmly of Abramoff and, as noted earlier, had gone on a much publicized golf outing to Scotland as the lobbyist's guest. Several former DeLay aides were implicated in the scandal as well. After Abramoff's guilty pleas, the idea that DeLay might try to return as their leader began to alarm Republicans in the House, and DeLay got the message. On January 7 he announced he would abandon the idea of ever regaining his leadership position.

Roy Blunt, who had been chosen as temporary majority leader when DeLay first stepped aside, now announced that he would seek the position permanently. Hartley became his unofficial campaign manager. A week later Blunt announced that he had the support of a majority of House Republicans, but his announcement was premature. In secret balloting on February 2, Congressman John Boehner of Ohio defeated Blunt 122–109.

In March a Republican opponent won nearly 40 percent of the vote running against DeLay in a primary—an ominous sign of his declining political fortunes at home, subsequently confirmed by polls taken for DeLay. The polling showed DeLay's increasing unpopularity; his high negatives had created an opening that a Democrat might exploit to beat him in November. Then Tony Rudy, once one of DeLay's most important aides, pleaded guilty to conspiring with Abramoff to corrupt public officials and defraud Abramoff's Indian clients in return for gifts and favors. The Abramoff scandal now threatened to engulf DeLay. The man who had dominated the House, intimidated his colleagues and opponents, led a crusade to impeach Bill Clinton, and done everything he could to ensure a Republican House majority in perpetuity, announced that he would not run for re-election to Congress. The Republican revolution of 1994, the Gingrich-DeLay revolution, was dead.

Two years earlier, Hartley had dismissed the early stages of the Abramoff scandal as a typical and insignificant Washington "controversy," but by the time of DeLay's announcement it had upended Hartley's political universe. The final jolt came on November 7. Because of scandal and the unpopularity of the Iraq War, the Republicans lost control of both the House and Senate.

Just as Hartley had completed the job of reconstituting Cassidy & Associates as a predominantly Republican firm, Republicans were out of power. Hartley's patron, Blunt, was now the minority whip of the House, hardly a seat of great influence. Hartley's vaunted connections were suddenly worth a great deal less than they had been.

Hartley was surprised by the election results. At first he expressed the hope that they represented a temporary setback. "We forgot what it meant to be Republicans," he explained when asked why his party had been beaten so badly. This was a common explanation from conservative Republicans who realized, too late, that their willingness to spend money like drunken sailors on earmarks and other favored expenditures hadn't looked very responsible, or very Republican. In December 2006, Hartley expressed the hope that in two years his team would be back.

Nevertheless, he knew he needed to "restructure" the lobbying firm again to accommodate the new realities. "I have to hire Democrats," he said in January 2007. He said he wanted to make the firm at least half Democratic and bigger, implying that he could make it more Democratic without having to fire Republicans.

But none of this happened. The firm hired no prominent Democrats in 2007 or 2008. It lost one, Amos Hochstein, who left the firm to be the foreign policy advisor to Senator Christopher Dodd's presidential campaign. When Dodd dropped out of the race, Hochstein decided not to return to Cassidy. An ambitious Democrat looking for a position as a lobbyist had many attractive alternatives in the Washington of 2008, but Cassidy & Associates was not one of them.

Washington was changing again. Republican members began announcing plans to retire from the House—thirty of them by mid-2008. This was taken as a sign that they expected Democrats to retain their majority in the House for some time. Cassidy and Hartley's Republican lobbying firm began to look a little anachronistic. For the first time in his long career, Cassidy had not prepared for a new turn of events in the capital. "I'm not convinced Cassidy & Associates can adapt this time," Hochstein said in June 2008.

Cassidy & Associates began to slip down the list of top lobbying firms. From second place in 2003, when Hartley came to the firm, it fell to fourth in the 2007 rankings. More ominously, its revenue declined by nearly 15 percent in those five years, from $28 million to $24.3 million. In 2003 it was just $1.4 million behind Patton Boggs, the leader; in 2007 it was $17.6 million behind. The other top firms were growing; Cassidy was not. Early in 2008, the firm lost one of its marquee names. Jack Quinn, the former congressman from Buffalo, decided to give up lobbying and to accept the presidency of Erie Community College in his hometown.

Many of the new, big-name clients fell off the list of Cassidy accounts, among them the Business Roundtable, Deutsche Telekom, Fidelity Investments, General Electric, Lucent Technologies, News Corporation, Swift, Wal-Mart, and Walt Disney. Five years into the Hartley era, 123 of the 203 clients added since his arrival had already left the firm.

"Cassidy & Associates has gone into eclipse," said an old friend of Cassidy's who had worked in the firm for many years. This old hand liked and admired Gregg Hartley, but worried that "he might not be the right man for the job" after the Republicans lost control of Congress.

The problem, ironically, was that Gerry Cassidy had fallen out of step with the town he had lived in for four decades. Cassidy himself insisted all was well because he and Russo maintained close ties to important Democrats. "Marty is genuinely like family" to the Democratic Speaker of the House, Nancy Pelosi, Cassidy said. Russo's relationships with his old Capitol Hill roommates—Senator Charles Schumer of New York, Richard Durbin of Illinois, the deputy leader of the Senate, and George Miller, chairman of the House Education and Labor Committee—were invaluable, Cassidy insisted. Cassidy's relationships with Senators Inouye and Harkin and Congressman Steny Hoyer of Maryland, the House majority leader, were all good too. Yes, and Cassidy was wealthy beyond his most outlandish fantasies, worth more than $100 million.

But the firm that bore his name belonged to a conglomerate, a Republican was running its day-to-day affairs, and its revenue number was slipping farther and farther behind the new leading firms in town. The fantastic journey that had carried Cassidy from Red Hook to the top of the Washington heap hadn't ended, but his magic carpet was slowing down. He was nearing seventy. He was surrounded by younger competitors with big appetites. Once the firm had been unique; for years it enjoyed huge competitive advantages. All that was gone, as the numbers made clear.

Nevertheless, the changes in Washington and its politics that Gerry Cassidy had witnessed, and often contributed to, endured. The nation's capital was now a big-money town, its politics utterly dependent on money. Tens of thousands of lobbyists worked the corridors of power—it was impossible to count them accurately. According to the filings that lobbyists and their clients had to make under the law, customers spent nearly $3 billion to lobby the government in 2007, but that was a fraction of the real amount spent to try to influence decisions in Congress and the executive branch. Lobbying was Washington's biggest business, and business was still booming.

CHAPTER 24

A CORRODED CULTURE

Occasionally, Washington scandals erupt into episodes of historic significance, when habits are broken and rules are changed. The scandal named for Jack Abramoff became just such an episode. The havoc it ultimately wreaked was impressive: not only did it end Tom DeLay's career, but Congressman Robert Ney of Ohio went to jail, Senator Conrad Burns of Montana and Congressman Richard Pombo of California lost their seats, and Congressman John Doolittle of California announced an unexpected retirement. (All were Republicans.) By October 2008, five former congressional aides had pleaded guilty to criminal charges; one former Bush administration official was tried and convicted; three others pleaded guilty, one of whom went to prison; Abramoff himself will spend years in jail.

The politicians in Congress realized that the Abramoff affair had tainted them. Republicans understood that it had helped the Democrats regain control of Congress. Many Democrats ran for re-election in 2006 on promises to pass tough new lobbying legislation; Nancy Pelosi of California, the Democratic leader, introduced a bill that she promised would be voted on at once if the Democrats won control of the House. Harry Reid, the Democratic leader in the Senate, made a similar pledge.

Both houses did pass significant reform legislation during their first days in power in January 2007. New rules banned all gifts to members or staff from registered lobbyists or their clients; banned members from flying on corporate jets in most circumstances; and restricted travel paid for by outside groups. The new law criminalized any effort like DeLay's K Street Project whose purpose was to influence hiring decisions by private entities based on partisan considerations. A violator could go to prison for fifteen years, or be banned from public office. Under the new rules, lobbyists had to file disclosure reports quarterly instead of twice a year, and they had to report in more detail on their lobbying activities. For the first time they had to report on their own political contributions. The new law also required members of Congress, party committees, and leadership PACs to report any "bundling" of contributions for them by lobbyists that totaled more than $15,000 in any six-month period, but implementation of this rule was delayed beyond the 2008 elections. Lobbyists became criminally liable for violating the ban on gifts to members and staff—picking up a dinner tab could send them to prison for five years, theoretically. Lobbyists did stop picking up tabs, according to many of them. Parties that lobbyists and their clients used to throw at the national conventions were strictly limited and mostly did not occur in 2008, a real change.

The way earmarks were made also changed. Members had to attach their names to all requests. Lobbyists could not propose earmarks in states or districts whose Senate and House members had not explicitly asked for them. New procedures made it much more difficult to slip earmarks into appropriations bills without any scrutiny. The Abramoff scandal also brought an end to the gym privileges that former senators and House members, including Marty Russo and many others, had previously enjoyed.

All these changes were approved by overwhelming, bipartisan majorities. The new rules got the lobbying community's attention. Cassidy & Associates hired an experienced Justice Department prosecutor as a new general counsel; he would "oversee everything that we do in terms of complying with the new rules," Gregg Hartley announced.

But the limits of the reform impulse in the House were soon discovered when Pelosi tried to fulfill another campaign promise to make it more difficult for House members and their staff to pass through the revolving door from Capitol Hill to lobbying firms and trade associations downtown. She proposed extending the "cooling off" period during which former members or staff assistants were prohibited from lobbying after giving up their jobs on the Hill from one year to two. This proved to be an unpopular idea.

Mostly out of public view, members began to threaten Pelosi that they would block her reform bill if she insisted on this change. Michael E. Capuano, a Massachusetts Democrat, was one of the few who explained their opposition publicly. "What makes two years a magical number?" he asked a reporter. "I'm sorry, but I'm not a millionaire." To another reporter he said the provision would mean "that I cut off my profession," because respecting a two-year hiatus would probably make it impossible to become a lobbyist. Before coming to Congress Capuano had worked as a lobbyist in Boston. "Funny," editorialized his hometown newspaper, *The Boston Globe*, "we thought Capuano's profession was public servant, not lobbyist-in-training."

On May 17 Congressman John Conyers of Michigan, the new Democratic chairman of the House Judiciary Committee, convened a hearing to "mark up" the Honest Leadership and Open Government Act of 2007, Pelosi's reform bill. Conyers offered an amendment to eliminate the provision extending the cooling-off period to two years. Conyers explained: "I have discussed this issue with numerous members on both sides of the aisle . . . who have expressed concerns about the potential unintended consequences on the ability of the members and committees to attract and retain top-flight staff" if the two-year period were adopted. In other words, Conyers was suggesting, good people would not accept staff positions in Congress unless they could count on converting them into lucrative lobbying jobs when they left. The amendment carried by voice vote, without objection. So much for that reform.

Requiring a two-year hiatus actually would have slowed down the revolving door. Lobbying firms that had been willing to pay fat salaries to members and senior staff for a year when they could not lobby (as Cassidy had paid Hartley, for example) would have resisted doing so for two years. "Former members command such large salaries that having them sit around unable to lobby their colleagues for two years is a really high cost for firms," Paul A. Miller of Miller/Wenhold Capitol Strategies explained. "The same applies to staffers, who I believe lose their value twice as fast."

It was true, as Conyers implied, that young people routinely took jobs on Capitol Hill to punch their Washington ticket en route to K Street. Making a career as an aide on Capitol Hill had become unusual—brief stopovers on the way downtown were much more common. This was a big change, which had evolved over many years. But Conyers's use of that argument to kill the two-year waiting period was disingenuous. The first worry of the members who opposed this provision was not about attracting top-flight staff. As Congressman Capuano made clear, they were worried about their own prospects.

By 2007, everyone in the system took it for granted that a high percentage of members and staff would eventually pass through the revolving door, because so many already had. A 2007 directory of Washington lobbyists listed 188 former members of the House and Senate who were registered to lobby. A study done by Public Citizen, an advocacy group, found that half the senators and 42 percent of House members who left Congress between 1998 and 2004 became lobbyists. Another study found that *3,600* former congressional aides had passed through the revolving door. Appointees from the executive branch followed the same path. In early 2008 the Center for Responsive Politics, a watchdog group, identified 310 former appointees of George W. Bush who had become lobbyists or Washington representatives. The center identified 283 former Clinton administration officials who had done the same.*

These numbers aren't just statistics; they describe the entrenched culture of modern Washington. The essential nature of this culture could not be quickly changed by a ban on congressmen flying in corporate jets or accepting meals or travel from lobbyists, or even by a two-year cooling-off period. In Washington it had become *normal* to use government experience—in Congress and the executive branch—as a stepping-stone to lucrative work in the "private sector" that is devoted to influencing the government.

There was nothing subtle about this culture, as Senator Trent Lott of Mississippi demonstrated in November 2007, when he announced, to the surprise of the political village of Washington, that he was resigning from Congress. Lott, the former Republican majority leader, had just been reelected a year earlier. He had just won a new leadership post from his Republican colleagues. In his re-election campaign he had given no hint that he would serve only one year of a six-year term. But of course when he ran, he did not know that Republicans would lose control of the Senate, and he would lose most of his legislative influence. Once that happened he began to consider his alternatives.

A second recent development had affected his thinking. Though Conyers had eliminated the two-year waiting period from the House reform bill in May, the Senate's version did include a mandatory two-year hiatus for senators. It would come into effect on January 1, 2008. Lott later acknowledged that he had been talking for years to his old friend John Breaux of Louisiana about setting up a lobbying firm together. Breaux, a conservative Democrat who had retired from Congress in 2004, was already a lobbyist in the firm of Patton Boggs. With the new two-year rule in effect, setting up a new firm with Lott would have been much more complicated. By resigning at the end of 2007, Lott evaded the new rule.

---

* The new rules that Congress approved in 2007 imposed a two-year cooling-off period on executive branch officials. Those who became lobbyists could not lobby their former government agencies for two years.

In early January 2008, a press release announced the formation of the Breaux-Lott Leadership Group with offices at Fourteenth and F streets in downtown Washington, two blocks east of the White House. Lott and Breaux both had sons who were experienced lobbyists (another common feature of the Washington culture); Chet Lott and John Breaux Jr. joined the new firm as well. In a matter of six weeks, Trent Lott abruptly wound up a thirty-five-year career in Congress, abandoned his constituents in Mississippi, and opened a business that Washington rivals estimated would soon be earning millions of dollars a year.

Was this proper? No one even asked.

The political culture of Washington, which was also the political culture of the United States, had been deteriorating for decades. By the time the Breaux-Lott Leadership Group was established—thirty-three years after the birth of Schlossberg-Cassidy & Associates—this degradation had taken a heavy toll.

Washington was thriving. It was the center of a vast industry devoted to influencing the American government on behalf of big business, small business, foreign governments, and the multitude of interests and interest groups comprised by the modern United States. The captains of this industry—and its lieutenants, sergeants, and corporals too—were all doing well. Their fat paychecks and big bonuses helped make the Washington region one of the country's two richest. Also doing well, curiously, were the members of the House and Senate whom the influence-peddling industry sought to influence. For years, incumbent senators and congressmen had been reelected at unprecedented rates—more than 95 percent by the early twenty-first century.

But the United States government was routinely ineffectual or incompetent. It did not attract many of the best and brightest young Americans. The quality of the Congress had declined profoundly over the previous generation. The country faced staggering challenges: how to pay for the retirement of the baby boom generation, how to provide health care to American citizens, how to cope with the largest influx of immigrants in American history, how to protect America from terrorists, how to preserve American prosperity in a complex global economy, how to save the earth. For years these challenges all shared one peculiarity: the politicians in Washington avoided or ignored every one of them.

The sad political realities of the early twenty-first century were not the product of any decision to undermine American politics and government—there is no mastermind or villain in this story. Gerry Cassidy did not hope for this outcome—indeed, he deplored it. Neither Newt Gingrich, nor Tip O'Neill, nor George W. Bush set out to do harm. What corroded American politics and government was the perfect storm of new developments that transformed campaigns for public office from the 1970s onward. These coincided with unprecedented growth of the federal government, whose influence spread wider and deeper in American life from the 1960s onward. "Liberals" and "conservatives" in power produced the same result—a more intrusive government, more important to the well-being of more Americans. This in turn was the great impetus to the astounding growth of the lobbying business; the more industries, institutions, individuals, and interest groups saw their own fate at stake in Washington's debates on public policy, the better the market for lobbyists.

The mess was created by ordinary people responding logically to powerful incentives. In the memorable phrase of George Washington Plunkitt of New York City, holder of numerous public offices in the late nineteenth and early twentieth centuries, these men and women "seen [their] opportunities and [they] took 'em."

This is just what Gerry Cassidy did for most of four decades. Cassidy was more aggressively opportunistic than most, but the logic of his choices was nearly always clear. Cassidy came to Washington almost by accident, the beneficiary of coincidences he could never have foreseen. Once there, he took the measure of the place and realized that it was a suitable setting for his efforts to reinvent himself and fulfill his immense ambitions. His timing was perfect. Just as he took his big plunge in 1975, the stars were aligning in fortuitous ways. Not only was the federal government more important in the life of the country than it had ever been, but a newly invigorated entrepreneurial spirit was abroad in the land: the politicians in Congress who could help a lobbyist needed support in forms that Cassidy could provide, from cash money to political bacon that would please their constituents. Cassidy soon realized that there was big money to be made as a fixer, a facilitator. He could charge clients large fees to help them navigate the complex structure and arcane procedures of the government in Washington to advance or protect their own interests. He could teach members of Congress how to earmark federal funds for their constituents' benefit. His success created an incentive to others who became his competitors.

Cassidy constantly pushed the edge of the envelope, looking for an advantage. He often grasped what the opportunities were before others did, which helps explain why he got richer than others in his line of work. But a great many lobbyists got rich and contributed to the one big arrangement that came to define modern Washington: the mutually dependent relationship that evolved in the years after 1975 between members of Congress and the ever-growing tribe of Washington lobbyists. All the participants in this relationship responded to compelling incentives.

In electoral politics the most persuasive incentive is fear—fear of defeat. Survival in office is the paramount concern. Over the last three decades the means by which survival could be secured were revolutionized by new technologies. Once it was clear that combinations of polling, television advertising, direct mail, and marketing actually won elections, no politician could resist them. Even those with relatively safe seats— a majority of the total membership in the House—could not resist ensuring their re-election in every practical way. But the new political technologies were expensive, and the politicians had to find the money to pay for them. The graph line that described the cost of campaigns for the House and Senate after 1974 went up and up, as if propelled by an irresistible force. The last elections were always the most expensive ever.

As the new technologies became entrenched in the 1980s, their practitioners became increasingly influential—and rich. Pollsters and consultants became a new elite. Though they and the politicians they served shared a common interest in disguising their importance, it could not be hidden. In an academic survey conducted as early as 1989, 44 percent of the consultants interviewed reported that their clients were uninvolved in deciding which issues would be emphasized in their own campaigns. Two-thirds said the candidates played no role in determining the tactics of their campaigns.

The growing importance of consultants and pollsters created a classic *dis*incentive for some potential candidates. What sort of people would want to run for office if they were expected to leave decisions about issues, strategy, and tactics to the hired hands? This is one reason why Americans today would have such a hard time identifying true leaders in their Congress. With a handful of exceptions, there are none to be found.

"The beautiful science of the random sample," said Raymond Strother, the consultant who had to persuade Senator John Stennis to raise money from defense contractors, had taken the ideas out of politics and replaced them with numbers. "It is hard to produce a true statesman from an environment so cautious and calculating. How will this look on TV? Or How will my opponent use this against me becomes the pressing question, instead of What's best for the country?"

The people who were encouraged to run for office in this environment were rarely future statesmen; they were more likely to be men and women who could raise money and follow instructions. Fund-raising—or being wealthy—became a critical political skill. "Money dictates the candidates," said Jack Quinn, the former Republican congressman from Buffalo who worked for Cassidy from 2005 to 2008. "Good people get aced out, shoved out. It's my belief that there are probably a lot of really good candidates out there who never run because of the money. . . . All too often I've been hearing lately, 'How much money have you got? How much can you raise?' "

Increasingly, the candidates are wealthy citizens looking for a second career in politics. They have money of their own to spend on a campaign. In November 2007, the National Republican Congressional Committee boasted publicly that it was recruiting wealthy individuals to run in the 2008 election—"credible Republican challengers . . . [who] happen to have access to personal financial resources." Most senators in 2008 were millionaires; so were a large number of House members. "That's scary," Quinn said. "I think you leave out a whole pool of people who would be good members."

Leon Panetta despaired of the quality of people now running for Congress. "If you're not independently wealthy, you're a person who has to sell your soul to a lot of interests so you can raise the money you need to run a campaign. . . . We're not going to get back to getting the kind of people we want in politics unless we can break this addiction to money."

And what do we get meanwhile? Douglas Bailey, the former Republican consultant, offered an answer: "The intellectual quality of our politics, the capacity of our politics to deal with tough issues, is very limited. I just think the quality of our politics is at one level, and the severity of the issues is at another level altogether."

But issues are secondary in modern politics. "It's all about winning, it's not about governing anymore," Panetta said. "If all you care about is winning, you're not going to care about solving problems." The technicians of politics could win races (as they helped George H. W. Bush win the presidency in 1988) with essentially negative campaigns that offered no solutions to the country's problems. What became known as "wedge issues" remained effective from the 1980s through at least 2004. If you could win voters' alliance with your opposition to gun control or gay marriage or flag burning, or by being tough on criminals and terrorists, who needed solutions to big national problems?

Douglas Bereuter, the Nebraska Republican who abandoned a congressional career that had lost its appeal for him, thought that for "an increasing number of people who run for Congress and serve in Congress, politics is their real love. Many of them have very little interest really in legislation or in being legislators. . . . I think there's a very high proportion of people in politics today for whom the thrill of the race, the thrill of the competition, the thrill of beating your opponent . . . is more important than addressing the nation's problems. The sophistication of the process, the mechanics of getting elected today, the mechanics of putting together an organization—for a lot of people today these are the intriguing part of running for office and serving, and continuing to be reelected."

Panetta and Bereuter were both describing the permanent campaign. If political power and political survival were at stake, risks would be taken, ethical compromises would be made. So, for example, Tom DeLay cut corners to raise money to support Republican candidates for the state legislature in Texas. In 2002, when they won a majority for the first time in 130 years, DeLay pushed them to redraw the congressional districts in Texas to produce more Republican seats, although Texas had just completed a redistricting after the 2000 census. This worked—in the 2004 election, after the legislature's new Republican majority had drawn a new map, Texas gained five Republican seats in the House. But then in September 2005, as we've seen, DeLay was indicted by a Texas court on charges of conspiring to direct illegal corporate contributions to Republican candidates for the Texas legislature. The indictment, of course, set DeLay on the downward path that led to his resignation from Congress nineteen months later.

More subtly and more consequentially, the permanent campaign has turned disputes over issues into all-out political battles. In the heat of battle, facts can be the first victim. When the purpose of debate is to gain political advantage, establishing the truth or seeking actual solutions to complicated problems both lose significance. Instead the campaigners use propagandistic arguments to tell voters that what they want to hear is in fact the case. "Facts" offered in these debates are often not facts at all, but convenient arguments intended to "promote one's cause against others," as Hugh Heclo wrote in his essay on the permanent campaign. And the permanent campaign has encouraged the hardening of ideology on both left and right. So Republicans keep promoting tax cuts, no matter their actual impact on the government's gigantic debt; Democrats avoid all serious discussion of Social Security and Medicare, despite the fact that both programs are headed over a cliff. In the permanent campaign, public opinion is not the voice of the people, but something to be leveraged and massaged "to make it serve one's own purposes," in Heclo's words.

The American public is generally unsophisticated about politics and public policy issues. America has long been apolitical. But Americans can demonstrate common sense. "Eighty percent of the people are frustrated because government is not addressing what only government can address to make their lives better," observed Bill Bradley, the former Democratic senator and presidential candidate. Bradley thought this explained public disenchantment with politics and politicians in the last generation.

Peter Hart, the pollster, prides himself on staying in touch with public sentiment, partly by running regular focus groups around the country, most often for corporate clients. "We have a public that is just absolutely repulsed by everything that is going on in Washington," Hart said as the 2008 presidential campaign was beginning in 2007. "Essentially, they can't stand all the lobbying, they can't stand all of the special interests, they don't think the public interest is represented. It is something they understand—the cesspool that they think we [in Washington] operate in."

Money became the great preoccupation of the politicians in Washington in the era of the permanent campaign. Senator Chris Dodd of Connecticut spoke of it emotionally in September 2006, the day after he attended a regular luncheon meeting of the Democratic Senate caucus with all his Democratic colleagues:

"I was looking around the room, and I'm seeing some people who are up [for re-election] in a couple of years, and I'm watching their faces as almost the entire luncheon was devoted to money—at a caucus lunch! These used to be, when I first came [to the Senate in 1981], a place for great debates and discussions—one of the best speeches I ever heard, from Tom Eagleton [senator from Missouri, 1969–87], on what it meant to be a national Democrat. I mean they were wonderful moments, those lunches. And it's now basically all money. . . . It's changed dramatically, I mean *dramatically*. I don't want to sound melodramatic, but the republic's at risk. Truly at risk because of this."

Dodd was providing a glimpse of a political money culture in Washington that is rarely seen by the public. For those involved, raising money is a chronic condition, a constant subject of conversation, and the basis for a little-known Washington industry of political action committees and professional fund-raisers. Michael J. Fraioli is a big player in this world.

Fraioli learned fund-raising from a master, Tony Coelho. A native of California's Central Valley, Fraioli worked in Coelho's first House campaign there in 1978. When he won, the new congressman invited Fraioli to join him in Washington. At first he worked on Coelho's personal staff, then followed him to the Democratic Congressional Campaign Committee, where Coelho made his mark as a fund-raiser. In 1987, after six years at the DCCC, Fraioli established Fraioli & Associates, one of Washington's first fund-raising firms.

"I was filling a void," Fraioli remembered. "The thirst for money in campaigns has just grown and grown and grown." His former colleagues at the DCCC referred candidates looking for fund-raising help. Fraioli quickly realized there was going to be more business than he could handle. He developed his own system. First, "we size up the candidate." An incumbent is relatively easy—his past supporters are the starting point. A challenger is more interesting. It is much easier to raise money for a challenger who is seen as having a fighting chance, so "the first question is, How will the conventional wisdom view their prospects?" Money can help shape that conventional wisdom; just getting some money into the candidate's bank account can make a significant difference. Politicians study each other's campaign treasuries (which have to be reported periodically to the Federal Election Commission). A big war chest can deter challengers; a surprising amount of cash on hand can scare an opponent, including an incumbent.

Of the four thousand registered PACs, "there may be five hundred that have serious money to spend" on Democratic candidates, the only kind Fraioli represents. He and his colleagues (who numbered six in 2008) will "keep cutting that list down until we come up with a legitimate target list for that candidate." Usually it's a long list: "There's a lot of people giving away money in this city." Then it's Fraioli's and the candidate's job to meet the PAC directors (another Washington subculture) and make their pitch. This isn't like fund-raising for a charitable cause from people who aren't sure they want to make any donation. PAC directors live to give, literally. The challenge is to persuade them to give to a particular candidate. Over the years Fraioli's firm has built a database that in 2008 contained more than thirty thousand records of proven donors, prospects, and local contacts for corporations, unions, and trade associations. Using the computer, the firm has organized donors by the issues they care about and the kinds of candidates they tend to support. It isn't the least bit awkward to go back to the same PAC directors and donors over and over again for different clients, Fraioli said: "No problem whatsoever. That's the business they've chosen, and that's the business we've chosen."

Fraioli's other regular target is the city's lobbyists. "Many of them know my phone number by heart," he said, "because they're tired of getting calls from us!" The lobbyists he aims at first are "the alumni, former Democratic members and staff that are now downtown. It's not an absolute that they're going to give, but of the however many thousands of lobbyists there are downtown, a lot will respond."

In the early years of the firm, business was cyclical, and slow in non-election years. That changed in the 1993–94 cycle, which produced the first Republican takeover of Congress in nearly half a century. "It's odd, but the fund-raising never stops anymore," Fraioli said. "It never stops. You go all the way to the election, and the day after the election begins a new cycle. If you have a debt, you get on the phone, start raising money for the debt."

The phone is the basic tool of his trade. A member facing a competitive campaign routinely devotes eight to ten hours or more every week to dialing for dollars. Fraioli's description of the process is sobering. His firm prepares a call list for every client. It usually includes the giving history of each person on the list, phone numbers to try, sometimes reminders of a spouse's name or where the member met the potential donor. "It isn't easy to get on the phone and to just start punching numbers, and to keep going through the list, because you get a lot of rejections, a lot of voice mail, whether you're calling individuals or organizations." This is how America's elected representatives spend at least one day of their workweek, month after month, year after year.

Fraioli is paid by his clients' campaign committees. Some of his competitors charge a percentage of the money they raise, but Fraioli charges a fixed fee of $3,000 to $6,000 a month. In 2008 he had twenty-one clients; his firm was taking in about $700,000 a year. So his line of work is not as lucrative as big-time lobbying, but Fraioli is making many times the salary he earned as an aide to Tony Coelho.

The market for his services is strong; at least three-fourths of the Democratic candidates for the House and Senate hire a professional fund-raiser, he estimated. Of course they don't like to talk about fund-raising publicly, or to attract attention from the news media: "There's never a good story about political fund-raising. Some are less objectionable than others, but there's never a good story."

Long-term prospects for the business are bright. Fraioli expects the cost of campaigns to keep climbing, assuring future demand. Could the price of running keep rising *forever?* "I don't know," he replied, "but I don't see what would stop it."

As we have seen, money changes public policy. All the participants in the modern system realize this to some degree, and many of them expect it.

But in public all parties usually deny that money can influence votes or policy outcomes. Then in early 2008, the National Association of Home Builders (NAHB) confirmed the realities with a brazen display of public pique.

Congress had just approved an emergency "stimulus package"—legislation intended to persuade voters that the government was doing something to try to head off a recession. The largest part of the package gave a tax rebate—cash—to most taxpayers in the hope that its recipients would spend it and thus stimulate the economy. The home builders had pushed several ideas they thought should be included in this package, including tax breaks for builders and expanded authority for state governments to issue tax-free bonds to finance cheap home mortgages.

The Senate Finance Committee drafted a version of the stimulus legislation that included the home builders' ideas—gravy for themselves, obviously. But the final version of the bill dropped those provisions. The president of the NAHB then announced that its PAC would stop giving money to all politicians. BUILD-PAC was the seventh-biggest business PAC; it had given $1.5 million to candidates since the beginning of 2007, and had more than $825,000 in the bank, ready to be donated. The president's statement made clear the home builders' frustration: "More needs to be done to jump-start housing and ensure the economy does not fall into a recession." The suspension of political contributions "will remain in effect until further notice."

The statement raised eyebrows all over Washington. The NAHB had broken one of the cardinal rules of the game. "Lobbies like to pretend that congressional action and their donations aren't tied," observed Melanie Sloan, executive director of a watchdog group called Citizens for Responsibility and Ethics in Washington. "But the home builders just confirmed that they are."

The home builders' suspension of contributions lasted just ten weeks. During that time housing legislation became a hot item in the House. The Banking Committee drafted a bill intended to stimulate the moribund industry. The NAHB announced that it had a new priority for this legislation, a $7,000 tax credit for first-time home-buyers. The House embraced this idea, including it in its housing bill. At the end of April, the NAHB resumed making political contributions. "Our message has been heard," said Ed Brady, an official of the association's PAC.

The home builders took on a challenging goal—to persuade Congress to act affirmatively on their behalf. One of the maxims of the lobbying business is that affirmative action in your own interest is always harder than blocking a proposal that helps somebody else. Managers of hedge funds and private equity funds confirmed this in 2007 and 2008.

These investment funds operate as partnerships, and pay low taxes. In 2007 Charles Rangel of New York, then the new chairman of the House Ways and Means Committee, proposed a simple change in the tax code that would have raised the tax paid by hedge and equity fund managers on their earnings, from 15 to 35 percent. The 15 percent rate, less than most working Americans pay on their income, was based on a loophole in the law that allowed these managers to define their earnings as capital gains (normally money earned on investments held for a year or longer) rather than ordinary income. These were people who earned some of the biggest salaries paid in America. Rangel proposed, in effect, to close their loophole.

Rarely if ever had an industry responded so dramatically to a perceived threat in Washington. The Center for Responsive Politics, which tracks these numbers, found that the hedge funds, private equity funds, and investment firms and their associations jacked up their spending on Washington lobbying from less than $4 million in 2006 to $20 million in 2007. The same category of interests increased political contributions to candidates from $11 million to nearly $20 million from 2005–06 to 2007–08.

Rangel's plan was blocked. Its most effective opponent was the congressman's fellow Democrat from New York, Charles Schumer. He became the investment industry's leading advocate in the Senate, a role that benefited him in his job as chairman of the Democratic Senatorial Campaign Committee, which collected millions from investment company executives while Schumer staved off legislation the industry opposed.

Long before Rangel proposed the tax change, Schumer was arguing against any federal regulation of hedge funds. In June 2006, the Senate Judiciary Committee held a hearing to look at the funds. Schumer, a member, came to the hearing to tell his colleagues that they had no business looking at this subject—the Banking Committee had jurisdiction over such matters. Schumer was a member of that committee as well, so he knew that it was well disposed to his New York constituents in the securities and financial industries, and not interested in new regulations for hedge funds.

This episode caught Gerry Cassidy's attention, and stimulated his liberal instincts. After describing Schumer's behavior at the Judiciary Committee hearing, Cassidy said: "It was the damnedest thing I ever heard of. . . . It's mind-boggling that you can have a force like [hedge funds] in the market, have it be unregulated, and have members defending it being unregulated." If a liberal Democrat had argued in favor of dereg- ulating an important segment of the financial markets in the 1960s or 1970s, the idea "would have been laughed out of town. Now it happens and guys run to the committee to defend it. It's just a remarkable change."

When pressed, Cassidy readily acknowledged what had happened in the country and in Washington over the years he had been there. The well-off had become much better off, while working people's incomes stagnated from the early 1970s into the twenty-first century. Didn't this show, Cassidy was asked, how well the wealthy could defend their interests in modern America?

"I refuse to argue the obvious. It's true. How could you look at it and say it wasn't true?" said Cassidy. "There has been a huge redistribution of income and you can't blame just the Republicans, because it has happened through Democratic presidencies, and through Democratic and Republi- can Congresses. It's just true, largely because they [poorer citizens] have less representation—you look at the movements out there, there is no anti-hunger movement out there, there is no committee on the Hill look- ing into poverty."

As Senator Bob Dole had said in 1982: "Poor people don't make cam- paign contributions."

Joe Rothstein was thirty-four when he came to Washington for the first time right after the 1968 election. He had just helped his old friend Mike Gravel win a seat in the Senate from Alaska. Rothstein had taken a leave from his job as a newspaperman on the *Anchorage News* to manage the Gravel campaign. Gravel had hired Joseph Napolitan, one of the first modern campaign consultants, who used a gimmick he had perfected in a Pennsylvania governor's race in 1966. Napolitan made a slick, half-hour film about Gravel's life that was shown on every television station in Alaska at the same time on a Sunday night nine days before the primary election. Thanks to the film, which depicted Gravel as a fighter for little people against the establishment, he defeated the incumbent senator, Ernest Gruening. Then he won the general election in November. Gravel sent Rothstein to Washington to hire a staff and organize his office.

"I'd never been to Washington," Rothstein said. "I was green as grass about what happened here. And I started getting phone calls from lobby- ists, union guys, and others. They wanted to take me to lunch, or have me come down to their office and have a chat, and so on. Washington didn't really support Gravel in that election, he got very little Washington money. So I get to Washington, and I have lunch with one of these people who didn't know Gravel and needed to catch up in a hurry, a guy from one of the unions. The guy says, Here, take this back to Mike—it was $5,000 in a brown paper bag, in cash.

"So I get back up on the Hill, and I have a few people I've started to rely on, wise old heads. And I say I have a feeling I should report this, to the authorities, who should I report this to? And they looked at me like I was nuts. They said, 'That's the way Washington works, that's the way you get money here, everybody does it.' And what I soon found out was, everybody did it! I mean, the best people—all the people you know and love who were big in town at the time. That's how they got money— brown paper bags and cash and what-not."

Rothstein (who later built on the lessons he learned from Napolitan to become a successful political consultant himself) told this story to discourage the belief that there had once been a period of pristine American politics untainted by money. There was no such time. Money has been part of American politics forever, on occasion—in the Gilded Age or the Harding administration, for example—much more blatantly than recently. But there was one important, qualitative difference, as Rothstein acknowledged: in recent decades "the scale of it has just gotten way out of hand." The money may have come in brown paper bags in earlier eras, but the politicians needed, and took, much less of it than they take through more formal channels today.

Fred Wertheimer has been an agitator for reforms to reduce the influence of money in Washington for more than three decades. Wertheimer is a lobbyist himself, but for a nonpaying client: his own vision of a cleaner American government.

Wertheimer noted that since the Nixon era, Congress itself has removed many egregious forms of corruption: cash contributions to politicians (like that bagful of money that Rothstein collected for Mike Gravel), which once were as common as Capitol Hill spittoons; direct employment of members of the House and Senate—as lawyers or advisors, for example—by corporations, also common until the 1970s; cash for speeches that went directly into members' pockets, the honoraria; unregulated soft money contributions from individuals, unions, and corporations that largely funded the 1996 and 2000 elections, banned in 2002. Wertheimer, who has the optimism required of anyone engaged in a long-term crusade to improve human behavior, noted proudly the Senate's decision to accept a two-year cooling-off period in 2007, when the House rejected it. He was pleased that earmarks were being debated seriously for the first time in decades. He also took heart from the provisions of the 2007 reforms that banned nearly all forms of gifts from lobbyists and lobbying organizations to members, from dinner at a Washington restaurant to a golfing vacation in Scotland. "The biggest change made by the new rules is a cultural one: making members pay their own way as opposed to their traditional view that they were entitled to trips, meals, etc., paid for by others," he said. If the culture of freebies could be altered, Wertheimer argued, so could other deleterious aspects of the Washington political culture. Not that Wertheimer was satisfied: "We still haven't solved the problem of campaign money."

Another optimist was Bill Bradley. Significant change in the culture of politics might require "a revolution," but why rule out the possibility of a revolution, especially when the country was so fed up? "The current approval rating of Congress has never been lower," he said—only a slight exaggeration when he spoke near the end of 2007. "The only way this is going to change is with a popular uprising. . . . I believe you can catalyze this latent revolution, you can direct it."

Curiously, Gerry Cassidy had a similar view: "I believe there's a day of reckoning coming," he said, when asked if America's politics could be revived. At some point Americans would realize that they were being gypped by an unresponsive government: "When you have to provide people the health care they expect, and you have to provide Social Security, and you have to meet the needs for an economy that has to generate jobs, and those pressures [are all] on one source of revenue, the American taxpayer, that is going to create a mass of policy issues and I think will finally bring about a level of public attention that will be focused. People will really come to understand that they are stakeholders."

The culture will change, it always does, and it could change for the better if some future Congress destroys the system that developed from the 1970s through the 2000s. Destroying it is legally possible. Congress could provide for public financing—money from the Treasury—for all elections to federal office, something it tried in the 1970s for presidential campaigns. That system worked until 1996, when Bill Clinton's re-election campaign stretched it so far that it effectively broke down. (Clinton did this by accepting public financing and simultaneously raising tens of millions of unregulated soft money for the Democratic Party to spend promoting Clinton's re-election.) Congress could ban any registered lobbyist and any institution that hires a registered lobbyist from raising or soliciting contributions for federal candidates and officeholders. A new law could also reduce to a nominal amount—say $250 or $500—the maximum a lobbyist could give personally to a campaign for federal office. Cooling-off periods could be lengthened and strengthened to make it difficult if not irrational for an elected or appointed official to consider moving from a government job through the revolving door to lobbying. New laws could require broadcast television stations to provide free time to political candidates, a reform idea that has bounced around Washington for years, but not yet found much support. Lobbyists could be required by law to report publicly on every meeting and conversation they hold with a public official. History confirms that moral behavior cannot be enforced by passing laws, but laws can certainly make immorality a lot more difficult.

But to pass such reforms would upend the culture that has evolved in modern times, the culture that has served today's incumbent politicians well. "You don't have many on the Hill who want to change the system," as Raymond Strother observed, because the system has been good for incumbents. In recent times incumbents have been reelected at rates without historical precedent. The avid supporters of real reform on Capitol Hill are few, the cynics many.

And the cynics' skepticism is hard-earned. Reforms have repeatedly had unintended consequences—the massive growth of PACs, for instance, was an unexpected result of the post-Watergate reforms of the 1970s. Already in 2008, in the first months after the latest reforms were put in place, lobbyists who could no longer buy dinner for a member or take them to a ball game realized that their ability to raise and donate money was going to be more important than ever. Under the latest rules, social events devoted partly to fund-raising remained legal.

Lawrence O'Brien III, a prominent Democratic lobbyist and founder of a successful bipartisan firm, observed in 2008 that the latest reforms "have shifted the emphasis over to political fund-raising. Now writing checks and raising money is the simplest pathway to completely legal, personal face time with members and their senior staff." Giving to the party committees—the Democratic Senatorial Campaign Committee, the National Republican Senatorial Committee, and the two comparable House committees—was more important than ever "because they can organize fund-raising events that create opportunities to interact with multiple members and staff at one time." Access remained the coin of the realm.

O'Brien noted another counterintuitive consequence of reform. It was going to cost him more money. The law known as McCain-Feingold passed in 2002 "indexed" the maximum allowable individual contributions to candidates, PACs, and party committees to the rate of inflation, so it would go up every two years. In the 2008 cycle it was $108,200—or $216,400 if a husband and wife decide to contribute the maximum, as O'Brien and his wife (and the Cassidys) have. So over the years to come, lobbyists like O'Brien and Cassidy who give the legal maximum every year will be relatively more important to candidates and campaign committees as time passes.

"The business used to be a lot about generating political contributions," O'Brien said. "And now, it is even more so."

Jack Abramoff's biggest contribution to the history of his time was to demonstrate how serious the corruption of Washington had become. But Abramoff was also the source of subtler revelations. The fact that not just editorial writers but also his fellow fat-cat lobbyists were shocked by his behavior was a reminder that there can be a code of honor even among rogues. The Washington lobbyists who were genuinely appalled by Abramoff's crimes (and that was most of them) could simultaneously condemn him, envy his success, and use many of the marketing and lobbying tactics he had employed. Life is complicated.

Americans have always had conflicted feelings about wealth and those who accumulate it. Andrew Carnegie was both a selfish and cruel captain of industry and a great philanthropist. Most of the great tycoons of American history have similarly ambivalent reputations.

Gerry Cassidy is no paragon, as he would readily admit. But he, his colleagues, and competitors do not constitute an alien force in our midst; they are not trying to undermine the American republic. These are recognizably American entrepreneurs who are devoted to the great American pastime, which is not baseball, but making money. Rapacious capitalists are as American as cherry pie.

Washington's thousands of lobbyists include a large number of pretty good citizens. They are interested in politics and public life, serious about the role of government in society, and capable of compassion and generosity. They make fine neighbors and Little League coaches. The city of Washington has benefited from the boom in the lobbying industry not just through tax revenues, but also from civic improvements that lobbyists assisted or made possible. One of Gerry Cassidy's biggest fans is Father John Adams, a Catholic priest who founded So Others May Eat, a social service agency for the homeless and impoverished of Washington. Cassidy has personally donated and raised hundreds of thousands of dollars for SOME. "He's been one of our major contributors," Father Adams said. Cassidy also gave to the Children's Inn, a residence for families of young

patients at the National Institutes of Health, and to the Shakespeare The-
atre Company, on whose board he sat (though he rarely attended a meeting). His biggest recorded gift was not to a Washington institution but to
Villanova, his alma mater—$5.25 million as part of a capital fund drive of
which Cassidy was the chairman.

These recent decades when Gerry Cassidy made his way in Washington were a time of rising inequalities in American life. Workers' income
did not keep pace with their bosses', and the fortunate few on top accumulated wealth at rates not seen previously in the country's history. Money
has always talked in America, but it has been talking louder of late than it
did in the first three decades after World War II. The unexpected rise of
Washington as a venue for getting rich was actually part of a national
trend. It had disruptive effects in many communities, and particular ones
in Washington.

Cassidy described one of the human consequences: "When I moved
here there was a level of respect for civil servants. The economics of the
city have changed enormously. People who had a high GS rating [senior
civil servants] lived very well in what was then a nice home—not these
extravagant homes that they are [now] tearing down the old ones to build,
but they lived very well. They had positions where their salary was equal
to people in the private sector. They were respected. That has been beaten
down to nothing."

The devoted public servants Cassidy described were from another
time, another America. Unlike the lobbyists and others who benefited
from the new realities, committed government employees were examples
of the Americans who were not enticed by the new incentives to get rich.
They marched to their own drummers.

Robert Strauss, a great Washington fixer, gets the last word. Cassidy
worked for Strauss in 1973, soon after the Texan came to town, when he
was the chairman of the Democratic National Committee. Strauss built
his law firm into a powerhouse. Its $31.4 million in lobbying revenue in
2007 put the Strauss firm second in the official standings, just behind Patton Boggs, two slots and $7 million ahead of Cassidy & Associates.

Why, Strauss was asked, did the lobbying business prosper so in the
years when he and Gerry Cassidy were part of it? Strauss paused for a long
moment. "There's just so damn much money in it," he finally replied.
"There's so many people with issues in Washington, and people are more
and more turning to the government because it is involved in their lives.
It's a company town, and the business is lobbying."

Acknowledgments

Many people helped me write this book, but no one gave me more assistance than Gerald S. J. Cassidy. When I showed up in his elegant office in 2004 and said I intended to learn everything I could about him and his business, he could not have been pleased. For whatever reasons, he eventually decided to cooperate. He sat for many long, recorded interviews, then went over the transcripts of our conversations with care. He shared not only his own life story, but also many of the insights he has accumulated over nearly forty years in Washington. Cassidy is smart and shrewd, and I benefited greatly from our exchanges.

Kenneth Schlossberg, Cassidy's original partner, was also extremely helpful, as was his wife, Sophia. The Schlossbergs both have remarkable memories. Ken left Washington years ago, but remains a thoughtful student of the city and its ways. He gave me many hours of his time.

Cassidy authorized friends and associates to talk freely with me, another boon to my reporting. The Notes make clear how many of them agreed to be interviewed on the record. I thank them all. Many of Cassidy's former associates were similarly helpful.

Numerous Washington lobbyists answered my questions. Jim Free, Larry O'Brien III, Dan Tate Sr., and Tom Downey were especially helpful.

Two dozen current and former members of Congress shared insights and gave me useful information. I would like to particularly thank Bill Bradley, Douglas Bereuter, Dick Clark, Chris Dodd, Mickey Edwards, Barney Frank, Chuck Hagel, Daniel Inouye, Mike Kopetski, Bob Livingston, and Leon Panetta.

Two former members of the House Appropriations Committee staff were also generous with their insights: Scott Lilly and Jim Dyer. I also had great help from practitioners of the modern arts of electoral politics, especially Doug Bailey, Mike Fraioli, Peter Hart, Joe Rothstein, and Ray Strother. Bill Satchell helped me understand how businesses like Cassidy's work, how to read company filings and related documents, and how employee stock ownership plans work. Altogether I conducted several hundred interviews for this book.

My largest debt is to *The Washington Post*, my employer since 1963. My association with the *Post* has opened doors in Washington for me for four decades—there is no better calling card. In 2004 I persuaded Executive Editor Len Downie, Managing Editor Phil Bennett, and Assistant Managing Editor Jeff Leen to let me undertake a reporting project on lobbying in Washington. I soon decided to focus on Cassidy and his firm, and worked on the reporting for many months. We produced the first online series in the *Post*'s history; it ran in twenty-seven installments in the spring of 2007 under the title "Citizen K Street." Most of the episodes appeared on the *Post*'s Web site, washingtonpost.com, whose creative editors were great allies. Leen edited the project; he was patient, helpful, and insightful. The project can be found at http://blog.washingtonpost.com/citizen-k-street/.

The idea of using the Cassidy story in a big book about Washington and American politics over the last thirty-five years came to me early in the reporting. Amanda Urban, the world's most loyal and supportive literary agent, encouraged the idea, and Jonathan Segal, my editor at Alfred A. Knopf, thought it could work. Jon helped me shape this book. He is a gifted editor, smart and subtle of mind, a former journalist himself who understands the importance of reporting. If this book is at all successful in explaining how Washington really works, he deserves much of the credit, for this is the question he kept pressing me to answer.

Seven friends volunteered to read the manuscript and suggest improvements: Tom Mann of the Brookings Institution and Norman Ornstein of the American Enterprise Institute, co-authors of *Broken Branch*, the best book about the failings of the modern Congress; Fred Wertheimer, who has been struggling to improve our politics for four decades and is now president of Democracy 21; Larry Smith, wise old hand on Capitol Hill; Professor Samuel Popkin of the University of California, San Diego, a distinguished political scientist; and Dan Morgan and Jeff Leen of the *Post*. All helped me avoid embarrassments, and all made large contributions to the final product.

Alice Crites, a gifted researcher, started work on this project by tracking down Ken Schlossberg in Brookline, Massachusetts. I had no idea where he was at the time. Over the many months we have worked together, Alice produced one miracle after another. She can find the unfindable. I could not have completed this book without her.

In my private life I am surrounded by wonderful women: my wife, Hannah Jopling, and daughters, Charlotte and Emily. Charlotte has brought Nick Peterson into our lives, a huge addition. All of them helped keep me going.

I have dedicated this book to Paul Corso and Andy Sumner, two brilliant physicians, who saved my life in 2003 by diagnosing (Sumner) and then surgically repairing (Corso) an aortic dissection, a rare and often fatal medical catastrophe. The dedication is a modest offering that does not begin to express my gratitude to these two men.

Notes

CHAPTER 1   A SCANDAL FOR OUR TIME

I conducted interviews with Gerald Cassidy, Arthur Mason, Scott Reed, Lester "Ruff" Fant, Larry Grossman, Daniel Inouye, William Cloherty, Greg Schneiders, Chuck Hagel, and Leon Panetta.

4 *Both sides fulfilled:* The statistics here come from the Web site of the Center for Responsive Politics, Open Secrets.org, http://opensecrets.org/bigpicture/ptytots.asp?cycle=2004#hard.

12 *said Gregg Hartley:* "Special Interests" column, *Washington Post*, March 25, 2004.

12 *"The financial arrangements":* "Probe Finds $10 Million in Payments to Lobbyist," *Washington Post*, March 30, 2004.

13 *"His explanation at that time seemed credible":* Cassidy memo to the author, January 31, 2007.

13 *"There's no truth":* Scott Reed interview with the author.

18 *"a hairline's difference":* "Russell B. Long, 84, Senator Who Influenced Tax Laws," *New York Times*, May 11, 2003.

20 *The warning, published:* "The Greening of Washington," *New York Times*, May 14, 1986.

20 *belittled his Indian clients:* "Gimme Five—Investigation of Tribal Lobbying Matters," U.S. Senate Committee on Indian Affairs, June 22, 2006.

CHAPTER 2   LOOKING DOWN ON THE CAPITOL

Gerald Cassidy invited me to the thirtieth birthday party. I had just begun my reporting at the time.

27 *in an angry speech: Congressional Record* for July 24, 1989.

CHAPTER 3   THE ART OF SELF-INVENTION

I conducted interviews with Gerald Cassidy, Philip Costanzo, Robert Cartwright, William and Loretta Dow, Mickey Kantor, Michael Foster, Charles Luckey, Bill Smith, and Kenneth Schlossberg.

48 *The committee was created in 1968:* Peter K. Eisinger, *Toward an End to Hunger in America* (Washington, D.C.: Brookings Institution, 1998).

48 *The president joined the chorus:* Gordon W. Gunderson, "The National School Lunch Program, Background and Development," USDA Food and Nutrition Service, undated.

48 *Facing up to the realities of poverty and hunger:* Homer Bigart, "Hunger in America: Poverty Leaves Migrants Prey to Disease," *New York Times*, February 17, 1969.

50 *Schlossberg wrote a statement:* "McGovern Expresses Shock at Fla. Poverty," *Washington Post*, March 12, 1969.

CHAPTER 4   A WASHINGTON THAT WORKED

I conducted interviews with Gerald Cassidy, Kenneth Schlossberg, George McGovern, Marlow Cook, Marshall Matz, Jack Rosenthal, John Holum, Eli Segal, Frank Mankiewicz, Carol Casey, Robert Strauss, Nancy Amidei, Robert Shrum, and Alan Stone.

53 *Its creation contributed to the growth:* Statistics on the growth of Senate staff were provided by the Office of the Senate Historian, "Legislative Branch Employment: Trends in Staffing, 1960–2000," Congressional Research Service, 2001.

53 *The nutrition committee was an example:* Legislative history of the select committee published in September 1968 by the Senate Committee on Labor and Public Welfare, Washington, D.C.: U.S. Government Printing Office.

57 *In the speech:* "Attention Must Be Paid," *Washington Post*, March 29, 1972.

CHAPTER 5   A NEW KIND OF BUSINESS

I conducted interviews with Gerald Cassidy, Kenneth Schlossberg, Chip Goodman, Bill LaMothe, Jack Rosenthal, Alan Stone, and Peter Krogh.

72 *Flood was treated gratis for stomach cancer:* "Georgetown Wins Friends and Funds on Hill," *Congressional Quarterly Weekly*, June 4, 1988.

75 *Brooke called the hearing to order:* All quotations from this hearing are in *Hearings Before the Subcommittee of the Committee on Appropriations, United States Senate,* Ninety Fifth Congress, First Session, On HR 9375 (Washington, D.C.: U.S. Government Printing Office, 1977).

CHAPTER 6   CORRUPT OR CORRECT?

82 *These merchants offered "treats, dinners, attentions":* William Maclay's diary quoted in Robert C. Byrd, *The Senate, Addresses on the History of the United States Senate,* Volume II (Washington, D.C.: U.S. Government Printing Office, 1991).

82 *Webster reminded Biddle:* Quoted in ibid.

84 *It first appears:* Jesse Sheidlower, editor-at-large of the *Oxford English Dictionary,* interviewed on NPR *Weekend Edition,* January 22, 2006.

84 *But in fact:* Ibid.

84 *That era has been called:* The term was coined by historian V. L. Parrington.

84 *One who benefited:* The rich story of how the railroaders corrupted and were corrupted by Washington in the 1860s is vividly told in David Haward Bains's *Empire Express* (New York: Viking, 1999), from which these examples are drawn.

85 *Ward was a swashbuckling figure:* Lately Thomas (pseudonym of Robert V. P. Steele), *Sam Ward: King of the Lobby* (Boston: Houghton Mifflin Co., 1965). This is an entertaining account of a remarkable life.

85 *"No country except the United States": Daily Telegraph* (London) obituary, published in *The Washington Post,* June 8, 1884.

86 *Yes, he readily acknowledged:* The transcript of this hearing is quoted at length in Thomas/Steele, *Sam Ward.*

87 *Trist v. Child:* 88 U.S. 441.

90 *famous piece of muckraking:* David Graham Phillips, *The Treason of the Senate,* reprinted as a book (New York: Monthly Review Press, 1953).

91 *The last of the progressive presidents, Woodrow Wilson: The Messages and Papers of Woodrow Wilson,* with editorial notes and an introduction by Alfred Shaw (New York: George H. Doran, undated).

92 *Kenneth G. Crawford explained:* Kenneth G. Crawford, *The Pressure Boys* (New York: Julian Messner, 1939).

94 *This speech and the hearings won Black national acclaim:* This account of Black's efforts is based on Byrd, *Senate, Addresses,* and Crawford, *The Pressure Boys.*

95 *As William H. Rehnquist:* Rehnquist's statement to the National Commission on Public Service, July 15, 2002.

96 *The records of the initial settlement in Jamestown:* Raymond C. Bailey, *Popular Influence Upon Public Policy, Petitioning in Eighteenth-Century Virginia* (Westport, Connecticut: Greenwood, 1979). This section on Virginia is based on Bailey's wonderful piece of scholarship.

CHAPTER 7   EARMARKS BECOME ROUTINE

I conducted interviews with Gerald Cassidy, Kenneth Schlossberg, Sophia Schlossberg, Bill Cloherty, Tom Murnane, John Silber, Bernie Bulkin, Terry Holcombe, Michael Sovern, and James Fabiani.

98 *One article in the weekly:* "Wheeling and Dealing on Capitol Hill," *Chronicle of Higher Education*, November 28, 1977.

101 *The story was not:* "The Rise of Imaging Sciences," *New York Times*, March 28, 1984.

103 *Cassidy recounted accompanying Byron:* Cassidy interview with Daniel S. Greenberg, editor of *Science & Government Report*, Vol. 13, No. 19, November 15, 1983.

106 *a story by Colin Norman:* "Universities Find Funding Shortcut," *Science*, June 3, 1983.

106 *When the full House voted: Science*, June 3, 1983, and *Congressional Record*, for May 12, 1983.

106 *Their real debut:* Greenberg, *Science & Government Report*.

108 *Written by Burt Schorr:* Burt Schorr, "Breaking Tradition, More Colleges Go Directly to Congress for Funds," *Wall Street Journal*, March 5, 1984.

109 *In 1984, a member of Congress:* Historical information on salaries of members of Congress can be found at http://www.senate.gov/reference/resources/pdf/97-1011.pdf.

CHAPTER 8   A GREAT AWAKENING

I conducted interviews with Norman Ornstein, Robert Strauss, and Gerald Cassidy.

114 *At the time a member of the House could collect:* Historical information on salaries of members of Congress can be found at http://www.senate.gov/reference/resources/pdf/97-1011.pdf.

115 *In the congressional elections of 1974:* Congressional Research Service study of May 7, 1982, quoted in Center for Responsive Politics, "Money & Politics: Campaign Spending Out of Control," Washington, 1984. Laws passed in 1973 and 1974 required candidates for Congress to report their spending to the then new Federal Election Commission.

116 *In 1974, as PACs were just coming into vogue:* All statistics in this paragraph, ibid.

118 *John Adams Wettergreen:* John Adams Wettergreen, "The Regulatory Revolution and the New Bureaucratic State," a Bradley Lecture at the Heritage Foundation, April 2, 1988, www.heritage.org.

119 *It was the work of Lewis F. Powell:* The full text of Powell's memo is at http://reclaimdemocracy.org/corporate_accountability/powell_memo_lewis.html.

120 *The founders of the Heritage Foundation:* Lee Edwards, *The Power of Ideas* (Ottawa, Illinois: Jameson Books, 1998).

CHAPTER 9   A MARRIAGE UNRAVELS

I conducted interviews with Kenneth Schlossberg, Sophia Schlossberg, Gerald Cassidy, Bill Cloherty, Jimmy Collins, Lester "Ruff" Fant, and John Silber.

124 *Ten years earlier they had been making:* Report of the Secretary of the Senate, from January 1, 1975, through June 30, 1975, lists their final, monthly Senate salaries: $3,090 (Schlossberg) and $2,670 (Cassidy).

CHAPTER 10   "WOULD THAT BE PROPER?"

I conducted interviews with Dick Clark, Peter Hart, Gordon Humphrey, Don Madden, Tony Coelho, Leon Panetta, and Raymond Strother.

134 *This was enough to elect Jepsen: Des Moines Register,* November 15, 1978.

134 *Robert C. Dopf, an attorney:* "Anti-Abortion Activists Help Scuttle Clark in Iowa," *Washington Post,* November 9, 1978.

135 *Humphrey and Jepsen both benefited:* Richard Viguerie, *The New Right: We're Ready to Lead* (Falls Church, Virginia: Viguerie Company, 1981).

136 *But in 1965 he quit that job:* Richard A. Viguerie and David Franke, *America's Right Turn* (Chicago: Bonus Books, 2004).

136 *"He was a creature of direct mail":* Sidney Blumenthal, *The Permanent Campaign* (New York: Simon & Schuster, 1980).

137 *"direct mail is a form of advertising":* Ibid.

137 *"one method of mass commercial communication":* Viguerie, *The New Right.*

137 *"Single-issue direct mail can make that difference":* Viguerie and Franke, *America's Right Turn.*

137 *"consciously thought of themselves" and other quotes:* Ibid.

139 *"We found bills in the Georgia Senate":* These quotations from L. H. Carter can be found in "After Political Victory, a Personal Revolution," *Washington Post,* December 19, 1994; and "Newt Gingrich: Shining Knight of the Post-Reagan Right," *Mother Jones,* November 1984.

141 *But the Church-led investigation:* " 'Dirtiest' Campaign Laid to Church Foes," *New York Times,* October 25, 1980.

141 *In an interview with National Public Radio:* Interviews with Church conducted by Bill Buzenberg of NPR, broadcast on *Morning Edition* and *All Things Considered,* October 29, 1980.

142 *Republicans had been losing races:* Brooks Jackson, *Honest Graft* (New York: Alfred A. Knopf, 1988).

143 *Coelho grew up:* What Coelho thought and did is wonderfully described in Brooks Jackson's book, ibid. In the 1980s Jackson was an investigative reporter for *The Wall Street Journal.* He persuaded Coelho to let him watch the congressman and his staff prepare for the 1986 congressional elections. Jackson had access to Coelho's meetings with staff, with donors, with members of Congress and their assistants. There is no better book about the ways the campaign finance reforms enacted in the 1970s were vitiated by both parties in the 1980s, when money transformed politics. I have drawn on Jackson's *Honest Graft* for details about Coelho's operations and for the quotations used here.

147 *As a member of the Speaker's Club:* The New York Times acquired a copy of the brochure: "For $5,147 a Year, Welcome to the Speaker's Club," *New York Times,* March 24, 1983.

147 *"The thing we've done basically":* "Rep. Coelho: Democrats' Fund-Raiser Extraordinaire," *Washington Post,* August 26, 1982.

147 *Reporters in Washington began to find cases:* "Special Interest Money Increasingly Influences What Congress Enacts," *Wall Street Journal,* July 26, 1982.

148 *Dole's comments appeared:* Albert R. Hunt, "Cash Politics," *Wall Street Journal,* July 26, July 29, August 2, 1982.

148 *Coelho had a similar moment of candor:* Jackson, *Honest Graft.*

149 *Bolling published an article:* Richard Bolling, *Annals of the American Academy of Social and Political Science,* Vol. 486, July 1986.

150 *A poignant, unpublicized exchange:* Strother tells the story in his wonderful memoir, *Falling Up* (Baton Rouge: Louisiana State University Press, 2003). He added more details in an interview with the author.

CHAPTER 11   A MONEY MACHINE

I conducted interviews with James Fabiani, Terry Holcombe, Vincent Versage, Philip Costanzo, Gerald Cassidy, Elliott Fiedler, Carol Casey, and Scott Giles.

CHAPTER 12   DISASTER AVERTED

I conducted interviews with John Danforth, William Danforth, Jonathan Orloff, Carol Casey, Gerald Cassidy, James Fabiani, Tom Mathews, Bob Livingston, Norm Dicks, and Vincent Versage.

166 *He noted that "the bill before us":* All quotations from the debate are from the *Congressional Record,* Vol. 132, No. 74, Issues 74 and 75.

167 *The Pentagon's stance:* "Over a Pork Barrel: The Senate Rejects Peer Review," *Science,* Vol. 233, July 1986.

172 *Carnegie Mellon had prevailed:* "U-MD Loses Bid for Software Center," *Washington Post,* November 15, 1984.

174 *Danforth began the debate:* Quotations from the June 26, 1986, debate are from the *Congressional Record,* Vol. 132, No. 74, issues 88 and 89.

180 *One of the favors Cassidy did for members in the 1980s:* Dan Morgan, "Congress and a Company: An Alliance Fed by Money; Firm Uses Gifts, Honoraria to Boost Business," *Washington Post,* June 13, 1988.

182 *Well, not always as simple as that:* "Behind Jim Wright's Book, His Friends," *New York Times,* June 12, 1988.

182 *The book wasn't sold in bookstores: Report of the Special Outside Counsel in the Matter of Speaker James C. Wright Jr.,* Committee on Standards of Official Conduct, U.S. House of Representatives (Washington, D.C.: U.S. Government Printing Office, February 21, 1989).

CHAPTER 13   TRICKS OF THE LOBBYING TRADE

I conducted interviews with Gerald Cassidy, James Fabiani, Donald Smith, Neil Buck-lew, and Dan Morgan. Senator Robert Byrd declined to be interviewed.

183 *On June 13, 1988, all of Washington learned:* Dan Morgan, "Congress and a Com-pany: An Alliance Fed by Money," *Washington Post,* June 13, 1988.

188 *Just a year later, Morgan published:* Dan Morgan, "As Federal Funding Tightens, Lobbyists Find a Surer Way," *Washington Post,* June 18, 1989.

190 *Explaining this switch:* "Byrd to Give Up Leader Post," *Washington Post,* April 13, 1988. Wikipedia lists thirty-eight things named for Byrd in West Virginia, from the Robert C. Byrd Academic and Technology Center at Marshall University, Huntington, to the Robert C. Byrd Visitor Center at Harpers Ferry National Historical Park, Harpers Ferry.

191 *But he had no real pals:* "A Minority Leader Highly Skilled at Being . . . A Major-ity Leader," *Washington Post,* May 31, 1981.

193 *Speaking in favor: Congressional Record* for July 26, 1989.

CHAPTER 14   THE NEW TECHNOLOGY OF POLITICS

I conducted interviews with Peter Hart, Douglas Bailey, and Bill Bradley.

198 *Ailes's approach was recorded memorably:* Joe McGinniss, *The Selling of the President, 1968* (New York: Trident, 1969).

199 *Roger Ailes loved negative commercials:* I have drawn on Paul Taylor's good book on the 1988 election, *See How They Run* (New York: Alfred A. Knopf, 1990), for many of the details in this account of the Bush campaign.

200 *"If I can make Willie Horton":* Ibid.

201 *For example, incumbent Democrats in relatively close races:* Statistics provided by the Campaign Finance Institute.

202 *Interviewed in 1988, Bailey summarized:* "Simple Messages Help Bush," *Washing-ton Post,* October 15, 1988.

203 *Blumenthal published:* Blumenthal, *Permanent Campaign.*

CHAPTER 15   DISORDER IN THE HOUSE

205 *Instead he organized the Conservative Opportunity Society:* From an interview with Vin Weber for a 1996 Public Broadcasting System documentary on Gingrich. It can be found at www.pbs.org/wgbh/pages/frontline/newt/newtintwshtml/ weber.html.

206 *On May 8, after their colleagues had gone home: Congressional Record* for May 8, 1984, p. 11,430.

207 *By rising to their bait:* "OUTBURST: Speaker O'Neill and Republicans Clash Fiercely in House Debate," *Washington Post,* May 16, 1984.

207 *When the House convened the next day: Congressional Record* for May 15, 1984. p. 12,201.

208 *as* The Washington Post *called him:* "OUTBURST."

208 *They called the film:* "It's 'Tip's Greatest Hits,' Electrifying a Closed House GOP Circuit," *Washington Post,* May 29, 1984.

209 The Washington Post *editorialized:* "A Seat for Mr. McIntyre," *Washington Post,* February 11, 1985.

211 *"If Wright consolidates his power":* Gingrich is quoted in: John M. Barry, *The Ambition and the Power* (New York: Penguin Books, 1990). Barry interviewed Gingrich at the time.

211 *"The number-one fact":* Ibid.

212 *long investigative report:* "Speaker's Royalty 55 Percent," *Washington Post,* September 24, 1987.

212 *"The more he has been scrutinized":* "72 Republicans Ask Panel to Probe Wright's Finances," *Washington Post,* May 27, 1988.

212 The Washington Post *disclosed:* "Gingrich's Book Venture," *Washington Post,* March 20, 1989.

213 *published another revelation:* "Coelho Campaign Listed as Junk Bonds Buyer," *Washington Post,* April 13, 1989.

213 *Coelho shocked Washington:* "Rep. Coelho to Resign from House," *Washington Post,* May 27, 1989.

213 *"There's an evil wind blowing":* "Wright to Resign Speaker's Post, House Seat," *Washington Post,* June 1, 1989.

213 *In his speech announcing his resignation:* "Partial Text of Wright's Resignation Speech," *Washington Post,* June 1, 1989.

CHAPTER 16 BECOMING A CONGLOMERATE

I conducted interviews with Gerald Cassidy, James Fabiani, John Silber, Don Smith, Elliott Fiedler, Lester "Ruff" Fant, Jody Powell, and Dale Leibach.

215 *Cassidy expected more than $21 million in revenue:* "As Federal Funding Tightens, Lobbyists Find a Surer Way," *Washington Post,* June 18, 1989.

222 *It was, as* The New York Times *later wrote:* "Clark Clifford, a Major Advisor to Four Presidents, Is Dead at 91," *New York Times,* October 11, 1998.

223 *"Actors Eat Cakes": New York Times,* October 18, 1924.

223 *Bernays (1891–1995) was one of the most important:* I have drawn the quotations from Bernays that follow from a wonderful chapter on Bernays, based on his writings and a long interview, in Sidney Blumenthal's *The Permanent Campaign.*

CHAPTER 17 INFLUENCING POLICY FOR PROFIT

I conducted interviews with Gerald Cassidy, Daniel Inouye, Vincent Versage, Jody Powell, Jim Turner, Robert Gillcash, Chris Dachi, Christopher Dodd, Joseph Lieberman, Bruce DeMars, William Bonvillian, Sam Gejdenson, Victoria Leon Monroe, Colin Mathews, Natale Bellocchi, Gerald Felix Warburg, Charles Robb, Peter Tomsen, Winston Lord, Sandy Berger, Leon Panetta, and Kurt Furst.

228 The Boston Globe *caught on:* "Ocean Spray's Little Secret," *Boston Globe,* October 9, 1988.

235 *Offering "a personal opinion":* "Admiral Opposes Bush Plan to Kill Submarine," *New York Times,* April 2, 1992.

236 *So Senator Arlen Specter:* Dachi interview.

240 The Washington Post *carried an item:* "Lobbyists Help Save General Dynamics' Seawolf Sub," *Washington Post,* September 14, 1993.

245 *Democratic Congressman Gejdenson:* Associated Press Worldstream, February 9, 1995.

CHAPTER 18 PUBLIC SERVICE, PRIVATE REWARDS

I conducted interviews with P. X. Kelley, Gerald Cassidy, James Fabiani, Marty Russo, Douglass Bobbitt, Leon Panetta, Tony Coelho, Jody Powell, Dan Tate Sr., Bill Cloherty, Peter Madigan, and Dale Leibach.

252 *"When I first got out":* Smathers's recollections appear in an oral history that he gave in 1989 to the Senate historian. It can be found at http://156.33.195.33/artandhistory/history/oral_history/George_A_Smathers.htm.

254 *He was one of 122 members:* "Former Members: Where Are They Now?," *Roll Call,* February 1, 1993.

255 *a document subsequently filed with the Securities and Exchange Commission:* This was an S-1, described in detail in Chapter 20. It can be found at http://www.secinfo.com/dv8Nc.7m2.htm.

CHAPTER 19 RADICAL ENDS, RADICAL MEANS

I conducted interviews with Gerald Cassidy, Douglas Bereuter, Jim Dyer, and Mike Kopetski.

261 *Two weeks before the 1994 election: Washington Post*–ABC News Poll in *The Washington Post,* October 25, 1994.

261 "Language, A Key Mechanism of Control": The full memo can be found at http://web.utk.edu/~glenn/GopacMemo.html.

262 *With Gingrich installed as speaker:* My account of the first year of Republican control of the House draws heavily on the wonderful book *Tell Newt to Shut Up* (New York: Simon & Schuster/Touchstone, 1996), by David Maraniss and Michael Weisskopf, two *Washington Post* reporters who spent 1995 reporting and writing about the Republicans. They produced a brilliant series of articles, which are collected in this book.

263 *challengers running against Democratic incumbents in competitive districts:* Statistics provided by the Campaign Finance Institute.

267 *"We're just following the old adage":* Maraniss and Weisskopf, *Tell Newt to Shut Up.*

267 *Over the course of the next decade:* Thomas E. Mann and Norman J. Ornstein, *The Broken Branch* (New York: Oxford University Press, 2006).

271 *The relentless fund-raising:* Hugh Heclo, "Campaigning and Governing: A Conspectus," in Norman Ornstein and Thomas Mann, eds. *The Permanent Campaign and Its Future* (Washington, D.C.: Brookings Institution, 2000). This is a brilliant essay.

272 *The amounts of money raised in those two cycles:* Statistics here are from the Campaign Finance Institute and opensecrets.org, the Web site of the Center for Responsive Politics.

272 *Before they were broadcast:* "Gingrich Orchestrated Lewinsky Ads," *Washington Post*, October 30, 1998.

CHAPTER 20   CASH COW ON THE POTOMAC

I conducted interviews with Gerald Cassidy, James Fabiani, Geoff Gonella, Dan Tate Sr., Douglass Bobbitt, Elliott Fiedler, Lester "Ruff" Fant, Daniel Inouye, Bob Beckel, Greg Schneiders, Glenn Cowan, Bob Livingston, Tom Griscom, Michael McCurry, Paul Costello, Stephen Conafay, and Michael Petruzzello.

279 The Wall Street Journal *learned about this meeting:* "Some of Washington's Influence Peddlers Reap Added Benefit of Stake in Firms They Promote," *Wall Street Journal*, October 12, 1994.

283 *Cassidy's S-1, filed on July 21, 1998:* The full text of the S-1 can be found at http://www.secinfo.com/dv8Nc.7m2.htm.

288 *DLJ found a much richer:* A confidential source gave me a copy of the DLJ "Confidential Information Memorandum."

CHAPTER 21   ELECTIONS BOUGHT AND SOLD

I conducted interviews with Gerald Cassidy, Leon Panetta, Chuck Hagel, Douglass Bobbitt, Don Smith, Geoff Gonella, Larry Grossman, Jonathan Orloff, Dan Tate Sr., Carol Casey, John Feehery, and Douglas Bereuter.

290 *In the 2000 elections:* Statistics from Public Citizen and Campaign Finance Institute. The total spent in 1976 was $258 million; in 2000 that would have been worth $797 million, after adjusting for inflation.

296 *For example, Murtha received:* Federal Election Commission statistics.

297 *Congressman Romano Mazzoli:* Martin Schram, *Speaking Frankly* (Washington, D.C.: Center for Responsive Politics, 1995).

298 *Ocean Spray's totaled:* Statistics provided by the Federal Election Commission.

300 *"We may reach a point":* Albert R. Hunt, "Cash Politics," *Wall Street Journal,* July 26, July 29, August 2, 1982.

301 *The Center for Responsive Politics . . . calculated:* The Center for Responsive Politics, http://www.opensecrets.org.

CHAPTER 22 POLITICS, THEN GOVERNMENT

I conducted interviews with Gerald Cassidy, Chuck Hagel, David Obey, John Feehery, Bob Livingston, Scott Lilly, Peter Hart, and Dale Leibach.

302 *Paul O'Neill . . . revealed how politics:* O'Neill collaborated with journalist Ron Susskind on his book, *The Price of Loyalty: George W. Bush, the White House, and the Education of Paul O'Neill* (New York: Simon & Schuster, 2004). He also gave a damning interview to *60 Minutes* that can be found at http://www.information clearinghouse.info/articles5510.htm.

302 *Weeks later Richard Clarke:* Clarke spoke out in March 2004 on *60 Minutes* and in a book published the same month, *Against All Enemies* (New York: The Free Press, 2004). An account of the CBS interview can be found at http://www .cbsnews.com/stories/2004/03/19/60minutes/main607356.shtml.

303 *Scott McClellan, told reporters:* "White House Fires Back at O'Neill in Iraq," *Washington Post,* January 13, 2004.

303 *adding nearly $2.5 trillion to the national debt:* Statistics of the Center on Budget and Policy Priorities.

304 *Rove's publicly delivered advice:* "GOP Touts War as Campaign Issue," *Washington Post,* January 18, 2002.

305 *Early in 2004 Obey recalled what happened:* Obey told the author this story in an interview. Later he published a version of it in his book, *Raising Hell for Justice* (Madison: University of Wisconsin Press, 2007).

309 *The Bush administration actually hid its own estimates:* "Inquiry Confirms Top Medicare Official Threatened Actuary over Cost of Drug Benefits," *New York Times,* July 7, 2004.

309 *According to Congressman Walter Jones:* Jones was quoted on *60 Minutes,* July 29, 2007.

309 *Finally, Frist and Hastert stepped in:* "For GOP Leaders, Battles and Bruises Produce Medicare Bill," *Washington Post,* November 30, 2003.

310 *The gavel finally fell:* I have drawn on the account of this drama in Mann and Ornstein, *The Broken Branch,* an excellent account of the deterioration of Congress in the years of Republican control.

310 *Hastert defended his handling of this vote:* "Address by House Speaker J. Dennis Hastert," *U.S. Newswire,* November 12, 2003.

311 *In the 2002 election cycle:* Center for Responsive Politics. Statistics available at http://www.opensecrets.org/industries/indus.asp?Ind=H04.

311 *Gingrich, for example, declared in 1992:* From a Gingrich speech on the House floor, January 3, 1992.

312 *By 2002 the number of individual earmarks:* "Grand Old Porkers," A Report of the Minority Staff of the House Appropriations Committee, 2006.

CHAPTER 23   HARD TIMES

I conducted interviews with Jody Powell, David Whitmore, Lester "Ruff" Fant, Stephen Conafay, James Fabiani, Gerald Cassidy, Carol Casey, Vincent Versage, Don Smith, Colette Godfrey (widow of Frank), Jean Davis, Steve Whitaker, Marty Russo, Al Gordon, Rudy DeLeon, Larry Grossman, Gregg Hartley, and Amos Hochstein.

324 *Texas Tech had paid Cassidy $580,000:* Lobbying reports filed with the clerk of the Senate show the fees paid by clients like this one. Photocopies of the reports can be found at http://sopr.senate.gov/cgi-win/m_opr_viewer.exe?DoFn=0.

325 *Versage had a close personal relationship:* David J. Schmidly, then the president of Texas Tech, confirmed in an interview that "Vince [Versage] was the person who had really delivered for us," which was why he moved his business to the National Group.

331 *someone leaked the story to the* Post: "GOP Whip Quietly Tried to Aid Big Donor; Provision Was Meant to Help Philip Morris," *Washington Post,* June 11, 2003.

337 *The polling showed DeLay's increasing unpopularity:* "DeLay Departing on Own Terms," *Washington Post,* April 5, 2006.

CHAPTER 24   A CORRODED CULTURE

I conducted interviews with Gerald Cassidy, Jack Quinn, Leon Panetta, Douglas Bereuter, Bill Bradley, Peter Hart, Douglas Bailey, Christopher Dodd, Michael Fraioli, Joe Rothstein, Fred Wertheimer, Raymond Strother, Lawrence O'Brien III, John Adams, and Robert Strauss.

342 *Cassidy & Associates hired:* "Cassidy Hires Full-time Compliance Guru," *Roll Call,* February 13, 2008.

342 *"What makes two years":* "Lobby Bill Doesn't Slow 'Revolving Door,' " *Congressional Quarterly Weekly,* May 24, 2007.

342 *"cut off my profession":* "Lawmakers Feel the Pull of Future Paychecks," *Washington Post,* May 22, 2007.

343 *"Funny," editorialized his hometown newspaper:* "It Came from the Ethics Swamp," *Boston Globe,* May 2, 2007.

343 *"I have discussed this issue":* Markup of H.R. 2317, *Congressional Quarterly Transcripts,* May 17, 2007.

343 *"Former members command":* "Lawmakers Feel the Pull of Future Paychecks," *Washington Post,* May 22, 2007.

343 *A study done by Public Citizen:* "Congressional Revolving Doors: The Journey

from Congress to K Street." The report can be found at www.lobbyingingo.org/documents/RevolveDoor.pdf.

344 *Another study found:* The Center for Responsive Politics maintains a "Revolving Door Database." It can be found at http://www.opensecrets.org/revolving/index.asp.

346 *In the memorable phrase:* Plunkitt's original observation was personal: "I seen my opportunities and I took 'em," he told journalist William L. Riordon, explaining how he got rich as a politician. Riordon recorded Plunkitt's wisdom in 1905 in *Plunkitt of Tammany Hall: A Series of Very Plain Talks on Very Practical Politics* (Boston: Bedford Books, 1994).

347 *In an academic survey:* Cited in Marshall Ganz, "Voters in the Crosshairs," *American Prospect*, November 2002.

347 *"The beautiful science of the random sample":* Strother, *Falling Up.*

348 *In November 2007:* "Short of Funds, GOP Recruits Rich to Run," *New York Times*, November 26, 2007.

349 *"promote one's cause against others":* Heclo, "Campaigning and Governing," in Mann and Ornstein, eds., *The Permanent Campaign.*

353 *"More needs to be done":* National Association of Home Builders press release, February 1, 2008.

353 *The statement raised eyebrows:* "Home Builders Halt Campaign Funds After Setback," *Washington Post*, February 14, 2008.

353 *The home builders' suspension:* "Builder Group Resumes Campaign Contributions," *Washington Post*, May 6, 2008.

353 *"Our message has been heard":* ibid.

Index

A NOTE ABOUT THE AUTHOR

Robert G. Kaiser was born in Washington, D.C., and has lived there for six decades, leaving only on foreign assignments for *The Washington Post*, his employer since 1963. Kaiser's first job in journalism was as a copy boy for the Associated Press in the House of Representatives Press Gallery when John F. Kennedy was president. Since then he has written about foreign and domestic policy, Congress, the White House, lobbying, and political campaigns. As a foreign correspondent he was based in London, Saigon, and Moscow. He spent sixteen years as an editor of the *Post*, serving as the paper's managing editor from 1991 to 1998. He is now associate editor and senior correspondent. Kaiser is the author or co-author of seven books. He lives in Washington with his wife, Hannah Jopling, an anthropologist. They have two grown daughters.

A NOTE ON THE TYPE

This book was set in Janson, a typeface long thought to have been made by the Dutchman Anton Janson, who was a practicing typefounder in Leipzig during the years 1668–1687. However, it has been conclusively demonstrated that these types are actually the work of Nicholas Kis (1650–1702), a Hungarian, who most probably learned his trade from the master Dutch typefounder Dirk Voskens. The type is an excellent example of the influential and sturdy Dutch types that prevailed in England up to the time William Caslon (1692–1766) developed his own incomparable designs from them.

Composed by North Market Street Graphics, Lancaster, Pennsylvania

Printed and bound by Berryville Graphics, Berryville, Virginia

Designed by Soonyoung Kwon